Frontispiece, Illustrations and Maps

TRAITOROUS HERO

The Life and Fortunes of

BENEDICT ARNOLD

by

WILLARD M. WALLACE

For comment about this book, see back of jacket

Here is the first modern, authentic biography of one of the boldest and most fascinating figures in American history, a man whose name is a synonym for treachery, yet who was one of the most courageous soldiers of his time. A brilliant commander, an impetuous lover, Benedict Arnold blazed an enigmatic career which rose to glory, ended in ruin—and which has never been completely understood until now.

It is the story of a man who loved the battlefield, wealth, and women, but himself above all these. It is the authentic account of a strange, romantic personality who did his utmost first to win, then to lose the war of the Colonies against England.

SINCE WILLARD WALLACE'S discovery of fresh evidence relating to the treason plot, Arnold's strategic genius and his plan to betray his cause are seen in a new light. A leading authority on the great personalities of the Revolution, and on its military history, Mr. Wallace graphically depicts, as no other biographer, the sweeping decline of Major General Arnold, a trusted favorite of Washington and husband of one of the prettiest ladies in America, through his desperate post-treason years to ultimate degradation.

Loring Studios

Willard M. Wallace, a professor of history at Wesleyan University, is the author of *Appeal to Arms, A Military History of the American Revolution*. Much of the research for this biography was done by Mr. Wallace while on a Guggenheim Fellowship in Canada and England. Mr. Wallace lives in Connecticut with his wife and two daughters.

Traitorous Hero

THE LIFE AND FORTUNES OF

BENEDICT ARNOLD

Also by Willard M. Wallace

☆

APPEAL TO ARMS

A Military History of the American Revolution

Major General Benedict Arnold, engraving based on a pre-treason
portrait by Pierre Eugene Du Simitière.

Traitorous Hero

The Life and Fortunes of

BENEDICT ARNOLD

by

Willard M. Wallace

HARPER & BROTHERS PUBLISHERS

NEW YORK

For

Betts, Joy, and Pam

The Dark Eagle comes to claim the wilderness. The wilderness will yield to the Dark Eagle, but the Rock will defy him. The Dark Eagle will soar aloft to the sun. Nations will behold him and sound his praises. Yet when he soars highest his fall is most certain. When his wings brush the sky then the arrow will pierce his heart.

> —Natanis to Arnold (according to tradition), at their first meeting in autumn, 1775.

Arnold had fought and would fight again in bigger battles, but never for bigger stakes. It was the American cause that was saved that day. Had Ticonderoga been taken and held that winter, Burgoyne's campaign of 1777, starting from that point, would have almost certainly succeeded.

> —Claude H. Van Tyne, writing of the action off Valcour Island (*War of Independence, American Phase*, 372–3).

. . . it was his doing.

> —Burgoyne to Clinton, Oct. 25, 1777, attributing to Arnold the cause of his defeat at Bemis Heights.

Had this plan succeeded it must have put an end to the war. General Arnold did but just escape, and upon his arrival in New York was appointed a Brigadier-General in our service by Sir Henry. Had the scheme answered, no rank would have overpaid so important a service.

> —From the Narrative of Lieutenant George Mathew of the Coldstream Guards.

Arnold (according to tradition) to an American captain taken in Virginia, "What would be my fate, if *I* should be taken prisoner?"

The captain to Arnold, "They will cut off that leg of yours wounded at Quebec and at Saratoga, and bury it with all the honors of war, and then hang the rest of you on a gibbet."

Let his name sink as low in infamy, as it was once high in our esteem. . . . On this stage, all good men will unite in execrating his memory to the latest posterity. Even villains less guilty than himself will not cease to upbraid him and tho' they "approve the treason they will despise the traitor!"

> —Lieutenant Colonel Eleazer Oswald to Colonel John Lamb (former friends of Arnold), Dec. 11, 1780.

ACKNOWLEDGMENTS

WRITING this biography of Arnold has placed me in debt to many people and institutions, to all of whom I am most grateful. I wish, however, to make especial acknowledgment to the following: the John Simon Guggenheim Memorial Foundation for making it financially possible through a fellowship to travel to distant centers of research; the President and Trustees of Wesleyan University for granting me a sabbatical semester; the Research Committee of Wesleyan University for stenographic funds; the Olin Library at Wesleyan University, particularly Miss Gertrude McKenna; the W. L. Clements Library at Ann Arbor, Michigan; the Library of Congress; the National Archives; the Historical Society of Pennsylvania; the New York Historical Society; the New York Public Library; the New Haven Colony Historical Society; the Sterling Library at Yale University; the Connecticut State Library; the New Brunswick Museum in St. John, New Brunswick, notably that most helpful of archivists, Miss Margaret Evans; the Library Archives of the University of New Brunswick, and Miss Frances Firth in particular; the British Museum in London; the Public Record Office in London; the late Carl Van Doren for his magnificent study of conspiracy and treason, *Secret History of the American Revolution;* Mrs. F. P. Albertine and Mr. Raymond B. Case of Norwichtown, who contributed more than they realized by their interest in Connecticut; Mr. Chauncey H. Clements of New Haven for his lavish hospitality and for generously sharing his vast fund of knowledge of Arnold and Colonial Connecticut; Colonel James R. Case of Bethel, Connecticut, for shrewd judgment on several points in Arnold's life, including his relations with General David Wooster; Dr. Esther Clark Wright of Fredericton, New Brunswick, for her warm interest and for giving me valuable time to uncover information concerning Arnold's sojourn in New Brunswick; Mrs. Jean M. Sweet of St. John, New Brunswick, for kindly supplying me with a copy of one of Arnold's unpublished letters; Professor D. Upton Hill of Acadia University, Nova Scotia, for several helpful suggestions on Arnold; Mrs. Gerda A. Foster of Wellesley, Massachusetts, for a number of "leads"; the late Professor Malcolm Foster of Wesleyan University, whose interest in this study was always keen and whose advice and encouragement meant much to me; Professor Burton C. Hallowell of the Economics Department at Wesleyan University for patiently helping me to arrive at an approximate figure of Arnold's treason price in modern dollars; my colleagues in the History Department at Wesleyan University for numerous suggestions and practical assistance, Professors S. Hugh Brockunier, Eugene O. Golob, Sigmund Neumann, and Carl E. Schorske, and Mr. Malcolm Stearns, Jr.; my friends, Mr. Donald Herzberg, for many kindnesses in facilitating my research in Washington, and Mr. John W. Paton, for assistance with illustrations; my brother, Mr. Oscar T. Wallace of South Portland, Maine, for checking certain data for me; Mr. John Fischer of Harper & Brothers for patient and understanding guidance; Mr. John Appleton, also of Harper & Brothers, for his interest and wholehearted co-operation; Mrs. Esther Carling of Middletown, Connecticut, for being an ideal secretary; lastly, the one to whom I owe most, my wife, Elizabeth Mueller Wallace, whose unstinting contributions would be too numerous and varied to specify but without which this biography could not have been written.

WILLARD M. WALLACE

Wesleyan University
Middletown, Connecticut

CONTENTS

ILLUSTRATIONS

Traitorous Hero

THE LIFE AND FORTUNES OF

BENEDICT ARNOLD

· I ·

From Glory to Infamy

THE STOCKY little man, in his blue coat with gold epaulettes, strode impatiently out of his tent to watch the American Continentals and militia hurl back the reconnaissance in force by British General John Burgoyne. His pale eyes glittered in exasperation as the rolling terrain, the woods in the scarlet and russet of autumn, and the clouds of white smoke shut off his view of the conflict. Meanwhile the discharge of cannon, the clatter of musketry, and the shouts and yells started him pacing restlessly back and forth. This was the great day of reckoning with the invading British and Germans, and Major General Benedict Arnold, instead of leading his division into battle on Bemis Heights, had no command at all.

Arnold's thoughts were indeed bitter on the sunny afternoon of October 7, 1777. This frustrating inaction seemed the end of all his efforts: his march through the Maine wilderness to Quebec in 1775, his siege of the city through the worst winter in a generation, his naval struggle on Lake Champlain in the autumn of 1776, his relief of Fort Stanwix during the past summer, and his energetic role against Burgoyne in the battle at Freeman's Farm last September 19. Involved in the struggle for command between Generals Philip Schuyler and Horatio Gates, his sympathies had been all too obviously with the former, and, with Schuyler's departure, he had become, in Gates's eyes and in those of Schuyler's partisans, the leader of the Schuyler faction. Whatever Gates's reasons, the general had neglected to mention him or his division in the official report of the action at

I

Freeman's Farm. Arnold had had no doubts that the oversight was calculated. Storming into Gates's quarters, he told him off in summary fashion, and demanded a pass to General Washington. The long-nosed Horatio, once friendly but now cool to him, quickly complied; what better way of getting rid of a troublesome subordinate than to relieve him at his own request?

But once he had his pass, Arnold refused to leave camp. Schuyler's friends and Arnold's own officers had persuaded him to remain, pointing out the imminence of another fight with Burgoyne and the flattering probability that only he could achieve the final victory over the theatrical but stubborn Briton.

Still, there appeared little he could do since Gates had assumed command of his division and had given the right wing of the army to fat, easy-going General Benjamin Lincoln. And in the present battle, as in that of Freeman's Farm, Gates clung to his headquarters two miles back of the lines, where much of what was happening was hidden from him. Arnold's regimental commanders were thus left with no immediate field leader, a realization that twisted Arnold's full lips in anger and contempt. Gates, as the army commander, naturally belonged in the rear, but, as a divisional commander, he should have been with his troops, the very place where Arnold himself longed with all his heart to be on this day of days. Finally he could tolerate the situation no longer. In spite of Gates, this was his battle, and he would not be denied. Quickly he ordered his bay mare saddled. To his astonished but delighted aides he is said to have exclaimed in his staccato voice, "No man shall keep me in my tent today. If I am without command, I will fight in the ranks; but the soldiers, God bless them, will follow my lead. Come on!" [1]

Then he leaped on his horse with the athletic ease that had enabled him to jump over an ammunition wagon when a youth, whipped out his sword, and galloped toward the firing.

At his appearance, the startled troops shouted his name and cheered him wildly. Infused with fresh vigor by his arrival, they followed him in one furious assault after another. Now he tried the defense of the young Lord Balcarres and his Light Infantry in the British center, now he scattered the Canadians and Loyalists at the Earl's right, and at last he stormed the redoubt manned by "Butcher" Breymann and his blue-coated Brunswickers. It was here that the mare went down and a German bullet pierced Arnold's left leg, the same leg that had stopped a British musket ball in the attack on Quebec.

But the victory was his, and he knew it. So did Burgoyne, who gave him the credit. Even Gates had a gracious word of praise for him in his report to Congress, while Washington presented him with a set of epaulettes and sword knots. Though Gates received greater recognition, Arnold's name was not forgotten in toasts drunk to the triumph that eventually brought France into the war on the side of the United States. The savor of such acknowledgment for his services was doubly sweet, coming after rebuffs by Congress and character assaults by his enemies. He had demonstrated beyond question his brilliance as a field commander. He was a national hero with an unlimited future before him.

Notwithstanding this success, within two years, Benedict Arnold—the real hero of the victories at Saratoga—made the first secret move in the tragic game that was to forfeit his reputation and his future as an American; within three years, he wore the scarlet and gold of a brigadier in the Britsh Army; and from that time to this, his name has been considered a very synonym for treason.

The reasons for the descent of such a star in the national firmament confused many of Arnold's contemporaries and have continued to puzzle people ever since. On the face of things, he appeared to have everything to gain by remaining loyal to the oath of allegiance which he and the other officers of the Continental Army signed at Valley Forge, the winter after Saratoga. But the motivations of treason are rarely easy to establish, as the treason trials in our own age have amply demonstrated. It is convenient, of course, to try to ascribe a single dominating motive to proved or suspected traitors, whether to Arnold, Aaron Burr, Copperhead leader Clement Vallandigham, Army traitor Martin Monti, or atomic spies Julius and Ethel Rosenberg. This, however, is a gross oversimplification; most of the known American traitors have operated under complexes of motives. Among these motives have been the need of money, frustration, a craving for recognition and prestige, love, revenge, racial or religious prejudice, respect for another form of government, devotion to a different social or economic philosophy—and these are but a beginning.

Arnold was the first great American traitor in point of time, a dubious distinction indeed. No individual in American history, moreover, has plummeted so swiftly from adulation to execration. Had his treason succeeded in accomplishing its objective, the Revolution might have bowed to the superior power of the British and many of our eminent political and military figures have at last graced the gibbet, a fate of which Benjamin Franklin had warned his colleagues in Congress during the drafting of the Declaration of Independence. Fortunately Arnold failed, but the country has never forgotten the shock and horror of those days, and treason has become the most odious offense in the catalogue of crime.

The conception of treason has acquired narrower limits since the great English treason law of 1352, when Parliament conceived of it as a breach of loyalty owed a superior, and included in its definition a wife's betrayal of her husband. At the same time, the moral responsibility attached to treason has increased and, similarly, the opprobrium with which the act is viewed. In committing treason, an individual strikes not simply at another individual but at a government, an entire society, a way of life. The fact that this is even truer now than in Arnold's day in no way lessens the gravity of his offense. On the contrary, it becomes more desirable than ever to determine the precise nature of his treason and, if possible, his motivations. Though the mid-twentieth century is farther removed from the late eighteenth than the mere passage of time would indicate, and though the interim developments have created new dimensions to treason, the constant factor is man himself. A study of Arnold's career, the opening chapter in American treason, may therefore help one arrive at a clearer understanding of the nature and motivations of treason in our own turbulent era.

· II ·

Youth

Aᴀ RNOLD was born at Norwich, Connecticut, on January 14, 1741, a critical period in the world's history. Europe was convulsed by war because of Frederick the Great's seizure of the Austrian province of Silesia. England, Austria's ally, faced France, Prussia's ally, in addition to Spain, with whom she had been disastrously at war in Florida, the West Indies, and Central America ever since 1739 when a questionable character, a sea captain named Jenkins, had shown the House of Commons a pickled ear in a bottle, declared it his own, and pointed an accusing finger at the Spanish Coast Guard off South America. An Anglo-Colonial expedition was now assembling on the North American mainland for an invasion of Cuba, while New Englanders eyed with apprehension the powerful French fortress of Louisburg on Cape Breton Island. Within Connecticut itself people were experiencing the joys and anguish of the Great Awakening, a religious revival that was to attain rapturous heights when George Whitefield, the evangelist friend of John and Charles Wesley, swept through the countryside with a voice like the angel Gabriel's. Conservative men, Old Lights, denounced the furor so bitterly that the disciples of the Great Awakening, New Lights, soon broke away and formed new churches. Their counter-criticism of the conservatives created such tumult and rancor that the Assembly in Hartford called for peace within the Congregational Church. It was thus in a disturbed world in general and a troubled province in particular that Arnold passed his childhood.

He came of a family that moved about. Ironically, in view of the man's ultimate fate, the name Arnold is derived from an early English word meaning "honor," and appears to have originated with a Welsh prince in the twelfth century whose descendants settled in Warwickshire, England. William Arnold, who was born in 1587, crossed the Western Ocean for religious reasons and hoped at first to settle in Boston. But William was a liberal-minded man and liked the iron-handed theocracy of Puritan Massachusetts no better than the rigorous rule of Archbishop Laud in England. Hence he followed the persecuted Roger Williams to Rhode Island and built a home on the Pawtuxet River in 1636. His son, Benedict, moved to Newport, became wealthy, and served as governor of Rhode Island for several terms. Governor Arnold's son, also named Benedict, sat in the Assembly for a while but had financial troubles because of a lack of ability in managing his landholdings and his accounts. His son, the third Benedict born in Rhode Island, was apprenticed to a cooper. This Benedict and his brother Oliver, deciding in 1730 that Connecticut offered better opportunities for making a decent living than Rhode Island, took passage for Norwich aboard a sloop owned by Captain Absalom King of that port.[1]

Benedict did very well for himself. Not only did he pursue his trade as a cooper but he also ventured into the coasting and West Indies trade. Very likely this was after he married the gouty King's pretty widow. In September, 1732, King was returning from having sold a sloop in Ireland when he died of smallpox in mid-ocean. Benedict, who seems to have admired Hannah King ever since his arrival in Norwich, now wooed and won her; they were married on November 8, 1733. Hannah, whose father, John Waterman, had been one of the original settlers of the town, brought her new husband a considerable estate.

Benedict soon found being a sea captain and a merchant more attractive than mere coopering. Carrying on where King left off, he sent several sloops and schooners plying the waters of Long Island Sound and scudding down to the West Indies with barrel staves, lumber, and pork in return for molasses, sugar, and rum. Before long, he bought several acres and a big gambrel-roofed house on what was later known as Washington Street. Presently, too, his fellow townsmen began to elect him to such offices as surveyor, collector, lister (assessor), constable, and selectman. They thought they knew a sensible man when they saw one, a family man as well as a man of substance. Six children, three boys and three girls, were born to the Arnolds, but of these four died. With the primitive knowledge of medicine then available, such was often the fate of colonial families. The two survivors were a girl named Hannah and a boy, the future general and traitor, who was given the same name a deceased older brother had received, Benedict.[2]

Benedict Arnold's mother, Hannah King Arnold, was a woman of admirable traits according to contemporaries, one testifying that she was a saint on earth. Certainly it would appear that the inscription on her tombstone was close to the truth in describing her as a "Pattern of Piety, Patience, and Virtue." She needed all the fortitude furnished her by her religion and her character, for, in the late 1740's and the 1750's, with trade falling off, her husband, hitherto so reliable, spent more and more time over a bottle of Madeira wine or a jack of rum. Yet if his disintegration was steady, he succeeded in outliving his worried, hard-working wife. Hannah's husband, however, was not the only member of the family who gave her concern. The other was her son.

Arnold displayed at an early age qualities of aggressiveness and self-confidence. There are tales of cruelty by him, of glass strewn in paths to cut the feet of playmates and of birds' nests robbed. But most children can at times be cruel, whether innocently or mischievously, and it is likely that such tales were given undue importance by contemporaries eager to testify, after Arnold's treachery, to the blackness of his youth. He was in all probability neither better nor worse than other children, though perhaps more energetic, proud, and willful than most. If he had had a father capable of guiding him, one whom he could have admired and emulated, he might have learned restraint. Unfortunately there was little to admire or copy in his father during the very years when Arnold needed a firm hand, though, in spite of his growing addiction to heavy drinking, the older Benedict appears to have retained a certain respectability in the eyes of his neighbors. The responsibility for the family clearly devolved upon Hannah. Ambitious for her son, and eager to place him under intelligent discipline, she sent him to a school run by a Dr. Jewett in Montville, then, when he was eleven years old, to Canterbury, fourteen miles up the winding Quinebaug River from Norwich, to another school kept by the Reverend Dr. James Cogswell, whom she entreated not to spare the rod and spoil the child.[3]

Canterbury is a little farming village dominated by a white meeting-house brooding on an eminence back of the Norwich road. Its inhabitants are quick to point out the gracious colonial house where, in 1833, the first school for Negro girls was established in this country, but of Dr. Cogs-

well's school there appears little knowledge and none at all that it was
ever attended by Benedict Arnold. Perhaps, after Arnold went over to the
British, Canterburians were as eager to obliterate any evidence of contact
with him as was the Norwich mob that stormed into the old cemetery in
Norwich and removed the gravestones belonging to Arnold's father and
the baby brother who had died before the traitor's birth simply because
they, too, bore the Christian name of Benedict. Notwithstanding the
present ignorance, Cogswell's school was well known in eastern Connecticut in the mid-eighteenth century. Cogswell himself enjoyed a reputation
as a skilled logician and an exacting schoolmaster; a president of Yale,
Naphtali Daggett, received his early education from him. The Norwich
section of Connecticut flourished with schools taught by clergymen, who,
like Cogswell, gave their students instruction in Latin, Greek, and sometimes Hebrew, also in mathematics and effective speaking.

At the Canterbury school, where Cogswell considered him a bright boy
given to pranks, Arnold displayed special ability in Latin and arithmetic.
In fact, nothing could be further from the truth than the contention,
occasionally stressed, that Arnold was virtually an unlettered man. Not
only did he receive a substantial schooling from Cogswell, but it is likely
that in subsequent years he learned French. He was too shrewd a trader
and carried on too extensive a trading business with Canada and the
French West Indies to rely solely on an interpreter. Furthermore, his
choice of books for the store he opened in New Haven was hardly that of
an uneducated man nor exactly that of a mere tradesman with a sharp
eye on what was selling well in the book market. On the other hand,
though Dr. Cogswell helped Arnold improve his mind, the boy's hasty
manner of using his voice brought frequent corrections from the minister,
who was himself a facile, graceful speaker. Yet Arnold's fastidiousness in
the care of his person and clothes must have won the approval of Mrs.
Cogswell, to whom Hannah Arnold wished constantly in her letters to be
remembered.

Those letters to Arnold abound with a mother's love and concern. In
August, 1753, yellow fever swept through Norwich, and all the Arnolds
came down with it. Struggling with her own misery, and with two daughters wasting away, Hannah wrote Arnold a long letter telling him of the
family and begging him to improve his time and to pray to God for guidance lest death overtake him unprepared. But much as she wanted him
with her, she would not think of having him enter such danger. The letter
ends on a homely note: "My love to you—beg you would write us. I have

sent you 1 lb. choclat." Another letter, in April, 1754, testified to the family means and generosity. "I have sent you 50 shillings," said Hannah. "Use it prudently, as you are accountable to God and your father." Then she added, "Your father puts in twenty more"; the older Benedict had evidently not forgotten that he was once a boy. In the same letter Hannah gave her son some old-fashioned advice. "Keep a steady watch over your thoughts, words and actions," she warned him, obviously all too aware that Arnold possessed a hot temper and a fierce pride. "Be dutiful to superiors, obliging to equals, and affable to inferiors, if any such there be. Always choose that your companions be your betters, that by their good examples you may learn." [4]

By the spring of 1755, however, his father's condition and the family circumstances had declined to such an extent that Hannah withdrew the boy from Dr. Cogswell's charge; and, suddenly freed from the restraints of school, Arnold had a wonderful time. Indeed in hilly Norwich at the head of navigation on the Thames River there was much to interest a lively boy in the 1750's. The days were still not too far distant when Indians menaced the town and Bean Hill received its name because of a woman's huge pot of beans that was hastily brought into a blockhouse to feed the garrison. Very old people remembered how Uncas and his Mohegans sided with the whites against King Philip. So Arnold and his mates played the deadly game of Indian warfare all over again as boys nowadays wage the eternal battle of cops and robbers.

Arnold also roamed over the waterfront with its graying wharves, long warehouses, sail lofts, and ropewalk. The air was often fragrant with the odors of freshly sawed lumber destined for Bermuda and Barbados and hogsheads of molasses just arrived from the Sugar Islands. He picked his way like a cat over the brigs and sloops at the wharves, learning every sail and rope. No boy could climb to a masthead more quickly than he, then catch a backstay and slide like lightning to the deck, his dark hair streaming behind him. None could dive so deeply from the stern of a vessel or swim across the river and back so swiftly. He could sail a catboat with easy skill, taking advantage of every capful of breeze and every eddy in the river. Though never more than five feet seven inches tall, he was broad-shouldered and very muscular with a kind of bouncing energy that lent itself to turning cartwheels and handsprings, climbing a rope hand over hand, and jumping for height or distance. Passionately fond of approval and intensely proud, he took the lead in every kind of boyish mischief and would permit none to excel him. How responsible his lack of height was in motivating his desire to dominate, both as a boy and as a man, is a matter of speculation, but Arnold had a fiercely competitive spirit that would probably have expressed itself whatever his size.

His strength and daredevil zeal often made him reckless. Once, when sent with corn to be ground at the local grist mill, he startled the boys with him by grabbing one of the arms of the millwheel and letting it carry him high in the air and then under the waters of the stream. At another time, on the occasion of a British victory over the French, he and a number of other boys swarmed over to the cannon on the green. Up-ending the piece, Arnold poured in a horn of powder, then plunged a flaming torch into the muzzle. He was lucky to escape with only his face and hair singed. More serious was an incident on Thanksgiving Day. The custom of the times called for a bonfire that night. Deciding to make it a real blaze, Arnold and his gang slipped down to a shipyard, seized a number of barrels, and started to roll them up to the green. The irate owner summoned the local constable, who rushed to the scene and pre-vented the boys from burning their spoil. Arnold was so furious that he stripped off his coat and offered to fight the constable then and there. Refusing to tolerate such impudence, the officer collared the angry boy and dragged him home to his mother.

These had been the pranks of a restless, high-spirited lad with too much time on his hands, but the affair with the constable convinced Hannah of the truth of the old saw that "An idle mind is the devil's work-shop." Accordingly she consulted her cousins, the Lathrops, who ran an apothecary shop on the way to the meetinghouse and Bean Hill. As a result of her conversation with them, they accepted Arnold as an ap-prentice.

Daniel and Joshua Lathrop were successful apothecaries. Daniel had graduated from Yale in 1733, went to London to learn his trade, returned with a large store of medicines, and established a business in Norwich. His brother Joshua, after finishing at Yale in 1743, soon joined him. In the beginning they imported from England drugs, dried fruits, wines, and goods made in both Europe and India. A member of the firm or one of its agents regularly sailed to England to place orders. It is said that the Lathrops operated the first drug store in Connecticut and the only one on the route between Boston and New York. Certainly it was no small con-cern that Arnold had joined, and it was rapidly expanding its volume of business since the Lathrops had contracted to furnish the army in the Lake George area of New York with surgical equipment.[5]

Shortly after Arnold began his apprenticeship, the Seven Years War broke out and lasted from 1756 to 1763, though fighting for control of the Ohio Valley had started as early as 1754. Young George Washington and his Virginia militia had suffered a severe defeat at Fort Necessity, and, in 1755, the year in which Arnold left school, General Edward Braddock had led his redcoats into an ambush near Fort Duquesne in the Pennsylvania wilderness. The frontier was thus exposed to the torch and the scalping knife even before Europe plunged into the conflict. During the war, England, Prussia, and Hanover faced practically all Europe. While at first England fared disastrously in the colonies and at sea, she ended as a winner of dazzling victories, of which the most important occurred in the autumn of 1759 when General James Wolfe defeated Montcalm at Quebec. News of the triumph brought to the colonies vast relief and a joy that was tempered only by sorrow at the hero-general's death on the field of battle.

The great struggle found young Benedict Arnold burning to become a soldier. Life in the apothecary shop was like prison to a boy with such vigor and so intense a love of the outdoors. He welcomed almost any diversion, whether, as on one occasion, it was a thunderstorm so shattering that he grew exhilarated and swung his cap and shouted at each blast, or the rat-a-tat-tat of the drum and a glimpse of the bright uniforms of a recruiting officer's detail. Eagerly he followed the course of the war and longed to share in the excitement of the military life.

At last, in 1758, when spring arrived early with one of those unseasonable spells of weather when the air is warm and soft and the buds swell to bursting, Arnold slipped away from home and started walking down the dusty road toward New York Province where service bounties were higher than in Connecticut. He enlisted on March 30 in Captain Reuben Lockwood's company drawn from Westchester County. Though his name still appeared on the muster roll of the company on April 22, legend is persistent and perhaps authentic that his mother and the Lathrops, who were shocked at his running away, entreated a prominent minister, the Reverend Dr. Lord, to intercede through the authorities in Hartford and have him returned to his home. Lord was evidently successful, for Arnold was soon back in the dreary routine of the Norwich apothecary shop. But his few weeks of service had only whetted his appetite. When the call for volunteers sounded throughout the colonies in the spring of 1759 for the grand campaign against the French, Arnold finally convinced his mother that he should go. Reluctantly she consented, and again he hastened across the border to New York. On March 16, he enlisted in the militia company of Captain James Holmes, who had been a lieutenant in Lockwood's company.

This time, however, Arnold discovered that a soldier's life is often more attractive at a distance. Moving northward, his company was soon hard at work training for Amherst's expedition to Ticonderoga and Montreal. Although Arnold had an eye for excitement and glory quickly gained, liking to shoot and to impress people with his strength and agility by jumping over ammunition wagons and wrestling, he showed less stomach for the routine tasks of drilling, marching, and clearing the forest roads. This kind of war was an organized bore, as the late Justice Holmes has characterized war in general. Furthermore, word reached Arnold that his mother was gravely ill. This was all that he needed to make up his mind. The French could wait; he could not. Leaving camp one night, he made his way home from the lake region, sleeping in haylofts, catching rides with farmers and peddlers, and likely, when asked by the curious why he was not with the army, telling tales of a furlough to be spent at home with his ailing mother. At any rate, he had to move carefully because of a notice that appeared in Weyman's *New York Gazette* for May 21, 1759 offering a reward of forty shillings for his arrest as a deserter. He was described as "18 years old, dark complexion, light eyes and dark hair."

Desertion has never been a light offense even in times of peace; in wartime its penalties are rigorous. Yet men have ever deserted, notwithstanding the threat of possible death upon recovery. This has been especially true in countries such as the colonies where a firm military tradition had not been established. Desertion from colonial armies and from those of the Revolution was a fairly common occurrence and not regarded by society at large with quite the disapprobation now accorded it. There is, however, a fine line between desertion and what is known in military jargon as being "absent without leave." The difference is not alone one of time but one of intent as well. It is possible that Arnold intended to return to service after he had seen his mother, knowing that, once the campaign against the French had opened in earnest, he would have little or no opportunity to obtain a furlough. At any rate, he rejoined the Provincial forces in Captain Joshua Bloomer's company from Westchester County on March 26, 1760 with no record of any action against him for having gone AWOL the previous year. Even so, during the early summer of 1759, when recruiting officers entered Norwich, his mother hid him in remote places of the Arnold house or in the houses of friends.[6]

Hannah King Arnold died on August 15, 1759. Possibly her husband was shocked into temporary sobriety and, with a stricken conscience, made vows of improvement; if so, he soon forgot them. The tall blonde daughter, also named Hannah, who was not quite a year younger than her brother, undoubtedly contained herself, realizing that the care of the father would fall to her until her brother could settle down. As for Arnold, though his mind could be coldly calculating, he possessed a warm heart, and, for all his wildness, he had a deep respect and affection for his mother. Her death removed one of the steadying and protective influences of his life, and he felt an acute sense of loss.[7]

It is difficult to be certain just what he did next. Very likely he went back to the apothecary shop until he rejoined the army. When he finally enrolled in Bloomer's company, he was in service for only a short time since, with the French conquered, the main task of the military forces was garrison duty and most of the men were released. Though he came back to Norwich in 1760, he soon shipped as supercargo in a vessel bound for the West Indies. Later he frequented trading establishments in Middletown, Hartford, and New Haven. Eventually he sailed to London, which, in view of his lively spirits, he probably "did" as had few colonials before. He also bought drugs, books, merchandise, and a passage for the return to Norwich.

Older now, and with his sensitivity increasing with his pride, he found his father a source of anguish. The older Benedict had got himself arrested for drunkenness in 1760 but still could not resist the bottle. At last he died in 1761, the fair promise of his earlier years almost literally washed away by alcohol. Interestingly enough, though Arnold subsequently developed a love of rich living which included a taste for fine wines, he never drank immoderately himself, and he could not tolerate drunkenness in others. The memory of the old captain, his father, staggering home to the jeers and laughs of bystanders and often having to lean on the strong arm of his son, must have been constantly vivid and unpleasant. It may not be unreasonable, therefore, to suppose that Arnold's fierce desire to excel in all things, to become accepted as an eminently respectable citizen, and to defend his name from all slights and aspersions originated in part in the humiliation which his father's intemperance had brought upon his family.[8]

With his father's death, Arnold made up his mind to move to New Haven, a larger and more flourishing place than Norwich, and a town, moreover, where there were no associations of sorrow and shame. Besides, his father's brother, Oliver Arnold, lived there, a man of modest means but of becoming sobriety who might be helpful to him. Hence, while Hannah, his sister, remained in the family homestead pending its sale, Arnold set out for New Haven. His hopes were soaring. He was young, strong, and healthy; he had a trade and stock; he had seen a little of the world; he was tremendously ambitious; and he was his own master. These were incomparable attributes which, he was determined, would quickly bring him the fame and fortune his proud spirit demanded.

· III ·

Druggist and Merchant

Arnold wasted no time in setting up a business in New Haven. He first leased a store on Chapel Street about fifty yards east of the present Hotel Taft, then one on Church Street near the site of Sears Roebuck and Company, and finally one on Water Street. He filled his store with the drugs and merchandise from England, and he hung over it a black sign with the following legend in gilt letters :

B. ARNOLD

Druggist, Bookseller, &c.

From London

Sibi Totique

The Latin inscription, meaning "For himself and for all," was singularly appropriate, at least the first part. Certainly Arnold threw himself into his business with the utmost zeal, taking a progressively greater pride in the respect his clients held for him as "Dr. Arnold." [1]

Like the Lathrops, Arnold carried a wide range of items in his store. In fact, in its variety of offerings, his shop combined the features of the larger chain drug store of today and an old-fashioned general store. Among the preparations included in an advertisement of Arnold's were "Essence Balm Gilead," "Pectoral Balsam Honey," "Francis' Female Elixir," "Greenough's Tincture for the Teeth," and "James' Fever Powder." He sold mace, cinnamon, cloves, rosemary, figs, currants, and

Arnold wounded at the Battle of Bemis Heights, engraving made after Chappel's painting in 1858.

Major John André, from
a miniature attributed to
himself.

LE GENERAL ARNOLD un   des Chefs
de l'Armée Anglo Americaine

An idealized French conception of
General Arnold.

A famous imaginary portrait of Colonel Arnold, published after the
expedition against Quebec.

Webster Collection, New Brunswick Museum

and themselves forced to tithe to a Popish clergy. Alexander Hamilton contended that so many Catholics would now come to the New World that the Protestant colonies would soon be surrounded by "a Nation of Papists and Slaves." The intolerance of 1774 did not suddenly burst forth; it had a tradition of long standing. Arnold was therefore scarcely an exception in his prejudices. Furthermore, he considered it hardly proper for Hannah to see the dancing master alone. When he noticed that she did not discourage the man's attentions, he grew furious.[3]

Arnold could be dangerous when he was crossed. Although he expressed his sentiments in forthright fashion to Hannah, she ignored his protests. Deeply angered, he told her he would take strong measures if he ever found the fellow again in the house. Thereafter the two young people saw each other only when they were sure Arnold was not around. Unfortunately for their courtship, Arnold arrived from New Haven one evening and, glancing through the windows of the front room, saw in the candlelight the Frenchman conversing with Hannah. Arnold at once requested the friend who had accompanied him to knock at the door and enter the house as if he himself were Arnold. Meanwhile Arnold drew a pistol from his saddle bag, loaded it, and assumed a position in front of the house. When the friend knocked and entered, the terrified Frenchman threw open a window and leaped out. Instantly Arnold fired. Luckily for the dancing master, Arnold shot over the man's head simply to frighten him away. He was successful, for the Frenchman decided that Norwich was not a healthy place for him and soon left town. There is a story that the two men met again in the West Indies, that the Frenchman issued a challenge to Arnold which was promptly accepted, and that Arnold severely wounded the man.

It is significant that the four women who played important roles in his life—his mother, his sister, and his two wives—were without exception devoted to him. Though they must have been all too aware of his shortcomings, he had a way of retaining their loyalty. Perhaps this was because, virile and proud and independent as he was, he paid them the subtle compliment of needing them; certainly to a woman they responded. Hannah, his sister, was almost as proud as he was, and, because of Arnold's behavior toward the Frenchman, had every good reason for never wanting to see her brother again. Even so, however deep her grief at her young man's departure, and notwithstanding her indignation at Arnold, she forgave her brother and agreed to go to New Haven to keep his books and help him run his store. In 1764, therefore, Arnold sold the

Norwich property for £700 and presently expanded his activities in New Haven to become a merchant trading with Canada and the West Indies.[4]

Recourse to force was becoming characteristic of Arnold. It cropped up in his business affairs on more than one occasion. When ships from the same port or of the same nationality regardless of port found themselves together in a foreign roadstead, it was common practice for a round of visiting to occur. Usually the oldest captain or the captain of the largest ship would initiate the festivities by extending an invitation to his fellow skippers. Once, when in the Bay of Honduras, Arnold ran afoul of this custom. Several British and colonial ships were riding at anchor, and one Captain Croskie, an Englishman, invited the other masters to come aboard his vessel for the evening. At the time, Arnold was too busy getting his papers in order and arranging for his departure to accept, and, with the final loading going on, he could spare no seaman to row over to Croskie and explain his absence. The next day, however, he hastened to Croskie to offer his apologies in person. Croskie was a crusty character with a high regard for courtesy, and may also have been suffering from the morning-after effects of an excessive number of toasts the night before.

"You damned Yankee!" he shouted when Arnold came aboard. "Have you no manners?"

His face darkening with anger, Arnold challenged the man to a duel, and Croskie accepted. The duel was to take place on a small island near by, and Arnold, his seconds, and a surgeon were waiting on the shore before the early morning mists lifted. When Croskie failed to appear at the appointed time, Arnold was about to leave. Then one of the group spied a boat approaching with the Englishman, his seconds and his surgeon, and a half dozen natives. The presence of the natives excited Arnold's suspicions. Leveling his pistol at the boat, he forbade those aboard to come nearer or he would shoot, and he demanded an explanation from Croskie. Though the Englishman muttered some excuse, Arnold refused to accept it. Instead, he permitted only Croskie and the authorized members to come ashore, and he ordered the natives to row the boat away until the duel was over. The incident must have rattled Croskie. As the challenged party, he fired first, but the bullet went wide. Arnold's shot, however, plowed a furrow along Croskie's arm. When Croskie's wound was dressed and the pistols were again loaded, Arnold turned sharply toward the man.

"I give you notice," he said in an angry staccato, "if you miss this time, I shall kill you!"

Something in Arnold's voice and manner must have warned Croskie that his opponent meant exactly what he said. Promptly the Englishman apologized, and the hot-blooded Arnold, his honor satisfied, accepted the apology.[5]

More serious in a number of ways was the Boles affair, which cuts directly across the problem of colonial smuggling and certain basic causes of the American Revolution. The trade and navigation acts aimed to set up an economic system closed to all but one's own nationals, a policy common to all the maritime nations of Europe. If such a system had its advantages, such as the bounties offered on certain rare products and naval stores, the exclusion of foreign competitors, and the protection afforded by the navy, it had less desirable aspects, too. The colonists could find markets for their products only in Britain or her possessions. They could manufacture nothing that competed with manufactures in Britain. They could import molasses and sugar only from the British West Indies. Yet, until the Seven Years War, the acts gave little difficulty, largely because prime ministers paid little heed to their enforcement. The colonists made smuggling almost respectable by the regularity with which their brigs and sloops slipped home from the French and Spanish West Indies with cheaper-priced molasses and sugar in their holds than they could possibly obtain in British Jamaica.

The Seven Years War and the peace brought changes. The war had been so enormously expensive that the British government decided America should bear its share of the burden. Certainly the trade laws should be enforced, part of the army stationed in America, and Americans compelled by taxation to help defray the cost of army maintenance. Customs officers were harried out of their comfortable offices in England and sent over to their American jobs, the navy was instructed to assist in apprehending smugglers, while illicit traders were to be tried in admiralty courts and informers richly rewarded. Henceforth Americans were to be taught to respect the laws of the Crown. The new provisions naturally roused terror and anger in the colonies. Their objections soared to a violent crescendo in 1765 when the British government resolved to raise a revenue by requiring that official stamps be attached to wills, contracts, mortgages, and other articles, including dice. The excitement, however, quickly subsided when the government withdrew the Stamp Act. But, two years later, when the government, with Charles Townshend as the guiding spirit, resorted to indirect taxation by imposing taxes on tea, glass, paper, and lead, irritation broke out again and mounted so appreciably as the new system of customs collection became effective that violation of the laws became tantamount to a patriotic act.

In no other place than Connecticut, and New Haven especially, was opinion more sharply divided over these policies; and Arnold, as an active merchant, was solidly against the government. He attended many of the meetings of the radicals, as the opposition was called, and soon became recognized as one of their leaders. He had little patience with the conservatives, who included a number of the well-to-do merchants and most of the landed interests, notably the influential Old Lights of the First Ecclesiastical Society and the Episcopalians of Trinity Church. The radicals, on the other hand, drew their strength from the New Lights of other parishes; from most of the faculty and two-hundred-strong student body at Yale, whose president was Naphtali Daggett, an old Canterbury pupil of Dr. Cogswell; and from many of the shopkeepers, small merchants, sailors, and youth of the town. This last group in particular welcomed Arnold's appeals to use force if necessary in opposing Crown policies. They had less to lose by violence, and many of them comprised the rougher elements of the town's population to whom force was a solution at once simple and effective.

Arnold sincerely felt that the conservatives could see only as far as their own noses and interests. Compelled to trade in the expensive British market, the small merchant had to go out of business, plunge deeply into debt, or follow the example of the illustrious John Hancock of Boston and turn to smuggling. If recourse were had to the last, then the government might seize cargo, ship, and owner as well as master. All this seemed to Arnold, as it did to most people in the shipping business, a distorted and unnecessarily costly conception of the traditional English freedom. Hence he met frequently with crowds of radicals in the rum-and-smoke-laden atmosphere of the taverns and harangued them in his harsh, strident voice on the desirability of continuing to defy the customs officials and on the need of asserting their rights as Englishmen. Moreover, if he and those who thought like him could not seize control of the town meeting from the conservatives, they could at least challenge that control in other ways. One of the outstanding instances was the Boles case of 1766.[6]

Peter Boles was a sailor on the *Fortune,* one of Arnold's vessels. When the *Fortune* put into New Haven in January, 1766, Boles demanded wages that Arnold was unwilling to pay. Boles's demand looked like blackmail since he then went on January 24 to the customs house to inform the King's agents that Arnold was a smuggler. He failed to find the collector in, but he met one of the assistants, a man named Sanford, and inquired of him what share of a cargo seized by the Crown would be granted to an informer. When Sanford either could not or would not tell him, Boles refused to reveal what he knew. He said instead that he would withhold his information until the collector returned after the Sabbath.

On Monday, January 29, Arnold learned of Boles's action. At once he hunted him down and, as he later admitted, "gave him a little chastisement." Boles left town but soon returned. Arnold then cornered him again and forced from him a written confession that he had attempted to inform on Arnold, that he was instigated by the devil, and that he justly deserved a halter for his actions. He further declared that he would never again purvey information about any person in the colony, and he swore that he would leave New Haven immediately and never come back.

Several hours later, Arnold heard a noise in the street. Inquiry revealed that a gang of sailors had gathered at the dwelling house of John Beecher, a tavern keeper, where Boles, in defiance of Arnold, had resolved to remain. Deciding to make an example of the informer, Arnold bounded outdoors, took charge of the gang, broke into Beecher's house, and man-handled Boles into the street. Then, dragging Boles to the green, the men stripped him, tied him to a whipping post, and, in the presence of spectators attracted by the excitement, gave him forty lashes with "a small cord." Afterward, Arnold's gang ran the man out of town.

For some time the conservatives in New Haven had felt intimidated by the recklessness and violence of the radicals. Now, however, they rose up indignantly at Arnold's deed, and two members of the grand jury, John Wise and Tilley Blakeslee, at once prodded their fellow townsman, Roger Sherman, a justice of the peace, into ordering Arnold and nine others bound over for trial. Wise and Blakeslee had their courage with them, for the very next day, January 30, a mob roamed the streets hanging and burning them in effigy. Not only was this a demonstration in Arnold's behalf, it was also an expression of popular hatred of informers and a warning to those who defended them even if the law was on their side. But Sherman, like the jurymen, refused to be cowed by the mob, or impressed by the rather surprising fact that Jared Ingersoll, the stamp collector, acted as Arnold's attorney. Evidently Ingersoll saw nothing inconsistent in serving in one capacity as a government official bound to support the laws and in another as defense counsel for a man charged with breaking the laws. At any rate, in the subsequent trial Arnold lost his case and paid a fine of fifty shillings.

Arnold's infraction has the ring of vigilante justice or of a Ku Klux visitation, and at first blush one is apt to condemn him outright as a blackguard. This would be as unjust as it would be to excuse him. Instead, one should place the action in the context of the time in which he lived. Smuggling was popular, even patriotic, with his group, and was to become even more so as customs enforcement grew more rigorous. Throughout the colonies the King's officers and prominent Loyalists were living in constant jeopardy as Sons of Liberty resorted to bathing them in hot tar and feathers, subjecting them to the cruelly painful treatment of riding them out of town on a fence rail, and destroying their property. Boston street rowdies provoked the famous Massacre in 1770 by their menacing attitude toward British soldiers. Rhode Islanders burned the British sloop *Gaspé* in 1772 in their anger at a common navy device to which the law usually closed an eye, the use of the press gang to shanghai sailors aboard. Arnold's whipping of Boles was therefore of a piece with the increasingly violent opposition to the policies of the Crown.

Given the regard in which smuggling was held by the radicals, informers could expect but short shrift. Hence Arnold was especially exasperated that he had been singled out for legal action, action which he construed as indicative of New Haven's approval of the informer's attempted betrayal of him. Back at the high desk in his office, he dipped his quill and dashed off a furious letter to the press.

Is it good policy [he asked with bitter sarcasm], or would so great a number of people, in any trading town on the continent, (New Haven excepted) vindicate, caress, and protect an informer—a character particularly at this alarming time so odious to the public? Every such influence tends to suppress our trade, so advantageous to the Colony, and to almost every individual, both here and in Great Britain, and which is nearly ruined by the late detestable Stamp and other oppressive acts—acts which we have so severely felt and so loudly complained of, and so earnestly remonstrated against that one would imagine every sensible man would strive to encourage trade and discountenance such infamous informers.

To a man of Arnold's explosive nature the extent to which the law could be made the tool of expediency was often more important than its inherent principles of justice. Or, to put it differently, perhaps as Arnold himself would have looked at it, there was a higher law than that which protected a man against arbitrary punishment at the hands of his fellow citizens. Call it patriotism, call it enlightened self-interest, call it what one would, it took precedence over other considerations, and countenanced infractions of such legal regulations and rules of conduct as opposed its operation. Naturally such a loose interpretation of justice deeply offended conservatives to whom only the justice obtained through the regular and orderly processes of law was valid. Englishmen of that day often deplored the lawlessness of American colonials even as Easterners of a century ago denounced the strong-arm methods of frontier justice in the West. But though Arnold's act was no worse than the behavior of many of his contemporaries, it could hardly be excused on such grounds, or even excused at all. It was an act of terrorism in an age when terrorism of the sort was fast rising to the point of approval. Ironically it was Arnold's peculiar misfortune to be residing in a town that decided the time had come to scotch such violence and prosecute the offender.[7]

The following year, 1767, Arnold was in financial difficulties like many a Connecticut merchant. As colonial trade expanded, the demand for hard money grew. It was hoped that Parliament would permit a circulation of paper currency in order to facilitate the payment of obligations by colonial merchants, but Parliament was cool to the idea. The result was that, with specie tending to move toward England, the colonists were pushed closer to the wall. The situation was further complicated by the recklessness of a number of Connecticut merchants in involving themselves deeply in contractual obligations. Thus living beyond one's means is hardly a recent American folkway. In 1766, a firm in which the future governor, Jonathan Trumbull, was a partner failed, and Trumbull found himself in debt chiefly to British merchants in the amount of between £10,000 and £15,000. Benjamin Gale of Killingworth and Joseph Chew of New London were other important merchants loaded with debt. One Englishman said that Connecticut people "are all mortgaged to the full to the Bostonians and New Yorkers," that they were "very great rogues, no money amongst them, and nobody would live amongst them that could possibly live anywhere else!" Arnold himself owed London merchants more than £1,700 and was forced to make a conveyance of his sloop *Sally* and her cargo to them. Very possibly, as more than one authority has pointed out, there was a pretty direct relationship between the growth of radicalism with its anti-British feeling and the existence of a debtor class.[8]

His stringent situation impelled Arnold to try to beat the exchange the same year, a common practice indeed at the time. Bernard Lintot, legal counsel in America for London merchants with whom Arnold and many colonial merchants traded, had seized the *Sally* in May and wrote Jared

Ingersoll in August that he had worked out a satisfactory arrangement with Arnold with respect to the rum, dry goods, and freight money that would reduce Arnold's indebtedness to £1,160. Then Lintot added, "A difficulty seems to arise between Mr. Arnold & me respecting the exchange, which Mr. Arnold calculates at the nominal exchange in the colony; but as bills rise and fall, & are generally higher than the rate he calculates at, I think it but just that it should be calculated at the price I actually can buy bills at; otherwise I am not paid the proposed sum." Despite Arnold's attempt at sharp dealing, ultimately Lintot was more successful in collecting from Arnold than Arnold himself was from a merchant named John Remsen, who refused to repay Arnold money that was due him.[9]

Notwithstanding such financial devices and his leadership of the radicals, Arnold was by no means unacceptable to many of the "better" families of New Haven. No doubt there were people in the stately white houses behind the towering elms who considered him too aggressive, too ambitious, and perhaps too loud, but others welcomed him into a close convivial relationship. This was especially true of the Masonic Lodge in New Haven. Masonry stresses fortitude, temperance, prudence, and justice, encourages the practice of the Golden Rule, and believes in one God. In the eighteenth century, with the age of reason and reasonableness replacing the political and religious passions of the seventeenth century, the Masonic emphasis on tolerance proved very popular throughout western Europe and the colonies. In fact, Masonry became an especially select society. It numbered among its members many of the most eminent men in the colonies, including George Washington and Benjamin Franklin. Arnold was also a Mason. Admission to the society in one place, however, did not necessarily assure acceptance at another place. But Arnold, though probably admitted at one of the many lodges in the West Indies, was accepted at the lodge in New Haven on April 10, 1765. His acceptance was of considerable significance. The New Haven lodge was very small but had on its roll the names of such distinguished citizens as Colonel David Wooster, a veteran of two wars with the French, Colonel Nathan Whiting, who was not only an able military man but became a beloved and renowned professor of divinity at Yale, and Samuel Mansfield, high sheriff of the county. Nathan Whiting presented Arnold for membership. Had Arnold been so completely the rascal he is sometimes represented to have been in New Haven, it seems hardly possible that this small group of "first citizens" of the town would have accepted him into their fellowship.[10]

Further evidence of the growth of Arnold's social status is seen in his marriage in the winter of the very year in which he subsequently experienced temporary financial embarrassment. Late in 1766, he began to court the modest, attractive daughter of a fellow Mason, Samuel Mansfield. The Mansfields were one of the most prominent families in New Haven, and it is unlikely that the high sheriff of the county would have given his daughter to anyone whom he considered not respectable. As a Mason, he had had an unparalleled opportunity to observe Arnold for nearly two years. He could not have regarded the Boles case as a sufficient obstacle; indeed it is highly probable that the importance of the Boles incident has been exaggerated by critics eager to build it up as an indictment of Arnold's character and ripping it out of its context in their zeal. Possessor of a fair education, an expanding business, and a reputation for being ambitious and enterprising, Arnold was a very eligible bachelor. Besides there was something of the glamour of the gentleman sport about him since he was an excellent horseman, a good shot with a pistol, and a superb skater, and always dressed in the height of fashion; in a day when gentlemen took pride in displaying a well-turned stockinged calf, Arnold liked to sheathe his legs in the finest white silk. His young lady, who had a number of suitors on her string, was a real catch herself, but soon succumbed to the dark-faced Arnold's impetuous wooing. On February 22, 1767, he married the sheriff's daughter, the first of the two Margarets who were to become his wives.[11]

So far as is known, Margaret Mansfield was Arnold's first love, and he adored and respected her. "Peggy," as he called her, was a gentle, affectionate, rather pious girl, three years younger than himself. Despite a certain fragility of health, she successfully bore him three sons: Benedict, born February 14, 1768; Richard, born August 22, 1769; and Henry, born September 19, 1772. Arnold surrounded Peggy with luxuries which at times were beyond his capacity to afford because of the fluctuating fortunes of the trading business. Though he became a rich man, Peggy must have been distinctly uncomfortable on occasion. In January, 1774, Arnold wrote her from the West Indies a letter that revealed something not only of the husband and father but also of the wife's responsibilities:[12]

Jany. 21, 1774

Dear Peggy:

Inclosed is Captain Sage's remit for ten joannes, and Jon Barrett's, which he is to sell in Turk's Island and remit you the proceeds—which I expect will be six joannes more—this is all I could possibly send you at present. I hope those people I owe will rest easy until I return. If not you must get Mr. Chauncey to put of[f] matters until I return, when they may all depend on being immediately paid.

I a few days since heard of the death of Mrs. Babcock and Polly Austin, which surprised me much—they were in the prime of life and as likely to live as any of us; how uncertain is life, how certain is death; may their loud and affecting calls, awaken us to prepare for our own exit, whenever it shall happen. My dear Life, pray by no means neglect the education of our dear boys, it is of infinite concern, what habits and principles they imbibe when young. I hope this will find you all well, and that the Almighty may preserve you in health and happiness is the sincere prayer of d[ea]r Peggy

Your loving husband
Benedict Arnold

With his wife and sister keeping an eye on his business when he was away, Arnold plunged ever more deeply into trade. On January 24, 1766, a year before his marriage, he had advertised in the *Connecticut Gazette* for "large, genteel, fat horses, pork, oats, and hay," and mentioned his desire to sell "choice cotton and salt, by quantity or retail: and other goods as usual." He controlled at that time three small ships, the *Fortune,* of forty tons; the *Sally,* of thirty tons; and the *Three Brothers,* of twenty-eight tons. Though he temporarily lost the *Sally* in 1767 when Lintot seized it, he retained the others and kept them active. He continued to buy horses, pork, wheat, and barrel staves, and sold them in the West Indies for molasses and rum. He kept a sloop plying between Quebec and Barbados. He learned to know well the city of Quebec with its steep, narrow streets, where merchants recognized him as a shrewd horse trader, and where he struck up a friendship with John Dyer Mercier, merchant and coroner of Quebec. He roamed through Albany, the Lake Champlain country, and the Sorel River Valley to Montreal, where he talked trade and politics with a rich merchant and fellow Mason named Thomas Walker, formerly a King's commissioner for the peace. Thus in days of peace he became familiar with country over which the storms of war were so soon to break, with Arnold himself in a position of paramount responsibility and command.[13]

After his marriage, Arnold was more anxious than ever to make as much money as possible, whether in Canada, the West Indies, New England, or New York. Not only did he have a growing family to provide for, he also had plans for building a house that would reflect his increasing affluence and importance. In 1770, construction started on property that he had bought on Water Street. The house was completed in 1771. It was, to use a favorite adjective of the day, an "elegant" white clapboard mansion, having two stories, two chimneys, a portico, pillars, a marble fireplace, and panel work on the first floor. Each bedroom in the second story had a fireplace, and there were roomy closets throughout the house. In a little hall just off a side door, Arnold had a large shoebox built to hold the many pairs of shoes that captured his fancy. Under each chimney in the cellar was a large arched area where he stored his wines. There was also a secret staircase that landed one in a large closet opening into a front room on the first floor. In front of the house stood a white picket fence, while behind lay stables, a coachhouse, and gardens with graveled walks. Fruit trees, elms, and maples grew in abundance on the nearly three acres of land. On the waterside stretched Arnold's wharves, and, adjacent to them, was the new store into which he moved. Whether in his house or store, he had an unrestricted view of the harbor and Long Island Sound, and, with the aid of a glass, could identify his own ships homeward bound. So attractive was the site that his father-in-law built a house next to it; it was more convenient now for the sheriff to drop in on Peggy, whom he dearly loved, and walk down to Arnold's store, chat with Hannah, and order the prodigious quantities of rum he drank.

After Arnold's treason, the state confiscated the property, then sold it. Noah Webster acquired the house in 1812 while working on his dictionary, but soon got rid of it and fled inland because of his fear of a British invasion. Eventually the house, long known as 155 Water Street, was torn down to make way for a lumber company. At the time Arnold owned it, however, the house was one of the finest in New Haven, and, for some time after he lost it, its spacious and beautiful gardens attracted visitors throughout the city, lingering evidence indeed of Arnold's dream to create a fitting background for the daughter of Samuel Mansfield, provide a substantial legacy in real estate for his sons, and express in mortar, wood, and land the aspirations to the social standing and recognition that he cherished.[14]

While building his new house, Arnold became extremely exercised over scurrilous tales circulating in New Haven concerning his conduct in the Bay of Honduras. A shipmaster named Brookman, whose own behavior suggests that he was a friend of the Captain Croskie whom Arnold had wounded, provoked a quarrel with Arnold for the latter's refusing to pay him a courtesy visit aboard his ship. Brookman, a skilled fencer, chose the sword as his weapon, but in the duel that resulted he had no better fortune than Croskie. Arnold's strength, nimbleness of foot, and supple wrist made him a dangerous opponent, though he possessed greater skill with a pistol. His triumph did nothing to enhance his popularity in that quarter of the world, where he drove hard bargains, loaded and unloaded his vessels with alacrity in his awareness that the first ship into port commanded the choicest prices in the market, and often disregarded the social amenities.

Shortly after his defeat of Brookman, the rumor spread in New Haven that the duel had occurred because of Arnold's wanting to take from Brookman a woman the latter was keeping, while another story became current that Arnold had contracted venereal disease in the Bay. These tales threw Arnold into a rage. He sent down an agent, Elihu Hall, to obtain depositions from business acquaintances in the Bay. As he wrote them, the last report in particular "has hurt my character here very much and given my family and friends much uneasiness." His acquaintances could attest to "my being in perfect health all the time I was in the Bay" since they had been aboard daily. "I . . . shall take it as a particular favor," he declared, "[if] you'd give Hall your deposition in regard to my character in the Bay my manner [of] living, with regard to drinks when at your house and the compy I kept which I believe no one can say was of bad character, but the most reputable people. . . . " He also sought depositions in regard to the true nature of his difficulty with Brookman.[15]

The situation contained elements with which he had to contend throughout his life. He was now a capable businessman even as later he became a brilliant general, and his success in both fields caused deep and vindictive jealousy. Had he possessed a gentle, tractable disposition, his competitors could have found little in him to criticize; he would have lacked the qualities that made him conspicuously successful. He evinced an unusually quick intelligence, a driving energy in his work that was almost ferocious, and an aggressive will that was often ruthless. As if these were not sufficiently disconcerting to his rivals, he also exhibited an insufferable arrogance, an atrocious lack of tact, and a self-righteousness that was nothing short of smug. Frequently unable to contend openly against him, enemies resorted to sniping at him, maligning his intentions and conduct, indulging in whispering campaigns of the vilest character.

Whether there was any truth in these tales of his deportment in the Bay is an open question. Certainly there was none concerning the cause of the duel, while venereal disease of the type evidently meant can be sufficiently incapacitating temporarily for Arnold not to have dared ask business acquaintances, who also did business with his enemies, to testify that he was healthy if indeed he had been ill. On the other hand, it is likely that in his business ethics he was troubled by few scruples, though in all fairness it must be acknowledged that the age in which he lived was not remarkable for an elevated moral code in commercial affairs. What is significant, however, is that he roused in business the same general type of opposition that he provoked when a soldier. He could publish every deposition he could obtain, and there would still be those who believed the worst, even as later a Congressional board of investigation would clear him of charges made by enemies and there would remain in both the army and in politics men who continued to believe him a villain.

Hard man of business though he was, Arnold was devoted to his family, and he grieved when letters failed to arrive from Peggy. Not only were mails irregular but Peggy was a poor correspondent as well. "I have now been in the West Indies seven weeks and have not heard one syllable from you since I left home, which . . . gives me a great deal uneasiness," he wrote from St. Croix in May, 1766; "[De]ar girl it seems a whole age since I left you." On August 8, 1768, once again in St. Croix, he said, "I have not had the pleasure to receive any letters from you, though there has been several vessels from New Haven. . . . I hope a few days, every one of which seems an age, will make me happy with you and my friends in New Haven." Five days later, he added reproachfully, "I assure you I think it hard you have wrote me only once when there has been so many opportunities . . . you cannot imagine how anxious I am to see you." Peggy, however, refused to change, nor did Arnold ever become reconciled to her negligence. From Quebec, in the fall of 1773, where he had trouble with informers again and with a lack of ready cash to pay off a debt, exasperation mingled with concern when he wrote, "I am now under the greatest anxiety and suspense, not knowing whether I write to the dead or the living, not having heard . . . from you this four months." He had "expected answers" to his letters but had been "disappointed." About to leave now for Barbados before heading for New Haven, he hoped she would not trouble herself about his debts but would "rest easy until I return." He was always solicitous that she not worry about him, but her deficiency as a letter writer caused him much concern about her.[16]

By 1775, only thirty-four years old, Arnold had come far. A few years later, to a court-martial sitting in Morristown, New Jersey, he said of these prewar days that he was in easy circumstances and enjoyed a fair prospect of improving them. There is little valid reason to believe that he was exaggerating. Though his fortunes varied with the ebb and flow of the tides of commerce and the ups and downs of the exchange, he had his spacious home, store, warehouses, wharves, and vessels. He was a merchant and an apothecary, and successful in both respects. If his social standing was still dubious in the opinion of a number of the older families in New Haven, he enjoyed the confidence of other families as respectable and as well endowed. His leadership of the radical elements, moreover, was firmly established. He was a man to watch, he knew it himself, and his resolve was high to make his name one not to be quickly forgotten.

· IV ·

The Call to Arms

WHILE Arnold was improving his fortunes in the early 1770's, feeling between Britain and the colonies sharpened appreciably. Although the government rescinded all duties except a threepenny tax on tea, it retained that as a symbol of its right to tax, and its admiralty courts continued to condemn American ships for smuggling. The anniversary of the Boston Massacre of 1770 became an occasion for flights of sulphurous oratory against alleged British tyranny. Meanwhile King's officials and Loyalists lived hazardous lives. American radicals were coming to look upon loyalty to the Crown as a hostile attitude, and Sons of Liberty organizations increased their terrorist activities. Not even clergymen were immune to the manhandling tactics of these vaunted patriots. In fact, with the pulpit such a powerful instrument for influencing opinion, the Sons considered it especially necessary to silence ministers who still dared to speak out boldly for compliance with Crown policies.

Arnold thoroughly approved of these demonstrations of opposition. His main fear was that his countrymen would meekly submit to the dictates of the Crown; this was particularly true when he learned of the Boston Massacre. On hearing the news in June while trading at St. George's Key in the West Indies, he wrote at once to a New Haven merchant friend and future selectman, Benjamin Douglas. "Good God," he exploded, "are the Americans all asleep and calmly giving up their glorious liberties, or, are they all turned philosophers, that they don't take immediate vengeance on such miscreants. I am afraid of the latter and that we shall all soon see ourselves as poor and as much oppressed as ever heathen philosopher was." In Arnold's opinion there was no sense in the colonists' further beguiling themselves that their relations with Britain could be settled on a reasonable basis satisfactory to all.[1]

Four years later, he and David Wooster, subsequently a general in the Revolution, are alleged to have attempted to use force on the Loyalist clergyman, the Reverend Samuel Peters. This clergyman was a stormy petrel in Connecticut. A native of Hebron, he strongly supported the King and denounced the action of the Boston "Mohawks" who boarded the three tea ships of the East India Company in the harbor and dumped their cargoes overboard. In August, 1774, a Sons of Liberty band searched his house. A month later, a mob of several hundred radicals from Hebron and towns near by roughed him up and forced him to make a confession repenting of his position. Peters at once left town, rode to Hartford, and sought the protection of Governor Trumbull, whom he held chiefly responsible for the outbreak. Failing to obtain the satisfaction he sought from the governor, who officially disapproved of the mob activities, Peters fled to New Haven, where he applied to the Reverend James Hillhouse for protection.

In his account of his New Haven adventure, Peters said that Hillhouse replied, "My house is your protection, yet I want protection myself against the mobs of Colonel Wooster and Dr. Benedict Arnold, who are mobbing the Sandemanians [a Christian sect of Scottish origin notable for its Loyalist affinities] for having spoken against the outrageous conduct of the destroyers of the teas in Boston harbour. But as you decline my offer, I advise you to put up at the house of the Rev. Dr. Hubbard, and, if any disturb you, warn them to keep out of the yard and house upon pain of death; and if they break the gate, shoot them, and kill as many as enter the yard. I will raise men and come to your assistance."

In a spirit of charity Hubbard let Peters enter the house, but he wisely removed himself and his family elsewhere on hearing that Arnold and Wooster intended to pay Peters a visit. Meanwhile, promising to repay Hubbard for any damage that might occur, Peters obtained twenty muskets, distributed them among his servants and a friend, barred the gate, and awaited the New Haven patriots.

At about ten o'clock that evening, Arnold arrived in front of the house. Finding the gate barred, he called on Peters to open it.

The clergyman, however, holding his musket ready, retorted, "The gate shall not be opened this night on pain of death!"

At this defiance Arnold's gang grew angry and roared for their leader to break down the gate so that they could get at the minister. Thus encouraged, Arnold called for an axe.

But Peters heard him and shouted from a window, "Arnold, so sure as you split the gate, I will blow your brains out, and all that enter this yard to-night!"

After a long moment of hesitation, Arnold prudently withdrew. Though he was brave to the point of rashness, there was a ring of determination in the preacher's voice that was utterly convincing. And when his followers suddenly taunted him with being a coward, he turned on them. "I am no coward," he said sharply, "but I know Dr. Peter's disposition and temper, and he will fulfill every promise he makes; and I have no wish for death at the present."

Since no one expressed by word or deed the contrary wish, the mob soon broke up. Wooster's gang arrived a half hour later, but when Peters again made his threat to kill any intruder, Wooster likewise retired. Peters eventually made his escape to Boston and British protection.

The only account of the Peters incident that has survived in detail is that of Peters himself in his *General History of Connecticut,* a book filled with rancor, prejudice, and misstatement. There is little doubt that Peters had an unpleasant experience in New Haven, and Arnold may indeed have been involved as Peters related. Though Arnold had been in the West Indies in the winter and spring, and though a study of the customs house reports suggests the possibility that he may still have been there at the time of the incident, there is no conclusive evidence that he was not present in New Haven. Furthermore, in view of his strong opinions and his addiction to the use of force, he could have led a Sons of Liberty gang against Peters.

But Peters's inclusion of Wooster as well makes one wonder about the minister's veracity or the reliability of his information. Wooster's entire character runs counter to the allegation that he was a rabble-rouser. If ever there was a conservative and law-abiding man by instinct and reputation, it was Wooster. A veteran, he deplored the use of force wherever it could be avoided, and deeply regretted the necessity of a break with Britain, though he warmly supported such an event when it occurred, even to giving his life. At the time of the Peters affair, he was sixty-four years old, hardly an age to engage in street brawls. It is possible, of course, that Peters may have been correct in regard to Arnold and Wooster. On the other hand, he or his informants may have been mistaken concerning the identity of the mob leaders; or, writing in 1781, four years after Wooster had died as a result of battle wounds and one year following Arnold's treachery, he may have considered them convenient whipping boys in castigating the province that had treated him so harshly.[2]

Arnold's alleged raid on Peters was symptomatic of the times. Throughout New England, Loyalists were being hounded by mobs. In Connecticut, in addition to Hebron and New Haven, mob violence broke out in Fairfield, New Town, Windham, Farmington, and Hartford, where the radical Whigs rose against Peters's brother, Jonathan, riding him out of town on a rail and excoriating him as "a Tory, a Tory, a cursed damned churchman." Although radicals denied that these gatherings were mobs, those Loyalists who were so unfortunate as to experience a hasty exit on a fence rail, with or without the "New fashion dress of tar and feathers," had little ground for doubts. And men of Arnold's impulsive, emotional nature, prone to violence, had a field day.[3]

Not long after the closing of the port of Boston as a result of the famous tea party, Arnold received a singular honor. With militia companies springing up throughout the colonies, a group of sixty-five New Haven "gentlemen of influence and high respectability" (the expression sounds like Arnold's), as they called themselves, met on December 28, 1774, and signed articles of agreement forming themselves into a company, hiring an instructor to teach them "the military exercise," and providing that each member equip and uniform himself. Arnold was one of the original members of this group and, in the middle of February, 1775, was appointed to a committee of three "to make inquiry how a stand of arms can be procured in the best way." On March 2, the group petitioned the General Assembly to be constituted as the "Governor's Second Company of Guards," with all the rights and privileges possessed by the First Company organized in Hartford in 1771. The Assembly at once granted them a charter. According to this charter, the election of officers took place on March 15 under the supervision of a colonel of militia, Leverett Hubbard. Arnold, whose zeal was clearly evident from the start, was chosen captain of the company. Membership in the Footguards, as they were subsequently called, conferred a certain prestige, while the command position conferred both prestige and power, particularly in the event of hostilities; it also signified a real recognition of leadership and ability.

Such a post was dear to Arnold's heart, and he was soon to have an opportunity to demonstrate its importance.[4]

Arnold's great career as a soldier really began after the news of the fighting at Lexington and Concord arrived in New Haven. That fateful day, April 19, 1775, had been a Wednesday, a day that Governor Trumbull had set aside in Connnecticut for fasting and prayer. New Haven people went to church to ask God's blessing on King George III "that he may have the divine direction in all his administration, and his government be just, benign, gracious and happy to the nation and these colonies." On Friday, about noon, one Israel Bissell galloped into town with news that the King's troops had fallen short of being gracious at Lexington and Concord. Within an hour, two events occurred that fanned into a blaze the excitement sweeping the town.[5]

The first was the summoning of a town meeting at the "Middle Brick" Church, the stronghold of the conservative Old Lights. At the meeting the conservatives who had supported Jared Ingersoll for years missed by only one vote keeping the choice of the radicals, Roger Sherman, from being elected moderator. As a radical, Sherman was hardly in the same class as Arnold, but he was definitely on the side of those who favored supporting the Massachusetts rebels. Notwithstanding his chairmanship, the conservatives decided against sending armed aid to the rebels, and appointed a committee, most of whom were conservatives, to look after the interests of the town.

These people reckoned without Benedict Arnold, who was responsible for the second incident of note. When Bissell reached town with his intelligence, Arnold suddenly realized that the time had at last arrived when the measures he had advocated must now be adopted. Force on the part of the government could only be countered by force on the part of its subjects; and as a man of action he welcomed a test of the policies of the Crown, which were becoming as humiliating in their political implications for the colonists in general as they were for merchants like himself in particular. Furthermore, this was a glorious opportunity for himself and his Guards to show that they could do more than act as a splendid ornament to New Haven. Knowing that most of the Guards were available since they had held a meeting the night before and had agreed to invite all the clergy in New Haven to dine with them on May 2, he sent runners to assemble the group. Once together, fifty of them enthusiastically agreed to Arnold's proposal that they march for Cambridge the very next day, Saturday, April 22. Several Yale students who asked to join them were at once accepted. The town buzzing with rumors of these two contrary actions, Arnold then went home.

Though greatly excited, Arnold realized that this leavetaking of his family possessed a potential finality. Heretofore he had faced the hazards of land journeys and sea trips, ventures that had indeed placed his life in the balance, but this time, with military action imminent, the hazards were multiplied. Arnold, however, was not one to shrink from danger. While it was painful to bid farewell to his family, of whom he was very fond, and while he disliked leaving his business, which Peggy and Hannah must carry on as best they could in his absence, Arnold followed his sense of duty and the siren call to glory. The next morning, in the company of his wife, his three small sons, and his sister, he headed for the green.

His company made a vivid splash of scarlet on the sprouting grass, and none looked more colorful than the short, energetic Arnold himself in the uniform adopted by the organization: a scarlet coat trimmed with silver-wash buttons, with the lapels, collar, cuffs, and facings of buff; a ruffled shirt; white waistcoat and breeches; and black half-leggings. Parading the Guards before a large crowd, he inspected their arms, uniforms, and equipment. Then, after the company listened to an exhortation by the Reverend Jonathan Edwards, Arnold sent a request for powder and ball to the selectmen, who were meeting in a tavern near by with the committee appointed the day before. The selectmen bluntly refused to comply with the request. His choler rising, Arnold briskly marched his company to the tavern and dispatched a messenger to inform the city fathers that if the keys to the powder house were not delivered to him within five minutes he would order his men to break open the door to the magazine and help themselves.

Arnold was hardly popular with the civic leaders, but undoubtedly there were those present who remembered the Boles affair and Arnold's reputation where violence was concerned. In a desperate effort to dissuade him, they sent David Wooster to reason with him. Wooster knew better than to order Arnold to dismiss his company; instead, he urged him to wait for orders from the proper authorities before marching.

"None but Almighty God shall prevent my marching!" Arnold retorted hotly.

Perceiving that the captain meant what he said and that his impatience was increasing, Wooster returned to the tavern. After a few minutes of heated discussion, the keys were handed over to Arnold.

A short time later, supplied with powder and ball, the company formed ranks again. Its flag, emblazoned in gold with the arms and motto of the colony, *Qui transtulit sustinet* (He Who brought us across supports us), rippled in the breeze, a drum began to roll, a fife struck up, and, at a crisp command from their leader, the Guards marched up the road toward Hartford, while the crowd cheered lustily and small boys and dogs raced madly after them.[6]

Arnold spent the second night in Wethersfield, where he and his men were warmly entertained. The Sabbath was more than welcome, for they had marched nearly twenty miles for each of the two days, no mean feat for men just out of the store, the office, and the classroom. While in Wethersfield, probably on Monday morning before leaving for Cambridge, Arnold and the Guards signed a singular type of document. They agreed to conduct themselves decently and inoffensively in relation to themselves and their countrymen. They pledged themselves to avoid, and to discourage in others, all drunkenness, gaming, profanity, and "every vice of that nature." Finally they swore to obey their officers, who should in no event enforce their orders by blows, and they declared that if any member should persist in being incorrigible, he should be expelled from the company "as totally unworthy of serving in so great and glorious a cause." The covenant has a highly moral tone throughout and expresses the exalted sense of fellowship and dedication that animated Arnold and his men in those early days of the Revolution.[7]

Once they reached Cambridge, Arnold billeted them in the mansion formerly occupied by Lieutenant Governor Oliver, a Loyalist who had been forced to flee. Because of their soldierly appearance, they were detailed to deliver to General Gage the body of a British officer who had been wounded and captured at Lexington, and who had since died. It is said that another British officer, one of a group appointed to receive the body of their comrade, expressed surprise at seeing an American unit so well trained and equipped. One can easily imagine the pride that Arnold must have felt at such a compliment.[8]

But Arnold chose not to continue as just another officer in the army outside the beleaguered city of Boston. On his way from Hartford to Cambridge he had met Colonel Samuel H. Parsons returning to Connecticut to recruit. Parsons expressed his concern at the defenseless state of the American siege lines because of the want of cannon. Possibly relying on his own observations during his travels in the region, but more likely drawing on information recently acquired from other sources, Arnold, unfortunately for his aspirations to early fame, mentioned the deteriorating condition of Fort Ticonderoga and the abundance of brass cannon there. After the two officers went their separate ways, both began to turn the matter over in their minds. By the time they had reached their destinations, they had also reached the same decision: to capture Ticonderoga, then defended by one Captain William Delaplace and a small detachment of the 27th Foot.

Parsons arrived in Hartford the same day on which he had talked with Arnold, and soon set in motion a train of events that, in the end, was to expose Arnold to the most acute humiliation. He conferred with prominent citizens, including Colonel Samuel Wyllys and Silas Deane. They decided to procure men, money, and supplies for the task without waiting to consult the Assembly. Then someone remembered that a Vermonter was in town, a man named Heman who was on business for that leather-lunged, free-swinging semi-outlaw of the Green Mountains, Ethan Allen. Sending for Heman, this committee explained its intention and hurried him homeward with a commission for Allen to muster a force of Green Mountain Boys and take the fort. The committee also promised reinforcements and money.[9]

While Heman was spurring northward, the Hartford group raised £300 and sent it along with two able recruiting agents, Noah Phelps of Simsbury and Bernard Romans of Hartford, an engineer who had spent many years of service in Florida. Shortly after Phelps and Romans departed, a sober-sided soldier, Captain Edward Mott, entered Hartford from Cambridge to assemble a company for service there. He, too, talked of the cannon at Ticonderoga; perhaps he, like Parsons, had encountered Arnold. The Hartford people quickly persuaded him that he would be more valuable to them than to the army in Cambridge, and appointed him supreme commander of the expedition. Mott soon reached Castleton, Vermont, where Allen, who had independently decided to take Ticonderoga, now awaited the Connecticut party after Heman had dashed into Ethan's lair at the Catamount Tavern in Bennington with word of the Hartford plans and the promise of funds.[10]

On their way through Pittsfield the Connecticut men were joined by forty Massachusetts recruits and two important officers. One was Colonel James Easton, a tavern keeper of forceful presence, but a man who could be coarse, garrulous, and slippery. The other was Major John Brown, an energetic, glib-tongued young lawyer who had graduated from Yale, read law with Arnold's cousin, Oliver Arnold, attorney general of Rhode Island, and married Oliver's sister. Brown, who had recently been in

Canada for the Boston committee of correspondence, had written of the urgency of seizing Ticonderoga at the outbreak of hostilities. Thus the idea of capturing the fort was very much in the air, having occurred to Arnold, Brown, Allen, Parsons, Mott, and possibly others as well. At any rate, the Connecticut arrivals now conferred with Allen and his officers in Castleton on May 7 and 8. Mott, who held the money bags, was elected president of the council of war. Since Mott had promised the men enlisted that they would serve under their own officers, and since Allen had raised most of the men, Ethan was given command of the assault force. That night, when the council was over, Allen left for Hand's Cove, at which point both men and boats were to assemble for an attack across Lake Champlain during the night of May 9–10.[11]

While the plans for this expedition were maturing, Arnold had developed his own project for capturing the fort. Soon after arriving in Cambridge, he presented his plan to the Massachusetts committee of safety, describing on April 30 the ruined condition of the fort, its small garrison, and the large stores of ordnance available. The committee at first dispatched a messenger with the information to its counterpart in New York as the likely body to authorize the seizure. Then, thanks to Dr. Joseph Warren, dynamo of the Patriot cause, it decided on May 3 not to wait; it appointed Arnold to a colonelcy, commissioned him to raise a force not to exceed four hundred men in western New England, and ordered him to take Ticonderoga. He was also supplied with munitions, ten horses, and £100 in cash for his enterprise, a ludicrously inadequate sum. Reaching Stockbridge, Arnold learned of Allen's expedition. Alarmed and angry that he might be too late, he left an officer to proceed with the recruiting and galloped for the north. At Castleton on the evening of May 9, Arnold confronted the Connecticut council of war that had appointed Allen, and with bold assurance demanded the command for himself on the ground that the council had no "proper" orders. When the council refused to surrender the command to him, Arnold rode after Allen, all the officers following for fear he might prevail on Ethan.[12]

For Arnold the issue was of the utmost importance. The personal element, of course, can never be omitted in any consideration of Arnold. Capture of Ticonderoga would bring great fame to the leader of the attacking force, and Arnold was zealous of achieving a military reputation of the first order. But apart from personal prestige, Arnold felt that the venture was too important to entrust to an irresponsible freebooter like Allen, whose commission emanated from an irregularly constituted committee. On the other hand, there was no question of the legality of his own commission, and he had no doubt that he could carry out the attack far more efficiently than Allen. He seems not to have considered, however, that his insistence on sole command was likely to jeopardize the success of the undertaking, which was scheduled to come off within a few hours.

Arnold caught up with Allen at Hand's Cove early in the morning, and the scene between the proud, hot-tempered, little Arnold in his scarlet regimentals and the fiery giant from the Green Mountains in a uniform of his own invention—green coat, buff breeches, and huge gold epaulettes—must have been an interesting one. Both were adventurers, both had nimble tongues, and neither was disposed to humility. As he had done before the council, so now Arnold produced his commission from the Massachusetts committee of safety and demanded the command in his most rasping, imperious tone. It was an awkward moment—the boats were assembling, daylight was not far off, and Allen was anxious to make full use of what cover of darkness remained. At the same time, he was one man that Arnold could not intimidate.

"What shall I do with the damned rascal—put him under guard?" Ethan is reported to have asked a friend, Amos Callender.

"Better go side by side," Callender replied.

At once the men standing around raised a violent protest. They were all for marching home: "Damn the pay . . . they would not be commanded by any others but those they engaged with." When Allen and Easton hurriedly assured them that Arnold would not command them, Arnold, his face congested with rage, shouted that this was not so. At this point, Allen suddenly proposed a kind of joint command whereby Arnold was to march with him at the head of the column as Callender had suggested but was to give no orders. Realizing that this was the best arrangement he could obtain, Arnold reluctantly agreed. Though Allen's partial submission may have occurred in part because Arnold's commission had been granted by an official committee of safety whereas his own was simply from an informal group in Connecticut, Ethan's awareness of time running out was undoubtedly the crucial factor that impelled him to compromise.[13]

The force, about two hundred, now moved to the boats. There was room aboard for only about eighty-five at one crossing, including Allen and Arnold, and, once ashore north of the fort, the leaders dared not waste further time waiting for the rest. It was already three o'clock, with a paleness showing in the eastern sky. After briefly exhorting the men,

Allen led them down a road skirting the east wall of the fort to a wicket gate on the south side. A sleepy sentry snapped his musket, but the gun misfired; and the man took to his heels as Allen and Arnold, with the Green Mountain Boys at their backs, swarmed into the fort. It was quickly over: the garrison subdued, the sword of the commander, Captain Delaplace, reposing in Ethan's hand, and the invading horde drunk for liberty and joy on the captain's rum. Allen and Arnold had taken the first offensive action for the colonies, and it had ended in a bloodless victory of enormous value. But the triumph was also the first important military frustration that Arnold encountered at the hands of his countrymen; it was Ethan Allen's name, not his, that the colonists identified with the capture of the great fortress.

· V ·

The Disputed Command at Ticonderoga

THE CAPTURE of Ticonderoga with its vast stores of military supplies and cannon, which were to prove so helpful in driving the British from Boston the next winter, was not even hours old that May morning before Arnold again brought up the command issue. The Green Mountain Boys possessed courage but no discipline, and celebrated their triumph in true buccaneering fashion. Disgusted at the drinking and plundering which he sought vainly to prevent, Arnold renewed his demand for the sole command. Again the troops threatened to quit if they had to serve under him, and it took a great deal of persuasion by Allen and Mott to convince them that Arnold would not be permitted to command them. Then the two officers turned on Arnold and told him once more that, since he had brought no men along, he could not expect to command theirs. But Arnold refused to be impressed by Mott's dour looks or Allen's bluster; he continued to insist that they possessed no legal orders. At this point, Mott resolved to end the fantastic situation. As the real leader of the Connecticut expedition, holding his commission from the Hartford committee, he directed Allen to retain command of the fort until further orders were received from Connecticut or the Continental Congress.[1]

It was an unhappy day for Arnold. A committee consisting of Mott,

Phelps, Easton, and one Epaphras Bull wrote an account of the capture and the dispute and sent it to the Massachusetts Congress by Easton, with whom Arnold had such harsh words that Easton swore to do him all the injury in his power. Oddly enough, notwithstanding the quarrel, Arnold also gave Easton a letter to deliver to the committee of safety; he could not have been greatly surprised to learn that the committee never received it. To make life less congenial for him, Allen's drunken followers openly derided him and actually shot at him on two occasions. Arnold's anger at these insulting actions was hardly less acute than his sense of humiliation. He had left his family and his business and volunteered for what appeared at the time as a patriotic duty. But to what end? The answer was all too clear to him: to become the butt of ridicule for ignorant louts with no soldierly qualities or conception of discipline, men who were led by a loud-mouthed brigand scarcely more cultivated than themselves. Still if Arnold thought of quitting the fort, he gave no indication. He was certain his day would come. One can discern the measure of his disgust in the fact that he found the company of the captured officers, Captain Delaplace and his second-in-command, Lieutenant Jocelyn Feltham, infinitely more agreeable than that of his own compatriots.[2]

But presently Arnold's fortunes improved. On May 14, a schooner arrived from Skenesborough (now Whitehall); it had belonged to the great landowner in those parts, Major Philip Skene, a Loyalist, whose estate had been captured by some of Allen's men. Aboard the schooner, sailed by a young New Haven distiller who was one of Arnold's Footguards, Eleazer Oswald, were a few of Allen's men and a body of fifty recruits enlisted by Arnold's agents. With a new project in mind, Arnold now shook off his gloom and discussed with Allen what could be done to obtain command of the lake. Seth Warner had seized Crown Point, but the lake could scarcely be considered secure until a large sloop at St. Johns on the Sorel River was captured. A council of war, hurriedly summoned, authorized Arnold to take command of the schooner, arm her, and move quickly down the lake to surprise the sloop while Allen followed in bateaux to seize the town.

Why Allen should consent to give Arnold this command is a matter of conjecture. Possibly Ethan hoped to appease Arnold by the assignment, or was simply trying to get him out of Ticonderoga. The real reason, however, was probably the obvious one, namely, that, since Arnold was an experienced ship master, he was the logical officer to take charge of the schooner. It is also likely that Allen felt less certain of his own strength,

with Easton leaving for the Massachusetts Congress, Mott heading for
Hartford with news of the capture, and Bull departing with the prisoners
for Hartford by way of Albany. At any rate, Arnold wrote the Massachusetts Congress that "Mr. Allen's party is decreasing, and the dispute
between us subsiding." Whatever the reason for his appointment, Arnold
leaped to his new responsibility, mounted carriage and swivel guns aboard
the schooner, and, accompanied by two bateaux, stood down the lake to
Crown Point, where he arrived on the 15th.[3]

His expedition was swift and not without glory. Though head winds
slowed him on the following day, he approached, on the 17th, to within
thirty miles of St. Johns, then manned his two bateaux with thirty-five
men, rowed all night, and landed in the early dawn. At six o'clock that
morning, he pounced on the town, and his attack was completely successful. He captured a small detail of British regulars, the sloop, and nine
bateaux, of which he destroyed five. Learning that reinforcements were
expected at almost any minute, Arnold weighed anchor two hours after
the attack, picked up a favoring wind, and sailed for Crown Point with
the captured flotilla and his prisoners.

By noon he sighted Allen's crowded bateaux with one hundred and
fifty men aboard. Salutes were fired by both parties three separate times—
Allen's men with muskets and Arnold's with cannon—before Ethan
climbed aboard the sloop to meet the triumphant Arnold. Not to be out-
shone by Arnold's glory, Allen announced his intention of going on to
occupy St. Johns. This, said Arnold, "appeared to me a wild, impracticable scheme, and provided it could be carried into execution, of no
consequence, so long as we are masters of the lake." But such appreciation
of the value of sea power was beyond Ethan Allen, who went on to what
Arnold termed his "rash design," was surprised in his slumbers the next
morning by a force of regulars, and compelled to flee. Arnold would have
been less than human had he not thoroughly enjoyed his rival's dis-
comfiture.[4]

Arnold returned to Ticonderoga and plunged into furious activity. He
armed the sloop and appointed one John Sloan master. He also rearmed
the schooner and gave her to a Captain Isaac Mathews. He inventoried
the ordnance and stores found at both Ticonderoga and Crown Point,
sending a number of cannon at the latter down to the southern end of
Lake George as directed by the committee of safety. He urgently requested men, powder, and supplies. He also dispatched to the committee
Captain Jonathan Brown with his report of the attack on St. Johns.

Jonathan Brown, unlike John Brown, the lawyer, was trusted by Arnold, who thought he might prove helpful in counteracting Easton's complaints.[5]

As many of Allen's men returned to their farms, and as Arnold's force steadily increased, Arnold assumed command of both Ticonderoga and Crown Point. Learning that the British were contemplating an attack up the lake, he set up his headquarters at the more advanced post, Crown Point. Throughout this bustle of activity he never asserted to the committee of safety that he was indispensable to any operation. He had insisted on assuming the command initially, and now he virtually possessed it alone, though Allen was loath to recognize this. Yet as even earlier, when Allen and the others had frustrated him, he had expressed to the committee a desire to be released from "this troublesome business," so now, on May 19, he repeated his request to be relieved. "I find it next to impossible," he explained, "to repair the old fort at Ticonderoga, and am not qualified to direct in building a new one." Four days later, he wrote again to the committee, "I hope some gentleman will soon be appointed in my room here." Arnold was not one to shrink from danger, nor was he modest about his own capacities. It is possible, of course, that he really never wanted to be relieved. On the other hand, he liked a clear-cut situation as to command, and he could not help but feel himself compromised by Allen's continued presence. Furthermore, sensitive as he always was concerning what people thought of him, particularly people in responsible positions, he was worried about the slander that he suspected Allen's friends were spreading in both the Massachusetts Congress and the Continental Congress. Finally, the intelligence he was receiving (and Arnold had a real knack for obtaining and evaluating intelligence) may have persuaded him that this venture had about played itself out. Some other project might afford greater opportunities for action, the command, for example, of an expedition to invade Canada.[6]

The idea of an attack on Canada occurred to both Arnold and Allen. The latter would have liked to avenge his humiliation at St. Johns, while both men were glory-seekers. On May 27, they scrapped their differences long enough to meet on Arnold's flagship, the sloop, considered the possibility of landing on Isle-aux-Noix, then decided to take an advanced defensive position on the west side of the lake at Point-au-Fer, a few miles south of Canada, while the Continental Congress made up its mind what to do about the recent conquests. As Allen pointed out in a letter to Congress, a vigorous invasion of Canada would be the best means of circumventing the able Governor Guy Carleton. Otherwise, if the Americans remained supine, Carleton could "discourage our friends, and encourage our enemies, and form those that are at present indifferent into combinations against us." [7]

But the very next day disturbing news arrived from Philadelphia. The Continental Congress had grown cautious of maintaining an extensive establishment at Ticonderoga. It advised New York to build another post at the northern end of Lake George, fortify it with cannon from Ticonderoga, and take a careful inventory of the ordnance and stores removed so that everything could be returned to the Crown intact when harmony should be re-established. At the same time, it urged New York to ask New Hampshire, Massachusetts, and Connecticut to send reinforcements. The three colonies were agreeable to this request, but they protested vigorously, as did the Albany committee of safety, against abandoning the northern posts. So did Arnold and Allen. On May 29, Arnold wrote the Continental Congress, noting the consternation among the hundreds of inhabitants when the Congressional decision was known. Furthermore, he pointed out, "Ticonderoga is the key of this extensive country, and if abandoned, leaves a very extensive frontier open to the ravages of the enemy, and to continual alarms, which will probably cost more than the expense of repairing and garrisoning it." [8]

While Arnold waited for Congress to change its mind and for the colonies to decide which of them should shoulder the main responsibility for dispatching reinforcements, he and Allen abandoned the plan to land men at Point-au-Fer. Ethan returned to Ticonderoga, while Arnold remained at Crown Point. He had found a companionable spirit in Romans, the engineer. Both spent much time together strengthening the fleet and the fort. Presently, however, Allen appeared with Easton, who brought word that the Massachusetts Congress had heartily approved the seizure of the Champlain forts. This was all very fine, but Arnold had early suspected, and with good reason, that, while at Cambridge, Easton had lost no opportunity to belittle him or to embellish his own reputation. Trouble might have broken out on the day Easton arrived, June 6, had not Arnold left before dawn on patrol down the lake.

With Arnold off on a reconnaissance, Allen began again seriously to consider a possible invasion of Canada. Intelligence reports from agents in Canada had Carleton appealing to the Canadians to take up arms against the Americans, the Canadians themselves uncertain what to do, and a French leader of the Indians, St. Luc la Corne, trying to whip up his braves to take the warpath. Allen wrote the Continental Congress on June 9, setting forth the intriguing possibilities of capturing Canada if enough men were made available. To consider the idea further, he called a council of war for late the next afternoon. Among the eighteen officers present were Allen, his brother Ira, Easton, Seth Warner, and Major Samuel Elmore, a recent arrival from Connecticut. The council had just settled down to the matter at hand when an orderly reported that Arnold's fleet was putting into the anchorage.[9]

What Allen may have thought at Arnold's arrival can only be imagined, but what Arnold thought is clear enough. He considered himself the sole legal commander by virtue of his authority from the Massachusetts committee of safety and of the superior numbers of men now at his disposal. In fact, he had assured the committee less than a fortnight before that Allen had entirely given up his command. Now, when he returned from the north, confident of his authority, he learned to his deep anger that Allen had summoned a council of war without his knowledge. Sending for Elmore, whom he may have known, he bade him go back with a message dismissing the council. As Arnold commented in his journal, "I wrote the council that I could not consistently with my duty suffer any illegal councils, meetings, etc., as they tended to raise a mutiny, that I was at present the only legal commanding officer and should not suffer my command to be disputed, but would willingly give up the command when anyone appeared with proper authority to take it." The council accordingly broke up, but, before doing so, inscribed a note to the Continental Congress praising Allen.[10]

On the following day, the Sabbath, the bad feeling between Arnold and Easton came to a head. Early in the morning, Arnold went ashore and ordered the guard doubled to prevent any disorder. While he was there, Allen, Easton, and Elmore left by boat for Ticonderoga. To their great annoyance, Captain Sloan of the sloop halted them, and, when they could produce no pass, sent them back to Crown Point. Elmore explained the situation to Arnold and requested permission for the group to go its way. But as Arnold started to speak, Easton interrupted him in the coarse, breezy manner that Arnold found so intolerable. His hatred suddenly blazing up, Arnold completely lost his temper with the tavern keeper. "I took the liberty," Arnold confessed, "of breaking his head, and on his refusing to draw like a gentleman, he having a hanger [cutlass] by his side, and case of loaded pistols in his pocket, I kicked him very heartily, and ordered him from the point immediately." Another account, possibly also written by Arnold, mentioned the incident as occurring to "the satisfaction of a number of gentlemen present." [11]

Such conduct on the part of one who considered himself the commanding officer was hardly that of a gentleman; certainly it was most unmilitary. But Arnold could not tolerate arrogance and rudeness in others, though those very elements were by no means lacking in his own bearing. Least of all could he put up with Easton, who cordially reciprocated his feeling. Subsequently a newspaper from the east arrived in the lake country with an account crediting to Easton the capture of the lake forts. This enraged Arnold. And Arnold, perhaps with Romans's aid, may have been the author of a letter signed "Veritas" which reduced Easton's part in the seizure of Ticonderoga to a pusillanimous role. A letter from the British commandant, Delaplace, also helped expose Easton's contribution to the capture as grossly exaggerated. "Veritas" dilates further on the Arnold-Easton antipathy, the author mentioning his having heard Easton often abuse Arnold behind his back "in a base and cowardly manner" though "always very complaisant before his face." Notwithstanding his dislike, however understandable, and possibly justified, Arnold had committed an outrageous breach of propriety and authority by his assault upon the tavern keeper.[12]

With the troublesome officers out of the way, Arnold busied himself with further strengthening Crown Point and contriving a plan to invade Canada. This plan he addressed on June 13 to the Continental Congress. He stated that he had received intelligence from a friend in Montreal (probably Thomas Walker) who was "a merchant and gentleman of probity" that the Indians were determined not to assist the British troops, that the Canadians were becoming impatient at the delay of the Americans in invading Canada, and that they would join the Americans whenever the latter appeared to support them. After an analysis of the British position in Canada, Arnold produced a plan to take both Montreal and Quebec with an army of two thousand. Arnold had only one condition to the composition of this army—there must be no Green Mountain Boys! St. Johns and Chambly were to be secured by one division of the army, while another moved on to Montreal; then a concerted drive should be made on Quebec, seizure of which would provide "an inexhaustible granary" since a half million bushels of wheat were shipped annually from that port. On the question of leadership for this army Arnold declared that "if no person appears who will undertake to carry the plan into execution, (if thought advisable,) I will undertake, and, with the smiles of Heaven, answer for the success of it, provided I am supplied with men, etc., to carry it into execution without loss of time." Actually the plan was well conceived, and was substantially the one adopted for General Schuyler's army in the fall. But Arnold stressed one element that was essential to the success of the scheme, once an army was assembled: the necessity of moving quickly. This element was neglected, and failure to heed its importance cost the Americans their objective and heavy expenditure in casualties and money.[13]

A few days after Arnold developed his invasion plan, which he entrusted to Oswald to take to Philadelphia, additional trouble began to brew for him. On June 1, the Massachusetts Congress had written him acknowledging his letters of May 19 and 23, expressing great satisfaction in his conquests, and conveying its regrets that he continually requested a replacement. It assured him that it had the utmost confidence in his "fidelity, knowledge, courage, and good conduct"; and it wished he would dismiss all thought of quitting his command. He was, in fact, requested to continue in command of the Massachusetts forces "until the Colony of New York or Connecticut shall take on them the maintaining and commanding the same agreeable to an order of the Continental Congress." Only the day before these deliberations, the Continental Congress, after a lot of backing and filling, finally decided to retain Ticonderoga and Crown Point, and urged Connecticut to send men and supplies. Accordingly Connecticut dispatched Colonel Benjamin Hinman and one thousand men to the Lake Champlain district.[14]

As a follow-up to Hinman's appointment, the Massachusetts Congress, despite its kind words for Arnold, resolved to investigate the command situation at Ticonderoga and Crown Point. Arnold referred to himself as the commanding officer, while, as late as June 4, Ethan Allen also spoke of himself as "At present the principal commander of the army"—and this notwithstanding an earlier public declaration that he would give up his command entirely to Arnold until "matters were regulated and an officer appointed to take command." The Massachusetts Congress had evidently heard enough from Arnold, from his enemies, and from Connecticut men in the area to want an end to these controversies when Hinman arrived. It therefore appointed a committee to proceed to Ticonderoga and inform itself how Arnold had executed his commission. The members were particularly to inquire if he had enlisted a greater number of men than specified in his instructions and to place him and his men under Hinman's command. After acquainting themselves with his spirit, capacity, and conduct, if they judged it proper to discharge him, they were to direct him to return to Massachusetts to "render his account of the disposition of the money, ammunition, and other things, which he received . . . and also of the charges he has incurred, and the debts which he has contracted in behalf of this Colony." The committee, consisting of Jedediah Foster, James Sullivan, and Walter Spooner as chairman, left at once for the west.[15]

The arrival of Hinman, and subsequently of the committee, startled and angered Arnold. When the former appeared on June 17 at Crown Point and requested Arnold to turn over his command to him, Arnold refused since Hinman could produce "no regular order." With admirable restraint the pacific Hinman chose not to make an issue of the situation. Six days later, when the committee arrived and Spooner handed Arnold a copy of the instructions given the committee, Arnold, according to Spooner, "seemed greatly disconcerted, and declared he would not be second in command to any person whomsoever." The next day, June 24, he submitted his resignation to the committee.

To say that Arnold was exasperated at his treatment would be a ridiculous understatement; he was utterly furious. His experience from the time he had ridden westward from Cambridge had been one of conspicuous unpleasantness: unsuccessful contention with Mott's committee and Allen over the assault command, insufferable indignities at the hands of Allen's wild crew, a running fire of argument with Ethan over the post command ever since the occupation of Ticonderoga, savage quarrels with Easton, praise by Massachusetts that was obliterated almost at once by the appearance of Hinman evidently with the sanction of Massachusetts, and finally the arrival of the Spooner committee. Notwithstanding Arnold's own efforts, others received the credit, while his intentions and endeavors were belittled and vilified.

Massachusetts, in his opinion, had treated him shabbily. He considered the inquiry into the execution of his commission to be an intimation that the Massachusetts Congress was dubious either of his rectitude or of his abilities. It seemed to him extraordinary, moreover, that the Congress should first appoint an officer and then, after he had already executed his commission, appoint a committee "to examine if he was fit for his post"; such an examination, Arnold contended, should have occurred beforehand. He further thought it "a most disgraceful reflection" on him and his troops that, after he had carried out his instructions, the Congress should acquiesce in giving the command of the forts and the fleet to a younger officer of the same rank. Finally, Arnold strongly objected to the failure of the Congress to send him funds to discharge "the small and unavoidable debts" he had contracted for "necessaries for the use of the army," articles for which he had pledged his own credit. He was therefore reduced, he said, to the necessity of leaving his post with dishonor or waiting until money arrived from home to pay the debts from his own resources; this last he was determined to do.[16]

Disgusted with the committee's instructions, Arnold not only resigned, he also disbanded the two to three hundred men under his command. To his even greater disgust and humiliation the committee then promptly re-enlisted as many of his officers and men as would volunteer, appointed Easton as their commander and Brown as Easton's second, and placed both under Hinman's command. Gloomy beyond measure, Arnold went aboard his flagship. He later asserted that, while at dinner, he was confined to the main cabin by crew members who were fearful of not being paid and who sent a boat after the committee. Edward Mott wrote Governor Trumbull of Connecticut that some of Arnold's men said their erstwhile commander intended to deliver the fleet to the British at St. Johns and that, when the committee went aboard the vessels, Arnold confined them under armed guard for several hours. Mott's colorful account of such a mutiny, however, was not borne out by the Spooner committee in its detailed report, which would seem to discredit Mott's letter in part as a compound of prejudice, rumor, and misapprehension. What evidently happened is that the crews actually became "dissatisfied and mutinous," as Spooner acknowledged. Many of them told the committee that they had been informed (possibly by the disgruntled Arnold) that they were likely to be defrauded out of their pay for the services they had rendered. They detained both Arnold and the committee until, as Spooner said, the committee, "in order to quiet them, engaged . . . that as soon as the rolls should be made up and authenticated, they should be paid for their past services." After that, the men permitted Arnold and the committee to go ashore.[17]

Arnold was henceforth finished with this first Lake Champlain campaign in which the command issue played so important a part. Colonel Samuel Parsons had been greatly amused by the struggle. It was a "matter of diversion," he said, "to see the various competitors for the honor of

concerting and carrying this matter into execution, contending so strenuously about a matter in the execution of which all concerned justly deserve
applause: but some can not bear an equal, and none a superior, and all
make representations at the expense of truth, to monopolize what ought
to be divided." But the brother of Silas Deane, Barnabas Deane, who was
also on the ground, was less Olympian than Parsons. In Deane's opinion,
"Col. Arnold has been greatly abused and misrepresented by designing
persons, some of which were from Connecticut. Had it not been for him
every thing here would have been in the utmost confusion and disorder;
people would have been plundered of their private property, and no man's
person would be safe that was not of the Green Mountain party." Similar
testimony to Arnold's merit came from inhabitants of the area. Regretting
to see him leave, many of them addressed him in a memorial in which
they expressed their appreciation for his "humanity and benevolence" in
supplying them with provisions and for the "uncommon vigilance, vigour,
and spirit" with which he had achieved and protected his conquests and
furnished security for themselves.[18]

The command issue had been the rock on which unity and reputations
had been shattered. In the last analysis, there were other parties as much
at fault as Arnold and Allen. The colonies themselves were jealous of one
another, Connecticut and Massachusetts in particular contending for the
honor of capturing Ticonderoga. As between the two principals, Arnold
had the only legal basis for assuming command, and it is likely that Allen,
more than Mott's group, was impressed with Arnold's authority; otherwise
he would have paid scant attention to the little man. It was unfortunate
that the arrangement of a divided command that prevailed during the
actual seizure of Ticonderoga broke down so soon afterward. On the other
hand, a rupture would probably have occurred eventually; divided commands have rarely succeeded, and few more egocentric competitors could
have been found than Benedict Arnold and Ethan Allen. In the fall, the
latter started out against Montreal in a venture that ended in his own
capture and subsequent condemnation by Washington and Schuyler for
imprudence and unwillingness to subordinate himself to others. Arnold, if
more prudent and far more skillful, possessed an even greater impatience
at subordinating himself to authority.[19]

The entire Ticonderoga episode, except for the raid on St. Johns, was
largely one of intense frustration for Arnold and a breeding time of
trouble that hounded him until his act of betrayal, and contributed to its

causes. Arnold, like most successful men in whatever field, believed in efficiency and discipline, qualities in which Allen and his followers were notably lacking. Though not trained extensively as a soldier, Arnold had soldierly instincts that were deeply offended by the slovenly behavior of Allen's troops, the nature of his leadership, Mott's assumption of authority in giving Allen the command, Easton's insulting deportment, and the politicking activities of both Easton and Brown. In fact, these last two officers roused in the Massachusetts Congress and the Continental Congress suspicions of Arnold's character that never completely subsided; the subsequent reluctance of the latter organization to take proper cognizance of Arnold's services during the Revolution, treatment that bitterly and profoundly offended him, had its origin thus early in the struggle.

The crushing blow to Arnold at Ticonderoga, however, was delivered not by any individual but by Massachusetts. In view of the situation obtaining at Ticonderoga, the intervention of Massachusetts in sending the Spooner committee with power was probably wise, though the Massachusetts Congress appears to have been motivated in part by an excessive courtesy and regard for the good will and co-operation of Connecticut that took little account of the role its own representative had played during the campaign. Actually, whatever the merits of its decision to settle the controversy and place Arnold under Hinman's command, Massachusetts had in a sense repudiated its own leadership. It had also exposed Arnold to a humiliation that cut him to the quick, and hence added to the resentment that he already felt toward individual officers such as Allen, Easton, and Brown. While one may denounce his discharge of his men as an act of peevishness, it would have required a large measure of tolerance indeed, far more than Arnold or most men possessed, to have continued under the new conditions.

After lingering in the Champlain area for more than a week, Arnold went down to Albany, where, on July 11, at General Schuyler's behest, he submitted to the Continental Congress a critical report on the condition of the troops and defenses at Ticonderoga, Crown Point, and Fort George. But Arnold's heart was no longer in this work. He felt his honor impugned by what had happened, and his pride was sorely hurt. He had public monies to account for to the Massachusetts Congress, and he considered himself personally short of $2,500 because of having provided provisions and clothing out of his own pocket. He was suffering from the gout and fretted at his inactivity. To fill his cup to overflowing, he learned while at Albany of the death of his wife, only thirty years of age, on June 19. Quickly deciding that his financial report to the Congress could wait until he had arranged his personal affairs, he left for Connecticut.[20]

It was thus a chastened and sorrowing Arnold who rode homeward to comfort his motherless boys and visit his Peggy's grave in the crypt of the Center Church in New Haven.

· VI ·

The Wilderness March

The SUMMER of 1775 was for Arnold an interlude, sad and exasperating, between his Lake Champlain controversies and one of the most arduous, heroic, and painful experiences of a career filled with toil and derring-do, the Canadian venture. Little is known of Peggy Arnold's fatal illness, but her death had tragic implications that went far beyond the immediate grief it evoked; had she lived, the circumstances of Arnold's private life would have been so different that it is doubtful he would have become a traitor. At the time of her demise, a serious domestic problem was naturally created. With three motherless boys, aged seven, six, and three, Arnold had either to remarry or to find some woman to look after them. It was now that Hannah Arnold took upon herself the care of his children, and to the end of her days she remained devoted to them and loyal to her brother. In fact she assumed charge at once, and, only four days after Peggy died, she enrolled Benedict and Richard in a school in New Haven.[1]

Meanwhile Arnold had to attend to his business affairs, interrupted by the months of service since word had arrived of the fighting at Lexington and Concord. He was worried over the possible capture of a sloop bound for Quebec. Moreover, expecting a brig home from the West Indies, he bought up a cargo of sixty thousand hoops and barrel staves. Hardly had he done this when he went to bed with the gout. While he was ill, the brig arrived, but, for the time being, he could do nothing about her. By the last of July, when he recovered, he knew he could no longer delay reporting to the Massachusetts Congress. Accordingly, though far from well, he rode up to Cambridge, intending to return as soon as possible to supervise the loading of the brig. Actually it was many months before he again saw New Haven. In his absence, Hannah assumed charge of his business affairs and sought the good offices of Silas Deane to obtain permission from the Continental Congress to ship to the West Indies the cargo Arnold had bought. Deane proved a good friend to the Arnolds, and agreed with his brother Barnabas that Arnold had been badly treated at Ticonderoga.[2]

In Massachusetts, Arnold's accounts were given sharp scrutiny. An amount of over £1,060 had to be explained, including £44 for oxen and sheep left at Crown Point, £107 for horses and saddles listed as not delivered pursuant to order, and £38 for sixty-four blankets charged to one company. Certain wages paid by Arnold appeared rather high, while it was difficult to secure a breakdown of the sum he admitted to having paid out of pocket for commissary supplies. The Massachusetts Congress, on August 1, gave the matter to a committee of five chaired by the amiable and able Dr. Benjamin Church, a man deep in American counsels but one who was shortly to be exposed as a British informer in the pay of General Gage. Six days later, a number of the orders drawn by Arnold on the Congress to pay various individuals and endorsed by them were allowed. Not until August 19, however, was the committee ready to deliver its full report. It considered the sum for the blankets not admissible in this account since the captain to whose company they were charged had already received an excess in his payroll. As for the animals, Arnold was informed that no payment could be made until he presented a receipt for them signed by Colonel Easton. Acting on the recommendation of the committee, the Massachusetts Congress then paid to Arnold the niggardly total of £195. Indignant that he had not been more justly treated, Arnold transmitted to Silas Deane a full account of his expenses and disbursements. Deane accordingly secured from the Continental Congress in January, 1776, a draft on the Treasury for the balance. This amount, consisting of $819, Deane forwarded to Hannah Arnold, her brother then being in Canada. It hardly seems likely that the balance would have been paid at all had the Continental Congress, which was certainly not noted for its financial generosity, detected any significant discrepancies in Arnold's accounts.[3]

Meanwhile plans were developing for an invasion of Canada. In the west Schuyler was preparing to besiege St. Johns, then to take Chambly and Montreal, and finally to drive toward Quebec. Soon after he invested St. Johns in early September, Schuyler had to retire to Ticonderoga because of illness, leaving the conduct of the field army to a quiet, gallant brigadier, Richard Montgomery, late of the British army and now of New York. Despite the illness among his poorly trained troops, their lack of equipment, and their insufficient members, Montgomery seized Chambly in October, and both St. Johns and Montreal in early November. During the campaign, he received effective assistance from two of Arnold's enemies, Colonel James Easton and Major John Brown. The latter was to prove especially troublesome to Arnold long before the Canadian campaign was over. In the meantime, Arnold was engaged in a far more strenuous but less conspicuous venture for power and glory, a march through the Maine wilderness to the fortress city of Quebec.[4]

The idea of invading Canada through Maine no more originated with any single individual than had the idea of capturing Ticonderoga, though, in both instances, Arnold proposed a plan of action. The course followed by the Chaudière, Dead, and Kennebec rivers had long been considered as a possible avenue of war, convenient for the French and Indians in raiding Massachusetts and equally convenient for the colonists in attacking Quebec. But, except for Indian war parties, the route had never been used. In 1761, two years after Wolfe's victory over Montcalm at Quebec, British General Murray had sent a military engineer, Lieutenant John Montrésor, to explore and map the route from the north. Now, in 1775, sometime in the spring, Colonel Jonathan Brewer of Massachusetts suggested to the Massachusetts Congress a plan by which he would lead a force of five hundred men through the wilderness to Quebec. It is likely that Washington had learned of the plan. It is also possible that Washington began to consider such an expedition seriously when his adjutant, Horatio Gates, laid on his desk a similar plan by Arnold, drawn up while the latter was waiting for the final decision of the committee reviewing his accounts. Employment of the energetic Arnold undoubtedly seemed to Washington to ensure a reasonable chance of success for the enterprise, while incidentally it would provide the fire-eating colonel, for whom Washington felt considerable sympathy, an opportunity to exercise his abilities in an independent command and would get him away from under the suspicious eyes of the politicians.

But the commander-in-chief was cautious. Unless Schuyler's invasion of Canada down the Sorel and the St. Lawrence and Arnold's expedition through Maine were synchronized, the latter project would be sheer folly and the former might also fail. Hence Washington wrote at length to Schuyler on August 20, the day after the Massachusetts committee finished its examination of Arnold's accounts. Washington pointed out the advantages of the Kennebec expedition. Carleton would be obliged to withdraw to Quebec, thus leaving a clear passage for Schuyler's forces, or else he would have to let Quebec fall to Arnold. Dispatched to Schuyler by express, the letter called for a swift reply. There was little that was wrong with Washington's strategy of this campaign, and he felt that in Schuyler and Arnold he had the lieutenants to effect its success.[5]

For Arnold the expedition meant literally the opportunity of a lifetime. It would be his first independent command—no more humiliating situations as at Ticonderoga where rival officers like Allen or Easton or a sovereign authority such as the Massachusetts Congress might contrive to cut the ground from under him. He would be primarily responsible to the commander-in-chief, not to civilian politicians who did not seem to understand either the strictly military problems or the financial exigencies of a campaign. He would be in a position to vindicate himself before men into whose eyes his detractors may have cast the dust of suspicion (for misguided scoffers he had nothing but contempt, but for his enemies he believed in the Mosaic law of reprisal, and he was sure his time of retribution would come). Above all, he craved the approval of Washington. There appeared little in common between the tall, aristocratic Virginia planter and the short, chunky Connecticut merchant and apothecary. On the other hand, both liked to dress well, loved horses, and possessed famous tempers; more important, both wanted to win the war in the shortest possible time and were willing to take at least a calculated chance to achieve this objective. With Washington's chilly eye on him, Arnold felt his measure being taken, and he resolved to disappoint neither the commander-in-chief nor his own future should Schuyler agree to the Canadian plan.

Though everything depended on a favorable response from Schuyler, Arnold began to organize the expedition. At Washington's direction he had a long conference with a Kennebec shipbuilder then in Cambridge, Reuben Colburn. Arnold followed up the conference with a letter in which he conveyed to Colburn the commander-in-chief's desire for Colburn to inform himself as to the shortest time he could construct two hundred bateaux capable of carrying a half-dozen men with their provisions and equipment, the quantity and price of beef in the Kennebec area, and such intelligence as existed concerning the carrying places and the depth and rate of flow of the rivers in the fall season. It is likely that Arnold also interviewed five Indians of the St. Francis tribe whom Colburn had brought to Cambridge on August 14; the Indians were reputed to know something about the route and the number of troops in Quebec. Arnold was thus securing every scrap of information he could lay his hands on, including Montrésor's map and journal.[6]

Yet as the days passed and no reply came from Schuyler, he grew impatient. He could not forget the brig lying idle at his wharf in New Haven, the lumber weathering in the summer sun, or the Quebec-bound sloop, which was probably seized by the enemy. He was furious at his treatment by the Massachusetts Congress, and may well have wondered whether he could expect any good word from the lakes, where he had but recently suffered humiliation. He was actually on the point of giving up any part in the Canadian affair and returning to Connecticut when Horatio Gates called him to a conference on August 24. Whatever acrimony developed between Gates and Arnold during the Burgoyne campaign, there was none at this time. On the contrary, the older man went out of his way to accommodate the impulsive Arnold. Gates secured his pledge not to go home until Schuyler's reply arrived, and this could not be reasonably expected for several days. To confirm his conversation, Gates sent Arnold a friendly letter, stating that it was Washington's request for him to remain until the return of the courier; an adjutant general's friendship can mean a great deal in any army to one seeking grace or favor of the commander-in-chief.[7]

When Schuyler's answer arrived on September 2, bearing strong approval of the Kennebec expedition, Arnold sped preparations. With General Montgomery closing in on St. Johns, it was imperative that the expedition move quickly. Conferences ensued between Washington and Arnold. On September 3, Colburn, again in Cambridge, was hurried down east to Gardiner on the Kennebec with instructions to build two hundred bateaux, to organize a maintenance crew and guides, to order all the pork and flour he could obtain, and to inform the inhabitants that a commissary officer would soon be on hand to buy salted beef.

Arnold also began to round up volunteers for the expedition. To many of the troops around Boston, men sweating in the late summer heat and bored by the interminable siege, Quebec had a magical inducement; the lure of a cooler climate and the chance for action were irresistible. Ten companies of New Englanders used to the musket were enlisted in two

battalions, one led by Lieutenant Colonel Roger Enos of Vermont and
Major Return Jonathan Meigs of Connecticut; the other, by Lieutenant
Colonel Christopher Greene, son of a Rhode Island supreme court justice
and a cousin to General Nathanael Greene, and Major Timothy Bigelow
of Massachusetts.

The choicest units of Arnold's little army were two companies of
riflemen from Pennsylvania and one company from Virginia, tall, rangy
frontiersmen, each armed with rifle, tomahawk, and scalping knife and
dressed in a long, fringed hunting shirt, leggings, and moccasins. When
the eight companies of riflemen authorized by Congress had first arrived
in Cambridge, their dress excited ridicule among both the New Englanders and the British. But there "shirt-tail men, with their cursed twisted
guns" were presently labeled by the British as "the most fatal widow-and-
orphan makers in the world." Arnold appointed to command of the riflemen Captain Daniel Morgan of Virginia. A veteran of Braddock's expedition and a huge, powerful man catlike on his feet, Morgan was severe in
manners, just and prudent in the performance of his duties, and affectionate to those whom he chose as friends. He was far more capable than the
commander of one of the Pennsylvania companies, Captain Matthew
Smith, a handsome, garrulous ruffian overly fond of liquor and one of the
notorious "Paxton Boys" who had murdered friendly Indians in Lan-
caster County, Pennsylvania. William Hendricks, captain of the other
Pennsylvania company, was of a splendid, long-suffering character, well
liked by his men but lacking in forcefulness.[8]

Arnold also took with him several "casuals." Included as gentlemen
volunteers were two young Princeton College classmates, Aaron Burr and
Matthias Ogden. Eleazer Oswald, who had served Arnold faithfully at
Ticonderoga, went along as Arnold's private secretary. It was to be
Oswald's odd lot to be closely associated with both Arnold and General
Charles Lee, men who performed valiant service but who fell from grace;
in fact, Oswald was one of the two individuals present when Lee died in
1782. Also going along with the expedition, sharing all its hardships and
enjoying universal respect, were the wives of two Pennsylvania riflemen, a
Mrs. Grier and a Mrs. Jemima Warner, both doomed to die violent deaths
at Quebec. The entire expedition numbered approximately 1,050.[9]

Despite the urgency and Arnold's prodding, the expedition got off to a
slow start because the men were concerned about their families. The next
pay day would find them deep in the forests of Maine, so that what they
could now send home meant a great deal. Though the rifle companies

took the road without delay for Newburyport, where a small fleet was gathering to transport the men to Gardiner, several of the companies refused to march until they received a month's pay in advance. Arnold recognized the justice of the soldiers' claims and accordingly had the advance pay issued to them either in Cambridge or, as in Captain Henry Dearborn's company, on the march to Newburyport.[10]

Arnold himself remained in Cambridge until Friday morning, September 15; then, after receiving his last instructions from headquarters, and shaking hands with Washington, he rode northward, dining in Salem and reaching Newburyport by nightfall. Over the weekend he was entertained by the great merchant, Nathaniel Tracy, in all the splendor of white damask and gleaming silver. He also attended the service on the Sabbath conducted by his chaplain, the Reverend Samuel Spring, who preached on the text, "If Thy presence go not with me, carry us not up hence." A Presbyterian, Arnold would have agreed with the Reverend Spring, but he would likewise have subscribed to the old saw that the Lord helps them who help themselves, and he was determined to afford the Deity every reason to assist him.

Arnold had hoped to embark on Saturday aboard the eleven vessels that Tracy had assembled, but wind and weather delayed the sailing. That day, however, he sent out three patrol boats to scout the coast for British cruisers. When, on Monday, one of them scudded into port with word that the coast was clear of the enemy, the troops went aboard the "dirty coasters and fish boats," as Private Simon Fobes described the craft. The next morning, the wind blowing at last from a favorable quarter, Arnold stood out to sea in his flagship, the topsail schooner *Broad Bay*. That night, one of wind and thunder, brought his seasick expedition well down the coast. Although fog, the numerous islets about the mouth of the Kennebec, and the tricky channel of the river slowed their progress, most of the vessels, by Saturday, September 22, lay at anchor off Colburn's shipyard at Gardiner. None was more relieved than Arnold that the voyage, which he wrote Tracy as being "very troublesome indeed," was over.[11]

But Arnold's troubles were just beginning. He inspected the bateaux that Colburn and Agry, the chief carpenter, had constructed, and growled in a letter to Washington, "I found the batteaus completed, but many of them smaller than the directions given, and very badly built; of course, I have been obliged to order twenty more, to bring on the remainder of the provisions, which will be finished in three days." Though Arnold's criticism was justified, Colburn and Agry had had to do a "rush" job finishing two hundred of the craft in eighteen days; furthermore, it is likely that neither understood exactly what was required for a boat to navigate the

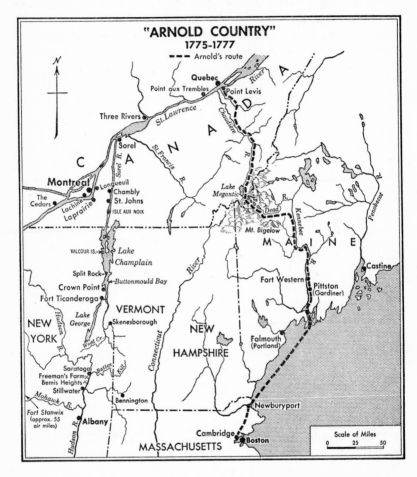

remote reaches of the upper Kennebec. For that matter, Arnold must have been as ignorant as they, else he would not have chosen the bateau as the type of craft for the expedition. Canoes, more maneuverable in the water and lighter to carry over the numerous portages, would have been preferable. Whoever suggested the heavy bateau rather than the canoe—

whether Arnold himself, Washington, or someone else—made a bad error in judgment.[12]

Arnold also studied with care the report of a scouting expedition sent out by Colburn. This expedition had gone up the Dead River, where Natanis, the great Indian in those parts, said that he was employed by Governor Carleton to watch for an army expected from New England; that there were spies, a small patrol of soldiers, and a large number of Indians stationed along the Chaudière River; and that, if the Americans went any farther, he would report his suspicions of their designs to Carleton. Though the men kept on for a day more, they then returned.

One would have thought Arnold might have been discouraged that the scouts had learned so little about the course his army must traverse and that Carleton knew of the expedition, but this was not so. Arnold had a way of making light of obstacles, so great was his confidence in his own power to surmount them. This manner of thinking was born neither of self-confidence nor—like certain other famous commanders—of a superstitious faith in the stars. Though his life had had its share of good and bad fortune, he had not faltered in his resolve to rise. He possessed a strong belief in his destiny. While he might not be certain in precisely what mold that destiny was cast, he knew that in military life, as in nothing he had ever done, he was able to realize more fully his potentialities, to express his fierce love of action, and to experience a satisfaction that was tempered only by his impatience with men less zealous and less capable than himself. Absolutely fearless, he was also confident in the courage and ability of his little army, a picked group, and he refused to be intimidated by any obstacle that man or nature might impose. Hence he scoffed at placing much credit in the information obtained from Natanis, whom he considered "a noted villain," an unfair characterization since Natanis eventually proved a real friend. Arnold perused Montrésor's map and journal, hoped for much from the trail-wise St. Francis Indians due to accompany the expedition, and took his army up to Fort Western opposite what is now Augusta, where he arrived on Saturday, September 22.[13]

It was in the lower Kennebec that, according to legend of redoubtable longevity and fervor, romance came to one of the members of the expedition, handsome, young Aaron Burr. Reportedly he fell in love with the sachem of Swan Island, a half-breed Indian girl, part Abenaki and part French, named Jacataqua. Obviously she returned his regard, for, likewise according to legend, she went with him to Quebec. The troops formed such an affection for her, considered her such a good-luck talisman, that they spared her hound dog the gastronomical fate that befell other pets. Jacataqua was reputed on one occasion to have helped guide lost companies of the expedition to safety. Eventually, quite some time after the column had reached its objective, Burr and Jacataqua, who was now pregnant, were stooping to drink from a brook one day when they looked up to see a British officer opposite them. Gallantly he passed over his own drinking cup. Burr and he struck up a quick friendship which culminated in an arrangement whereby the Englishman agreed to take Jacataqua to one of the city convents for care. Romancers are not certain that the Indian girl passed out of the amatory Burr's life at this point; there are interesting stories to the contrary. Few legends, however, are as persistent as this one of Aaron Burr, the future vice-president and nemesis of Hamilton, and Jacataqua, the Indian sachem of Swan Island.[14]

Meanwhile, at Fort Western, Arnold set about organizing for the wilderness. He dispatched two reconnaissance parties in canoes, the first under a Lieutenant Steele and the second under a Lieutenant Church. Steele was to obtain intelligence from the Indians hunting in the area about Lake Megantic; Church was to survey the route to the Chaudière region. Arnold now divided the army into four parts under Morgan, Greene, Meigs, and Enos. He intended originally to have Greene lead the advance division with one company of riflemen and two of musketmen, but, all unwittingly, he stirred up a hornet's nest. Morgan, Smith, and Hendricks waited on him and insisted that it was their understanding that no militia officer should command the riflemen. Morgan might do so, as a Continental officer, or Arnold himself, since, before leaving, he had been accepted into the Continental Army in the grade of colonel, but not Greene. The rifle officers asserted that Washington supported their contention. Although, when Arnold later explained the situation, the commander-in-chief disavowed such a claim, Arnold felt that this was no time to bicker; conceding the point, he placed all the riflemen under Morgan. With physical violence sometimes necessary to keep certain of the untamed frontier spirits in line, the harsh, forceful Morgan was probably a wiser choice than the cultivated Greene, who, while he was later to prove his worth defending the Delaware forts, was as yet untested and relatively unknown. Morgan led his men north on Monday, September 25. His specific task was to cut a road across the Great Carrying Place between the Kennebec and the Dead River. The following day, Greene and Bigelow left with the second division, and, the next afternoon, Meigs set off with the third. The last division under Enos was slower to leave; by the 29th, however, even he was on the move upriver.[15]

Before Arnold departed, he had an unpleasant piece of business to settle. On the night of September 24, while the expedition lay at Fort Western, James McCormick of North Yarmouth, Maine, became so quarrelsome in a private home with a number of other soldiers that they turned him outdoors. This was too much for McCormick, who seems to have gone berserk, very likely under the double influence of wrath and rum. Running for his gun, he returned and fired into the room full of soldiers. One of them, Reuben Bishop, was hit and died of the resulting hemorrhage. At once Arnold impaneled a court-martial, which tried McCormick without delay, found him guilty, and sentenced him to hang, a sentence that Arnold approved. But when McCormick was brought before a hastily erected gallows, Arnold suddenly reprieved him and sent him and the evidence to Washington for the commander-in-chief's judgment. Though the man's guilt was clear, Arnold considered the circumstances extenuating. As he explained to Washington, "The criminal appears to be very simple and ignorant; and in the company he belonged to, had the character of being a peaceable fellow. . . . I wish he may be found a proper object of mercy. . . ." Arnold understood enlisted men and was unfailingly kind to them; it was with officers and civilian politicians that he had most of his trouble. McCormick, incidentally, is reported to have died in prison at Cambridge on the day set for his execution.[16]

With the expedition now on the way, Arnold hastened to the head of the column. The leaves were bright with color, the days exhilaratingly cool, and his spirits high. "I . . . believe, by the best information I can procure, we shall be able to perform the march in twenty days," he declared confidently on September 25. It was a proud boast, but even the sanguine Arnold could not foresee all the obstacles facing him and his army. Even before the troops reached Fort Halifax (Winslow), Caleb Haskell, one of the diarists in the expedition, said of this phase, "We begin to see that we shall have a scene of trouble to go through in this river, the water is so swift and the shoal full of rocks, ripples and falls, which oblige us to wade a great part of the way." Ticonic Falls provided a foretaste of the portaging ahead. The bateaux were run ashore and their supplies and equipment removed. Then handspikes were passed beneath, fore and aft, and the awkward four-hundred-craft, with much straining, heaving, and sweating, were borne to a point above the falls. Still farther up the river were the Five Mile Falls, which Arnold found very dangerous and the passage of which evoked Haskell's tart comment, "Now we are learning to be soldiers." [17]

Regardless of rips, swift water, and falls, Arnold kept his men moving as fast as possible. He himself arrived at the gorge in Skowhegan on October 1, and had little difficulty with it, but the same could not be said of the bulk of the army. The men were up to their waists in the foaming, swirling water, and their wet hands blistered and grew raw from poling and hauling the bateaux. Soaked to the skin when they lay down that evening, they woke to find their clothes, as Simeon Thayer remarked, "frozen a pane of glass thick." Though Arnold sympathized with them, he could not afford to be too softhearted, for beyond lay Norridgewock Falls, where there were three pitches, roughly a half mile apart, and a drop of ninety feet in the mile. The water here was so dangerous for the bateaux that they were again unloaded and most of them shouldered the long mile to quieter water above.[18]

Arnold now decided that, before the expedition could continue, the bateaux had to be repaired, for, under the battering of water and rocks, their seams had parted. Even more serious was the discovery that, because of the poor construction of the boats, large quantities of provisions had been ruined. Furthermore, inspecting the salt beef with Dr. Isaac Senter, Arnold saw that most of it had to be thrown away because of poor curing during the summer. Stifling his impatience as best he could, and still refusing to be discouraged, he personally supervised the repacking of the food that was still edible, and the repairing of the bateaux. Not until October 9 did he move forward again, this time with one of the companies of the last division.[19]

After leaving Carritunk Falls, Arnold began to enter the real wilderness. Habitations disappeared, while the woods and hills closed in on the river so that those men not in the boats marched along the ridges, sometimes a half mile distant. Occasionally a moose was brought down or a mess of salmon caught to supplement the waning fare. On October 11, Arnold reached the Great Carrying Place, overtaking the three leading divisions. Lieutenant Church now reported on his reconnaissance to the Dead River: rising ground and a bad trail ahead. The next day, Lieutenant Steele's party stumbled in, half starved, with word that no Indians had been discovered in the Chaudière region. This last was encouraging news, and it was not long before Arnold sent both lieutenants out again.

Meanwhile he struggled with the Great Carrying Place. Hard rains churned the route into a quagmire, and the men were obliged to carry all the bateaux and barrels of provisions through deep woods and over ledgy hills. "The boats," said one soldier, "were turned bottom up, and four men would take one on their shoulders and march along, the edge of the boat, being somewhat sharp, pressing very painfully on the flesh." Arnold also became much concerned over the increase of nausea and diarrhea in the army by reason of the men drinking the yellow, mucky water. Indefatigable, he sloshed back and forth along the straggling line, steadying a slipping trooper here, helping carry a heavy bateau up a steep hill, and cheering the men with his praise for their spirit and industry.[20]

On October 13, a raw day of high wind, he wrote four important letters. One of them was to General Schuyler, informing him of the progress of the expedition, expressing the hope of a meeting in Quebec within a fortnight, and requesting such intelligence as the general could furnish. The second—a fateful message indeed—was addressed to a friend of Arnold and of the American cause, John Manir (John Dyer Mercier). Arnold informed Mercier of his approach and of his intention to co-operate with Schuyler to "restore" liberty to the Canadians. Arnold urged Mercier to send him at once all available intelligence concerning the number of troops in Quebec, their commander, any advice he had received from Schuyler, what ships were at Quebec, and what action could be expected of the Canadians and of the merchants in the city. Arnold sent the letter by Eneas, an Indian considered more faithful than he proved to be. Eneas was also to give Mercier the letter to Schuyler for forwarding, and was to return with Mercier's reply. The third letter went to Lieutenant Steele, directing him to release from his command a man who spoke French, one John Hall. Hall was to accompany Eneas and an Indian companion to Sartigan, near Quebec. At that point, in addition to discovering information on his own, he was to hire a reliable Frenchman who should go to Quebec with the Indians, see that Arnold's letter was delivered, and await an answer. Hall was also directed to caution the Indians to keep their lips buttoned tightly about the Kennebec column. The fourth letter was to Washington. Arnold gave a brief account of the progress of the army, explained that he had received no intelligence from either Schuyler or Canada, and trusted that, in view of the obstacles encountered, the commander-in-chief would not be critical of the comparatively short distance covered so far. Arnold could not forget Washington's solemn warning before leaving that the safety and welfare of the whole continent might depend upon the success of the Kennebec expedition.[21]

In his letter to Washington, Arnold had expressed the hope that the greatest difficulty was already past, but within a few days of his writing he saw the expedition threatened with disaster. Provisions, particularly in the second division, began to run out with alarming rapidity. The Dead River, on which part of the army now floated, proved extraordinarily winding, then rose twelve feet and flooded its banks for a mile or more on each side in the course of a torrential downpour lasting three days. Small tributaries expanded, and those men marching by land had to cover great distances before finding a spot narrow enough to cross. Entire units went astray, while a number of the bateaux were swamped and their provisions lost. With the expedition almost literally drowned, the air bitterly cold, and food very short, Arnold called an emergency council of war of such officers as were within easy reach.[22]

It was a small, sober group that crouched around a fire inside a lean-to of dripping pine branches. Arnold, like the others, was soaking wet, and the heat from the feeble blaze seemed only to accentuate the common misery. Loosening his military cloak so that his soggy Footguards uniform was opened to the warmth, he knelt on one knee and drove the index finger of his right hand into his left palm to indicate his points. Occasionally he clenched his fist, and his voice rose harshly above the sputtering of the wet fagots and the coughs of the officers as the resinous smoke caught at their throats. His pale eyes burning with the smart of smoke tears and with the intensity of his emotion, Arnold stated the situation baldly. There was no denying that the expedition had encountered great and unexpected hardships. The boats were a failure and perhaps should never have been used. Food supplies were indeed short and would steadily diminish, while the weather and the invasion of hundreds of men into the wilderness had scattered game. The storm and the cold made everyone wretched. Worse still was the delay that these difficulties had created. But—and Arnold paused as the group admitted all this to be true and hunkered closer to the fire—all was not lost. On the contrary, said Arnold with a sardonic smile, there was much to be thankful for. No man had died; in fact, the expedition had enjoyed remarkable health. Of course the men were hungry, of course the rain and cold were uncomfortable to bear. Yet the remaining supplies would be evenly divided and, with strict rationing, should last until the French settlements were reached. As for the rain, it could not continue forever, while the cold would harden the sodden ground and make the going easier for those on foot. It was still possible to win this battle with the wilderness and hunger. And beyond lay

Quebec, on the capture of which depended the success of the whole campaign to take Canada, and perhaps the safety of their own country. Ahead lay more hardship, to be sure, but also great honor and glory.

His appeal was Spartan, soldierly, and effective. After a few moments of questions, the officers growled their readiness to keep moving. Then Arnold, his dark cheeks glowing with excitement, snapped out his orders in a brisk, cheery voice that infused the weary officers with something of the invincible spirit of their leader. The sick were to be sent back and orders were to go down to the two rear divisions, now the second and fourth, to send back their unfit, too. Captain Oliver Hanchet of Suffield, Connecticut, was to move ahead with a picked group of fifty men to the settlements along the Chaudière and forward supplies to the main body. Arnold himself proposed to set out at once with a small flying column to procure the supplies. "I have been deceived," he subsequently informed Washington, "in every account of our route, which is longer and has been attended with a thousand difficulties I never apprehended: but if crowned with success and conducive to the public good I shall think it but trifling." The next day, a day on which two inches of snow fell, the decisions were put into effect.[23]

Less resolute, however, was another sort of council on October 25 held by the leaders of the second and fourth divisions. Though Arnold's orders to Greene and Enos were to hurry on as fast as possible, the officers of these two divisions voted on the question of a retreat. Enos's division decided to return to Cambridge and refused to share the remaining flour with Greene. Enos later claimed that he had saved the lives of his men by his withdrawal, but his plight, had he continued, would scarcely have been worse than that of the divisions which remained true, while his defection jeopardized the entire expedition. It was days before Arnold learned of Enos's desertion. Though the news made him furious, it was too late for him to do anything about the situation. Refusing to despair, he wrote Washington with uncommon restraint, "Col. Enos's division . . . I am surprised to hear, are all gone back." "You could not be more surprised than I was at Enos's return," Washington replied. "I immediately put him under arrest, and had him tried for quitting the detachment without your orders." But Enos was honorably acquitted, thanks to a most enviable situation, the favorable testimony of his own officers and the absence of any opposition; Arnold and the faithful were still in Canada.[24]

As if to point up the faintheartedness of Enos and his men and to confirm their own faith in Arnold was the fortitude shown by the two women of the expedition, Mrs. Grier and Mrs. Warner. Jemima Warner, missing her dying husband, returned a few miles along the trail to succor him when to remain behind, in view of the near-starvation and cold, was to court death. After burying him, she rushed back, weeping, to join the column. As for Mrs. Grier, whose husband was a soldier in Hendricks's company, Henry, the young rifleman-diarist, said that "Entering the pond . . . and breaking the ice here and there with the butts of our guns and feet, . . . we were soon waist deep in mud and water. As is generally the case with youths, it came to my mind that a better path might be found. . . . Attempting this, the water in a trice cooling my armpits, made me gladly return into the file. Now Mrs. Grier had got before me. My mind was humbled, yet astonished, at the exertions of this good woman. Her clothes more than waist high, she waded before me to firm ground. No one . . . dared to intimate a disrespectful idea of her." [25]

While his depleted army toiled over the Height of Land, floundered astray in the swamps of the pond chain leading to Lake Megantic, and fought starvation by boiling moccasins, roasting moose-hide breeches, and making gruel of shaving soap and barber's powder, Arnold dashed ahead. Rescue depended on him. Though rationing had thinned his own stout frame, the man possessed an inexhaustible store of energy. Furthermore, it was his expedition, his great opportunity; he must not fail. Beating his way through swamps, bogs, thickets, and acres of fallen trees, portaging constantly, he reached Lake Megantic in the late afternoon of October 27. Earlier that day, he had met Steele and Church with one Jaquin, whom he had sent down to Sartigan to gather intelligence among the French. Jaquin reported the inhabitants ready to welcome the Americans, few troops in Quebec, and Governor Carleton at Montreal. This was encouraging news, but Arnold was disturbed by Hanchet's failure to make camp. Coming by land, Hanchet's men, instead of remaining on high ground, had waded two miles through water breast-high, and finally halted in a marsh. Arnold found them there, had his bateaux brought across for them, and reached camp with them about midnight. Hanchet had evidently not followed his instructions, and Arnold's former high opinion of the officer diminished.[26]

In the morning, while Hanchet again marched by land, Arnold set out with Steele, Church, Oswald, and thirteen men in four bateaux and a canoe. Using the canoe, Arnold flew ahead, cleared the lake by mid-morning, and, after the bateaux joined him, entered the Chaudière at noon, a river appropriately named "caldron." Swiftly the current bore them along for about fifteen miles when, without warning, they plunged into rapids that upset all the craft, smashing two boats to pieces, damaging the others, and causing considerable loss of equipment. Six of the men were forced to swim for their lives, and, after a long time in the water, were with difficulty saved. Dripping from his immersion, Arnold at first thought this mishap lamentable but soon considered it a "kind interposition of Providence." When he and the others had wrung out their clothing and were about to re-embark, one who had particularly sharp eyes and ears cried out a warning—falls ahead! Arnold admitted that, had the boats been carried over, they would have been dashed to pieces and all on board lost. After portaging and then ferrying another half mile, he discovered even more dangerous rapids, and therefore decided to spend the night before again engaging the perilous river.

The next two days, October 29 and 30, Arnold continued to whirl down the stream. The canoe hit a rock at the start, but fortunately Arnold was not in it at the time; its occupants crawled into the two remaining bateaux. Despite rapids, portages, and a raw east wind that cut him to the bone, Arnold finally reached the junction of the Chaudière and the River du Loup on the 30th. A little farther down, with darkness closing in, one of the men in the bow set up a shout that brought relief and joy to the tired, hungry party. Ahead shone the lights of the first house on the Chaudière.[27]

Though Arnold's remarkable journal breaks off at this point in the middle of a sentence (the last part of the journal has never been found), it is clear from his letters and from the journals of the other men that he wasted no time in getting supplies back to his starving column. He bought up oatmeal, flour, and cattle, and sent them back by land the next morning. Other provisions—mutton, meal, and even tobacco—he dispatched by canoe with Canadians at the paddles. At sight of the relief, the famishing troops raised hoarse, feeble cheers, and quickly fell upon the cattle, some devouring the flesh raw; others bolted the oatmeal uncooked. Arnold also hired horses to bring in those men lying in the snow. By November 3, food had reached all in the long, straggling line. With food in their stomachs it was not long before the men began to dicker for eggs, cheese, potatoes, and drink with the friendly Canadians and to eye with some doubt the group of painted Indians, including Natanis, who, after a harangue by Arnold, joined the column. Unbeknownst to Arnold and his men, Natanis and his warriors had kept their eyes on the expedition ever since it had left the Kennebec. Several times the men had seen what they were sure were signal smokes, and alarm had swept the column. Never, however, had they seen a redskin outside of the St. Francis Indians already with them until, on one occasion, a young brave from Natanis's band appeared as if from nowhere to guide several lost companies safely through the swamps.[28]

Establishing supply stations along the route, Arnold made his way northward, and, in the early morning hours of November 8, his vanguard reached the St. Lawrence, across which towered the formidable battlements of Quebec. By the 10th, the entire column had arrived, thus bringing to an end one of the great marches in our military history, a tortuous, wearisome course of 350 miles from Fort Western. It had been no retreat like many other celebrated marches but an advance conducted despite enormous physical obstacles and, as Arnold himself remarked, with "famine staring us in the face; an enemy country and uncertainty ahead." Of course, it is not surprising if certain critics have belittled this march through the wilderness, one of them scornfully asserting that it was about what Canadians would now consider a camping holiday! Carried out in 1775, in country poorly mapped and relatively unknown, with all the difficulties of getting a fighting column of a thousand men and their equipment through the rugged wilderness country, the march was a marvelous accomplishment, even if it took twenty-six days more than Arnold's prediction of twenty.[29]

The same high praise can be given to Arnold's leadership. It was his good fortune, of course, to have no superior officer of whom he could be jealous. Completely on his own, he gave himself unsparingly to attaining his objective. His intelligence and foresight, his courage and confidence, his vigor and compelling personality held most of the expedition together. Though writing in his old age, when Arnold's villainy had long since become an article of the national faith, Henry could state, "Our commander, Arnold, was a remarkable character. He was brave, even to temerity, was beloved by the soldiery." Henry, of course, had special reason to feel kindly toward Arnold. Stricken with illness when near the St. Lawrence, he collapsed. When Arnold came along the route and saw him lying in the snow, he personally paid a French-Canadian to take the soldier down by boat. But Henry was merely echoing, in a sense, Hannah Arnold's report of months before that the Footguards spoke of Arnold as "a very humane, tender officer." Likewise Abner Stocking could say, "Our bold though unexperienced general discovered such firmness and zeal as inspired us with resolution." Washington made no effort to disguise his admiration of Arnold's leadership. To Arnold himself he declared, "It is not in the power of any man to command success; but you have done more—you have deserved it. . . . My thanks are due, and sincerely offered to you, for your enterprizing and persevering spirit." In a letter to General Schuyler he said further of Arnold, "The merit of this gentleman is certainly great, and I heartily wish that Fortune may distinguish him as one of her favourites. I am convinced that he will do every thing that prudence and valour shall suggest. . . ." Schuyler, who had sought unsuccessfully to make Arnold his adjutant after the colonel's unhappy Ticonderoga experience, replied to this encomium with understandable smugness, "I have heretofore observed that Col. Arnold had great merit." Neither criticism nor the defects of his character—not even his subsequent treachery—could take from Arnold the credit due him for his great march.[30]

But however impressive Arnold's achievement, could he now capture Quebec? That was the question on the answer to which so much depended. As early as November 1, he had suspected that his Indian messengers had betrayed him to the British in Quebec, a fact all too true; and Mercier, to whom he had written, was a prisoner. Small though the garrison was under the old-maidish lieutenant governor, Hector Cramahé, the city was alerted and all the canoes and boats on the Point Levis side of the St. Lawrence were removed. The sloop-of-war *Hunter* and the frigate *Lizard* lay in the river, their patrol boats out on watch. Worse still, a letter Arnold had dispatched by two Indians to General Montgomery at Montreal on November 8 was intercepted by a loyal, crusty Highlander, Allen Maclean, who, with two hundred men, was leisurely headed for Quebec after having been driven from Sorel by units attached to Montgomery's army that were commanded by Colonel Easton and Major Brown. At once catching the import of the situation, Maclean sped for the capital.

Though Arnold's men, after much searching, managed to secure between thirty and forty canoes and dugouts, wind on November 10 lashed the St. Lawrence into foam-crested waves that would have swamped the craft. Impatiently shaking his head when he saw that a night crossing at this time was impossible, Arnold waited for three crucial days for wind and current to lessen. He knew now, moreover, that his letter to Montgomery had been seized, that Maclean's arrival would appreciably alter the chances of a quick capture of the city, that every hour of delay strengthened the defense. Though far from despair, Arnold was nearer discouragement than at any time during the march. To have come so far only to be checked at the very last was a cruel stroke of fate. For the moment, only the wind-whipped river stood between the former apothecary's apprentice and the fall of Quebec. But that moment was passing.[31]

The Quebec Assault

ARNOLD was pre-eminently a man of action, rarely disposed to be philosophical when frustrated, and the Quebec venture was one of the most frustrating campaigns in American history. Though Arnold's part in it was truly Homeric, his efforts seemed to be attended by a singular fatality. In the present situation, despite his having been plagued by wilderness, storm, hunger, and desertion, he had reached the St. Lawrence only to discover the city warned through the treachery of a messenger. Had the river not been high, moreover, he would have reached the city before Maclean and might still have succeeded in seizing it. The knowledge was bitter, too, that had his own enemies, Easton and Brown, not been successful in driving Maclean from Sorel, the Highlander would not have been available to reinforce the garrison; a superstitious man, or an officer less confident of himself than Arnold, might have seen in the irony an ominous portent. But Arnold would never admit he was defeated until he had done everything within his power to overcome the opposition, whether it was a forest, a personal enemy, or the British. Quebec was a challenge he had come a long way to accept, and he was determined to take the city.

Having received intelligence that the gates of the city were still open at night, Arnold was eager to attack as soon as he could get his troops over on the north bank of the river, and at a council of war on November 12 he and Greene agreed on this course. Though most of the other officers recommended caution, the ultimate decision was left to Arnold himself. Meanwhile he fretted at the delay but finally decided that on Monday night, November 13, wind and water had quieted sufficiently for the canoes to chance the trip. Accordingly, at nine o'clock, the darkness being intense, the fragile birch-bark canoes began to ply their way back and forth across the river.[1]

The crossing was not without risk, for boats were passing on hourly patrol between the *Lizard* and the *Hunter*. In the lead canoe, Arnold suddenly spied a boat moving between them and the shore. With a harsh, whispered command, he bade the men at the paddles be still, and peered tensely into the darkness as the moving blur ahead cut across his bow. But the patrol failed to notice the canoes, and Arnold again started toward the northern bank. Though the presence of the *Hunter* forced him away from the debarkation point originally designated, he went ashore just above the very cove where General Wolfe had landed in 1759 on his way to the great trial of strength with Montcalm. While the canoes returned for additional troops, Arnold posted security guards and sent out reconnaissance parties. But anxiously he kept his eye on the river. The ebbing tide was beginning to make the landing a more difficult undertaking. The wind, moreover, was rising, and the moon starting to break through the clouds. Then someone kindled a blaze in a deserted house to warm men who had been spilled into the icy river when their canoe fell apart in midstream. Almost at once a patrol barge spotted the flames and put in toward shore. Arnold hailed her and ordered her to heave to. When the crew refused, riflemen fired at them. Though several aboard were hit, the boat succeeded in backing off. Realizing that by this time further trips were unsafe, Arnold ended the crossings at four o'clock.[2]

What he should do now was not clear. He had only five hundred men on the Quebec side and no scaling ladders immediately available. Reports from his reconnaissance parties were that no sentries had been encountered, though their calls could be heard. Subsequently a story, which appears to have had some substance, became current that the St. John's Gate was wide open and that the invaders could easily have swarmed through to the city. Morgan, however, had led a reconnaissance party close to the walls and returned with no such report, though Morgan himself had been eager for an immediate assault. Furthermore, Arnold could not help but believe that the firing on the barge had revealed his presence to the British and that they were therefore prepared for him; ironically neither Cramahé nor Maclean knew of the barge incident until hours afterward. Arnold believed, too, that the forces in the city at least equaled, if not outnumbered, his troops on the north shore; he had no idea how disorganized and discouraged the British were. Knowledge gained later would indicate that Arnold should have taken a chance and assaulted the city at once, but, on the basis of the information he possessed at the time, he was undoubtedly wise in not hazarding his small force in an assault which, if unsuccessful, could well have been fatal to the general plan of campaign that Washington had contrived. Though disappointed at not being able to achieve at once the objective which he and his men had endured so much to attain, Arnold had little doubt that a more favorable opportunity would soon arrive. Hence, restraining his impatience, he climbed the bluff to the Plains of Abraham, posted sentries, and billeted most of his weary troops in the mansion and outbuildings belonging to Major Henry Caldwell, about a mile and one half from Quebec. The surprise element had been forfeited, but Arnold still hoped that he could tempt the garrison out of the city to do battle with him as Montcalm had accepted Wolfe's challenge in 1759.[3]

While the troops caught a few hours' sleep and Arnold wrote his reports, a British sergeant, with the aid of a few daring redcoats, sneaked up close to the American lines and kidnapped a sentry who was probably dozing, one of Morgan's men. When word of this reached Arnold, he sprang up from his camp desk, threw on his cloak and hat, and dashed outdoors. Maclean must be thinking of making a sally, and if he did so, Arnold knew he had the Highlander in his power. Quickly he turned his men out in force and marched toward the walls of Quebec. The Americans cheered and taunted the soldiers and citizens thronging the ramparts, and the people there returned the salutations in like manner. In no way, however, could Arnold induce Maclean to repeat Montcalm's maneuver of issuing from the gates to challenge the invaders. Moreover, when Arnold sent Ogden with a flag of truce to demand Cramahé's surrender, the British fired a cannon at him, a procedure repeated the following morning. Already chagrined at his failure to capture the city, Arnold looked upon the firing on his envoy as a personal affront. It was, he said, an insult he "could not have expected from a private soldier; much more from an officer." His only recourse for the present was to cut off supplies from the city, and the British, though possessing troops, marines, seamen, and loyal inhabitants in greater numbers than the Americans, commenced to worry that the French within the walls, if exposed to a food shortage, might mutiny.[4]

Arnold himself was having trouble because of a shortage of supplies. Though he distributed the captured supplies intended for the city, he instituted such strict rationing that Morgan, Hendricks, and Smith demanded more food for their companies. Morgan was upset by the failure to take the city, by the seizure of his sentry, and by the futile parading before the walls. It is said that "altercation and warm language" passed between him and Arnold, but Arnold refused to accede to Morgan's demands. He appears, however, to have reconsidered the matter after the interview because, the next day, the riflemen's ration was increased. Furthermore, despite their disagreement, Morgan and Arnold continued to respect and to co-operate with each other.[5]

More serious and humiliating for Arnold was a subsequent development. Intelligence received from friends within the walls on November 18 revealed that the men-of-war were to be laid up and their guns and men added to the garrison, that an armed snow (a bastard brig with a fore-and-aft sail abaft its mainmast) just escaped from Montreal with two hundred men aboard was near, and that the garrison, equipped with several good field pieces, intended to attack the Americans on the 19th. The movement of the *Lizard* upriver as if to harass a retreat lent color to the report of a sally. At once Arnold ordered an inspection of all arms and ammunition. To his astonishment and dismay, the inspection disclosed nearly one hundred rifles and muskets unfit, the larger part of the cartridges useless despite their serviceable appearance, and no more than five good rounds available for each man.

The discovery shocked him more than he cared to reveal to his subordinates. He had known, of course, that the rigors of the march had ruined supplies and equipment, but he had supposed that, of all things, the men would be extra careful of their weapons and ammunition. On the other hand, their hardships had been of such a character and their spirit so laudable that he could not find it in his heart to reprove them; besides, perhaps they were not entirely responsible. Yet this situation called for a decision that he knew he had to make, however sorely it lacerated his pride. He had led his expedition through the most incredible difficulties only to be foiled in his hopes of a quick capture of Quebec, and now even a siege was out of the question. He must give up thought of having his name linked for all time and with surpassing honor to the capture of Quebec, even as he had had to make a similar sacrifice at Ticonderoga. Though he would have dearly loved to continue the siege on the chance that he might still devise some scheme to secure the city, he realized he must ignore his own feelings. The only sensible course was to withdraw to some defensible spot and await the arrival of Montgomery's army and supplies of ammunition and clothing.

Arnold was never one to delay making up his mind. On the 19th, he sent orders to the detachment at Point Levis to march parallel to the river, and moved his ragged, shivering army about twenty miles up the St. Lawrence to Pointe-aux-Trembles, the frozen ruts cutting so many of the shoeless men's feet that one soldier said, "We might have been tracked all the way by the blood from our shattered hoofs." En route, while his men admired the spectacular scenery about the river, he studied a snow and a schooner that passed them bound for Quebec. Aboard the snow was Guy Carleton, escaped from Sorel, and while the Americans were still on the march, Arnold heard the cannon in Quebec welcoming the redoubtable governor. Perhaps it was just as well he did not know that Maclean had intended no such sally as the informants from Quebec had described, that indeed the informants had not been the friends they pretended to be. The retreat itself was bitter enough for Arnold.[6]

Once at Pointe-aux-Trembles, Arnold's sense of duty would not permit him to relax, which was just as well in view of the occasional spells of despondency that assailed him. He billeted his troops among the inhabitants and provided them with ample provisions from the countryside. Procuring a supply of leather, he set the men to making shoes for themselves. He dispatched reports to Montgomery and Washington. He sent Ogden down to Montreal for clothing and ammunition. He also brought over the Point Levis detachment. Word from Montgomery confirming the fall of Montreal was cheering news, but even more inspiring was intelligence from an express that the cannon and munitions shipped by Montgomery had arrived at a point just thirty miles away. Anticipating the rapid approach of the general, Arnold sent off a detail on November 27 to bring up the guns, and hurried Morgan the next day back to Quebec on reconnaissance. Yet, two days later, neither the guns nor Montgomery had arrived, and Arnold gave Aaron Burr an anxious letter of inquiry to take to the general. Within the next few days, however, Montgomery sailed up with several of the vessels captured at Montreal, while the guns, munitions, and plentiful supplies of clothing also appeared.[7]

From the beginning, Arnold and the tall, handsome Montgomery got along like brothers. Both were young and vigorous, Montgomery at thirty-seven being only three years older than Arnold. The generous-natured general had been an able officer in the British regular establishment and had participated in the siege of Louisburg under Amherst. Refusing to serve against Americans in a regiment designated to help enforce the Stamp Act, he emigrated to New York, married into the Livingston family in 1773, and bought a small estate on the Hudson. He was appointed a brigadier by the Continental Congress and, serving under Schuyler, had seized Chambly, St. Johns, and Montreal. Like Arnold, he had experienced difficulty holding all his troops together, hundreds of New Englanders having recently left for home at the expiration of their short-term enlistments. He frankly admired Arnold's march through the wilderness and made the Kennebec column a nice little speech on its achievement. He soon informed Schuyler that he found "Colonel Arnold's corps an exceedingly fine one. . . . There is a style of discipline among them, much superior to what I have been used to see in this campaign." Of Arnold himself he said, "He . . . is active, intelligent, and enterprising." Arnold, on his part, exhibited neither jealousy nor rancor toward Montgomery. It is interesting indeed that with truly able leaders like Washington, Schuyler, and Montgomery, men who understood and appreciated him, Arnold had no trouble. It was generally with the second-raters, officers who were often more interested in their promotions than in their jobs, that Arnold encountered difficulty. Now, eager to get on to their objective, the two officers took their combined forces, numbering scarcely one thousand men, back to Quebec.[8]

Before leaving for the fortress city, Arnold experienced some unpleasantness with Captain Oliver Hanchet. On December 2, Arnold ordered the Connecticut officer to convey cannon, stores, and provisions down to Celears, within a league of Quebec. Hanchet appears to have held against Arnold as a mortal offense a rebuke the colonel had administered when Hanchet had not followed instructions during the wilderness march and had lost his company in the swamps. Now he abruptly refused to obey Arnold's order, alleging the danger of the undertaking as "too imminent." Justly enraged at Hanchet's insubordination, and swearing to arrest him, a threat he did not carry out, Arnold sent for Captains John Topham and Simeon Thayer, and asked one of them to perform the duty. Both eagerly accepted and tossed a coin to decide which one should go. Thayer won, to his satisfaction. Nearly a week later, Hanchet refused to execute another order for the same reason. Why Arnold put up with the man's atrocious behavior can be explained only in terms of the enlistment problem. On the day of Hanchet's first infraction, the surveyor, John Pierce, reported that Captain Goodrich's men expressed their intention of leaving, while "Capt. Hanchet's men all paraded to march for home." It took many "promises and threats," as Arnold admitted, to persuade them to stay. Arnold had therefore to bury his anger against Hanchet personally and leave the offender alone if he was to hold him and his men in service.[9]

Meanwhile, by December 5, Arnold and Montgomery had brought the troops to Quebec, and Arnold's chance to "knock up a dust with the garrison," as he expressed it, came nearer to realization. Still the possibility of taking the city, ruggedly fortified by nature and man, was hardly better than before Arnold's withdrawal to Pointe-aux-Trembles. With Canadian volunteers and Natanis's Indians, the little American army was barely more than half the size of the garrison, which had been considerably augmented thanks to Carleton's energy, and which had the services of one hundred and fifty cannon. But Montgomery had hopes. In a letter as imperious as Arnold's to Cramahé, he summoned Carleton to surrender. Though the guard refused to receive the letter, Montgomery persuaded an old woman to smuggle a copy through to Carleton. The governor threw the letter into a blazing fireplace and had the woman imprisoned; while British guns, starting to cannonade American-occupied St. Roque and St. John, signified to Montgomery that the haughty Carleton would have no more traffic with him than Cramahé and Maclean had had with Arnold. American artillery, presently emplaced behind redoubts of ice and snow, opened on the city, but the heavy British guns soon shattered the redoubts and forced the American pieces out of action. Montgomery was only too right when he said, "To the storming we must come at last." He and Arnold now planned to assault the city on the first wild night.[10]

The approaching expiration of many of the men's enlistments kept both leaders in a state of anxiety, and this feeling was accentuated by the dissension that rose between Arnold, on the one hand, and several of his officers, on the other. By no means all the officers and men were in favor of storming Quebec, particularly those whose enlistments were due to end by January 1. The greatest malcontents were in the companies of Captains Hanchet, William Goodrich, and Jonas Hubbard, and the chief troublemaker was Hanchet. This insubordinate officer, supported by the other two captains, flatly refused to serve further under Arnold and wanted to form an independent corps under a field officer. Just who this last individual was remains something of a mystery, since he is mentioned in none of the contemporary writings. Major John Brown, Arnold's old enemy, had come to Quebec with Montgomery. On the other hand, of

Arnold's field officers—Christopher Greene, Timothy Bigelow, and Return J. Meigs—Bigelow had voted against scaling the walls, while Meigs admitted in his journal to having spent a whole day shortly before in Hanchet's quarters. Was he trying to dissuade Hanchet from his position, or was he sympathizing and planning with him? The choice among the possible offenders is wide open, but would appear to lie chiefly between Brown and Bigelow. The enmity between Brown and Arnold was so great, however, that it is difficult to see how Brown could have let this opportunity pass to make additional trouble for Arnold. Montgomery himself believed the offender to be Brown.

If this flare-up was embarrassing to Montgomery, it was humiliating for Arnold. He realized now that, regardless of its effect on enlistments, he should have taken disciplinary action against Hanchet for his previous insubordination. Had he done so, this near mutiny might not have occurred. Yet it must be met, and the situation was so delicate that he must turn it over to Montgomery to handle. To think that Montgomery had openly praised the discipline of his troops when the general first saw them! But short though his acquaintance with Montgomery, he knew that the general could be relied upon to be just.

And Montgomery was exactly that. Although every man was needed, he declined to accept the offer of the officers to remain as part of another corps. "This," he said, "is resentment against Arnold, and will hurt him so much that I do not think I can consent to it." Perceiving how he felt, the officers expressed their aversion to an assault. To this broadening of their position—and they seem to have held Arnold mainly responsible for suggesting the attack—Montgomery retorted that he would not compel them for he wanted none with him who would go reluctantly. All his Irish skill in persuasion and all his tactfulness, a quality in which Arnold was pathetically lacking, were needed before the mutinous officers finally agreed to an assault and to continued service under Arnold. The latter, however, could not help noting that, like himself, Montgomery had dared take no action against the officers, who, with their companies, were so necessary if the assault was to be made.[11]

Finally, on the afternoon of December 30, with smallpox making alarming inroads in the little army, and with hundreds preparing to leave for their New England homes at the expiration of their enlistments with the end of the calendar year, a few snowflakes fluttered down. As Arnold and Montgomery anxiously studied the leaden sky, the downfall thickened, and, with darkness, the wind began to rise. The men looked to their arms and hastily pinned pieces of white paper to their headgear to identify themselves. Meanwhile the officers were again briefed on the plan: a diversionary attack by a small force under Captain Jacob Brown (Major Brown's brother) above Cape Diamond, another diversion by the Canadians under Colonel James Livingston against the upper town, a push by Montgomery with about three hundred men against the lower town from Wolfe's Cove, and a solid drive by the Kennebec column, reinforced by Captain John Lamb's artillery unit from New York, against the lower town from St. Roque. Meeting in the lower town, Montgomery and Arnold were, if possible, to smash up Mountain Street to the upper town. It was an ambitious plan for not quite twelve hundred effectives.

Few as the Americans were, and widely separated though their points of attack, the plan might have succeeded but for a combination of bad luck, questionable leadership on the part of certain officers, and British courage and skill. In the first place, thanks to the desertion of American Sergeant John Singleton and to the escape of one of the menials in a house where American officers were billeted, the British knew all about the design of attacking on the first stormy night, and soon manned their posts after Captain Malcolm Fraser of the main guard sighted American signal rockets at five o'clock on the morning of December 31 and troops moving toward the walls. The diversionary attacks detained the British only briefly; Brown's was soon diagnosed for what it was, while Livingston's Canadians presently fled. Montgomery, stumbling over ice cakes strewing the river road, tried to infuse courage into his straggling New Yorkers by taking the lead in person. Breaking his way through two palisades, he raced through the driving sleet with a small group toward a house blocking his path. Unfortunately the house had been pierced for cannon and was manned by Royal Navy seamen and Canadian volunteers under Captain Adam Barnfare of the snow *Fell*. When he sighted the onrushing Americans, Barnfare fired his guns, crammed to the muzzle with grapeshot. Montgomery and a dozen others fell dead or dying, including his aide, Captain John MacPherson, whose father had built the gracious home in Philadelphia which, in 1779, was to kindle the fancy and strip the financial resources of Benedict Arnold. At the general's fall, his nerveless second-in-command, Lieutenant Colonel Donald Campbell, ordered a retreat that turned into wild flight despite Aaron Burr's efforts to rally the terrified men. Ironically, the blockhouse defenders had also grown panicky on suddenly receiving a report that Arnold had forced the barrier at Sault-au-Matelot and was smashing toward them. They fled just after their repulse of Montgomery's charge, and only returned when their officers threatened to kill them. Had the faint-hearted New Yorkers waited inside or outside the palisade but a few minutes longer, they could have walked into the blockhouse and subsequently have kept their rendez-vous with Arnold's troops. The entire outcome of the battle might have been vastly different.

The burden of the attack now fell upon Arnold. His route lay from the General Hospital through St. Roque, along the St. Charles River toward the first barrier at Sault-au-Matelot, and up the narrow street to its junction with Mountain Street, at which point Montgomery was to join him. Like Montgomery, Arnold was in the van, leading thirty men in "the forlorn hope," as advance parties in that day were called. Behind him came Lamb with a brass six-pounder strapped to a sled, and then Morgan heading the main body, about one hundred yards behind Arnold. All had been up since the assembly hour at two o'clock and, at five o'clock, moved to the attack. Wrapping the lapels of their coats about the locks of their guns to keep them dry, the troops bent their heads to the storm and raced forward single-file. Ignoring the spurts of fire from the hundreds of enemy muskets lining the bluff above, Arnold led the column past the Palace Gate to the first barrier. He had hoped Lamb's cannon might breach the barrier, or at least silence one of the two defending twelve-pounders. Lamb, however, was forced to abandon the weapon because of the snow that drifted higher than a man's head. There was no other course now than for Arnold to take the barrier without benefit of artillery support. With a shout of encouragement to his men, he dashed forward. One of the British guns, loaded with grape, went off with a brilliant burst of light, but the gun was aimed too high to cause much damage. Thankful to have escaped the blast, Arnold raced on. Then suddenly he staggered and fell headlong into the snow as a ricocheting bullet burned into his left leg.

Painfully he got up, but could put little weight on the wounded leg. As men crowded around him, insisting that he go to the rear, he refused until the main body came up. Supported by Chaplain Samuel Spring and a soldier from Morgan's company, he waited until the field officers agreed to let Morgan take charge since Morgan had seen service and they had not. Even then, Arnold could not leave. In an agony of frustration, sus-pense, and pride, he watched the scaling ladders rise despite the flaming muskets and cannon at the barrier and Morgan and his riflemen go bound-ing over the obstacle as those still waiting to mount burst into cheers.

"Rush on, brave boys!" Arnold himself shouted, so Simon Fobes said; while Henry remarked, "Arnold called to the troops in a cheering voice as we passed, urging us forward." [12]

His place was at the head of his troops, not back here, but in the greatest test of his life, he had been struck down, and the battle must go on without his fierce spirit. Still the spurts of pain and the warm gushing in his leg gradually forced his mind off the din of battle. In fact, he grew so faint from loss of blood that he had to be carried from the Palace Gate to the General Hospital.

Once on a cot, he suffered double anguish, from his leg and from the course of the battle. Dr. Senter's diagnosis of his wound was that the ball had "entered the outer side of the leg, about midway, and in an oblique course passed between the tibia and fibula, lodged in the . . . muscle at the rise of the tendon achilles." Before Senter had finished dressing the colonel's wound, Matthias Ogden came in with a bullet through his left shoulder and gloomed that the battle was lost. Further reports confirmed his pessimism. Morgan had driven through to the second barrier, the gate to which was actually open and the enemy in a panic. But Morgan had thought to meet Montgomery there, and though he himself was ready to go on, the other officers dissuaded him. They said that the orders were to wait for Montgomery at this point; that they had already taken so many prisoners that the latter might turn the captured cannon against them if left behind; and that the Americans were sure of conquest anyway if they but acted with prudence and caution. Morgan accordingly dared not override them and order the attack, a step that Arnold would not have hesitated to take. By the time the officers had changed their minds, Carleton had rallied his men, surrounded the Americans, and forced most of them to surrender, including Morgan, weeping with rage, Lieutenant Colonel Greene, Majors Bigelow and Meigs, and Captains Thayer, Topham, Dearborn, Ward, Goodrich, and Hanchet. Captains Hendricks and Hubbard were dead, while among the wounded were Lieutenant Steele and Captain Lamb. The total American casualties in the battle—48 killed, 34 wounded, and 372 captured—formed a staggering proportion of the small force that had attacked Quebec that terrible night. To make matters worse, scores of the survivors fled toward Montreal or deserted outright.[13]

Stricken as he was by the disaster, Arnold was utterly indomitable. Even before the struggle was over, he dashed off a letter of brilliant clarity and conciseness to General Wooster at Montreal, informing him of the critical situation and requesting assistance. Few men could have been more courageous or resolute when, on the face of things, it looked as if Carleton's troops might advance and destroy the besiegers entirely. "Under these circumstances," said Dr. Senter, "we entreated Colonel Arnold for his own safety to be carried back into the country where they would not find him . . . but to no purpose. He would neither be removed, nor suffer a man from the Hospital to retreat. He ordered his pistols loaded with a sword on his bed . . . adding that he was determined to kill as many as possible if they came into the room. We were now all soldiers, even to the wounded in their beds were ordered a gun by their side. That if they did attack the Hospital to make the most vigorous defence possible." [14]

However bleak the outlook, Arnold never despaired. He refused to remove the heavy guns and ammunition since to do so might discourage the Canadians, though he withdrew a number of cannon from the Plains of Abraham and placed them around the powder magazine. He dispatched orders to the militia captains in the villages near by to rally to the Americans, and succeeded in convincing a few to bring up their companies. He sought to check the flight of the fainthearted to Montreal, he sent a report to Congress and to Washington, and he kept prodding the lethargic General David Wooster, his fellow Mason and townsman, who was in command at Montreal. "For God's sake," he begged this old hero, "order as many men down as you can possibly spare, consistent with the safety of Montreal, and all the mortars, howitzers, and shells, that you can possibly bring. I hope you will stop every rascal who has deserted from us, and bring him back again." His fiery spirit infused new hope into the discouraged, smallpox-ridden troops. Though he resigned in favor of Campbell because his wound kept him prostrate, the other officers insisted that he retract his resignation. From the hospital bed that served as his headquarters, he therefore issued the orders that maintained the siege. "I have no thought of leaving this proud town, until I first enter it in triumph," he wrote Hannah. "I know you will be anxious for me. That Providence which has carried me through so many dangers, is still my protection. I am in the way of duty, and know no fear." This was not the bravado of a tin-horn braggart. The words were those of a man in deadly earnest, a dynamic, resourceful leader who was determined that catastrophic defeat, the menace of enemy and disease, and bodily disablement should not prevail.[15]

· VIII ·

Withdrawal from Canada

NEWS of the failure of the assault upon Quebec, with the death of Montgomery, the wounding of Arnold, and the loss of so many men, shocked the United Colonies. "My amiable friend, the gallant Montgomery, is no more; the brave Arnold is wounded; and we have met with a severe check . . . I tremble for our people in Canada," Schuyler lamented to Washington. "I . . . most sincerely condole with you upon the fall of the brave and worthy Montgomery and those gallant officers and men who have experienced a like fate," Washington replied, and added, "I am much concerned for the intrepid and enterprising Arnold." Thanks to vigorous measures by the commander-in-chief, Congress, and the colonies, troops from Massachusetts, Connecticut, New Hampshire, New Jersey, and Pennsylvania were raised to reinforce the American forces in Canada. These, however, did not start arriving in numbers for weeks, leaving Arnold at Quebec and Wooster at Montreal largely on their own until the latter part of February.[1]

Though Arnold pled with Wooster for men and guns, the general felt that he could spare few of either, his own forces were so small and his fears so great that the inhabitants of Montreal would rise against him. Critics have contended, rather unfairly, that Wooster's fears may have originated in part from the enormous quantities of flip he drank, but there is no question that he considered himself unable to give Arnold much help. The old general was a politician who provoked Schuyler by writing to Congress over his head and irritated Washington by the manner in which he handled his men and the excessive caution which prevented him from assisting Arnold. Furthermore, conservative that he was, he deplored Arnold's impetuosity. But Wooster, although he had left his military competence back in the wars with France, was honest. Whenever he could, he dribbled men and supplies down to Arnold and openly marveled at Arnold's ability to maintain the siege. He announced to Congress that "General Arnold has, in a most surprising manner, kept up the blockade of Quebec, and that with half the number of the enemy." To Washington he spoke even more warmly of Arnold. "General Arnold," he said, "has, to his great honour, kept up the blockade with such a handful of men, that the story, when told hereafter, will be scarcely credited." Still Washington already knew the military stuff of which Arnold was made. At least a month before receiving the encomium from Wooster, he had written his friend Joseph Reed, "I find, that Arnold was continuing the blockade of Quebec on the 19th [January, 1776], which, under the heaviness of our loss there, is a most favorable circumstance, and exhibits fresh proof of Arnold's ability and perseverance in the midst of difficulties." [2]

The recognition that came to Arnold gave him enormous satisfaction. Praise was sweet, but concrete evidence of appreciation was sweeter. As early as December 5, Washington had appointed him to command of one of the regiments being raised for the Continental Army. Even more flattering was the action of Congress. On January 8, before word of the storming of Quebec arrived in Philadelphia, Christopher Gadsden of South Carolina moved "that Col. Arnold may be made a Brigadier Gen. and receive the thanks of the Congress for his extraordinary march from Cambridge to Quebec and for his other spirited exertions." The motion was seconded by Richard Smith of New Jersey. After considerable debate, the motion was deferred until the following day, then deferred again until January 10, when it was passed unanimously. When Arnold learned the welcome news, he asked John Hancock, as president of Congress, to present that body with his "respectful compliments and sincere thanks for the honourable mark of esteem they have been pleased to confer on me, which I shall study to deserve." His gratitude for being appreciated was almost touching. To a letter from Washington expressing the commander-in-chief's hopes for the campaign and confidence in him, and mentioning his bravery and perseverance, Arnold replied, "I am greatly obliged to you for your good wishes, and the concern you express for me. Sensible of the vast importance of this country, you may be assured my utmost exertions will not be wanting to effect your wishes in adding it to the United Colonies." [3]

While Arnold sought to fulfill this proud resolve, he encountered trouble within his own command not only in the form of hunger and smallpox but also in the person of Major John Brown. This officer was a brave and capable soldier who was to die in 1780 defending Stone Arabia in western New York against an Indian raid. He was intensely ambitious, not entirely scrupulous, and as proud and vindictive in his way as Arnold, whom it is likely he knew before the war since he had married the sister of Oliver Arnold, Benedict's cousin. He had sided with Allen and Easton against Arnold at Ticonderoga and intrigued with Hanchet, Goodrich, and Hubbard against Arnold before the storming of Quebec. Now, during the siege, he felt that Arnold meant to make a Uriah of him by sending him with inferior forces to repulse sallies or to head an assault force in another storming of the city. He also assumed and insisted on the grade of colonel, which, he contended, Montgomery had promised him at Montreal. In an amazingly outspoken letter to the president of Congress, Arnold admitted this contention to be true, but added the following:

When Major Brown wrote to remind him of his promise, the General handed me his letter, and told me, at the same time, as Colonel Easton and Major Brown were publickly impeached with plundering the officers' baggage taken at Sorel, contrary to articles of capitulation, and to the great scandal of the American Army, he could not, in conscience or honour promote him, (Major Brown,) until those matters were cleared up. He then sent for Major Brown, and told him his sentiments on the matter very freely; after which I heard of no further application for promotion. This transaction Colonel Campbell, Major Dubois, and several gentlemen, were knowing to. As Colonel Easton and Major Brown have, doubtless, a sufficient share of modest merit to apply to the honourable Continental Congress for promotion, I think it my duty to say the charge beforementioned is the publick topick of conversation at Montreal, and among the officers of the Army in general; and, as such conduct is unbecoming the character of gentlemen or soldiers, I believe it would give great disgust to the Army in general if those gentlemen were promoted before those matters were cleared up.

To this letter Arnold appended a postscript:

The contents of the enclosed letter I do not wish to be kept from the gentlemen mentioned therein; the publick interest is my chief motive for writing. I should despise myself were I capable of asserting a thing in prejudice of any gentleman without sufficient reasons to make it public. [4]

This was an extraordinary communication, and its repercussions were to last for many months with severe effects on the careers of Arnold, Brown, and Easton. In view, moreover, of certain aspects of Arnold's subsequent career, one can hardly help being struck by the tone of self-righteousness, particularly in the postscript; yet this may indicate nothing more than a hypersensitivity to the opinion of his superiors and to the public at large. Arnold had obviously written during a period of great emotional strain. Indeed, when one considers the decisions he was called on to make, the frustration of being bedridden in these crucial weeks, and the presence of real physical discomfort, he was probably distraught most of the time, and understandably so. Now to have a man he deeply distrusted and disliked insist on an elevation in grade undoubtedly touched off his trigger-edge temper. At the same time, the charges were of so grave a nature that an officer in his position could scarcely have made them without having real grounds, or what appeared to him to be such. He must have realized, furthermore, that an aggressive officer like Brown, who was also an able lawyer, would not let him speak out without making a vigorous defense.

Brown was prompt to retort, once he learned of what Arnold had written, but his efforts gained at first little recognition. On June 26, 1776, he sent a petition to Congress, listing the sacrifices he had made under Montgomery's command, explaining the situation concerning the promised promotion, and labeling Arnold's allegation about himself and Easton as "false, scandalous, and malicious." He said that, on first hearing the charge at Quebec, he went to Arnold, challenged him to prove it, and demanded a court of inquiry, which Arnold "peremptorily refused." Subsequently Brown demanded a court of inquiry of Wooster, too, but Wooster "likewise refused." He later "did the same to the honourable Committee sent to Canada from the Congress, who refused." Finally he appealed for a court of inquiry to General Schuyler, at Fort George, "but the General thought it inexpedient." In view of Wooster's own dislike of Arnold, Schuyler's essential fairness, and the distinguished composition of the Canadian commission (Benjamin Franklin, Samuel Chase, and Charles Carroll), it is more than passing strange that no one accorded Brown the satisfaction he sought unless it seemed unlikely that Arnold had done the man a real injustice. But even with the commission's dismissal of his case, Brown was not through with his defense. In fact, as will appear subsequently, he went over to the attack and sought to make Arnold's life miserable for months to come.[5]

Having recovered sufficiently by the end of February to limp about, Arnold continued to keep the British bottled up in Quebec. He cut off supplies from the city, hammered back into the city several parties attempting a sally, mounted guns on the Levis side of the river, and prepared fireships to send against British shipping when the thaw arrived. Unfortunately smallpox gave little respite in its ravages, the temperature dropped to 28° below 0°, and desertion persisted. Almost as serious for Arnold was the shortage of specie. He was accordingly forced to issue a decree on March 4 authorizing circulation of paper money among the Canadians. For several weeks, dissatisfaction among many of the Canadians had been growing. As their hopes of American victory waned, their dread of British reprisals increased. They felt, too, that politically the Americans had neglected them, and certainly Congress had been remiss in not solidifying the political bonds between Canada and the United Colonies. Relations between American soldiers and the Canadians, moreover, had deteriorated since the failure of the assault. Furthermore, the arrest of priests loyal to the Crown roused great antagonism. Arnold's financial decree seemed for many the climax of disillusionment. Within three weeks, several hundred Canadians on the southern bank of the river rose in revolt, threatening the garrison at Point Levis. Instantly Arnold strengthened the garrison there and on Orleans Island, and sent troops that succeeded in routing the insurgents. By the influx of Canadians thereafter into his ranks and by the friendlier attitude evinced by the inhabitants in the troop areas at least, he considered that most of them were still hopeful of an eventual American triumph. Meanwhile he furthered his preparations for tightening the siege.[6]

Then on April Fools' Day came General Wooster. The proud old man had his own hopes and plans for capturing Quebec, and he chose not to share them with Arnold. To the latter, the general's secretiveness was intolerable, particularly since Arnold had borne the burden of the siege and still limped from his wound. Furthermore, he despaired of the old veteran's ever being able to do more than look like a soldier, and a pompous, slow-thinking one at that. Taking Quebec was a young man's task, and if Wooster believed he could do more than he, Arnold, had done, the general was as sorely mistaken as he had been when he thought he could prevent the Footguards from marching to Cambridge. The feeling between the two officers was thus not only a clash of two opposing natures, it was also a conflict of generations. Perhaps it was just as well, therefore, that on the very next day Arnold's horse (only a week before, Arnold had started again to ride) slipped on the Sillery road to St. Roque and fell, violently bruising the wounded leg. After nursing his leg and his pride for ten days, he asked permission to go to Montreal. Wooster readily granted him a leave of absence until his leg had recovered. At Montreal, however, he explained in a letter to Schuyler, "Had I been able to take an active part, I should by no means have left the camp; but as General Wooster did not think proper to consult me in any of his matters, I was convinced I should be of more service here than in camp." [7]

Arnold was hardly established in Montreal when he had to receive the commissioners who had been belatedly dispatched by Congress. The purpose of the commission was to represent to the Canadians the essential commonness of purpose that existed between the United Colonies and Canada in the struggle against Britain and to give the Canadians assurance of full religious and civil liberty. Few more distinguished representatives could have been sent than the shrewd, tolerant, and world-renowned Franklin, the resolute Samuel Chase, and the wealthy and temperate Charles Carroll of Carrollton. Accompanying the commissioners were a learned and liberal Jesuit brother of Carroll's, John Carroll, future archbishop of Baltimore, and a foreign officer with the rank of brigadier general in the Continental Army who turned out to be a drunkard, Baron Wilhelm de Woedtke. A salute of cannon heralded the approach of the commissioners, and Arnold warmly greeted them, then led them to his headquarters, the Chateau de Ramezay, residence of the wealthy Canadian rebel, Thomas Walker, who had been known to Arnold in prewar days. "We were received by General Arnold," said Charles Carroll, "in the most polite and friendly manner, conducted to headquarters, where a genteel company of ladies and gentlemen had assembled to welcome our arrival." Arnold loved to play the lavish host and could do it handsomely. Later, in the spacious, high-ceilinged chateau, he dined the commissioners, listened to the accounts of their travels, and discussed the campaign.[8]

As the commission turned to its tasks, Arnold found himself involved in a tragic and exasperating situation, the Cedars affair. Wooster had been hapless before Quebec, and on May 1 he was succeeded by General John Thomas, a man of decision. Thomas gave the defenses of the fortress city, the siege lines, and his army a thorough inspection, and, on May 5, ordered the siege raised. While the Americans were preparing to leave on the following day, heavy reinforcements arrived from England which Carleton threw into action at once. The Americans fled in panic toward

Montreal, abandoning most of their supplies, cannon, and equipment, even their sick; and Carleton dined off the still warm and untouched dinner of General Thomas, who was unable to check his frightened men. Though he subsequently rallied some of his units, he continued to withdraw up the river. It therefore became of the highest importance to hold Montreal. But Montreal itself was threatened by a force of British and Indians about thirty miles west of the town at a place called the Cedars, where the St. Lawrence makes a sharp turn. Colonel Timothy Bedell with a small party, presently reinforced by Major Isaac Butterfield with about four hundred men, commanded the post. Bedell liked neither the post nor the smallpox with which he was soon afflicted. Hence, leaving Butterfield in command, he set out for Montreal. On arriving, he announced that a combined force of British and Indians was hovering near the Cedars, and requested reinforcements. Arnold was at Sorel at the time, but Colonel John Patterson in Montreal sent out Major Henry Sherburne with about one hundred and fifty men as reinforcements.

Bedell's bad news was only too true. Under orders from Quebec, Captain George Forster of the British Army with approximately one hundred regulars and Canadians and four hundred Indians under the English-educated Mohawk chief, Joseph Brant, had approached the Cedars. The allies considered the stockade too strong to attack and were on the point of withdrawing when word reached them of the American flight from Quebec. At once they turned back, and Forster made it clear to Butterfield that unless he surrendered, the savages would give no quarter. With scarcely a show of resistance the cowardly officer submitted on May 19. Learning that reinforcements were on the way, Forster then ambushed Sherburne, who gave the enemy somewhat more opposition than Butterfield but also surrendered with upward of one hundred of his men; like Butterfield's troops, they were immediately stripped of their arms and clothing by the Indians. The way was now clear to Montreal, and it looked as if the American forces would be squeezed between Carleton and his new lieutenant, Burgoyne, on the one hand, and Forster and Brant, on the other.

But the American fainthearts and the British sympathizers in Montreal reckoned without Benedict Arnold. Shocked at Forster's triumphs and by reports of Indian barbarities on the prisoners, Arnold rounded up a hundred men and dashed toward the enemy. Entrenching at Lachine around a stone farmhouse, he defied Forster to attack him; soon he was joined by a few more troops. Though Forster pushed so close to the improvised fort

that Arnold heard his drums on the night of May 24, rumor reaching
Forster from Montreal exaggerated Arnold's force to fifteen hundred men
and eight cannon, with one thousand more men on the way. Possibly
Arnold himself was responsible for the rumor; he employed the same ruse
in relieving Fort Stanwix, the following year. At any rate, most of Forster's
Indians and Canadians fled in terror. He drew back to the Cedars with
but eighty men, though two hundred Indians rejoined him after they
learned of how few troops Arnold had with him. What to do with his
five hundred or more prisoners at first bothered Forster. Then, under the
threat of letting the Indians loose upon them, he extracted an agreement
from the captives for an exchange of prisoners in equal numbers. The
joker was that the agreement, or cartel, as it was called, provided that the
Americans should never again serve against England while British prisoners exchanged were under no such prohibition.

Meanwhile, reinforced by the 1st Pennsylvania Regiment and an additional four hundred troops, Arnold raced after the enemy. Ahead of him
he hurried several friendly Caughnawagas to the hostile Indians with the
threat that if any of the prisoners were murdered, he would follow the
culprits to their towns and destroy them "by fire and sword." He arrived
at St. Anne on the western tip of the island of Montreal only to see the
Indians with their prisoners fleeing from another island to the mainland.
Worse still, the Caughnawagas had returned with the reply that, if he
attacked, the Indians would kill all the prisoners and any Americans they
thereafter captured.

Arnold was never one to be impressed by the threat of force if he felt
he could do something to counteract the threat. Leaping to the boats he
had collected, he flew to the island and found five naked, starving soldiers.
All the rest had been taken to Quinze Chiens on the mainland except two
who had been sick; the Indians had butchered these. Deciding to reconnoiter the enemy, Arnold and his men were brought up short in their
boats by the brisk fire of two cannon on shore and a burst of musketry.
With darkness falling, he reluctantly withdrew to St. Anne and held a
council of war. He was all for going up the St. Lawrence at once and
flanking the enemy, but Colonel Moses Hazen, who had changed from a
Loyalist to a rebel in his affiliations, contended that the Indians could
not be surprised and would surely sacrifice their prisoners. Though the
argument grew warm between them, Arnold finally deferred to Hazen,
who had been a ranger in these parts, and to Colonel John de Haas of the

1st Pennsylvania, who supported Hazen. Arnold insisted, however—and his officers agreed with him—on an attack early in the morning.

At two o'clock that morning, a British officer arrived with a copy of the cartel. As Arnold read it by the light of a campfire, his famous temper rose. Arnold, aroused, was not an easy man to oppose. The blue-gray, bulging eyes shone hotly in contrast to the full, dark cheeks, while the heavy lower lip thrust out belligerently. There was a bulldog appearance as well to the powerful shoulders and the wide stance. Holding the paper with one hand and slapping it with the back of the other for emphasis, Arnold told the officer in terse, blunt language that he flatly rejected the article favoring British prisoners to be exchanged. He would only consider an exchange on equal terms. If Forster refused, he would attack him at once; and if the American prisoners were murdered, he would "sacrifice every soul who fell into our hands." Impressed by his messenger's report of Arnold's resolution, the American numbers, and his own inferior strength, Forster accepted the amendment and signed the agreement. Shortly afterward, Butterfield, Sherburne, and the others returned, while Forster retreated. Thus Arnold brought the humiliating incident to as honorable a close as was possible under the circumstances. Angrily he wrote the commissioners of Congress, "Word cannot express my feelings . . . torn by the conflicting passions of revenge and humanity." Congress confirmed Arnold's agreement but insisted that before any British prisoners were returned, the British commander in Canada should give up those responsible for the murders and indemnify the Americans for their loss of property after the surrender. Needless to say, these conditions were not met; consequently, British captives were not restored. Both Bedell and Butterfield, however, were court-martialed and cashiered for their conduct.[9]

Meanwhile, to his dismay, Arnold saw the Canadian venture, in which he had earlier borne so brilliant a part, turn utterly grim for the Americans. The army was without pay, food, clothing, tentage, or medicines, and so rotten with smallpox, caught naturally or by self-inoculation, that at one time two-thirds of the force at Montreal was incapacitated. General Thomas himself died of the disease. Arnold saw the proverbial handwriting on the wall, and, on May 31, he wrote a very frank letter to General Gates, who was in charge in northern New York and with whom he was on the best of terms:

I shall be ever happy in your friendship and society; and hope, with you, that our next winter-quarters will be more agreeable, though I must doubt it if affairs go as ill with you as here. Neglected by Congress below; pinched with every want here; distressed with the small-pox; want of Generals and discipline in our Army, which may rather be called a great rabble; our late unhappy retreat from Quebeck, and loss of the Cedars; our credit and reputation lost, and great part of the country; and a powerful foreign enemy advancing upon us,—are so many difficulties we cannot surmount them. My whole thoughts are now bent on making a safe retreat out of this country; however, I hope we shall not be obliged to leave it until we have had one bout more for the honour of America. I think we can make a stand at Isle-aux-Noix, and keep the lake this summer from an invasion that way. We have little to fear; but I am heartily chagrined to think we have lost in one month all the immortal Montgomery was a whole campaign in gaining, together with our credit, and many men and an amazing sum of money. The Commissioners [from Congress] this day leave us, as our good fortune has long since; but Miss, like most other Misses, is fickle, and often changes, I still hope for her favours again; and that we shall have the pleasure of dying or living together.[10]

One might have thought that, at this juncture, the American authorities would have appointed Arnold to the command of the decimated army as the general officer most familiar with the terrain and the campaign, and one whose qualifications for leadership had been so clearly demonstrated. Not so. The command had to go to a major general, in this instance to General John Sullivan, a New Hampshire lawyer and politician whose record of military failures in the course of the Revolution was hardly short of remarkable. He possessed not only "a little tincture of vanity" and an "over desire of being popular," as Washington observed, though the commander-in-chief liked and respected him, but also a tendency to act first and think afterward. Almost at once, his forces under General William Thompson suffered a severe defeat at Three Rivers on June 7. The outcome of this "bout," for which Arnold had longed but in which he had no direct participation, convinced him of the futility of the struggle. He wrote Sullivan on June 13 that "the junction of the Canadians with the Colonies . . . is at an end. Let us quit them and secure our own country before it is too late; there will be more honour in making a safe retreat, than hazarding a battle, against such superiority which will doubtless be attended with the loss of men, artillery etc. . . . These arguments are not urged by fear for my personal safety. I am content to be the last man who quits this country and fall so that my country rise—but let us not fall all together." [11]

The day after Arnold wrote him, Sullivan evacuated Sorel, and this movement necessitated Arnold's leaving Montreal. Up to the last, acting under orders from the commissioners of Congress, Arnold seized from Montreal merchants quantities of provisions and material for the army and sent them to St. Johns by way of Chambly. This legalized plundering was to become a point of intense controversy during the summer. While employed in preparing for a retreat, Arnold kept young Captain James Wilkinson standing by in a barge to take a last message to Sullivan. A mere boy, Wilkinson was to exhibit before many months some of the devious ways that helped contribute to one of the strangest and most disgraceful careers in our military history. On Saturday, June 15, Wilkinson spotted Carleton's fleet, the decks of its vessels crowded with soldiers, bearing down on Montreal. Racing ashore, he stole a horse and galloped to Arnold at the Chateau de Ramezay with the alarm. Arnold evacuated the garrison within two hours and headed across the flat country to St. Johns, destroying bridges and making what Sullivan later described as "a very prudent and judicious retreat with an enemy close at his heels." At St. Johns he was joined on the 17th by the inconsolable Sullivan, who left nothing but ruin behind him at Sorel and Chambly. Immediately Sullivan held a council of war, and the council recommended a retreat to Crown Point via Isle-aux-Noix. The boats assembled by the quartermasters started transporting the troops at once to the island.[12]

By evening of June 18, with darkness fast falling, all had gone save Arnold and young Wilkinson. Acrid columns of black smoke rose from the demolished defenses and waterfront of St. Johns, which was now virtually a ghost town. Nodding to his companion, Arnold rode back through the deserted streets. If his thoughts were as stark as the graceless countryside, it was understandable, for he was viewing the wreck of his own hopes as well as those of the American attempts to win Canada to the United Colonies. The expedition to Quebec had been an opportunity he had welcomed with all his heart. Success would vindicate him to those who mattered and would also confound his opponents. Though he had won fame of a sort, and had added greatly to his reputation, the failure of the campaign to take Canada made his achievements seem futile. He grew morose and angry when he thought of the sufferings of the Kennebec expedition, the assault on Quebec with its bitter harvest of death and disaster, the anguish of his own wound, the ordeal of the winter siege, Wooster's arrival to take the command when he was on the point of making an attempt to destroy British shipping in the St. Lawrence, and the humiliating affair at the Cedars. Who would have thought that Wooster, Thomas, and Sullivan could have made such a mess of the campaign?

But was not Congress also at fault for not supporting the campaign more strongly from the start? And what criminal folly these short-term enlistments were! Without them, Quebec would have fallen; of this he was convinced. Yet, with or without them, this cursed smallpox was everywhere. Stricken as it was, the army was lucky to have escaped. But it was still a question whether even a few miles of water could long hold up the energetic British.

Now near the edge of the town, Arnold stopped to listen. There was no mistaking the massive, muffled tread of many feet, the creaking of artillery wheels, the shouts of drivers to their horses, or the sharp commands in the high, piercing tone that British officers affected; Carleton's army was very close, with Lieutenant General John Burgoyne in charge of the vanguard. In a few moments a company of scarlet and white skirmishers appeared down the road from Chambly, then a group of mounted officers, and, after that, seemingly endless columns of scarlet infantry moving swiftly to the urgent thudding of many drums. There was no time to lose. Wheeling about, Arnold dashed back to the canoe he had reserved. Then he made two typically Arnoldian gestures: defiantly he shot his horse that it might not fall into the hands of the British; but, first, he removed the saddle and bridle and carefully placed them in the canoe. Wilkinson did likewise. The lad now gingerly climbed into the craft and picked up a paddle, while Arnold pushed the canoe from shore with his own hands. He had fulfilled his prediction to Sullivan: he was the last man of all that fateful expedition to leave the mainland of Canada.[13]

· IX ·

Summer of Controversy

"**I** AM sorry Arnold escaped," Lord George Germain, secretary of state for the colonies, wrote in reply to Burgoyne's report of his pursuit of the Americans. "I think he has shown himself the most enterprising man among the rebels." By early autumn, Arnold was to give the British cause for even greater regret by reason of his supervising the construction of a fleet on Lake Champlain and then leading it into one of the most gallant actions in American naval history. But during that breathless, exciting summer, while Carleton was also putting together a fleet and assembling an army at the northern end of Champlain, Arnold became involved in sharp controversies. One of them, not without pathos and humor, was with a stubborn officer of Dutch extraction, Jacobus Wynkoop, over command of the fleet. Another, a much more serious affair, grew out of the plundering of the Montreal merchants, and formed the basis for numerous attacks on Arnold's character. In addition to these difficulties, Easton and Brown carried their grievances against Arnold to Congress. For the time being, however, the gravest development was the plundering controversy, which was not long in developing after the army, following a ghastly ordeal of smallpox and malaria on Isle-aux-Noix, floated up to Crown Point and then to Ticonderoga, its casualties by capture, desertion, wounds, and death by battle or disease totaling about five thousand.[1]

While Arnold was at Montreal, the army was living from hand to

mouth and was pitifully short of clothing and equipment. Carroll and
Chase, the only active commissioners (Franklin, who was ill, had returned
home), tried desperately to procure provisions and supplies for the army's
needs and to stiffen its morale. It was as a result of their criticism that
Wooster was superseded at Quebec by Thomas. Their relations with the
energetic Arnold were singularly agreeable, and they frequently turned to
him for assistance. On May 15, he wrote Chase,

> I believe I know your sentiments in respect to provisions, and shall not let the
> Army suffer. I am fully of opinion with you in regard to persons holding
> criminal correspondence with our enemies, and shall treat them accordingly. The
> proclamation you hint I think is both just and reasonable, and the only resource
> we have left to maintain an Army in this country. . . . Blankets and coarse
> linens are exceedingly wanted. . . . Will it not be advisable and justifiable to
> seize on all such goods in Montreal as we are in absolute necessity for, and pay
> them the value? Government has set us many precedents, and necessity will
> doubtless justify retaliation. This I submit to your better judgment.[2]

The commissioners then authorized Arnold to make such seizures. He
could thus assure them on June 2 that

> I am making every possible preparation to secure our retreat. I have secured
> six tons of lead, ball and shot. Merchandise or the inhabitants I have not yet
> taken hold of; I intend it tomorrow. It is impossible to know one hour before-
> hand the necessary steps to be taken. Everything is in the greatest confusion; not
> one contractor, commissary, or quartermaster: I am obliged to do the duty of
> all.

Those were desperate days in early June, 1776, the destitute army close
to being a mere rabble, and capable officers lacking. Arnold threw himself into the work of confiscation with the same zeal that he showed in
battle, yet he kept General Schuyler and Sullivan apprised of his activities.
To Schuyler he wrote on June 6, "I am now removing a parcel of goods I
have seized for the use of the Army." Similarly, on the 10th, he told the
general, "I have received your instructions respecting the Tories and
their effects; most of the former had absconded; great part of the latter is
secured. I have sent to St. Johns a quantity of goods for the use of the
Army—some bought and some seized." [3]

Arnold presently learned that these goods, sent by way of Chambly,
fared badly. He therefore made no pretense at disguising his feelings to
Sullivan on June 13:

> The goods I seized at Montreal and sent to Chambly under the care of Major

Scott, have been broken open, plundered, and huddled together in the greatest confusion. They were taken in such a hurry it was impossible to take a particular account of them. Each man's [merchant's] name was marked on his packages. When Major Scott, arrived at Chambly, he received your positive orders to repair to Sorel. The guard was ordered to return, and the goods to be delivered to Colonel Hazen to be stored. He refused receiving or taking care of any of them, by which means, and Major Scott's being ordered away, the goods have been opened and plundered, I believe to a large amount. It is impossible for me to distinguish each man's goods, or ever settle with the proprietors. The goods are delivered to Mr. McCarthy. This is not the first or last order Colonel Hazen has disobeyed. I think him a man of too much consequence for the post he is in.[4]

A somewhat more temperate letter to Schuyler amplified the information given Sullivan:

Major Scott was sent with them [the goods], with orders to have them stored under the care of Colonel Hazen, who commanded at Chambly. On his arrival there he received orders to repair to Sorel. Colonel Hazen refused taking the goods into store, or taking charge of them; they were heaped in piles on the banks of the river. Colonel Hazen finally received them, and placed sentinels over them; they were, however, neglected in such a manner that great part were stolen or plundered. On receiving this intelligence I repaired to Chambly; the goods were sent to St. Johns by Colonel Hazen, in different parcels, all under the care of a French corporal; and through them I found the goods broken open, plundered, and mixed together in the greatest confusion, and great part missing. Mr. McCarthy has General Sullivan's orders, and is now receiving the goods.[5]

Arnold's letter to Sullivan, of which he sent Hazen a copy, prompted the latter to ask Sullivan for a court-martial or a court of inquiry to clear himself. The matter was referred to Gates on Sullivan's departure, and Gates set July 26 as the date of the court-martial. Hazen presently complained to Gates, however, that certain irregularities in procedure existed, namely that not all the officers being impaneled were of field grade and that they were being named by Arnold. Whether there was any truth in the second complaint is difficult to say, but if the implication was that the nominees would necessarily favor Arnold, the result of the court-martial would seem to disprove the allegation. President of the court was Colonel Enoch Poor, who opened the trial on the appointed date.[6]

Few court-martials have produced more fireworks. Arnold held Hazen responsible for the damage to the goods, and presented Major Scott as his principal witness. To his indignation the court rejected Scott as "so far interested in the event of Colonel Hazen's trial, as to render his testimony inadmissible." The reasons given for the court's deducing the manner and degree of Scott's interest were reasons which, as Arnold's most temperate biographer has justly declared, "went to affect his credibility and not his competency as a witness." After other witnesses were called, Arnold again requested the admission of Scott, adding that he would enter a protest on the minutes of the court if his request was denied. When the court still refused, Arnold declared, "As the Court have refused accepting my principal evidence, Major Scott, after my having declared to them, on honour, that he had punctually obeyed my orders respecting the goods he had in charge from Montreal to Chamblee, and of course is not in the least interested in the event of Colonel Hazen's trial, I do solemnly protest against their proceedings and refusal as unprecedented, and I think unjust." [7]

The court took offense at Arnold's action, and entered the following on its records:

General Arnold having offered a protest to the Court, for the entry of it on their minutes, which appears to them illegal, illiberal, and ungentlemanlike, for these reasons they have objected to its entry and refuse the same.

The Court likewise directed the President to demand satisfaction of the General; which he accordingly did, in the following words:

Sir: As you have evidently called in question, not only the honour, but the justice likewise of this Court by the illiberal protest you exhibited, the Court have directed me, and as President of this Court I esteem it my duty, to inform you that you have drawn upon yourself their just resentment, and that nothing but an open acknowledgment of your error will be conceived as satisfactory.[8]

Arnold's protest, if somewhat irregular, hardly merited such a reply. Furthermore, the reply was so worded that Arnold could not but conceive his honor had been impugned. Accordingly, on August 1, he dispatched the court a prompt and sharp rejoinder:

Gentlemen: The very extraordinary vote of the Court, and directions given to the President, and his still more extraordinary demand, are, in my opinion, ungenteel and indecent reflections on a superior officer, which the nature and words of my protest will by no means justify; nor was it designed as you have construed it. I am not very conversant with Courts-Martial, but this I may venture to say, they are composed of men not infallible. Even you may have erred. Congress will judge between us; to whom I will desire the General to transmit the proceedings of this Court. This I can assure you, I shall ever, in publick or private, be ready to support the character of a man of honour; and, as your very nice and delicate honour, in your apprehension, is injured, you may depend, as soon as this disagreeable service is at an end, (which God grant may soon be the case,) I will by no means withhold from any gentleman of the Court the satisfaction his nice honour may require.

Your demand I shall not comply with.[9]

Thus, for a moment, the menace of flashing steel filled the courtroom at Fort Ticonderoga. In the eighteenth century, the satisfaction of honor among gentlemen meant one of two things: swordplay at dawn or pistols at the usual twelve paces.

Angered by Arnold's "extraordinary answer," which, in the words of the court, "added insult to injury," the court turned all its records over to General Gates with a demand for Arnold's arrest. The "illiberal sentiments of the protest," said the officers, "was not the only injury offered us; the whole of the General's conduct during the course of the trial was marked with contempt and disrespect toward the Court." Faced now with a situation that might cost him the services of his ablest subordinate, the most daring and resourceful officer on the field of battle that the Revolution produced, Gates studied the data carefully, sent them to Congress as both Arnold and the court wished, and dissolved the court. As he explained to the president of Congress, "The warmth of General Arnold's temper might possibly lead him a little farther than is marked by the precise line of decorum to be observed before and towards a Court-Martial. Seeing and knowing all circumstances, I am convinced, if there was a fault on one side, there was too much acrimony on the other. Here again I was obliged to act dictatorially, and dissolve the Court-Martial the instant they demanded General Arnold to be put in arrest. The United States must not be deprived of that excellent officer's service at this important moment." Gates further begged Congress to consider "whatever is whispered against General Arnold as the foul stream of that poisonous fountain, detraction." In view of Gates's consistent support of Arnold from the time that the march to Quebec was being planned, it is all the more regrettable that by the time the Saratoga campaign rolled around, but a year hence, the two officers should have become hostile to each other.[10]

The situation that had ripened with the demand for Arnold's arrest had developed from the dislike and suspicions that Hazen entertained of Arnold. The two men had clashed over the Cedars affair, while at Chambly Hazen had clearly suspected that the boxes of goods arriving from

Montreal contained material that Arnold intended for his own profit rather than for the army's welfare. Whether or not Hazen's surmise was correct, his negligence in attending to the goods was an act of insubordination; if he lacked storeroom, he could at least have prevented their being plundered. As for Arnold's intending the goods for himself, this is at least debatable, though in view of his predilection for turning a penny wherever he could, one is disposed to believe him guilty. Writing in after years, when his own character was revealed as worthless, Wilkinson said that he considered Arnold's activities during those last days in Montreal to be "rather mercantile than military," and that when he mentioned this to Arnold, the latter said that he, Wilkinson, was "more nice than wise." Such a remark, coming from Wilkinson as an aspersion on Arnold's character, should be given little weight. The odd fact, however, is that the activities *were* mercantile in their nature but for a military objective, and Arnold was acting under orders from the commissioners of Congress. Moreover, as has been noted, he informed both Schuyler and Sullivan of what he was doing.[11]

It is possible, even probable, that Arnold hoped to reap some measure of personal gain. Distasteful as the idea of private profit from public service may be to most people today, such conduct was not at all peculiar, or even necessarily considered reprehensible, for the age in which he lived. Many officers in the British and other European armies looked upon certain appointments as opportunities to make their fortunes, and the attitude of their governments was much like that of a hotel establishment which pays its help but the minimum and lets them make what they can in gratuities. On the other hand, there is no positive proof that Arnold was engaged in this work for a mercenary motive. Acting, by his own admission and against his will, as contractor, commissary, and quartermaster, he was, of course, especially vulnerable to criticism, particularly by a lad like Wilkinson, whose idea of an officer's function seems to have been solely one of fighting, or by a man like Hazen, who was a friend of many of the merchants from whom the goods were seized, and whose own probity may well be open to question. This vulnerability was directly attributable to the shortage of competent officers, but it made Arnold the victim of suspicion that was both dangerous and persistent.

But if Arnold was justified in preferring charges against Hazen, both he and the court were at fault in their excitement over the Scott issue. This officer had little to gain from the conviction of Hazen. His zeal to testify might lead the officers of the court to think that he had a stake in the outcome, and it was undoubtedly annoying. Yet what was far more important was to establish the validity or speciousness of his testimony, testimony that, unfortunately, he was not permitted to give. Moreover, although Arnold's protest might be somewhat unusual, to contend that the court's action was "unprecedented, and I think unjust" was hardly, as the court objected, "illegal, illiberal, and ungentlemanlike." Nor was that part of Arnold's reply through his expression to leave the matter in the hands of Congress undecorous. From that point on, however, all the touchy, arrogant, Billy-be-damned side of his nature came to the fore. If the court, acting extraordinarily for a judicial body, demanded "satisfaction" and an "open acknowledgment of error," it would get none of the latter from Benedict Arnold, but all the "satisfaction" he could possibly furnish them, the kind of satisfaction he had rendered Captain Croskie in the Bay of Honduras. It was indeed a remarkable court-martial.

The decision to submit the matter to Congress was eminently wise, but not without danger to Arnold's reputation. The Congressional mill ground slowly, and, in the meantime, there were not lacking those who sought to turn the minds of Congressmen against him. Hazen was exceedingly active in his own behalf. So was John Brown, who hotly contended there was no doubt that Arnold had plundered the inhabitants of Montreal. This allegation was carefully considered in May, 1777, by the Board of War. Happily for Arnold, Charles Carroll, one of the commissioners from Congress, sat on the Board. None was in a better position to ascertain whether or not Arnold was justified in his "plundering." And in the Board's exoneration of Arnold may be seen the judgment of Carroll. Until more concrete and persuasive evidence of Arnold's guilt is amassed, material based on something more substantial than mere suspicion or surmise, there is no proper course but to consider him the overworked officer he was, pursuing faithfully and honestly his duty as he saw it. It was Arnold's misfortune that even the action of the Board failed to remove the suspicion or distrust of certain factions of Congress, if the attitude of that body toward future promotion for Arnold is any indication.[12]

Though Brown spent a busy anti-Arnold summer in 1776, Easton was initially more active in this direction. His regiment having been disbanded in the winter, Easton went to Philadelphia in April, seeking permission to raise another regiment for Canada and submitting a petition for a court of inquiry to consider the charge of plundering captured British officers' baggage made by Arnold against himself and Brown. Congress accordingly instructed its commissioners in Canada to hold such a court. Unfortunately for Easton, no sooner had he received this satisfaction from Congress than creditors had him clapped into prison in Philadelphia for debts totaling £1500. In another petition to Congress he explained the difficulties of collecting money due him in Massachusetts, funds that would have covered his indebtedness. He further stated that he ought to be on his way to Canada to settle his regimental accounts still outstanding and to meet with the commissioners concerning the court of inquiry. Though Congress then authorized his release and Easton hurried northward, he found the army in full retreat and the commissioners disinclined to pay him any attention. Thereafter the breezy colonel, disappointed not to have cleared himself, let Brown carry the burden of defense.[13]

Brown was of tougher fiber. For a while, moreover, his chances looked favorable, as, on June 27, 1776, Congress recognized his petition for vindication and referred it to a committee appointed to inquire into the causes of the disasters in Canada. The committee reported on July 30 that in the course of its investigation it had reason to believe the baggage of the British general captured at Sorel, General Prescott, had indeed been "plundered by some licentious persons, in violation of the faith of the capitulation." Congress therefore enjoined General Schuyler to favor Brown's petition by holding a court of inquiry. Three days later, Congress also allowed Brown the rank and pay of a colonel in the Continental Army retroactive to November 20, 1775. When Brown arrived at Albany with his papers, Schuyler directed Gates to impanel a court. Brown followed through by preferring a formal complaint to Gates on September 3 that Arnold be arrested for defamation of character. It was Brown's misfortune, however, that Gates considered Arnold's services indispensable at the time. Gates therefore ignored both Brown's request for a court and his plea for Arnold's arrest, and referred him to the Board of War. Recognizing the action as a complete rebuff, and aware that the Board would probably never get around to considering the case, Brown desisted. He would bide his time until Arnold's period of indispensability had passed. Then he would renounce defensive tactics and really expose his enemy.[14]

Arnold's current great value to the American cause, the value that had defeated Brown, was his endeavor to construct a fleet to meet the British when they had finished their own preparations. Sensitive to the need of possessing naval command of the lake, Arnold had written to Washington on June 25 concerning the question of a fleet. He thought it of the utmost importance that a frigate, twenty or thirty gondolas, row-galleys, and floating batteries be built without delay and at least three hundred carpenters immediately hired. The country was scoured for these and for axmen, blacksmiths, armorers, and artificers. Most of the carpenters obtained were house carpenters, but a group of ship carpenters from Maine, Massachusetts, Connecticut, and Pennsylvania provided a helpful nucleus of knowledgeable craftsmen. The chief shipbuilding center was established at Skenesborough, while most of the vessels, after launching, were sent to Ticonderoga to be rigged and armed. The states, especially the towns, were heavily pressed for canvas, cordage, nails, sailing needles, white lead, anchors, hawsers, and armament that ranged from swivels to 18-pounders.[15]

To muster the builders and supplies from the seaboard, to construct an ambitiously large fleet of green timber, and to man the vessels required an extraordinary degree of enthusiasm, sustained drive, and intelligent direction. Arnold gave Gates such able advice and energetic assistance that Horatio, in charge of Ticonderoga, sent him to Skenesborough to keep the carpenters sober and to push the construction along. Yet, while Arnold was away, Gates sorely wished he were at Ticonderoga "to give directions for putting our whole squadron afloat." Finally Gates, who frankly confessed his ignorance of naval matters, asked Arnold to take supreme command. "General Arnold (who is perfectly skilled in maritime affairs)," he wrote John Hancock on July 29, "has most nobly undertaken to command our fleet upon the Lake. With infinite satisfaction, I have committed the whole of that department to his care, convinced he will thereby add to that brilliant reputation he has so deservedly acquired." Not knowing of Gates's decision, Washington wrote him about the fleet command, "I trust neither courage nor activity will be wanting in those to whom the business is committed. If assigned to General Arnold none will doubt of his exertions." He was almost as relieved to learn of Arnold's appointment as was Schuyler, who told Gates on August 3 that he was "extremely happy that General Arnold has undertaken command of the fleet. It has relieved me from very great anxiety under which I labored on that account." [16]

Arnold's appointment was not happily received by at least one individual, Jacobus Wynkoop. In May, 1776, the pompous Jacobus, a New York infantry captain, had been appointed by Schuyler commander of such vessels as the Americans then possessed on Lake Champlain. Few men could have been so proud of an appointment, so tenacious in its retention, or so lethargic in discharging its obligations. Gates had no high

opinion of him. "The Commodore seems slow," he said impatiently. Gates
hoped Wynkoop might retain "all that prowess for which he says he was
so famous last war. It is of the greatest consequence to our affairs to have
the armed vessels commanded by men of firmness and approved courage."
On August 7, Gates issued orders to Arnold to stand down the lake as far
as Split Rock or even to Isle-aux-Têtes but to fall back to Ticonderoga if
the British fleet, then supposed to be advancing, proved superior. Arnold,
with eleven assorted craft, reconnoitered, found nothing to be alarmed
about, and returned to Crown Point. Ten days later, however, when the
enemy was again reported on the prowl southward and menacing an
American detail seven miles down the lake making oars, Arnold ordered
out two light schooners to cover the retreat of the detail. To his astonishment, Wynkoop, who commanded the schooner *Royal Savage,* twelve
guns, fired a shot off their bows and ordered them to heave to. The officer
then sent Arnold a note, stating, "I know no orders but what shall be
given out by me, except sailing orders from the Commander-in-Chief."
The note was signed, "Jacobus Wynkoop, Commander of Lake Champlain." [17]

For a moment, Arnold's mind reverted to the humiliating dispute, the
previous year, between himself and Ethan Allen. But this year there was
no question of his authority, and he stood for no nonsense. Rowing over
to Wynkoop, he dressed the Dutchman down aboard his own ship. "I am
surprised that you pretend to contradict my orders," he remarked sharply,
"as I acquainted you some time since that the Commander-in-Chief had
appointed me to take command of the Navy on the Lake. . . . You
surely must be out of your senses to say no orders shall be obeyed but
yours." At Arnold's threat to arrest him, Wynkoop protested to Gates,
asserting the priority of his appointment by Schuyler as naval commander.
But Gates, who had no love for Schuyler (the feeling was mutual),
derived considerable satisfaction in writing to Arnold the moment he
learned of the altercation and in peremptorily ordering Wynkoop's immediate arrest and transportation as a prisoner to Ticonderoga. Though
Arnold complied, he bore Jacobus no malice, and asked that the officer
not be cashiered since, as he explained to Gates, "I believe the Commodore was really of opinion that neither of us had authority to command
him." Gates respected Arnold's wish, but dispatched Wynkoop to Schuyler
at Albany with the request that he never be sent back to the lake. Schuyler, while considering Wynkoop a brave and reasonably able man, was

shocked at his disobedience and upheld the action of both Arnold and Gates despite Wynkoop's appeal to Congress.[18]

Thus beset, Arnold passed a hectic summer. It was not enough that he was charged with the construction of the fleet and the defense of the lake against the ever-growing British fleet and army. He was called on constantly to defend his authority and reputation. Of all difficulties, however, the accusations of his plundering the Montreal merchants troubled him most, accusations springing out of the Hazen affair and pressed strongly by Hazen, Brown, and Easton. Samuel Chase observed that the plunder reports prevailing in Philadelphia were injuring Arnold's character. "Your best friends," he added, "are not your countrymen." Always sensitive to what people in power thought of him, Arnold was especially outraged by the slander in the nation's capital. "I cannot but think it extremely cruel," he burst out in confidence to Gates, "when I have sacrificed my ease, health, and great part of my private property, in the cause of my country, to be calumniated as a robber and thief—at a time, too, when I have it not in my power to be heard in my own defense." While his critics might consider this an expression of the most consummate hypocrisy and even his friends see in it the exaggeration of self-pity, it was only too true that he had not then the power to defend himself. He could have demanded a court-martial to clear himself, but a court-martial would have taken time, and time was running out. It was early September, the fleet to train, and the scarlet host in the north about to move. In another month, Arnold was to engage in a desperate struggle with the British, the most hopeless combat of his career, and on his conduct of the fleet hinged the fate of the north, perhaps of the entire Revolution. Meanwhile, his conscientiousness and his love of glory holding him at the front, he had no alternative but to let the wolf pack of enemies within his own country snarl and tear at his reputation for integrity and ability.[19]

· X ·

Arnold's Naval Career
on Lake Champlain

Arnold's naval career in the Revolution embraced the summer and early fall of 1776. As a sea captain and a leader of men, he knew considerable about the handling of ships and crews, and could spur the shipbuilders along. In the art of directing a fleet, however, he was a novice; Gates had exaggerated his knowledge of naval matters. Yet in the severe actions on Lake Champlain even the British were impressed by his skill and admired his spirit, an opinion which a number of his countrymen refused to share.

The British were in a good position to know and appreciate the odds Arnold faced. Learning of American ship construction, Carleton had rushed the building of his own fleet as soon as he had recaptured St. Johns. Had it not been for the rapids in the Sorel, he could easily and quickly have secured command of Lake Champlain. But the rapids necessitated an extensive building program. Though flatboats and longboats might be drawn overland by oxen, heavy craft had to be constructed south of the rapids. A ship-rigged vessel at Quebec, the *Inflexible*, was taken apart, brought over the carry, and reassembled at St. Johns. The same was true of two schooners, the *Maria* and the *Carleton*. Drawing on the crews from the transports and men-of-war in the St. Lawrence, Carleton had no lack of carpenters and seamen. Altogether, he gathered a formidable force. The *Inflexible,* mounting eighteen 12-pounders, was capable of taking on most of Arnold's fleet by herself. The *Maria* and *Carleton,* mounting respectively fourteen and twelve 6-pounders, were individually more powerful than anything Arnold possessed. A heavy flatboat, or scow, the *Thunderer,* carried a number of 24-pounders; a gondola, the *Loyal Convert,* 9-pounders; twenty gunboats, one gun apiece ranging from a 4-pounder to a 24; and four longboats, each with a light howitzer. Captain Charles Douglas of the Royal Navy supervised the construction of the squadron, which was commanded by Captain Thomas Pringle and manned by nearly seven hundred officers and ratings of the Royal Navy. It was the most powerful fleet ever constructed up to that time in American inland waters.

Against this force Arnold mustered a heterogeneous collection of craft. These included two schooners, the *Royal Savage* carrying four 6-pounders and eight 4's, and the *Revenge* with four 4-pounders and four 2's; one sloop, the *Enterprise,* mounting twelve 4-pounders; four row-galleys, the *Washington, Congress, Trumbull,* and *Lee,* with eight guns ranging from 4- to 18-pounders; and nine gondolas with three guns apiece, one 12-pounder and two 9's. A sloop, the *Liberty,* and a galley, the *Gates,* were absent when the testing time arrived. Though Arnold's fleet was not small, his ships threw only about half the British weight in gun metal.[1]

Arnold had a difficult time getting crews for his ships. On September 18, he wrote Gates begging "one hundred good seamen as soon as possible; we have a wretched motley crew in the fleet .The marines, the refuse of every regiment, and the sailors, few of them ever wet with salt water— we are upwards of one hundred men short." On October 1, from Valcour Island, he dashed off another urgent letter for supplies and the "one hundred seamen, no landlubbers." Gates dispatched every article he could and added a plaintive note, "where it is not to be had, you and the princes of the earth must go unfurnished." Fortunately a number of reinforcements appeared on October 6 with the *Congress* and the *Washington,* which were hastily sent to Arnold before the outfitters could complete them. Arnold thus managed to have between seven and eight hundred men on hand, most of them half-trained and definitely out of their element.[2]

While Arnold was pleading for men, guns, and supplies, and anxiously awaiting the arrival of the row-galleys, he kept an interested eye cocked on the New York campaign to the south between Washington and Howe.

He saw the relation of the two campaigns, realizing that if Washington's army should be defeated by General Howe and the Northern Army by Carleton and if the two British generals should then effect a junction, the colonies would be split and could be conquered in detail. At first, Arnold could not believe the report that the Americans had evacuated Long Island. When General David Waterbury, Arnold's second in command, appeared with the two galleys, Arnold eagerly questioned him on developments to the south, but Waterbury could give him no information that he did not already possess. "I am very anxious for our army and friends below," Arnold wrote Gates. "It appears to me our troops or officers are panick struck, or why does a hundred thousand men fly before one quarter of their number. Is it possible my countrymen can be callous to their wrongs or hesitate one moment between slavery and death? . . . However . . . that Being in whose hands are all human events, will doubtless turn the scale in favor of the just and oppressed." [3]

The thought that the "Being" might have to intervene in his own behalf, as well as in Washington's, must have occurred to Arnold. Since mid-September, he had known that the British were building a large vessel at St. Johns. This ship, the *Inflexible,* would not have been constructed had the Americans not developed the keeled, two-masted, lateen-rigged row-galleys, which resembled the piratical craft that lurked in Algerian waters. On the other hand, without the galleys, which formed the backbone of Arnold's fleet, the British would have had little difficulty in establishing command of the lake; the galleys had been the American answer to the large British schooners. Yet, until October, Arnold had only two galleys available, and his knowledge that the British were likely to move at any time kept him in a fever of anxiety. Even after the galleys arrived and he had transferred his flag from the *Royal Savage* to the *Congress,* he worried about the lack of supplies and seamen and the formidable nature of the enemy's fleet.

Arnold had his own ideas with respect to how he would fight the impending battle. He wrote Gates on September 18 that he intended "first fair wind to come up as high as Isle Valcour, where is a good harbour, and where we shall have the advantage of attacking the enemy in the open lake, where the row-galleys, as their motion is quick, will give us a great advantage over the enemy; and if they are too many for us we can retire." On the 21st, he mentioned to Gates that he had sent boats to make soundings around Valcour, in the harbor of which he thought the fleet would be secure. At this time, he was in the narrow waters in the north, about twenty-five miles from St. Johns, and was driven from this position by shore batteries. Hence he retreated to Valcour on September 23 and anchored in a cove on the western side. In this position the island mass, thickly wooded and rising to one hundred and eighty feet, screened him from discovery by vessels in the channel east of Valcour, while a great shoal to the north protected him from a fleet movement southward between the island and the New York shore. Furthermore, as he told Gates on September 28, "We are . . . moored as near together as possible, and in such a form that few vessels can attack us at the same time, and those will be exposed to the fire of the whole fleet." He offered, however, to return if Gates did not approve of his position, but Gates replied that he was pleased to learn that Arnold and his fleet "ride in Valcour Bay, in defiance of our foes in Canada." Ironically Gates wrote on October 12; by that time, Arnold was no longer at Valcour but limping southward after a furious battle with the British.[4]

Carleton forced the issue on October 11. A northeast wind bellying his sails, he moved up the lake with all his ships, together with his gunboats filled with troops and upward of a thousand Indians in their war canoes. At eight o'clock in the morning, an American vessel returning from patrol fired alarm guns at the enemy's approach, while lookouts ashore on the island shouted that they could see the enemy off Cumberland Head. At once Arnold called his captains aboard the *Congress* for a council of war. During the conference, Waterbury was anxiously insistent that Arnold change his battle plan. He contended that since the Americans were outnumbered and outgunned and could easily be surrounded, the wise course was to engage the British in the open lake and make a fighting retreat to the shelter of the protecting guns at Ticonderoga. No coward, Waterbury spoke with the voice of prudence.

But Arnold vehemently disagreed. To challenge the British in the open lake, as he himself had once thought of doing, would expose his fleet to the superior speed and gunpower of the British. His strength, he knew, lay in his present position. If the British should try to come down from the north between him and the mainland, they would fetch up on the shoal. If they passed the island to the east, they would have to attack from "to leeward," an awkward maneuver that would expose their broken line to the concerted fire of the American fleet. There was always the possibility, too, that they might miss him altogether and go ramping down the wind to Ticonderoga, in which case Arnold could sweep northward and destroy the vast collection of boats and canoes being assembled to transport the

British troops. Arnold reasoned well, but he knew he could be surrounded and possibly starved out. This was a chance he had to take. Every day he could delay the advance of Carleton's army brought winter that much closer and the campaigning season nearer to an end. Simply by pressing the fleet construction on the scale that he had, he had forced the British to spend valuable weeks to match and then surpass him. Now the issue was to be joined, and his only recourse was a stout defense. Arnold therefore told his captains that the fleet would retain its crescent battle line in the bay of Valcour and await the enemy. Waterbury, the voice of prudence, must have returned to his galley, the *Washington,* wondering if Arnold's zeal had not unhinged his sense of judgment.[5]

Arnold now cleared for action. The guns were loaded, additional powder and shot brought up from below, wet blankets draped about the powder magazine, and rope matches lighted to touch off the cannon, while sand was strewn on the decks lest they become slippery with blood. The men worked with the zeal they later showed in battle. Yet as Arnold watched the ragged crews, he could only hope that the few weeks of training and discipline he had been able to give them would show to good effect.

Presently, his tension growing, he saw the British burst into view. For a few moments he thought the enemy might not discover him as, with its flags streaming in the wind, Carleton's fleet swept southward. Indeed it is possible that the British might have missed him entirely, for Carleton and Pringle had neglected to send craft to reconnoiter the island. Unfortunately some incident not described by the British—perhaps a movement by some American ship—turned their eyes back toward Valcour and Arnold's battle line. At once the British came about and headed toward the bay, though the square-rigged *Inflexible* and the *Thunderer,* square-rigged but with no centerboard, were brought up to the wind only with the greatest difficulty. Even the schooner *Maria,* with General Carleton and Captain Pringle aboard, had trouble. Nearer and more maneuverable, the *Carleton* slowly worked her way into position. Closing in rapidly, however, was the huddle of gunboats looking like so many crawling bugs with their single big gun in the bow and their oars slashing the water.

Arnold quickly saw his chance in this disorder. With the larger British ships tardy in their approach, he sent the *Royal Savage* to cut off the gunboats, and followed with the three powerful row-galleys. Though he did not succeed in his maneuver, he exchanged shots with the gunboats and with the *Carleton.* Then he headed back toward the bay. It was on the return that he suffered his first loss. Poorly handled, the *Royal Savage* fell behind, took severe punishment from the gunboats and the *Inflexible*, and ran ashore on the southern point of Valcour. Though Arnold lost his papers and his belongings, which he had not transferred to the *Congress*, the men were saved.

Arnold had no time to lament this first loss. The big *Carleton* and the gunboats were challenging the American battle line. And, as if to warn him that he was left no retreat, the enemy landed hordes of Indians on both the island and the mainland. The savages kept up a din of horrid shrieks and yells and blazed away with their muskets at Arnold's decks. Fortunately Arnold had anticipated this maneuver and had raised an effective barricade of young trees as fascines on his ships' sides.

Far more dangerous than the Indians was the British naval assault, which, from half past twelve throughout the afternoon, was strongly pressed. Though only the gunboats and the *Carleton* were able to get close enough until late in the day, they hammered away with round shot and grape at musket range. The action, as Arnold admitted, became "very warm," while Baron Riedesel, aboard a British ship, said, "The cannonade was tremendous." The *Carleton*, under Lieutenant Dacres, daringly anchored in the very middle of the American crescent, and Arnold at once called for a concentration of fire on her. Lacking gunners, he limped about the shot-torn deck of the *Congress* and personally aimed the cannon. His face and clothes smudged with black powder, he could hardly be distinguished from the lowliest powder monkey. But inspired by his example and by the driving urgency of his voice, his crews fought like veteran sea dogs.

And under the American fire the *Carleton* began to careen. Dacres, hit by a flying splinter, fell unconscious. Another officer lost an arm. Then an American shot severed the schooner's cable, and her bow swung toward the Americans. Anxiously Captain Pringle signaled her to retire, but she was unable to move. Seeing this, young Edward Pellew, later Lord Exmouth, one of England's great naval commanders, gallantly climbed out on the bowsprit to kick the jib over to windward. When the schooner, her guns now silenced, still could not move, Pringle sent two artillery boats to tow her out. She finally anchored out of range, two feet of water in her hold, eight men killed, and eight wounded.

The action, however, was by no means over. Arnold pounded the gunboats relentlessly and sent one skyward with a shot in its magazine. In fact, his fire became so lethal that, as one British officer, Lieutenant

William Digby, admitted, "the boats' advantage was not to come nearer than 700 yards, as whenever they approached nearer they were greatly annoyed by grape shot." He was but reiterating the testimony of a fellow officer, Lieutenant George Pausch, who described Arnold as firing "rapidly and effectually." At last Pringle called off the battered gunboats and let the *Inflexible*, now in position, take over. She loosed five heavy broadsides, but when Arnold still held his position, she, too, retired. Pringle then anchored his vessels in a line to cut off Arnold's retreat.

While the British licked their wounds and repaired their ships, Arnold called a council of war aboard the *Congress*. It was a gloomy meeting of officers. The *Congress* had been hit twelve times, seven of the shot entering at the waterline, and had suffered numerous casualties. The *Washington* looked like a sieve, and Waterbury had lost his captain, executive officer, and sailing master. Of the officers on the gondola *New York* only the captain remained. The gondola *Philadelphia* plunged to the bottom of the lake within an hour after the fighting ceased, while two more gondolas were barely afloat. Ammunition, moreover, was so short that the fleet could not have sustained another such prolonged engagement even if the vessels were in fighting trim. From this situation there appeared no escape, certainly not to the mainland because British troops and Indians were bivouacked abreast of the fleet, the Indians making the night hideous with their yells. Indeed, as if to remind Arnold that the British were in complete command of the situation, Pringle sent a boarding party to the *Royal Savage* to blow her up lest Arnold try to recover the schooner. The ear-splitting roar and the brilliant flash seemed to symbolize the end of Arnold's efforts, and the cabin became very glum after the explosion revealed to each captain the tense, strained faces of his fellow officers.

Gloomy though the prospect, Arnold refused to admit the game was up. He was always best in adversity, quick to contrive some bold or ingenious maneuver to meet an emergency. Discovering that fog was setting in, he came up with a plan now. Its execution called for brave spirits and steady nerves. Arnold proposed to take advantage of the fog to have the fleet in single column slip between the British and the shore. Each vessel except the last, which should be Arnold's, was to show at its stern a dim lantern hooded, probably, in a canvas sack. There was always the chance of discovery, either by the enemy afloat or by the enemy ashore, but, unless the chance was taken, surrender was inevitable. If they got away, the Americans might still reach Ticonderoga and come back to fight another day. As Arnold presented his plan, his voice harsh with fatigue but immensely hopeful, his captains caught something of his truly great courage and resourcefulness. They agreed to his project.

At seven o'clock, darkness having fallen and the fog obscuring the night, the movement started. Colonel Edward Wigglesworth, a stout fighter, led off in the *Trumbull*, followed by smaller vessels, with the *Washington* and *Congress* bringing up the rear. Carrying just enough sail for steerageway, the ships picked their way carefully along, preserving the strictest silence. Though Arnold could hear voices and hammering aboard the British squadron as the carpenters made repairs, he saw none of the enemy's ships. Nor did they see him. Probably to the amazement of his own officers, certainly to the chagrin of the British, his plan succeeded. He passed, wraithlike, through the midst of the enemy and escaped undiscovered to Schuyler's Island, eight miles from Valcour.

When, at daybreak, Carleton awoke to find that Arnold had eluded him, he was furious and ordered an immediate pursuit. Yet no sooner had he got under way than he realized that he had not left instructions for the troops ashore. Even so, he continued the search for a while until convinced that Arnold had made good his escape and until an adverse breeze slowed his pursuit to a mere crawl. Then, after sending out scouts to bring him information of Arnold's whereabouts, he returned to Valcour.

Meanwhile Arnold strove desperately to plug the shot holes in his vessels and make them seaworthy. In this he was only partially successful; two of the gondolas were in such hopeless condition that he sank them. But by two o'clock in the afternoon he was moving again, though pitifully slowly because of damages and a contrary wind. He wrote Gates to send ammunition to Crown Point, which was the fleet's objective, and he also begged the general to dispatch a dozen well-manned bateaux to tow the ships to safety. Unfortunately there was no chance for the bateaux to arrive, for, by evening, Carleton, having heard from his scouts, was again heading southward. During the night, the breeze moderated, and the morning of October 13 found Arnold still twenty-eight miles from Crown Point, fourteen from Valcour, and only eight from the British. While the southerly breeze continued to impede his progress, the enemy caught a fresh gust from the northeast and came booming down under full sail, the *Inflexible* and the two schooners heading the pack.

Arnold now urged his lighter craft ahead and lingered behind to cover their retreat. The battered *Washington* was wallowing and his own ship doing hardly better, yet he proposed to fight it out, and opened fire at eleven o'clock on the *Maria,* the nearest opponent. When the enemy came abreast of him at Split Rock, Arnold, supported at long range by four crippled gondolas, exchanged broadsides with the heavier British vessels. The enemy, however, concentrated on the *Washington* and simply overwhelmed her. Though Waterbury had earlier sought Arnold's permission to run her ashore, Arnold had ordered him to continue the fight. Now it was becoming clear that perhaps he should have let Waterbury beach the galley. But Arnold was a dogged fighter and had hoped the *Washington* might still hold up her own end of the struggle.

Soon his own great trial arrived. When the British had received Waterbury's surrender, they swarmed around the *Congress* instead of chasing the rest of the fleet. For two and one half hours, the *Inflexible,* the *Carleton,* the *Maria,* and four other craft pounded the galley, killing the first lieutenant and several others of her already decimated crew, and shattering her sails, rigging, and hull. Yet even when faced with utter disaster, the swarthy soldier-skipper refused to give up. Gamely he limped across the deck, cluttered with tangled gear and wreckage, and aimed and fired the guns. How he or any aboard managed to survive the storm of round shot and grape was hardly short of miraculous.

Arnold, however, was a realist. If he continued the one-sided contest, sooner or later he was bound to surrender or go down with his ship. He declined to do either. Signaling the crippled gondolas, which the British had evidently considered theirs once they had finished with the *Congress,* Arnold, by means of hard rowing, slipped through the cordon and headed for the Vermont shore. When the enemy, having to beat to windward, slowly pursued, he blasted them once more with all he had left. Then, like a sheepdog working his flock homeward, he herded the gondolas ashore in Buttonmould Bay on the east side, ten miles from Crown Point, and set them afire with their flags flying. He personally applied the torch to the *Congress,* was the last man to leap from the ship, and kept the crews standing by on shore with small arms until all five vessels were sheets of flame and beyond seizure by the enemy's small boats. Afterward, he marched his men quickly through the woods to Crown Point and, as he admitted, "very luckily escaped the savages, who waylaid the road in two hours after we passed."

It had been a costly struggle, as costly for the British in one sense as for Arnold in another. Arnold had lost ten vessels, not to mention more than one hundred men captured aboard the *Washington* and eighty casualties in dead and wounded; the *Congress* alone reported twenty-seven men killed or wounded in a crew of seventy-three. Meanwhile the

British, though suffering forty casualties, had demonstrated their superiority over Arnold's fleet in everything but fighting spirit, and the fall of Ticonderoga appeared imminent. But Carleton was by no means elated; he told Burgoyne that since the victory had been over fellow subjects, it was not cause for rejoicing. Furthermore, after seizing Crown Point and sweeping to within sight of Ticonderoga, he hesitated to make the kill. The siege would take time, the season was well advanced, and his troops were far from a base of operations. With the American fleet out of the way, he felt that he could afford to wait until spring and then swoop down on Ticonderoga when siege operations would be more favorable. Hence he withdrew to Canada.[6]

Carleton's decision clearly saved the young country. But had not Arnold taken every possible measure to delay the British by pressing the fleet construction through the summer and by boldly challenging their offensive threat, Carleton would not have had to make his decision. He could easily have moved up the lake, taken Ticonderoga, and subsequently joined forces with Howe. The Revolution would have sputtered out in a series of rearguard actions. Arnold had won for the Americans valuable time to organize for the crucial campaign the ensuing summer. As the great authority on sea power, Admiral Alfred Thayer Mahan, in writing of the naval activities of this period, declared, "That the Americans were strong enough to impose the capitulation of Saratoga was due to the invaluable year of delay secured to them in 1776 by their little navy on Lake Champlain, created by the indomitable energy, and handled with the indomitable courage of the traitor, Benedict Arnold."[7]

Arnold's heroism and resolution were warmly celebrated. In a letter to Governor Trumbull, Gates generously praised "the gallant behavior, and steady good conduct of that excellent officer [Arnold]" and, in general orders, thanked him for his "gallant defense." British officers mentioned his courage and ability, calling him "a spirited fellow" and admiring the manner in which he had extricated himself from Valcour and fought his ships. Richard Varick, an aide to Schuyler, thanked Providence for Arnold's safe return. And truly, as Gates wrote of him to Schuyler, "Few men ever met with so many hairbreadth escapes in so short a space of time."[8]

Despite the encomiums, there were contrary voices. General William Maxwell, writing from Ticonderoga to Governor Livingston of New Jersey, was no admirer of Arnold:

"You must have heard that a few days ago we had a fine fleet and tolerably good army [he said bitterly], but General Arnold, our evil genius to the north, has, with a good deal of industry, got us clear of all our fine fleet . . . and he has managed his point so well with the old man, the General, that he has got his thanks for his good services. Our fleet . . . was much the strongest; but he suffered himself to be surrounded between an island and the main land. . . . In the night he gave orders to every vessel to make the best of their way, by which they became an easy prey. . . . This was a pretty piece of admiralship, after going to their doors almost, and bantering them for two months or more, contrary to the opinion of the army. Had we our fleet here, we would give ourselves little concern about the enemy.

Maxwell's opinion is especially interesting since it was a type that followed Arnold everywhere, an opinion compounded of misinformation and deep jealousy. A far more dangerous and persistent opponent than Maxwell also refused to be impressed by Arnold's feat. John Brown was on the warpath again, more eager than ever for Arnold's scalp; and Brown had influence in Congress.[9]

Not even Brown, however, nor men like Maxwell, could effectually dim the luster of Arnold's valorous struggle. His was an epic of resistance for which there are few equals in the colorful history of this country. And though defeated, he was justly acclaimed as if he had returned with the laurels of triumph.

· XI ·

Denial of Promotion

CARLETON'S withdrawal in November afforded Arnold an opportunity to which he had looked forward for weeks, namely, a chance to straighten out his accounts and to visit his family. With the guns of Valcour barely cool, he wrote that he had lost all his papers and clothes with the *Royal Savage,* while four days after the battle he informed Schuyler that he was sending him "a small box containing all my publick and private papers, and accounts, with a considerable sum of hard and paper money." Now, in November, he rode down to Albany, from which Gates notified Congress that Arnold was "anxious . . . to see his family, and settle his publick accounts." With a strange prescience, Gates added that "Should the motions of the enemy make his presence necessary below, I know his zeal for the service will outweigh all other considerations, and induce him to take the route that leads to them." [1]

But Arnold was delayed for several days in leaving Albany; John Brown and Moses Hazen had returned to the attack. Foiled by Gates in the autumn, and angry at getting nowhere with the Board of War, Brown, on December 1, preferred to Gates a formal charge for Arnold's arrest "for the following crimes." He listed thirteen specifications ranging from the Ticonderoga controversy of the previous year through Arnold's action with the fleet, which, he declared, had been lost through Arnold's "great misconduct." A number of the specifications were manifestly absurd, and the rest questionable, but Brown was determined this time to bring Arnold to account. "I have been led an expensive dance from generals to Congress, and from Congress to generals," he complained; and, but for his vindictiveness and the speciousness of his allegations, one could sympathize with him for having become a victim to the age-old game of "passing the buck." Yet if he thought he would finally secure favorable action, he was sadly mistaken. His impatience overcame whatever tact he possessed, for he prodded Gates twice the very next day. Annoyed because Brown was, in the general's words, "so importunate for an answer in writing" to his petition, Gates announced that he would submit the petition to Congress. Brown was thus forced to continue his expensive dance.[2]

Hazen had more success. On December 2, a court of inquiry was held at Albany to hear a complaint by the former Tory. Hazen charged that in June, while he had commanded at Chambly, Arnold had traduced his character by certain remarks on the back of a receipt given him at Chambly, and had passed on the receipt to the Congressional commission in Canada. Arnold had alleged that Hazen had kept for his own use brandy and tobacco belonging to the garrison and had delivered garrison rum to a French innkeeper. Of the rum, Arnold had written, "Colonel Hazen can best tell how much he sold." After hearing the case, the court, with Brigadier General Brickett in the chair and the other members being Colonel Cortlandt and Arnold's old ship commander, Colonel Wigglesworth, declared that Arnold's words were indeed "an aspersion of Colonel Hazen's character, and therefore think the complaint just." [3]

Soon after the hearing, Arnold left with several regiments to reinforce Washington. Although the commander-in-chief had ordered Arnold to the New England coast where "His presence will be of infinite service," Arnold was already in Bethlehem, Pennsylvania, when he received his orders. Before Christmas, therefore, he was off to New England; Clinton had seized Newport on December 8, and there still seemed a possibility that British forces in New York might descend on the Connecticut coast. Accompanying Arnold to the north was Colonel John Trumbull, the Connecticut governor's son, who was soon to resign from service and devote himself to painting those colorful canvases that constitute such a splendid pictorial record of the Revolution. Arnold thus missed by two days being part of the spectacularly successful move to revive the drooping spirits of the country by capturing the Hessian contingent at Trenton.[4]

Arnold's winter in New England, while not unpleasant, failed to bring the action for which he hungered. After visiting his children and sister in New Haven, and being given a triumphant reception on his way through his native state, he reached Providence on January 12. General Nathanael

friends to his support, and in the debates, which were described as "perplexed, inconclusive and irksome," one can be reasonably sure that Arnold's shortcomings were fully exploited.[9]

Congress had not deigned to consult Washington in its choices, and the commander-in-chief, disturbed by the omission of Arnold, rumor of which he first learned through the newspapers, begged his fiery lieutenant on March 3 not to "take any hasty steps" until further information was obtained. It was possible, he added, that the newspapers had omitted Arnold's name through a mistake. Privately Washington wrote Richard Henry Lee in Congress, declaring that he was

anxious to know whether General Arnold's non-promotion was owing to accident or design; and the cause of it. Surely a more active, a more spirited, and sensible officer, fills no department in your army. Not seeing him then in the list of major generals, and no mention made of him, has given me uneasiness, as it is not to be presumed (being the oldest brigadier) that he will continue in service under such a slight.[10]

On March 14 and 26, Arnold replied to Washington in two letters marked by deep distress and no little bewilderment. He viewed the action of Congress

as a very civil way of requesting my resignation, as unqualified for the office I hold. My commission was conferred unsolicited, and received with pleasure only as a means of serving my country. With equal pleasure I resign it when I can no longer serve my country with honor. The person who, void of nice feelings of honor, will tamely condescend to give up his right, and retain a commission at the expense of his reputation, I hold as a disgrace to the army, and unworthy of the glorious cause in which we are engaged. When I entered the service of my country my character was unimpeached. I have sacrificed my interest, ease and happiness in her cause. It is rather a misfortune than a fault, that my exertions have not been crowned with success. I am conscious of the rectitude of my intentions. In justice, therefore, to my own character, and for the satisfaction of my friends, I must request a court of inquiry into my conduct; yet every personal injury shall be buried in my zeal for the safety and happiness of my country, in whose cause I have repeatedly fought and bled, and am ready at all times to risk my life. I shall certainly avoid any hasty step . . . that may tend to the injury of my country.

Subsequently, after a fortnight more of anguish, he told Washington that he considered his being superseded as

an implied impeachment of my character . . . I believe the time is now at hand when I can leave this department without any damage to the public interest.

When that is the case, I will wait on your Excellency, not doubting my request will be granted, and that I shall be able to acquit myself of every charge which malice or envy can bring against me.[11]

Washington was genuinely moved by the situation. He was having difficulty smoothing many ruffled feathers at the time. General Andrew Lewis, who thought he should also have been made a major general, resigned, as did Colonel John Armstrong, who resented his omission from the list of colonels appointed to brigade command, while Colonel John de Haas was so tardy in acknowledging his appointment that Washington wondered if he still considered himself in the army. But Arnold's case was different, as was that of Colonel John Stark, who resigned when Congress moved several junior officers over his head, too; to both Arnold and Stark Congress had been unjust. Torn between loyalty to Congress and sympathy with a subordinate whose services he wished to retain, Washington wrote Arnold on April 3 a letter remarkable for its candor and tact:

It is needless for me to say much upon a subject, which must undoubtedly give you a good deal of uneasiness. I confess I was surprised, when I did not see your name in the list of major generals, and was so fully of the opinion that there was some mistake in the matter, that I (as you may recollect) desired you not to take any hasty step, before the intention of Congress was fully known. The point does not now admit of a doubt, and is of so delicate a nature, that I will not even undertake to advise; your own feelings must be your guide. As no particular charge is alledged against you, I do not see upon what ground you can demand a court of inquiry. Besides, public bodies are not amenable for their actions; they place and displace at pleasure, and all the satisfaction that an individual can obtain, when he is overlooked, is, if innocent, a consciousness that he has not deserved such treatment for his honest exertions. Your determination, not to quit your present command, while any danger to the public might ensue from your leaving it, deserves my thanks, and justly entitles you to the thanks of your country.

General Greene, who has lately been at Philadelphia, took occasion to inquire upon what principle the Congress proceeded in their late promotion of general officers. He was informed, that the members from each state seemed to insist upon having a proportion of genl. officers, adequate to the number of men which they furnish, and that as Connecticut had already two major generals, it was their full share. I confess this is a strange mode of reasoning, but it may serve to shew you, that the promotion which was due to your seniority, was not overlooked for want of merit in you.[12]

The concern Arnold evinced for rank and precedence was scarcely peculiar to him. When Congress, with its propensity for employing large numbers of foreign officers, showed signs, a few months later, of appointing a French officer, Philippe du Coudray, to major general, Generals Nathanael Greene, John Sullivan, and Henry Knox wrote almost identical letters of protest on July 1. As Greene said, ". . . if the report be true, it will lay me under the necessity of resigning my commission, as his appointment supersedes me in command." Piqued, Congress passed a resolution to transmit the letters to Washington with directions to him to let the offending generals know that their letters constituted an attempt to influence the decisions of Congress and were "an invasion of the liberties of the people." The generals were to make proper acknowledgments "for an interference of so dangerous a tendency" or resign. John Adams was believed to be the author of the resolution, and, hitherto friendly with Greene, sent the Quaker general a letter demanding that he acknowledge his error or give up his commission at once. Adams's insistence ended a personal correspondence that was not renewed for five years. In fact, Adams appeared to express the feelings of a large number of Congressmen when he declared that he was "wearied to death with the wrangles between military officers, high and low. They quarrel like cats and dogs. They worry one another like mastiffs, scrambling for rank and pay like apes for nuts." It was with a Congress thus touchy, thus arbitrary, that Arnold had to deal when he finally decided that he could no longer tolerate the injustice it had rendered him and must go to Philadelphia in person and seek an investigation.[13]

· XII ·

Heroism in Connecticut and Humiliation in Philadelphia

ARNOLD'S trip to Philadelphia proved exciting, both en route and once he arrived. While in New Haven, spending a short time with Hannah and the boys, he learned of the British raid on Danbury. British Governor Tryon of New York at the head of nearly two thousand troops embarked at New York on April 23 and landed at Compo, four miles east of Norwalk. From there the detachment marched to Danbury, where the troops destroyed enormous quantities of public stores and much private property; then, on the 27th, Tryon headed back for his transports.

Tryon's arrival had not gone unnoticed. General Gold S. Silliman at Fairfield ordered the militia to assemble and, on the 26th, marched with five hundred men toward the enemy. General David Wooster, hearing the news, ordered the New Haven militia to follow him and pushed toward Fairfield, thence to Redding. After him raced Arnold, lathering his horse to catch up with the others at Redding. From here the generals hurried to Bethel, four miles from smoking Danbury, but, on arriving at two in the morning, they learned that Tryon was withdrawing to his ships. After a few hours of rest for the weary militiamen, the generals moved out again, Arnold and Silliman with four hundred men to Ridgefield, Wooster with two hundred also to Ridgefield but by a different route. Now was the chance to harass the British in their retreat as Lord

Percy and Colonel Smith had been harassed in their painful withdrawal from Concord and Lexington.

The action that presently ensued was almost as severe as the Massachusetts encounter. Wooster suffered a mortal wound while trying to rally his men who had fled when the enemy brought up cannon. In the meantime, Arnold raced ahead of the enemy and threw a road block across his escape route. When the British approached with a force four times as large as his own, Arnold met them with a heavy fire. He was dislodged only when British General Agnew succeeded in getting flanking bodies into position. The last to leave, Arnold looked up to see a redcoat platoon charging down a ledge of rocks at him. As he wheeled his horse about, the platoon fired a volley at him. Though Arnold himself miraculously escaped injury, his horse went down hit by nine bullets. Seeing their leader fall, the Americans fled, and Arnold was near to being captured as he struggled vainly to extricate his feet from the stirrups. In that moment of helplessness a soldier lunged at him with a bayonet and shouted, "Surrender! You are my prisoner!"

"Not yet!" shouted Arnold; and, coolly drawing his pistol, he shot his assailant dead. Then, springing loose from his stirrups, he dashed into a swamp, followed by a shower of musket balls.

Lucky to get away, he was still not through with Tryon. While the British bivouacked that night within a mile of Ridgefield, Arnold, again in the saddle, rallied the militia. When Tryon pushed toward Compo beach the next day, Arnold attacked him constantly. This day he received able assistance from detachments of artillery under Colonel Lamb and Lieutenant Colonel Oswald and from militia under Colonel Huntington; Arnold's investment in Lamb's battalion was thus paying off as Arnold had never calculated. Beset at every turn of the road, and harassed by fire from every stone wall and tree large enough to shelter a militiaman, the weary British were only saved from capture by Sir William Erskine's action in landing a body of marines from the fleet off the beach. Though the militia now outnumbered the British, they fled before the marines' counterattack despite Arnold's exhortations, pleas, and threats. Arnold himself was all over the field, but even his magnificent display of courage and energy could not put heart into his terrified men. Recklessly exposing himself, he had his second horse disabled by a wound, while a bullet tore through the collar of his coat. He behaved, as one combatant observed, "with the greatest intrepidity and coolness, even to the best language under the most aggravating circumstances." If he lamented the enemy's successful withdrawal, he had the satisfaction of knowing the British casualties were nearly four times those of the Americans.[1]

The affairs at Ridgefield and Compo were much talked about, and the intrepid Arnold became the hero of the hour. Though he was justly so acclaimed, men passed over too quickly the brave exertions of old Wooster, who lost his life, and the gallantry of Lamb, who was painfully but not fatally wounded. At last impressed by his ability and exploits, Congress raised Arnold to a major general on May 2 but still refused to restore his seniority in rank. Neither Arnold nor Washington could make much sense out of this reluctance, and Arnold, by no means assuaged by the belated promotion, determined to get to the bottom of the matter. Hence he headed for the capital by way of Washington's headquarters at Morristown.[2]

His desire to go to Philadelphia was accentuated by the behavior of John Brown. Chagrined because he could obtain no favorable action from either Gates or Congress in his endeavor to arraign Arnold before a court-martial, Brown resigned from the army during the winter and, in the role of a civilian, published a paper in Pittsfield on April 12 that maligned Arnold's ability and character. The conclusion was couched in stinging words which, in retrospect, have a prophetic note: "Money is this man's god, and to get enough of it he would sacrifice his country." After conferring with Arnold, Washington wrote Congress on May 12 that Arnold was anxious to settle his accounts, to clear himself of the reports injurious to his character as a man of integrity, and to confer on the problem of his rank. "It is needless to say any thing of this gentleman's military character," Washington declared. "It is universally known that he has always distinguished himself, as a judicious, brave officer, of great activity, enterprize and perseverance." [3]

Once in Philadelphia, Arnold moved to secure vindication. In a letter to Congress on May 20, with which he enclosed a copy of Brown's handbill, he said that he was "exceedingly unhappy to find that having made every sacrifice of fortune, ease and domestic happiness to serve my country, I am publicly impeached (in particular by Lt.-Colonel Brown,) of a catalogue of crimes, which, if true, ought to subject me to disgrace, infamy, and the just resentment of my countrymen. Conscious of the rectitude of my intentions, however I may have erred in judgment, I must request the favor of Congress to point out some mode by which my conduct, and that of my accusers, may be inquired into, and justice done to the innocent and injured." [4]

Arnold's opinion was shared by at least two distinguished members of Congress, Richard Henry Lee and John Adams. On the same day that Arnold petitioned Congress, Lee wrote to Jefferson, "One plan now in frequent use, is, to assassinate the characters of the friends of America in every place, and by every means. At this moment they are now reading in Congress, an audacious attempt of this kind against the brave General Arnold." Two days later, Adams wrote his beloved Abigail, "I spent last evening at the war office with General Arnold. He has been basely slandered and libeled." [5]

Brown's efforts were a little too raw for Congress to accept. In a show of gallantry Congress voted, on the day that Arnold submitted his letter, "That the quarter master general be directed to procure a horse, and present the same, properly caparisoned, to Major General Arnold, in the name of this Congress, as a token of their approbation of his gallant conduct in the action against the enemy in their late enterprize to Danbury, in which General Arnold had one horse killed under him, and another wounded." Congress also referred Arnold's complaint at once to the Board of War. The Board, whose opinion Adams reflected in his letter to Abigail, submitted its report on May 23. The report declared that the Board had had a conference with Arnold "concerning the imputations upon his character, contained in an hand bill, dated Pittsfield, April 12, 1777, and subscribed John Brown, laid before Congress by the general in his letter to the president: that the general laid before the Board a variety of original letters, orders, and other papers, which, together with the general's account of his conduct confirmed by the relation of Mr. Carroll, one of the later commissioners in Canada, now a member of this Board, have given entire satisfaction to this Board concerning the general's character and conduct, so cruelly and groundlessly aspersed in the publication." [6]

Congressional approval of the report of the Board of War brought the case officially to an end, though Brown never relinquished hope that Congress might see Arnold in the same light as he. But Brown's obvious hatred of Arnold, his intemperate language, and his aggressiveness helped defeat his own efforts. Schuyler said that Arnold "will always be the subject of complaint, because his impartiality and candor will not suffer him to see impropriety of behavior with impunity." Schuyler was looking at Arnold through rose-tinted spectacles, but he had at least seen enough of Arnold to feel sympathy for a man in some ways as bitterly traduced as himself, and on as dubious grounds. Schuyler was correct, however, in considering Arnold a perpetual storm center. Few officers in American history have provoked more animosity than Arnold while he remained in loyal service, and few have been so intolerant of criticism or as relentless in defending themselves.[7]

Notwithstanding its approval of the Board's report and its own recognition of Arnold's services in the Danbury invasion, Congress failed to act decisively in regard to Arnold's accounts and the restoration of his seniority in rank. For the Canadian expedition Congress had allowed him $66,671; of this amount he could not account to their satisfaction for about $55,000. It was a simple thing for his enemies and detractors in Congress to assert or insinuate that he had mulcted the government of a great deal of this money. Most of these gentlemen, however, had spent the winter and spring in comparative security and comfort while he was enduring a campaign of the utmost hazard, bitter cold, personal suffering, and exhausting overwork. Criticism when by one's snug fireside comes easily.

Arnold's accounts ran from the time he left for Quebec to the naval actions on Lake Champlain. Throughout this time the army was poorly organized and grossly understaffed in its commissary and quartermaster departments, with the result that unit commanders were left with the total responsibility for purchases and disbursements. In February, 1776, while besieging Quebec, he begged Congress to appoint a paymaster to look after the "multiplicity of accounts." The appointment would "prevent many frauds, . . . greatly accelerate the public business," and leave him, as commanding officer, more time to attend to strictly military matters. At Montreal, Arnold pled in vain for contractors, commissaries, and quartermasters, and lamented to the Congressional commissioners to Canada that, with having to do the work of all, he had scarcely a minute to write. In June, 1776, he borrowed "several sums of hard money," declaring that "The poor soldiers receive no benefit from their pay (it being in uncurrent paper), and starve in the midst of plenty, with their pockets full of money." Arnold often spent from his own resources while in Canada and drew on his own credit to supply the lack. Owing to the confused army organization, the dearth of competent officers, and the rapid military developments in the early and late stages of the Canadian campaign, his accounts undoubtedly contained deficiencies which would not have appeared in the reports of officers trained to the work and having no other duties to fulfill. Though the money he could not satisfactorily account for was a large sum, it is neither fair nor accurate, given this distance in time, to assert that he had pocketed funds or padded expenditures when the Congressional committee appointed to investigate his accounts would not arrive at a definite decision. That he was guilty of peculation is entirely possible, but nothing conclusive has ever been proved.[8]

It was not alone the neglect or inability of Congress to clear his accounts that irked Arnold; its refusal to restore his seniority festered in the man's spirit. Temporarily his attention was diverted as General Howe moved menacingly across New Jersey toward Philadelphia and Congress hastily appointed Arnold to command of the militia along the Delaware. "Fight the enemy we must, whenever our reinforcements are in," he wrote Mifflin on June 12. "We cannot avoid it with honor; our men are in high spirits." Even so, conflict was avoided as Howe withdrew. Arnold, his popularity high among the enlisted men, returned to the capital to request once more the restoration of his rank. When the politicians, their fears of Howe subsiding, paid no attention to him, Arnold refused to submit longer to the situation. Following Stark's example, he resigned on July 11, prompted, he said, by his sense of injustice. He declared that, though he continued to love his country, and was still ready to hazard his life in her behalf, he believed that "Honour is a sacrifice no man ought to make; as I received, so I wish to transmit it inviolate to posterity." [9]

In this dark hour, had he but known it, a letter from Washington was speeding by courier to Philadelphia that would bring surcease from his frustration and injured pride and an opportunity again to demonstrate his military prowess. Even as Arnold had proved the thorn in General Carleton's flesh the previous year, so now did the commander-in-chief see need of him to help stop the rampaging invasion of General John Burgoyne, with his Anglo-German army supported by Loyalists and Indians. "Gentleman Johnny" had slashed up Lake Champlain and forced St. Clair to evacuate Ticonderoga by seizing Mount Defiance, on the top of which he mounted cannon that made the fort untenable. Then, closely pursuing the retreating Americans, he took Fort Anne, while his subordinates, General Fraser and the Brunswicker, General Riedesel, routed Seth Warner at Hubbardton. The old British plan of 1776 to sever New England from the rest of the colonies appeared perilously close to realization.

Recognizing the danger, Washington looked to Arnold as the man who could give General Schuyler, in command of the Northern Army, the kind of support he needed, particularly with the raising of militia. As Washington wrote the president of Congress on July 10:

> . . . there is now an absolute necessity for their turning out to check Genl Burgoyne's progress or the most disagreeable consequences may be apprehended. Upon this occasion, I would take the liberty to suggest to Congress the propriety of sending an active, spirited officer to conduct and lead them on. If General Arnold has settled his affairs and can be spared from Philadelphia, I would recommend him for the business and that he should immediately set out for the Northern department. He is active, judicious and brave, and an officer in whom the militia will repose the greatest confidence. Besides this, he is well acquainted with that country and with the routes and most important passes and defiles in it. I do not think he can render more signal services, or be more usefully employed at this time, than in this way. I am persuaded his presence and activity will animate the militia greatly, and spur them on to a becoming conduct; I could wish him to be engaged in a more agreeable service, to be with better troops; but circumstances call for his exertions in this way, and I have no doubt of his adding much to the honors he has already acquired.[10]

The very next day, July 11, Washington's letter was read to Congress. Interestingly enough, Arnold's letter of resignation was dated July 11. Since the resignation was not read until the day following, and since Congress was therefore officially in ignorance of it, the politicians resolved that an extract of Washington's letter, so far as it related to Arnold, be made out and sent to him. They further directed that he repair to headquarters and follow the orders of the commander-in-chief. In order to expedite the appointment, and at the same time leave no doubt in the minds of Congress, Washington reiterated his request for Arnold on the 12th, "Being more and more convinced of the important advantages that will result from his presence and conduct, I have thought it my duty to repeat my wishes on the subject, and that he may without a moment's loss of time, set out from Philadelphia for that purpose." [11]

Inspired by Washington's trust, and fired by the imminence of active work with troops, Arnold dashed off a letter to Congress requesting a suspension of action on his resignation. He said he would leave the request with them and doubted not that when he had discharged the duty ahead, they would listen to him. As he assured Washington when he reached headquarters, the fact that he might have to serve under men promoted over him, particularly St. Clair, would not trouble him, especially if it was for "the good of the service." Action, with the promise of glory, exhilarated him. Like a number of generals then and since, he was never at his best with politicians and rejoiced at the prospect of being back in the field. But, notwithstanding the appeal that action always exercised for him, his decision to serve after he had already resigned, and under conditions not altogether attractive, was both generous and patriotic.[12]

Perhaps it was as well for all concerned that the truculent little general was not in Philadelphia when Congress, on August 8, again showed unmistakably its opposition to restoring his seniority. On that day, a motion was made and seconded that a new commission, dated back to February 19, be made out for Arnold. After debate, another motion was made to amend the original motion by adding, "On account of his extraordinary merit and former rank in the army." Both the amendment and the original motion were lost, whereupon Henry Marchant of Rhode Island requested that the votes be recorded. The record, with its count of six for and sixteen against, showed four states, represented by one member each, voting in favor: Connecticut, Georgia, New Hampshire, and Rhode Island; these were supported by one member from New York and one from Pennsylvania. With the exception of members from Virginia and South Carolina, all of whom were either absent or abstaining, the rest of the Congressmen present voted down the motions. Of the three members from Connecticut, Eliphalet Dyer of Windham was the only one present; the others, Roger Sherman and William Williams, son-in-law of Governor Trumbull, were ill. It is doubtful that Sherman, who distrusted Arnold from the time of the Boles incident, would have cast affirmatively; his illness was therefore well timed. John Adams, favorable to Arnold in the Board of War investigation, now voted against restoring his seniority.[13]

The reasons for Congressional opposition to Arnold are not completely clear but appear to have had their basis primarily in the civilian's mistrust of, and failure to understand, the military mind, with its addiction to the use of force to solve problems, its concern for its honor, and its rigid attention to the niceties of rank. Congress, it must be said, was enduring a chastening experience at this time with officers, both native and foreign, contending for rank and authority. John Adams, sober constitutional lawyer that he was, could not understand what happens inside a man's mind when he receives a commission and a command; hence his scornful allusion to the scrambling of apes for nuts.[14]

Adams was far from alone in his view, which was probably held by most members of Congress. James Lovell, the former Boston schoolmaster and a precise man fond of cryptic remarks usually barbed with sarcasm, was the most articulate on "this mighty occasion," as he termed it. He wrote that Arnold "conducted himself almost without blemish in resigning, if a man may be said to do so, who leaves a patriotic exertion because self love was injured in a fanciful right incompatible with the general interest of the Union." More explicitly he declared the issue to be "really a question between monarchical and republican principles put at a most critical time." Arnold, an officer, was challenging the justice of a decision reached by the civil department of the government, and his action must have been particularly obnoxious to the Massachusetts delegation of John and Samuel Adams, Elbridge Gerry, and Lovell, all of whom voted against the motions. Feeling evidently ran high on the issue if one can accept Lovell's comment on the minority reaction, "They intend to have Mass [achusetts]. hanged on a tree we being all 4 of a mind. . . ." By no means vehement but thoroughly offended was Henry Laurens, newly arrived member from South Carolina and a man highly respected by John Adams. Laurens thought "the reasoning upon this occasion was disgusting." Arnold, he said, was refused "not because he was deficient in merit or that his demand was not well founded but because he asked for it and that granting at such an instance would be derogatory to the honour of Congress." [15]

Unfortunately men who could look at the problem with the fairness and objectivity of Laurens were few. Whether for geographical reasons, mistrust of the military, or suspicion and dislike of him personally, Congress had treated Arnold on both the promotion and seniority issues with flagrant injustice. There was even less reason for the opposition to restoring his seniority than for holding up his promotion, since, once the promotion was granted, the larger reasons motivating Congress were presumably removed. During its long career, which was virtually one crisis after another, the Continental Congress, on the whole, performed its duties with distinction. Like any political organization not run by angels, however, it made notable mistakes, and none was more glaring or more tragic in its consequences than the treatment of Benedict Arnold. The desire to be appreciated is among the most compelling urges of the human spirit, and when a man peculiarly susceptible to good opinion has performed extraordinary services and is denied recognition, he may wonder, in anger or despair, if the game is worth the candle. Not disposed by inclination or experience to be either philosophical or charitable when thwarted, Arnold was not likely to forget his humiliation by Congress. The background to the treason of 1780 was thus already being filled in with heavy strokes in 1777.[16]

· XIII ·

Relief of Fort Stanwix

ARNOLD found the situation of the Northern Army, when he joined
it at Fort Edward, scarcely enviable. Burgoyne's sudden advance and
seizure of Ticonderoga had struck a sharp blow at American morale.
That morale further deteriorated as his redskins, whom he sought vainly
to control, went to work with torch and scalping knife. It seemed that
all the good-natured, swaggering, play-writing Briton had to do to reach
Albany was to traverse the rugged neck of land between Lake Champlain
and Lake George, float his troops, cannon, and equipment down the
latter lake on flatboats, and push through the woods to the Hudson, from
which point he could go overland or continue by water to Albany. To
make the prospect even less auspicious for the Americans, Colonel Barry
St. Leger had landed at Fort Oswego and driven eastward to the carrying place between the Great Lakes and the Mohawk Valley with a force
of nearly two thousand regulars, Loyalists, and Indians, who were under
the command of Chief Joseph Brant. On August 3, St. Leger laid siege
to Fort Stanwix, which was commanded by Colonel Peter Gansevoort.
To assist Gansevoort, rugged old General Nicholas Herkimer marched
with a large force of Tryon County militia. Unfortunately Herkimer fell
victim to an ambush carefully laid by Brant and Sir John Johnson, and
one of the stubbornest and bloodiest battles of the war, proportionate to
the numbers engaged, then ensued in the dark woods near Oriskany.
Though the enemy drew off when Lieutenant Colonel Marinus Willett

sallied from the fort and raided his camp, Herkimer, mortally wounded, was forced to withdraw, leaving St. Leger to keep Stanwix under close siege. Unless relief soon reached the fort, its downfall appeared certain. Arnold was one of those who saw the overwhelming necessity of its remaining in American hands.

British successes were only part of the dismal situation. The controversy over the command of the Northern Army was also injuring morale, and Arnold was soon to become involved in the backwash of that altercation. If the quarrel between himself and Brown had been characterized by deep animosity, Gates's timely intervention had probably saved the country. But the controversy between Gates and Schuyler, restrained by none, endangered the national security. Schuyler was a great New York landholder who had to depend for troops mainly on the small farmers of New England, and these disliked him not only because he was an aristocrat but also because he was a native of the state that had long laid claim to Vermont. He was often arrogant and patronizing, with a pronounced lord-of-the-manor attitude. He found it difficult to allocate work to others for fear it would not be well done. He often expressed his discouragement in letters, thereby occasionally giving a mistaken impression of timorousness. Faults he had, but he was also a great-hearted man, large in his views, a thorough patriot, loyal in both directions of the chain of command, and an officer of great organizing ability with a penchant for being especially tenacious on the defensive. Arnold and Schuyler were on the best of terms. Schuyler had been the first general officer to see merit in the little man and wanted to make him his adjutant when Arnold turned up at Albany following his dismal experience with Ethan Allen and the Massachusetts committee back in 1775.

Schuyler's protagonist, Gates, was a very different person with a decidedly different background. A son of the housekeeper of the Duke of Leeds, he was also the godson of the famous contemporary diarist and letter-writer, Horace Walpole, and had been a British officer who had seen considerable service in America before he settled in Virginia in 1773. In 1775, he had fulfilled admirably his administrative functions as adjutant general to Washington. Usually mild-mannered, democratic in his political attitudes, though snobbish in his regard for the society of the rich and noble, he had early won the attention of John Adams, who made him the recipient of many confidences and who became his advocate for the command of the Northern Army. Though Gates possessed no small degree of courage, loyalty to those he liked, and more military ability than he is generally credited with, he could be malicious, spiteful, and underhanded. Beneath the friendly, gossipy, at times unctuous manner there was something felinely treacherous in the man. Despite a professed friendship with Washington, he made no report of his great triumph at Saratoga to the commander-in-chief but submitted it directly to Congress, thereby infuriating Washington. Later, as president of the Board of War, Gates made life very unpleasant for Washington. After Saratoga, he so antagonized Daniel Morgan that the backwoodsman refused to speak to him for several years, while his treatment of Arnold in the latter part of the Saratoga campaign was a notorious example of pettiness, jealousy, and poor leadership. Initially Arnold enjoyed excellent relations with Gates, as with Schuyler, but the tone of his letters to Schuyler shows an element of respect not so evident in his communications with Gates.

The contest between Gates and Schuyler was not new. In 1776, when in command of the field army, Gates felt himself straitjacketed by Schuyler at headquarters in Albany. Though both men may have been suffering from an attack of nerves, their relations went from bad to worse. After Carleton decided not to venture a winter siege of Ticonderoga, Gates joined Washington before Christmas. Washington offered him a command in the Trenton expedition, but Gates claimed his health was poor, and went instead to do battle in his own behalf before Congress. Both Washington and Congress wished him to resume his old duties as adjutant general, but the small, ruddy-faced, bespectacled Horatio had tasted the sweet grape of ambition; the Northern Army was to be his. Though he accepted the adjutant generalship for a brief period, he soon returned to dicker with Congress again. He was rewarded in March, 1777, by being given command of the Northern Department, Congress and Schuyler having fallen out over a minor issue. Two months afterward, Schuyler having come to Philadelphia to present his case, Congress reinstated the New Yorker as commander of the Northern Department. Though Schuyler hoped Gates would remain as commander of Ticonderoga, Gates refused to serve under Schuyler, and dashed back to Philadelphia to plead his cause. Small wonder, with all these comings and goings, that Arnold's arrival after the Danbury invasion had provoked Adams's testy comments on officers' ambitions. Gates antagonized several of the political gentlemen, who thought he should be taught a lesson in parliamentary good manners. Failing to gain anything substantial from his visit, Gates remained in the vicinity of Philadelphia, argus-eyed and politically alert, until Burgoyne's victorious advance brought down a storm of criticism on Schuyler's head, some of it not unwarranted but much of it purely partisan in nature. The New Englanders in Congress were wild at the New Yorker, John Adams even hinting darkly at an execution. Congress requested Washington to name a successor to Schuyler, but Washington declined to handle this hot chestnut. Congress then took a secret ballot on August 4, 1777, and voted overwhelmingly for Gates as the new commander. Though Gates may not have been the most gifted general of his time, few could match his ability to win political favor when he put his mind to it.[1]

Meanwhile, the new commander not arriving in the north until August was well along, Schuyler and Arnold labored manfully to resist Burgoyne. Arnold took charge of one division of the army, Schuyler of the other. They sent hundreds of axmen into the woods to cut down trees in the path of Burgoyne's troops and to remove such bridges as existed. Though these measures slowed Burgoyne to a mile a day, no mean pace for the British considering the obstacles, the Englishman could not be stopped. Schuyler, whatever his deficiencies in regard to St. Clair's fiasco at Ticonderoga, now refused to sacrifice his army by standing and fighting, as popular opinion demanded he should. Sooner or later he knew he would reach a point where it would not be wise to go back farther, but he hoped that by that time he would be strong enough to confront Burgoyne.

And indeed American resistance was gradually increasing as angry militiamen began to turn out in numbers because of fears for their homes roused by the murder of Jane McCrea. Jane, or Jenny, was betrothed to a Loyalist officer in Burgoyne's command, Lieutenant David Jones. On July 27, an Indian patrol seized her and a cousin of Burgoyne's General Fraser. In taking them to the British camp, they quarreled over Jane, the altercation ending only after Jane herself had been killed and scalped. Shocked, Burgoyne, a humane officer at heart, would have tried and executed her assailant if his subordinates had not warned that such action would lose him his Indian allies. Though these proved subsequently of small value to his army, they were rendering indispensable assistance to St. Leger, who maintained his siege of Fort Stanwix so tightly that Lieutenant Colonel Willett volunteered for the heroic feat of slipping through the enemy's camp on a stormy night to reach Schuyler and plead for help; unless assistance arrived soon, the fort was doomed.

Meanwhile both Schuyler and Arnold were doing their utmost to relieve the fort. Schuyler's decision to send a force against St. Leger was a brave one, made in the face of violent opposition from his New England officers, at least one of whom alleged that he was deliberately contriving to weaken the army. When he asked for a brigadier to head the relief expedition, none would accept the responsibility. Arnold, though a major general and, at the time, second in command, then volunteered. In fact, angry at the imputations of cowardice and treason leveled at Schuyler, and eager for action, he leaped at the opportunity. Schuyler gratefully accepted him, remarking, "It gives me great satisfaction that you have offered to go and conduct the military expedition in Tryon County." Raising the siege of the fort, as Washington himself observed, would be "a most important matter just at this time." [2]

When he started off with fewer than a thousand men on August 15, Arnold had no illusions that relieving the fort would be a simple matter. The trouble lay not only in the strength of the enemy but also in the fact that many of the Tryon County militia, usually so brave, were now reluctant to leave their homes after their Oriskany experience. They had suffered too severely at the hands of St. Leger and Brant to want to antagonize further such almost certain victors. With an eye to putting heart into people thus affected, Arnold issued a ferocious proclamation after arriving at German Flats. He threatened St. Leger's "banditti of robbers, murderers and traitors, composed of savages of America and more savage Britons" with "no mercy" if they persisted "in their wicked courses" and did not lay down their arms within ten days. The next day, August 21, however, a council of war attended by Brigadier General Ebenezer Learned and the half-dozen colonels of his brigade voted against moving on until reinforcements arrived; Arnold had available only nine hundred and thirty-three men and a handful of militia. Reluctantly Arnold deferred to the council's opinion, requested additional troops of Gates, and set about vigorously rounding up militia.[3]

But when word reached him only a few hours after the council meeting that St. Leger was closing in on the fort by means of the zigzag and parallel trenches so typical of eighteenth-century siege warfare, Arnold quickly scrapped his policy of waiting. Dashing off a note to Gates, he explained that he had resolved "to hazard a battle rather than suffer the garrison to fall a sacrifice." He assured Gates that "nothing shall be omitted that can be done to raise the siege; you will hear of my being victorious or no more, and as soon as the safety of this part of the country will permit I will fly to your assistance." From another officer these melodramatic words would have seemed absurd. Gates, however, had had sufficient acquaintance with Arnold as a fighter not to doubt that, high-sounding though his expression, he meant what he said. The man was capable of the most amazing feats and was utterly reckless of his own life.[4]

On the other hand, Arnold was not only "judicious," as Washington had described him to Congress, but wily, as well. To Arnold the "infernal savages, painted like furies" by whom so many people had been "inhumanly butchered" were children in their credulity. He therefore decided to employ a ruse which, if successful, would help supply in effect what he lacked in numbers. Among prisoners recently taken and condemned to death for planning a Loyalist uprising in Tryon County was a half-wit named Hon-Yost Schuyler, who was well known to the Indians. Hon-Yost was perhaps not so lacking in gray matter as he sometimes seemed, but the Indians thought of him as one under the special protection of the Great Spirit. When Hon-Yost's mother and another son, Nicholas, entered the American camp at Fort Dayton and obtained an audience with Arnold to plead for Hon-Yost's life, Arnold was at first adamant. Then he suddenly agreed, provided Hon-Yost would go to St. Leger's Indians and spread the frightening information that Arnold was coming with overwhelming forces; in the meantime, he would hold Nicholas as a hostage. To this the family eagerly assented. The half-wit's coat was then riddled with bullet holes to lend credence to his tale, and he was sent on his way. Arnold left little to chance; trailing Hon-Yost was an Oneida, a member of the one tribe of the Six Nations generally friendly to the Americans. The Oneida's task was to keep an eye on Hon-Yost and to confirm the half-wit's story to the hostile Indians.

Arnold's device was a stroke of genius. Hon-Yost burst among the Indians looking every bit the wild-eyed, tattered fugitive. Arnold, he exclaimed, was close behind. When the Indians demanded to know how many men Arnold had with him, Hon-Yost pointed to the leaves of the trees. The yells of dismay from the startled redskins caused St. Leger to summon Hon-Yost at once. The half-wit faithfully repeated the story of pursuit but was more explicit; Arnold would arrive in twenty-four hours with two thousand men at his back.

The Indians were unhappy. They had become increasingly restive and sullen as the siege dragged along and had turned cold to an affair so unremunerative in scalps and plunder. Furthermore, they had a highly developed respect for the fighting qualities of the little American general whom the Abenaki Indians had called "The Dark Eagle." Sorely troubled by Hon-Yost, they now received another shock, but one that was not without a measure of encouragement. As the Oneida had followed after Hon-Yost, he had met stray Indians whom he knew. Arnold, he told them, was coming to punish only the British and Loyalists, not the Indians; and the Oneida sought his friends' co-operation in convincing St. Leger's Indians. His friends agreeing to help him, the Oneida suddenly appeared among the hostile redskins and corroborated Hon-Yost's account. When his friends also arrived with even more fantastic tales of Arnold's numbers and prowess, St. Leger's Indians needed no further convincing; the woods and safety proved an irresistible attraction.

Faced with the disintegration of his army, St. Leger tried in vain to persuade the Indian chiefs to have their braves remain; the chiefs insisted on leaving immediately. When St. Leger declared that he would not go before sundown, the braves broke out of control, looting British military stores and stealing the officers' clothes and their liquor. St. Leger then reluctantly decided to raise the siege without further delay. But his was no orderly withdrawal. His men broke for the woods in a wild scramble, first the Loyalists and then the regulars, leaving cannon, tents, and other equipment behind. The liquored-up Indians now shouted that Arnold was upon them, and whooped in glee as the British floundered in panic through the woods at mention of the terrible general's name. And the British soon discovered to their horror the dripping scalps of their own stragglers swinging at the Indians' belts.[5]

Arnold was for a time ignorant of the extent of his triumph. Gansevoort wrote Gates on August 22 that at three o'clock in the afternoon several enemy deserters came into the fort with the report that St. Leger was retreating "with the utmost precipitation." Arnold informed Gates late the next day that he had heard the rumor of the enemy's withdrawal but that he did not know for sure whether St. Leger had actually retreated or had merely disengaged himself in order to intercept the relieving force. Still, believing that the enemy might truly be fleeing and that he could harass him, Arnold made a forced march of twenty-two miles, arriving at the fort on August 24 at five o'clock in the afternoon. Only then did he perceive the complete success of his ruse. Despite the fatiguing march, he sent out a pursuit party, but rain slowed the men so appreciably that they gave up the task as hopeless and returned to the fort. A small advance element, however, continued to Oneida Lake, where the pursuers arrived just in time to see the last of the enemy going off in boats.[6]

In this humiliation of the enemy ended the Mohawk Valley campaign, which, without Arnold's intercession, might have terminated in the fall of Fort Stanwix, the loss of the Valley, and the junction of St. Leger and Burgoyne. The latter was now like a man who had lost both his arms; not only had St. Leger fled but on the very day after Arnold had left General Schuyler for the relief of Fort Stanwix, Colonel John Stark, who had come out of retirement, Colonel Seth Warner, and their militiamen utterly smashed the German forces under Colonels Baum and Breymann which Burgoyne had sent toward Bennington to obtain horses and supplies. St. Leger's troops and Indians would have been invaluable reinforcements for Burgoyne now that he had lost so many of his Germans. Arnold, however, had spoiled this fine prospect. He could testify to Gates that, as for the Mohawk Valley, "there is nothing to be feared from the enemy in this quarter at present." Gates, in turn, could write to the crabbed, moody Stark, many of whose troops were bedridden with measles, "When the wings of General Burgoyne are . . . discomfited, I shall rejoice in yours and General Arnold's assistance to try our best with him and his main army." The way was now cleared for concentrating on Johnny Burgoyne, and Arnold returned in triumph, eager to take a decisive role in the issue which might well determine the fate of the young republic.[7]

Battle of Freeman's Farm

ARNOLD returned to the Northern Army to find a different commander and a different spirit. Gates, appointed to Schuyler's place on August 4, took a fortnight to reach Albany. True, he stopped off at Peekskill to confer with General Israel Putnam, but conversations with that fabulous hero of the wolf den could hardly have taken so long. When Gates finally reached Albany on August 19, Schuyler received him with the utmost graciousness, giving no hint of his own hurt feelings. Though he offered his assistance in any way possible, Gates ignored the offer. In fact, his treatment of the general who had been shelved provoked Gouverneur Morris to comment that "The new commander in chief of the Northern Department may, if he please, neglect to ask or disdain to receive advice; but those who know him will, I am sure, be convinced that he needs it." But Gates was keeping his own counsel; certainly he was not taking advice from Schuyler's "New York gang," as Gates's secretary, a civilian named William Clajon, sneered about Schuyler's aides and friends. If Gates confided in anyone, it was in young Colonel James Wilkinson, his adjutant, who, when he had learned of Schuyler's reinstatement in the spring, had exploded that were it not for the amiable lady dependent on his existence, he would wish no longer "to breathe the common air with ingrates, assassins, and double-faced villains." Had Gates been able to look into the future, he would have been horrified to see his loyal "Wilky" actually challenge him to a duel but a few months after the victory at Saratoga.[1]

Arnold, however, could not help noticing a change in the army. It might have been owing to the victories, and, if so, Gates could hardly lay claim to the honor; Bennington had been won before Gates arrived and Arnold himself was already off on his Mohawk Valley expedition. Nor had many militia as yet appeared despite Gates's appointment, a fact of which he complained to Washington on August 27. But the army had won two victories, Washington had responded to Schuyler's request for reinforcements by sending Daniel Morgan's regiment of riflemen, a magnificient legacy for Gates. Moreover, Burgoyne, badly hurt by Bennington, still hampered by a heavy artillery train, and slowed by American delaying tactics originally initiated by Schuyler and Arnold, was in the position of having to choose whether to continue to Albany or retreat to Ticonderoga; his line of communications was dangerously overextended. Gate's estimate of the situation led him to conclude that, with the menace from St. Leger over, his own best course was to advance a few miles to the high, defensible ground in the town of Stillwater where a man named Jotham Bemis ran a tavern. The morale of the army rose perceptibly at the reversal of direction. Unlike Schuyler, Gates came to enjoy a measure of popularity, particularly with the New Englanders in his army. Nor should it be forgotten that Gates possessed fine administrative and executive talents which he now had ample opportunity to demonstrate. This Northern Army, therefore, was on the way to becoming a confident army of nearly seven thousand men during those mid-September days.

The first act of the decisive drama occurred on September 19, just four days after Burgoyne, still confident of his ability to reach Albany, started to cross to the west bank of the Hudson above the Battenkill. For several days, Arnold had reconnoitered the area, helping to choose, with Kosciusko, the Polish engineer, the sites on Bemis Heights that the Pole subsequently fortified. Arnold also dispatched raiders against the enemy's fatigue details employed in road construction and repair. Gradually Gates concentrated most of the army at Bemis Heights, and the command of the left wing fell to Arnold. Gates planned on a holding action, trusting that Burgoyne would try to assault the American entrenchments. Arnold envisaged a contest that would be decided by an offensive thrust against Burgoyne. He could see no sense in giving Burgoyne the time and opportunity to emplace his heavy artillery, which might force the Americans to evacuate their favorable position. Unfortunately for Arnold,

Gates was the commanding officer and counted on winning by points rather than by a knockout.[2]

The battle that occurred on the 19th revealed the wisdom of Gates's plan as it developed up to a point and the opportunity that was missed by his refusal to permit Arnold to have his way. Determined to test the American lines, though he knew little or nothing of the strength of Kosciusko's entrenchments or the number of troops under Gates's command, Burgoyne sent out three columns through the woods, much of which is now open country. General Baron von Riedesel, the Brunswicker, and General William Phillips, the British artillery expert, were to march by the river road and engage the American right. Burgoyne, with three regiments in line and one in reserve, proposed to cross the ravine. After linking up with the third column, which consisted largely of Grenadiers and Light Infantry under General Simon Fraser and Colonel H. C. Breymann, Burgoyne intended to hit the American center and, if possible, have Fraser envelop the American left. Three reports from signal guns would notify Riedesel and Phillips that the battle was on. The direction of Burgoyne's attack would thus involve a heavy concentration on the American left wing, the portion of the army commanded by Arnold.

Prevented by Gates from going at once on the offensive, Arnold followed through with Gates's plan, which was that Morgan and Dearborn's regiments should receive the British attack, with the rest of Arnold's division in support. But after the British advance guards flushed the American pickets at Freeman's Farm, Gates let the battle develop considerably in front of the breastworks. As Morgan and Dearborn drove back the Canadians and Indians under Fraser, they lost formation, particularly Morgan. Arnold now sent in the regiments of Alexander Scammel and Joseph Cilley, which managed to check the enemy while Morgan's men, at his famous "turkey call," rallied to the side of their chief, who, weeping, had thought his unit ruined. Arnold presently hurled additional regiments against the British center. Though these troops pushed back the close ranks of redcoats by the accuracy of their fire, they themselves were driven from the clearing on Freeman's Farm once they tried to take possession of it. The American line now extended increasingly to the left, and had Fraser supported Burgoyne adequately by moving to envelop that left, Arnold's troops might have been in real trouble. As it was, however, the Americans hammered Burgoyne hard, particularly the weak spot that appeared between his right and Fraser's left. Fortunately for Burgoyne, relief was on the way as Riedesel and Phillips, stripping their own column, raced across country with men and guns to save the hard-pressed center.

Arnold was still confident that if Gates supplied him with reinforcements, he could deliver the finishing stroke. Though Gates ordered out Learned's brigade, he refused to let Arnold direct Learned's movements, with the result that Learned's troops went astray and, instead of rushing to assist their comrades against Burgoyne, blundered up against Fraser. According to Wilkinson, Arnold and Gates had been in front of the center of the camp listening to the rattle of small arms when Colonel Morgan Lewis, Gates's deputy quartermaster general, rode up. Questioned by Gates as to how the battle was progressing now that Learned was on the field, Lewis replied that the action was still indecisive. At this point Arnold exclaimed, "By God, I will soon put an end to it," and, clapping spurs to his horse, galloped off. Lewis, a toady of Gates, then remarked to the general, "You had better order him back, the action is going well, [and] he may by some rash act do mischief." Gates then dispatched Wilkinson, who overtook Arnold and remanded the furious general to camp. The consequence of Gates's action was that, lacking unity of direction, the Americans, though outnumbering the British and Germans, presently faded before the enemy counterattacks and, with darkness falling, left Burgoyne in possession of the field. Had not Gates restrained Arnold, a second battle might not have been necessary to convince Burgoyne that his luck had run out.[3]

· XV ·

The Quarrel with Gates and the Battle of Bemis Heights

WHILE the female camp followers of both armies stripped the dead and wolves often reached the bodies before burial details, Arnold and Gates tangled in bitter controversy. So far as is known, relations between the two men existed on an amicable basis until Arnold's return from the Mohawk Valley; certainly Arnold's letters to Gates from the Valley contain no suggestion of a rift. On the other hand, it is possible that while with Schuyler before Gates's arrival Arnold sympathized with the New Yorker. In the field after having vainly battered his head against Congress, Arnold was in a position to appreciate Schuyler's efforts and to realize that Schuyler had become a political sacrifice to military necessity: the New Englanders simply had to be appeased by Gates's appointment in order to enlist their support in the campaign.

Arnold had liked and respected both men, and had reason to be grateful to both. Gates had been especially helpful in shielding him against court-martial moves by Enoch Poor and John Brown the previous fall. Had Arnold been a complete opportunist, he would have been wise to drop his friendship with Schuyler, once the New Yorker was superseded, and hitch his wagon to Gates's star. But Arnold thought he could remain a friend of Schuyler while continuing to serve Gates. Unfortunately he reckoned without Gates's jealousy, his own vanity and over-quick temper, and the passionate attachment of the aides of Gates and Schuyler to their chiefs.

How soon trouble broke out is not clear, but from information in letters after September 19 between Arnold and Henry B. Livingston, one of Schuyler's former aides and now his own, one would judge that feeling had been building up for some time. Arnold's division had originally consisted of Poor's and Learned's brigades, while associated with them was Morgan's regiment, nominally under Arnold's command. On September 9, Gates wished Arnold to distribute the New York and Connecticut militia to such brigades as he thought proper. Accordingly Arnold attached the New Yorkers to Poor and the Connecticut militia to Learned. But the twenty-year-old Wilkinson, bumptious with authority as deputy adjutant general, published in general orders a directive attaching the New York militia to General John Glover's brigade. As Arnold complained to Gates, this act placed him "in the ridiculous light of presuming to give orders I had no right to do, and having them publicly contradicted." At the same time, Arnold mentioned it as undoubtedly Wilkinson's mistake rather than Gates's, but the latter very decently and properly protected his subordinate by asserting that the responsibility was his alone. Although he mollified Arnold by promising that the mistake should be mentioned in ensuing orders, it was never done. Thus even before the battle, differences had occurred, though nothing of a critical nature. Then came September 19, the disputed method of attack, and Gates's final restraint of Arnold.[1]

Arnold's indignation, already asimmer, boiled over at last on the occasion of two incidents. In his battle report to Congress, Gates made no mention of Arnold's division. Then, on September 22, in accordance with Wilkinson's suggestion, he directed Morgan, whose troops, he declared, were not attached to any brigade or division, to make returns and reports to his headquarters, from which source alone Morgan was to receive his orders. Arnold bulled his way into Gates's headquarters and demanded to know why his division had not been given full credit for its work on the 19th but had been alluded to merely as a "detachment from the army." He insisted, too, on an explanation for the change in arrangements for Morgan's regiment.[2]

At Arnold's imperious tone, Gates also flared up; and the quarrel became an old-fashioned hate-fest. Livingston declared that "matters were altercated in a very high strain. Both were warm. . . ." If Arnold was domineering and fiery, Gates, said Livingston, was "rather passionate and very assuming." Wilkinson, whose presumption had scarcely helped the situation, commented gleefully that Arnold, who was "in great warmth . . . was ridiculed by General Gates: high words and gross language ensued." Gates cattishly informed Arnold that he did not know that Arnold was a major general at all, since he had sent in his resignation to Congress before coming up to this part of the country, or that he had any command in the army. He further stated that when General Lincoln arrived in a day or two, Arnold would be relieved of his division. Heaping insult upon insult, Gates told Arnold that he was of little consequence to the army and that he would gladly be given a pass to leave it whenever he wanted to do so.[3]

Livid with rage, Arnold strode back to his quarters and dashed off a letter to Gates. In it he recounted the scene that had occurred and the train of unpleasant incidents ever since his return from the Mohawk Valley. "For what reason, I know not," he protested, "(as I am conscious of no offence or neglect of duty) but I have lately observed little or no attention paid to any proposals I have thought it my duty to make for the publick service, and when a measure I have proposed has been agreed to it has been immediately contradicted. I have been received with the greatest coolness at headquarters, and often huffed [*sic*] in such a manner as must mortify a person with less pride than I have and in my station in the army." Arnold therefore requested a pass for himself and his aides, Livingston and Richard Varick, who had been Schuyler's military secretary. He proposed to join General Washington, where he hoped it would still be possible to serve his country.[4]

The quarrel did credit to neither man. Arnold had become almost pathologically sensitive to criticism and evidently lost complete control of himself. Gates's failure to mention Arnold's division as such was galling to Arnold but not necessarily malicious in intent. Though Morgan's regiment was an independent unit, Gates had let it do duty with Arnold. Gates was justified, if it had suited his purposes, in removing Morgan from Arnold's supervision, but his tactlessness in not notifying Arnold of the change before its publication in general orders was inexcusable, whether it was intended as a deliberate slap or was an oversight. Livingston, moreover, confirmed Arnold's recent treatment at Gates's hands. In a report to Schuyler, he said that for some time past he had observed the coolness, even the disrespect, accorded Arnold at Gates's headquarters and the unceremonious rejection of his proposals.[5]

While such comments might be dismissed as the natural indignation of a loyal follower, an officer hardly unprejudiced, Livingston had a discerning mind, and undoubtedly put his finger on the real cause of the difficulty when he told Schuyler, "The reason of the present disagreement between two cronies is simply this: Arnold is your friend." Schuyler's own opinion, given to Varick when the general heard that Arnold was about to leave, was that Gates would probably be indebted to Arnold for the glory he might acquire from a victory. But "perhaps," Schuyler added, "he is so very sure of success that he does not wish the other to come in for a share of it." [6]

That Gates was jealous of Arnold may well be so; certainly he had struggled too long for this command to have a subordinate deprive him of the glory of winning the campaign. Yet it is probable that, though jealous of Arnold, he was also suspicious and resentful of the influence that he assumed Schuyler was still exercising through his former aides and other friends in the army. And, indeed, Varick and Livingston would have been less than human had they not compared in unfavorable terms for the benefit of any who might listen Gates's conduct with that of Schuyler under conditions fully as trying. According to Livingston, Gates had insinuated several times that Arnold's mind had been poisoned and prejudiced by members of his staff, and Livingston was the person usually indicated as the chief offender. Major Leonard Chester on Gates's staff consulted with Wilkinson as to what measures would be necessary to effect a reconciliation. He was told, Livingston informed Schuyler, "that some overtures were necessary on Arnold's side; that General Gates was jealous of me, and thought I had influenced Arnold's conduct, and that of course it was necessary to get rid of me to open a way for accommodation. When this was told to Arnold, he could scarcely contain himself, and desired Chester to return for answer: that his judgment had never been influenced by any man, and that he would not sacrifice a friend to please the 'face of clay.'" Though Arnold insisted on Livingston's remaining, the future Supreme Court justice made up his mind to leave camp the next day. Conceiving himself also affected by Gates's remarks, Varick likewise decided to leave.[7]

Meanwhile the Arnold-Gates controversy hotly continued. In answer to his request for leave, Gates sent Arnold not a regular pass but an open letter to John Hancock, president of Congress. Curtly Arnold rejected the communication, stating that if Gates wished him to convey any sealed letters to Hancock, he would be glad to take charge of them. In the meantime, he desired a pass to Philadelphia; and he remarked that he knew of no reason for Gates's conduct toward him unless he had been "traduced by some designing villain." Accordingly Gates sent him a pass and undoubtedly hoped that Arnold would soon depart.[8]

He was disappointed in this hope. When the army learned that Arnold intended to leave, the soldiers, said Livingston, were seized by a "great uneasiness." General Poor, moreover, drew up an address, petitioning Arnold to stay. Though Poor's officers signed it, General Learned's, while approving it in principle, refused to put their signatures to it on the ground that it might offend Gates. Poor then wrote a letter which all the general officers except Lincoln signed, entreating Arnold to remain. With action appearing imminent, Arnold agreed, and the officers breathed more easily. Benedict Arnold was a good man to have about when Burgoyne should decide to wrench out of the jaws of the trap that were slowly being drawn tighter.[9]

In the interim, the altercation flared up again. Arnold, without authorization from Gates, made a payment of fifty dollars as a reward to a soldier who had distinguished himself during the retreat from Fort Edward. Gates thunderingly rebuked him, whereupon Arnold promptly told Gates that he needed not to be reminded of army procedure. The soldier, he explained, had distinguished himself one day when General Schuyler was absent and when he, Arnold, had commanded the army; hence he conceived that he had the right to make the payment. The point of altercation was of a minor nature and the amount in question pathetically small. Though Arnold undoubtedly exceeded his authority by Gates's interpretation, Gates would have done well to let the incident pass without notice. It is indicative of the petty nature of the man, however, that he did not do so and in his reprimand used a sledge hammer to drive a tack. Inordinately jealous of his new authority, he was determined to resist any and every encroachment on it. After acknowledging Arnold's protest, Gates ignored him altogether, even to excluding him from staff discussions.[10]

For Arnold these were wretched days, and he exploded in helpless anger. He deeply resented being regarded "only as a cypher," believing that Gates's treatment "proceeds from a spirit of jealousy and that I have every thing to fear from the malice of my enemies." Even so, he was determined to remain. In sending him north, he argued with Gates, Congress and Washington must have thought him of some consequence and believed the commanding general would consult with him. Though Gates chose not to do so, he thought it his duty to acquaint the general with the fact that the militia, restless for action, were threatening to go home. He therefore entreated Gates "to improve the present time." But he hoped the general would not impute this hint as a wish to command the army or to outshine him; it proceeded rather from his zeal for the cause of his country.[11]

Arnold's letter, a monument of indiscretion, stung Gates into angry action. If he lacked decisiveness before this, refusing to do more than hope that Arnold would leave of his own accord, he did not lack for resolution now. To Wilkinson's delight and relief, he removed Arnold from command, gave Lincoln the right wing, and took over Arnold's division himself. Thus frustrated again, this time not by Congress but by its general, Arnold faced an immediate future void of any chance of realizing the aspiration that had buoyed him up through these troublesome weeks: being in at the kill when Johnny Burgoyne was finally driven to ground.

The day of reckoning, meanwhile, was drawing closer for the gay British general, who enlivened the campaign with his cards, his liquor, and Madame Rousseau, a commissary's wife, activities strongly disapproved of by Frederica Riedesel, the German general's lady. Detached by General Lincoln, Colonel John Brown, Arnold's old enemy who was now back in service, made a successful raid on Ticonderoga, capturing many prisoners though failing to take the fort itself. While such an assault upon his communications might have been a real inducement to Burgoyne to retreat, he changed his mind when he learned that Sir Henry Clinton was at last moving up the Hudson. Clinton enjoyed a startling success, seizing both Fort Montgomery and Fort Clinton on October 6. Clinton could then write Burgoyne, "*Nous y voici,* and nothing now between us but Gates; I sincerely hope this little success of ours may facilitate your operations." This letter, however, was intercepted by American scouts, and Clinton's luckless messenger was forced to vomit up the silver bullet containing the message and was then hanged. Unaware, therefore, of Clinton's victories, and having placed his troops on short rations on October 3, Burgoyne sought once again to test the strength of the American lines on October 7. He thought he spotted an elevation, possession of which would permit him to enfilade the enemy's entrenchments. Resolving to seize this elevation (none such exists!), he moved out in a reconnaissance in force with fifteen hundred British and Germans, supported by several cannon and one hundred and fifty Indians and Canadians. It was a brave venture but reckless and foolhardy; Gates had shrewdly calculated on the "old gamester," as he alluded to Burgoyne, making some such last desperate thrust.[12]

The contest that opened in mid-afternoon was sheer misery for Arnold to watch. Morgan's riflemen and Dearborn's light infantry assailed Burgoyne's right, Learned the center, and Poor, reinforced by two New York regiments and the Connecticut militia, the British left. Poor's attack on Major John Acland and the Grenadiers was so severe that, though the latter sold their lives dearly, they were overwhelmed and Acland, wounded in both legs, was captured. While Riedesel strove to rally a battalion of Germans in support, Morgan and Dearborn smashed back Burgoyne's right, where Lord Balcarres was stationed with the British Light Infantry. Balcarres, however, proved a stubborn fighter, and, though the Americans thinned his ranks, he gave ground grudgingly. Meanwhile, Burgoyne's center, consisting largely of Germans, remained steady. The issue thus continued undecided, but none was more keenly aware than Arnold that a climax was approaching. Restlessly he had paced up and down through the early part of the battle, muttering to himself. He possessed neither the authority to command nor the permission to fight. A spectator only, he was forced to observe the conflict from the vicinity of his tent but a few rods from Gates's headquarters.

Arnold at last reached the limit of his endurance. Jaw thrust out, bulldog fashion, and pale eyes afire, he harshly shouted that no man would keep him in his tent this day. Then ordering up his horse, he brandished his sword and galloped into the fighting, which Gates in his report to Congress described as "very warm and bloody." Furious at Arnold's departure, Gates ordered an aide, Major John Armstrong, to bring him back. As well order the whirlwind to stop! The young officer, who, toward the end of the war, was actually to propose in the brilliant Newburgh Addresses that the Continental Army mutiny against the Continental Congress, soon lost sight of the chunky, blue-clad figure on the flying bay mare. The future traitor had yet a last great service to render his country.

His performance was incredible. Later, some said he was drunk or had eaten opium; others, that he was mad. The latter were nearer the truth, for his mind was half shaken by frustration, and the battle stirred him to frenzy. The incident in the Second World War in which General George Patton slapped a soldier had something of a counterpart in the Revolution. During the heat of this battle, Arnold, while flourishing his sword and encouraging the troops, struck on the head a Captain Ball of Dearborn's infantry. By the time Ball raised his own weapon to protect himself, Arnold was already off in another part of the field. The next day, when Ball confronted him, Arnold confessed that he remembered nothing of the act and expressed his profound regret at its occurrence. Distracted by the conflict, Arnold had eyes only for what measures were necessary to defeat Burgoyne. In his furious concentration on this objective, individuals, least of all himself, counted for little. Call it madness, call it frenzy, call it a death wish or sheer heroism, his conduct of the battle from the time he arrived produced marvelous results.[13]

Arnold appeared on the field at a crucial moment. The enemy was sore beset and needed, to be defeated, only a kind of immediate direction that Gates could not furnish from two miles away. Arnold supplied the necessary direction and, this time, assumed personal leadership of the assault. As he dashed up, Learned's brigade was just moving to the attack. Some of Learned's men from Norwich and New London recognized him and raised a cheer that swept through the whole brigade. "God bless you!" Arnold shouted, waving his sword in acknowledgment. "Now come on, boys, if the day is long enough, we'll have them all in hell before night!" Truly, as Livingston remarked of the soldiers, "They would follow him to conquest or death." [14]

Though Arnold was not at first successful, he soon took steps to make the American pressure felt. His initial attack was repulsed by the steady Germans. Then, through a misunderstanding, Balcarres withdrew the Light Infantry. At once the Germans, their right uncovered, fell back to Burgoyne's entrenched camp. When General Fraser with the 24th Regiment and the Light Infantry made a stand to cover the retreating reconnaissance force, Arnold regretfully suggested to Morgan that Fraser was a legitimate target for his sharpshooters. Morgan turned the task over to one of his most reliable men, Timothy Murphy, who mortally wounded the stout-hearted Scottish general. With Fraser out of action, Burgoyne, who showed superb personal courage throughout the day, drew all his troops within his entrenchments.[15]

Arnold now turned to the assault. Picking up the brigades of John Patterson and John Glover, he stormed the center held by young Balcarres. But the huge Briton, reinforced, stood his ground. Then the little general on the big brown mare darted to the left between the two lines, hazarding the fire from both sides. Wilkinson, who called it "a mad prank," could not appreciate such courage. He declared that Arnold "exposed himself with great folly and temerity." Once in the clear,

Arnold saw Learned's brigade again, and led them in an attack that cleared the Canadians and Indians out of a number of log cabins in front of Colonel Breymann's Germans. This action uncovered Breymann's left. Arnold now galloped to the right, where he saw Morgan's riflemen moving up with two regiments in support. Instantly putting himself at the head of a body of riflemen and a portion of Colonel John Brooks's regiment, Arnold pointed his sword at "Butcher" Breymann's entrenchments and led the cheering backwoodsmen in a furious charge on the blue-coated Brunswickers. Breymann, it was said, killed four of his own men with his saber when they wanted to retreat before a fifth finally shot him dead. Staggered by the fierce assault, and now practically leaderless, the Germans gave way. But as Arnold spurred his horse through a sally port in the great redoubt, they fired a final volley before they fled.[16]

That last discharge was almost fatal to Arnold. His horse was killed, and as he fell heavily with the animal, a wounded German shot him in the leg that had also taken a ball in the storming of Quebec. But though in sudden agony, Arnold could not forget the battle. "Rush on! Rush on!" he called to the men who burst into the redoubt. Nor did he neglect to spare the life of his assailant. When a soldier rushed up to bayonet the wounded German, Arnold cried out, "Don't hurt him, he did but his duty; he is a fine fellow!" [17]

By this time, however, the long shadows of the autumnal sunset had given way to the deeper shadows of dusk, and the weary troops, unable to see more than a few yards, rested on their arms. Four of them now rigged a litter of poles and blankets and tenderly placed the bleeding general on it, while officers came up to express their regrets.

"Where are you hit?" asked Henry Dearborn, who had made the long march with Arnold to Quebec.

"In the same leg," Arnold replied grimly. "I wish it had been my heart," a sentiment echoed ever since, whether men have admired or hated him.[18]

Then Major Armstrong appeared with Gates's order for Arnold to return to camp. Why Armstrong had not been able to catch up, long before this, with the most conspicuous man on the field leaves one wondering ever so slightly about that young man. At any rate, it is difficult to think of him as being quite so callous as Gates, who was found by Wilkinson, on his return from the field, engaged in a warm dispute on the politics of the Revolution with a distinguished prisoner, Sir Francis Clark, Burgoyne's mortally wounded aide-de-camp. Gates became so enraged at Clark's spirited defense that, calling Wilkinson out of the room, he asked if Wilkinson "had ever heard so impudent a son of a bitch." [19]

But Gates, however unfeeling to Clark, was more honest to Arnold than Wilkinson. A pretty fair sample of the judgment of this devious officer, whom Gates considered a military genius, is his comment on Arnold's performance that seventh day of October, "It is certain, that he neither rendered service, nor deserved credit on that day." On the other hand, Gates, in his report to Congress, wrote that among the wounded was "the gallant Major General Arnold whose leg was fractured by a musket ball as he was forcing the enemy's breastworks." Even this was short shrift, perhaps, considering Arnold's efforts, but it was at least a favorable comment. In fact, had Gates dispensed from the first with the insidious Wilkinson, who was forever purring malice and bad advice into his ear, and possibly with Armstrong and Lewis as well, and had Arnold possessed other aides than Schuyler's former officers, the two generals might have continued on the friendly terms of the year before. At it was, their hatred was now mutual and profound. [20]

Neither Gates and Wilkinson, however, nor Gates's defenders then and since could take from Arnold the credit due him. Much praise was owing to Morgan, Poor, Learned, and the others, but until Arnold appeared they had achieved only a partial triumph. Gates himself did little more than make the original dispositions and order the attack begun. It was Arnold whose dynamic leadership chiefly co-ordinated the field efforts and whose flaming personal courage inspired the troops to follow him in those gallant attacks against Burgoyne's proud regiments. Only Balcarres's stout defense saved the British center, and only the advent of darkness prevented the Americans from capitalizing on their seizure of Breymann's redoubt. Capture of that redoubt turned Burgoyne's position. If he could not retake it in the very near future, he would have to retreat. The loss of the battle was therefore fatal to Burgoyne's hopes, and he knew, perhaps better than anyone else, that Arnold was responsible: ". . . it was his doing," he bluntly informed Clinton. In the next few days, Gates shrewdly cut off the possibility of a successful British retreat, and, with Clinton's sudden withdrawal to New York, Burgoyne was forced to surrender his battered army on October 17 at Saratoga. [21]

Though Gates received the accolade for the splendid triumph, Congress also thanked Arnold and Lincoln for their efforts. And, within a few weeks, Congress restored Arnold's rank within his grade. As Washington wrote Lincoln the following January, "General Arnold is restored to a violated right; and the restitution I hope, will be considered by every gentleman concerned, as I am sure it will by you, as an act of necessary justice." Recognition had not come easily to Arnold, far less so than to Wilkinson, whom Congress breveted a brigadier general simply for bringing to them the good news of Saratoga—and he was so inexcusably tardy that Sam Adams suggested Congress present him with a pair of spurs. But, however exasperating Arnold's experience with Congress and Gates, he was at last firmly established in rank and grade. He was also acclaimed by many as the real hero of the successful Saratoga campaign that brought to the side of the struggling republic the kingdom of France, without whose help the war could not have been won. In those waning months of 1777 and during the winter of 1778, Arnold rode the crest of his popularity, reveling, despite the discomfort of his wound, in the approval of his countrymen. An unknown future beckoned, bright with promise, and who was to say that a sun of greater glory than even that of Saratoga might not yet shine upon his path? [22]

· XVI ·

Convalescence, the New Command, and Money Ventures

Arnold's convalescence was slow, a condition evidently attributable not only to the gravity of his wound but also to his temperament. Dr. James Thacher recorded in his journal on October 12 that Arnold was "very peevish, and impatient under his misfortunes, and required all my attention during the night." Ten weeks later, Dr. J. Brown, one of the attending surgeons at the military hospital in Albany, compared Arnold unfavorably with General Lincoln, who was wounded the day after the battle. "General Lincoln," said the surgeon, "is in a fair way of recovery. . . . He is the patient Christian. . . . Not so the gallant General Arnold, for his wound, though less dangerous in the beginning than Lincoln's is not in so fair a way of healing. He abuses us for a set of pretenders." It requires little stretch of the imagination to hear Arnold's rasping, strident voice and see his choleric face with the full lower lip thrust out belligerently. Possessed of a nervous disposition and great physical vigor, Arnold made a wretched patient. Nevertheless, he informed Congress on January 11 that he was able to sit up and hoped to hobble out of his chamber within a few weeks with the aid of a crutch.[1]

By early spring he was well enough to return to New England in easy stages. In March he was greeted warmly in Middletown, Connecticut, where he was the guest of a shipping merchant now serving as a militia general, Comfort Sage. For several weeks, he remained with Sage and his wife. Occasionally he visited the better-class taverns of the river port where lawyers and merchants and important farmers in from the country would gather and, over a pipe and a glass of wine, discuss the pathetic state of the army at Valley Forge, the decaying shipping along the waterfront, and the deteriorating financial condition of the country. It is likely that Arnold had strong opinions on all these subjects and was not backward in expressing himself; he had visited Middletown often enough to feel at home.

While in Middletown, he sought once again to storm the heart of Betsy Deblois of Boston. Twenty times he had taken up his pen to write her, but his trembling hand, he vowed, had refused to obey the dictates of his heart, so great was his fear of giving offense. He said that he was unable to efface her image; the impression her charms had made was superior to time, absence, misfortune, and her own cruel indifference. Now he hoped her heavenly bosom would expand with friendship and let him know his fate. This request Betsy evidently complied with, and her reply shook this man of battle. She inspired him, he protested, with a pure and exalted passion, and he begged her to suffer her heart to expand with a sensation more tender than friendship and to consider well the consequences to her own happiness and his before she gave her final answer. But Arnold found Betsy's heart more difficult to assail than Breymann's redoubt. She would have nothing to do with the fiery little general, however valorous his reputation and pure and unsullied his motives. Thus rebuffed, Arnold relinquished his pursuit of the fair Loyalist but kept copies of the passionate letters he had written her.[2]

Presently he left for New Haven, arriving there on May 4. Word of his coming flew ahead of him, and his old command, the Footguards, marched out to meet him in all their panoply of scarlet. They were accompanied by blue-coated Continental and militia officers and a large body of soberly clad citizens described locally as "of the first respectability." People showed him every mark of esteem, including the firing of thirteen cannon in his honor. Thus the hero was home from the wars, adored by his sister and his children, admired and applauded by fellow townsmen of high and low estate. He had reached the pinnacle of local fame.[3]

Arnold did not linger long in New Haven, for by May 21 he reported to Washington at Valley Forge, "to the great joy of the army," said

Henry Dearborn. Though he had thrown away his crutch, he was by no means completely recovered. Informed of Arnold's condition, Washington had written him early in May, begging him not to hazard himself by coming too soon. As a testimony of his regard and approval, he sent Arnold, as well as the wounded Lincoln, a set of sword knots, and he closed his letter with the term, "affectionately." What all this meant to the praise-hungry Arnold can well be imagined. Certainly it quickened his desire to report at Valley Forge, where, on May 30, he took the

I *Benedict Arnold Major General* do acknowledge the UNITED STATES of AME-RICA to be Free, Independent and Sovereign States, and declare that the people thereof owe no allegiance or obedience to George the Third, King of Great-Britain; and I renounce, refuse and abjure any allegiance or obedience to him; and I do *Swear* that I will, to the utmost of my power, support, maintain and defend the said United States against the said King George the Third, his heirs and successors, and his or their abettors, assistants and adherents, and will serve the said United States in the office of *Major General* which I now hold, with fidelity, according to the best of my skill and understanding.

Sworn before me this 30th. May 1778 at the Artillery Park Valley Forge HKnox B Arnold B. Gen.

ARNOLD'S OATH OF ALLEGIANCE

famous oath of allegiance required of all officers of the Continental Army. Fat, friendly Henry Knox administered the oath to Arnold, who, because his wound still prevented him from field duty, had been appointed by Washington only two days before to the command of Philadelphia.[4]

Had Washington deliberately planned to crucify Arnold, he could not have treated him more cruelly. Philadelphia soon became the scene of bitter contests of authority between the powerful, state-conscious Council of Pennsylvania and the Continental Congress, whose power was inadequate to support its pretensions. Into this struggle was now interposed a third authority, of which both were suspicious and resentful, the military.

And to compound the difficulty, the military commander was Arnold, with his rash tongue, his arrogance, his avarice, and his intense resentment at the treatment which, until recently, he had received at the hands of Congress. Washington made both good and bad appointments during the war, but despite his best intentions none was worse, given the political situation, than the appointment of the temperamental Arnold as commander of Philadelphia.

Sir Henry Clinton having completed his evacuation of the city on June 18, Arnold moved in the following day. Almost at once he stirred up hostile opinion. Philadelphia contained a great deal of property belonging to Loyalists, and patriots returning to the capital had their own ideas of vengeance. With the idea of forestalling disorder, Congress directed Washington "to prevent the removal, transfer, or sale of any goods, wares, or merchandise, in possession of the inhabitants . . . until the property of the same shall be ascertained by a joint committee; consisting of persons appointed by the supreme executive council of the State of Pennsylvania, to wit, so far as to determine, whether any, or what part thereof may belong to the king of Great Britain, or to any of his subjects." Enclosing a copy of this resolution, Washington, in turn, directed the new commander of Philadelphia to take every prudent step to preserve order and to adopt such measures as should appear most effectual and least offensive for compliance with the views of Congress respecting the disposition of property.[5]

Arnold responded with a proclamation on June 19. Drawn up under the guidance of several prominent Philadelphians, especially Joseph Reed, member of both the Congress and the Executive Council of Pennsylvania, this proclamation established martial law. British and Loyalist property, "European, East or West India goods, iron, leather, shoes, wines, and provisions of every kind, beyond the necessary use of a private family" were to be reported "in order that the quartermaster, commissary and clothier generals may contract for such goods as are wanted for the use of the army." Until this procedure was completed, Arnold closed stores and shops throughout the city. This state of affairs lasted a week.[6]

The indignation that flared up may have startled even him. Although the action was a necessary and routine compliance with his instructions, many Philadelphians regarded it as a capricious exercise of authority for which Arnold alone was responsible. And as the succeeding weeks and months revealed Arnold's arrogance, love of high living, and desire for personal gain, public opinion unfriendly to him gathered weight and influence. It scarcely mattered that in this first instance he was but the instrument for executing the will of the civil authorities; his subsequent conduct served only to confirm and solidify the ill opinion in which he was now held.

One of his early acts that provoked criticism was his moving into Sir William Howe's headquarters, the John Penn house on Market Street, and living there as grandly as had the British general himself. Many people wondered how Arnold could afford such style. As a matter of fact, he could not, but living beyond his means was an old Arnold custom over which neither the responsibility of position nor prudence could prevail. If his income from his stagnant trading business and his officer's salary (now sadly in arrears) was insufficient, he explored other channels. One such channel evidently had its origin in an agreement with the clothier general of the army, James Mease, and Mease's deputy, William West. According to this arrangement, effected on June 23, it was agreed, first, that "by purchasing goods and necessaries for the use of the public, sundry articles not wanted for that purpose may be obtained" and, secondly, that "all such goods and merchandise which are or may be bought by the clothier general or persons appointed by him, shall be sold for the joint equal benefit of the subscribers and be purchased at their risk." This arrangement with its employment of public credit as capital and its private division of the proceeds realized on the purchase and sale of goods over and beyond the needs of the army was not known until after the treason, but it may well account for part of Arnold's income.[7]

Less certain as a source of income, and less reprehensible, were two arrangements which he made in July, one with John R. Livingston of New York, the other with Moses Seixas, a Newport merchant. On the chance that New York might fall to the Americans within a few months, Arnold directed Livingston to buy up a quantity of goods. As for the other, "Mr. Seixas," Arnold informed General Sullivan, who was besieging the British in Newport, "has a plan to propose to you which I believe will be agreeable. If so, I have promised him I will be concerned and think it may be of service to the public as well as conducive to our private interest. If you approve the plan, I will take one-third or one-fourth the risk." As the historian of the Arnold conspiracy declared, not in extenuation but in explanation, "Other American generals besides Arnold, paid in falling currency at a time of rising prices, even engaged in speculations, like many citizens whose love of country did not interfere with their love of profits." Though his arrangements with Livingston and Seixas may never have borne fruit, they indicate that Arnold was leaving no stone unturned in his search for additional income.[8]

Opportunity seemed to open for him in the vicissitudes of two ships, the *Charming Nancy* and the *Active*. The first was a New England-built schooner owned by Robert Shewell, a Philadelphian, and James Seagrove and William Constable, New Yorkers who found Philadelphia a more profitable place in which to operate while the British had been in possession. On June 4, a week after Arnold's appointment to the command of Philadelphia, Shewell visited him at Valley Forge requesting permission for the schooner to put into an American-held port and there sell her miscellaneous cargo. Unbeknownst to either Arnold or Shewell at the time, Congress, then sitting at York, passed, also on June 4, a resolution prohibiting the removal of property from the city, the very resolution which Arnold subsequently enforced by closing the shops and stores. Arnold gave Shewell the permission requested for the master of the *Charming Nancy* to take the schooner into any American port without "umbrage or molestation" by American officials. Although Arnold eventually possessed a substantial share in the enterprise, he appears to have had no such vested interest when he gave Shewell the pass.[9]

The *Charming Nancy* caused Arnold a great deal of trouble. Captured by an American privateer, she was brought into Egg Harbor, New Jersey, where a prize court released her. But suddenly the British swooped down on the port from the sea, and Arnold, disturbed, dispatched twelve government wagons to bring back part of the schooner's cargo to Philadelphia. Arnold never insisted that the cargo was public property, and he fully intended to pay for the use of the wagons. Furthermore, as the deputy quartermaster subsequently admitted, his use of the wagons at the time caused no inconvenience to the service. Back in Philadelphia by October 30, the property was sold, and Arnold received one-half the proceeds; his concern for the cargo can therefore be understood. Both his concern and his employment of the wagons point to a previous definite arrangement between Arnold and Shewell. If it was not effected on June 4, then it must have been made either between June 4 and the time the word was received of the British expedition to Egg Harbor, or immediately after news of the expedition arrived. In any event Arnold was not guilty of anything illegal, though he was wide open to attacks on his prudence and sense of propriety. His enemies in Pennsylvania were presently to try to make out a stronger case.[10]

Unlike the *Charming Nancy,* the case of the *Active* proved of long duration. The *Active* was a British sloop sailing from Jamaica with provisions and stores for the British in New York. Aboard her were four Americans now forced to serve as members of the crew and later to be sent to the prison hulks in New York. One of the Americans was the second mate, Gideon Olmsted, a singularly tough young privateersman from Hartford, Connecticut, who had been master of a privateer recently taken by a British cruiser. Determined not to rot aboard a prison hulk, he succeeded, with the others' assistance, in seizing the sloop at midnight, September 6, and he refused to be intimidated when the imprisoned British captain threatened to fire his pistol into a keg of gunpowder. Shortly after Olmsted changed the course for Egg Harbor, the *Active* was taken in charge by the Pennsylvania brig *Convention,* in company with the privateer *Gerard,* and brought into Philadelphia. The Pennsylvanians claimed that they had assisted in the capture, a contention Olmsted flatly denied. Unfortunately for him, a Pennsylvania admiralty court declared against him, and he received but one quarter of the prize money.

At this point, Arnold entered the situation. Olmsted was a brave man whose courage was of no avail in this rough treatment at the hands of Pennsylvania justice, and Arnold, who may have seen something of a parallel with himself, adopted Olmsted's cause as his own. He did this in two respects: not only did he provide for an appeal of the decision to Congress but he also made a secret agreement with Olmsted for a half interest in the ultimate return. In an affair which eventually involved upward of one hundred thousand dollars in prize money, such an interest was no inconsequential matter. Olmsted won his appeal, too, because on December 15 the Congressional committee on appeals ruled that after the costs and charges of the trial were paid, ship and cargo should be sold and the proceeds, minus the expenses attending the sale, be paid to Olmsted and the three other Americans.

But if Arnold's eyes gleamed at the golden harvest about to become his, it was not for long. In January, 1779, the Pennsylvania court not only challenged the committee's decision but seized the money realized on the sale of the cargo. Thus confronted with a show of Pennsylvania power, Congress refused to go farther on the ground that to press contempt charges might endanger the public peace. The case lingered in the courts until 1809 when the Supreme Court of the United States compelled Pennsylvania to pay Olmsted the money due him. Arnold lost heavily in the speculation. He had supported Olmsted and the others for months and had borrowed £12,000 from Jean Holker, the new French consul; he failed, however, to induce Holker to take a flyer in the case. Arnold's need for money clearly showed no signs of abating.[11]

Other schemes for making money included trading within and without the British lines and privateering. Together with Seagrove and Constable, he made an agreement in November, 1778, with James Duncan, a Canadian captain in American service. Duncan, who was going to New York (which was expected soon to be evacuated), was to buy up quantities of goods for what capital he himself could produce on the joint accounts and risks of the partners. If the British intended to remain in the city, he was to convey to the subscribers what goods he could get out. This last provision fell within the trade ban of Congress and was strictly illegal. The whole arrangement was, in fact, a strange one, but evidently it flourished; when Arnold submitted to the British a list of losses incurred because of his treason, he included £1200 as his share of profits on £10,000 worth of goods bought and sold jointly with Seagrove and Constable.[12]

As for privateering, Arnold's activities have been greatly exaggerated. During the war, he was concerned with only one ship, the *General McDougall*, formerly a British vessel. She was bonded for $10,000 to carry a letter of marque and was commissioned on April 6, 1778 while Arnold was still recuperating from his wound in Middletown, Connecticut. He was one of four owners. Hopes of realizing profits from this venture were illusory, because, the last of May, she was overtaken by a British man of war after a chase of eight hours and, though mounting ten guns, she hauled down her flag without firing a shot. By the time Arnold learned of this misfortune, he had already assumed command of Philadelphia and was exploring other sources of income.[13]

Arnold had not been in command of Philadelphia for long before he became bored and restless, and perhaps was none too well. Elias Boudinot thought that, in the last of June, Arnold had worked himself ill, while, on July 4, Major David Franks, aide to Arnold, wrote Washington that his commander was afflicted with "a violent oppression" in his stomach. Possibly these upsets occurred as a result of his fretting at inactivity. And it was probably this restlessness, combined with his need for money, that prompted him to try for a career in the navy. Though his wound still prevented him from taking the field, he was certain it would not be so great a handicap aboard ship, and he so informed Washington. But when he requested the commander-in-chief's sentiments respecting a naval command, Washington confessed that he was not a competent judge in marine matters. Arnold was reluctant to let the matter drop, and, in September, he presented to Congress a scheme for seizing British islands in the West Indies; at least that was the objective according to the first French minister to the United States, Conrad Alexandre Gerard. Unfortunately for Arnold, his naval hopes were never realized. Had it been otherwise, he might have won further fame and fortune, married a different woman or none at all, avoided the intense controversy that presently developed with Pennsylvania, and remained loyal to the country for which he had fought so hard. Or he might have finished the war in a British naval prison. The naval aspirations, however, are only one of the many fascinating "ifs" in Arnold's career.[14]

That summer of 1778, while Arnold was shaking down into the Philadelphia command for which he was so profoundly unsuited, he showed his gratitude in a practical way for kindness rendered him by a friend now dead. Among those killed at Bunker Hill was Dr. Joseph Warren, the man chiefly responsible for organizing an effective armed opposition in Massachusetts after the affair at Concord and Lexington. It had been Warren who was instrumental in sending Arnold to take Ticonderoga. Learning now that Warren's orphaned children were in want, Arnold sent a letter to Miss Mercy Scollay, who is alleged to have been engaged to Dr. Warren to become his second wife:

> About three months ago I was informed that my late worthy friend General Warren left his affairs unsettled, and that, after paying his debts, a very small matter, if any thing, would remain for the education of his children, who, to my great surprise, I find have been entirely neglected by the State. Permit me to beg your continuing your care of the daughter, and that you will at present take charge of the education of the son. I make no doubt that his relations will consent that he shall be under your care. My intention is to use my interest with Congress to provide for the family. If they decline it, I make no doubt of a handsome collection by private subscription. At all events, I will provide for them in a manner suitable to their birth, and the grateful sentiments I shall ever feel for the memory of my friend. I have sent to you by Mr. Hancock five hundred dollars for the present. I wish to have Richard clothed handsomely, and sent to the best school in Boston. Any expense you are at, please call on me for, and it shall be paid with thanks.[15]

When Congress neglected to do anything for the children, Arnold persisted in his interest. He sent Mercy five hundred dollars more on account in February, 1779, and continued to press Congress for action in behalf of the children. The greatest obstacle within that body was the Massachusetts delegation, Elbridge Gerry in particular doing everything he could to oppose Arnold's application. Gerry's reason was that Massachusetts should assume this expense. That state, however, proved dilatory, and a private subscription, also opposed by Gerry as dishonorable to Massachusetts and to Warren's friends and relations, failed miserably. Finally, thanks in good part to Arnold's refusal to admit defeat, Congress resolved to provide adequately for the children, a move of which Arnold had the pleasure of informing Mercy Scollay within seven weeks of the climax of his treasonous conspiracy. In a man whose name was forever blackened by the infamy of his defection it is refreshing to discover such willingness to assist the needy; for all too many death seems to cancel debts of gratitude.[16]

· XVII ·

Marriage to Peggy Shippen and Controversy with Pennsylvania

AMONG the wealthy families of Philadelphia, few enjoyed greater prestige than the Shippen family. William Shippen was surgeon general of the Continental army. Edward Shippen, his cousin, was a prominent jurist whose neutrality during the war did not prevent his subsequent elevation as chief justice of Pennsylvania. Edward lived on the west side of Fourth Street in a splendid house that proved a magnet for many of Sir William Howe's staff during the British occupation. The officers came not primarily because of Shippen, for all that he was no Anglophobe and possessed a fine legal mind, but because of his three daughters. All were attractive, vivacious, and fun-loving, and the most charming and graceful was Peggy. Born on June 11, 1760, and the youngest, she had been spoiled from childhood and was used to having her own way. Only recently, however, she had suffered a sharp disappointment. This was when her father refused to permit any of his daughters to attend the magnificent farewell revels for Howe, the Mischianza, because of the scandalous nature of the costumes they proposed to wear. Usually she encountered no such obstacle to her will.

Peggy found the British occupation a most enjoyable experience, thanks largely to Captain John André, a redcoat gallant and member of Howe's staff. André, before he joined the army, had fancied himself a poet. His suit rejected by blond Honora Sneyd in the Midlands of England, he discovered the army to be an invigorating change, and eventually went to Canada as a lieutenant in the 7th Regiment. Taken prisoner at Fort Chambly in November, 1775, he was subsequently exchanged. In the Pennsylvania campaign he served with conspicuous ability as a staff officer under General Charles "No Flint" Grey of Paoli Massacre fame. During the occupation of Philadelphia, André's charming, debonair presence and ready wit enlivened many an hour at the headquarters of General Howe, with whom he now served. He wrote plays, designed backdrops and costumes, and became both actor and impresario. He also paid assiduous attention to Peggy Shippen, who was captivated by the brilliant young officer. Whether or not he was seriously her suitor remains an unsettled question. At any rate, he often visited at the Shippen house and escorted her to various gay routs; he made a pen-and-ink sketch of her that shows a sweet, determined face with a hint of petulance about the mouth; he personally drew up the pattern for the Turkish-pantalooned costume which she was to wear at the Mischianza but was not allowed to; and he wrote to her after he returned to New York. Sir Henry Clinton, succeeding Howe in command of the British armies in America, found André's industry and charm indispensable. When the opportunity presented itself, he made him his adjutant general, a capacity in which André, promoted to a major, proved extraordinarily capable, particularly in his intelligence work.

For Peggy and the young ladies of Loyalist and neutral families who had lived gay lives indeed with the British, the departure of André and his comrades left a gap that the Americans appeared unable to fill. Arnold, however, tried his best to supply some color. He dashed about in his coach-and-four, entertained lavishly, and encouraged with his presence the performance of plays at the Old Southwark Theater. In this last activity he was presently thwarted, for Congress so vehemently disapproved of plays that it resolved in mid-October of 1778 to recommend to the states that theatrical entertainments, horse racing, and gaming be suppressed. Arnold's entertaining also brought rebukes in the press for its unseemliness, while charges were bitter that he included more than patriots in his invitations. Joseph Reed, who was becoming a far more dangerous enemy than John Brown ever was because of his membership on the Council of Pennsylvania, wrote indignantly to General Greene on November 5, "Will you not think it extraordinary that General Arnold made a public entertainment the night before last of which not only numerous Tory ladies and the wives and daughters of persons proscribed by the State and now with the enemy at New York, formed a very considerable number?" But as Arnold explained subsequently, "I have not yet learned to carry on a warfare against women or to consider every man as disaffected to our glorious cause who, from an opposition in sentiment to those in power in the state of Pennsylvania, may, by the clamour of party, be styled a Tory." [1]

Sometime during 1778, perhaps in the summer at a private party, Arnold met Peggy Shippen. It was an ill-starred day for both, had they but known it, particularly for the willful, impressionable Peggy. Arnold was quickly taken by the young beauty. On September 25, he wrote her a letter that resembled so closely the epistle he had addressed to Betsy Deblois in April that he must simply have drawn its copy out of his desk and reworked it. This was either economy of effort carried to a ludicrous extent or a conviction that he could never surpass in fervor and felicitous expression the language employed in the spring. Again he protested that twenty times he had taken up his pen to write but his trembling hand refused to obey the dictates of his heart. Peggy's charms, like Betsy's, had lighted an inextinguishable flame in his bosom, while her "heavenly image is too deeply impressed ever to be effaced." His passion was founded not simply on her personal charms but also on her sweetness of disposition and goodness of heart. On her alone his happiness depended. As with Betsy, he entreated Peggy to suffer her "heavenly bosom . . . to expand with a sensation more soft, more tender than friendship." "Consult your own happiness," he begged her, "and if incompatible, forget there is so unhappy a wretch; for may I perish if I would give you one moment's inquietude to purchase the greatest possible felicity for myself. Whatever my fate may be, my most ardent wish is for your happiness, and my latest breath will be to implore the blessing of heaven on the idol and only wish of my heart." [2]

The courtship proceeded in a decorous and unhurried manner. Perhaps, in fact, its movement was a little too stately for the impetuous Arnold. In October, Sarah Bache, Benjamin Franklin's daughter, wrote her father concerning her own baby daughter, Betty, "You cant think how fond of kissing she is, and she gives such old-fashioned smacks General Arnold says he would give a good deal to have her for a schoolmistress to teach the young ladies how to kiss." Though under close siege by the wounded hero, Peggy was evidently not letting her heart overcome her reason. [3]

In her cautious conduct Peggy was undoubtedly influenced by the counsel of her father. Judge Shippen was none too eager to see his youngest daughter become Arnold's wife. Very likely Arnold's crippled condition, the disparity in age, the general's already having three children dependent on him, and the fact that Arnold was a parvenu socially made the aristocratic Shippen wary of the match. Even before he wrote his impassioned letter of September 25 to Peggy, Arnold had observed the proprieties by writing Peggy's father for his daughter's hand. He declared that his fortune, while not large, was sufficient to make Peggy and himself happy. He hoped that his private character was irreproachable—his public character, he declared, was well known. Finally he expressed his trust that "Our difference in political sentiments will . . . be no bar to my happiness." [4]

Though Shippen eventually gave his consent, he did not wish the courtship hastened. On December 21, 1778, he wrote his own father, "I gave my daughter Betsy to Neddy Burd [Major Edward Burd] last Thursday evening, and all is jollity and mirth. My youngest daughter is much solicited by a certain general, on the same subject; whether this will take place or not, depends upon circumstances. If it should, I think it will not be until spring." Shippen fails to mention the circumstances he had in mind, but it seems likely that he blew now hot and now cold on the prospect and wished something might occur to prevent it. On February 15, 1779, twelve days after charges were preferred against Arnold by Pennsylvania, Shippen, in writing to a friend, said, "I see there are a number of things laid to the charge of General Arnold; I wish you would favor me with a few lines concerning that matter." [5]

In the last analysis, however, the decision depended on Peggy herself. Of Arnold's passion there was no doubt—and no attempt at secrecy, either. Mrs. Robert Morris remarked in a letter in November, 1778, "I must tell you that Cupid has given our little general a more mortal wound, than all the host of Britons could, unless his present conduct can expiate for his past—Miss Peggy Shippen is the fair one." In a letter felicitating Betsy Shippen on her marriage, Edward Burd's sister wrote on December 30, "Pray tell me, will Cousin Peggy follow your example? Every one tells me so with such confidence that I am laughed at for my unbelief. Does she know her own mind yet?" [6]

Edward Burd throws a little light on Peggy's coy behavior. To his brother-in-law, Burd wrote, "You mention a report of another wedding being likely to take place in the family. You may recollect my suspicion, when I last saw you notwithstanding the refusal [by the Judge, according to Shippen family tradition]. My expectations have been answered: I was almost sure it could not be otherwise. A lame leg is at present the only obstacle. But a lady who makes that the only objection, and is firmly persuaded it will soon be well can never retract, however expressly conditional an engagement may have been made. However we have every reason to hope it will be well again, tho' I am not so sanguine as he is with respect to the time; but the leg will be a couple of inches shorter than the other and disfigured." [7]

Peggy's reluctance amazed others in the family, too. Elizabeth Tilghman, first cousin to Peggy, wrote Betsy Shippen Burd a delightful, chatty letter on January 29, 1779 in which she alluded with some surprise to the situation: ". . . when is he [Arnold] likely to convert our little Peggy?" she asked. "They say she intends to surrender soon. I thought the fort would not hold out so long. Well after all there is nothing like perseverance, and a regular attack." [8]

Arnold's persistence eventually crumbled the defenses of the lovely Peggy and her cautious father. On March 22, Arnold secured possession of Mount Pleasant, a grand estate of ninety-six acres in what is now Fairmount Park, the house having been built by the father of Captain John MacPherson, General Montgomery's aide, who, like his commander, died in the assault on Quebec. Arnold settled the estate on himself and Peggy for life, but otherwise was content to rent it and continue in the Penn house until he found less expensive accommodations. A little more than a fortnight later, April 8, the thirty-eight-year-old Arnold and the eighteen-year-old Peggy were married in Judge Shippen's mansion. An eyewitness of the wedding reported that "Arnold during the marriage ceremony was supported by a soldier, and when seated his disabled limb was propped upon a camp-stool." For one of Arnold's temperament and pride such assistance must have been intensely humiliating, but at least he had scored another victory: Peggy Shippen's heart and hand were his at last. [9]

The same good fortune did not attend his public life. The authorities criticized him for his money-making activities, for his alleged favoritism to Loyalists, for his extravagant entertainments. One of his most unsparing critics was Timothy Matlack, Secretary of the Council of Pennsylvania, and with Matlack he ran into trouble as early as October, 1778. Matlack's son William was a Pennsylvania militia sergeant whom one of Arnold's aides, Major David Franks, sent for a barber. Thinking such duty not properly that of a soldier, William complained to his father. Timothy agreed with his son, and, in the manner reminiscent of certain fathers in more recent wars, he dashed off a letter of protest. Timothy's letter, however, was addressed not to a Congressman but to Arnold himself. Arnold replied on October 6 in a letter that summed up succinctly what, in his opinion, should happen when a man puts on the uniform of his state or country. "No man," he asserted, "has a higher sense of the rights of a citizen and freeman than myself. They are dear to me, as I have fought and bled for them, and as it is my highest ambition and most ardent wish to resume the character of a free citizen whenever the service of my country will permit. At the same time, let me observe, that whenever necessity obliges the citizen to assume the character of a soldier, the former is entirely lost in the latter, and the respect due to the citizen is by no means to be paid to the soldier any further than his rank entitles him to it; this is evident from the necessity of military discipline, the basis of which is implicit obedience, and however the feelings of a citizen may be hurt, he has this consolation, that it is a sacrifice he pays to the safety of his country." Arnold's was a hard doctrine in a land that prided itself on its individualism and freedom, but an army, by its very nature, can never be completely democratic.[10]

Far from mollifying Matlack, this letter threw him into a rage. Franks's order, he insisted, was highly improper, and if Arnold supported Franks, he, Matlack, would withdraw William from the service rather than submit him to further orders that would lower him in the esteem of the world. Furthermore, Matlack would consider it his duty to publish his reasons for so doing. To this announcement Arnold replied on October 12 that he could perceive that his sentiments were not clearly understood. But, he continued, "it is needless to discuss a subject which will perhaps be determined more by the feelings than the reason of men. If the declaration that you will withdraw your son from the service and publish the reason is intended as a threat, you have mistaken your object. I am not to be intimidated by a newspaper. To vindicate the rights of citizens I became a soldier and bear the marks upon me; I hope your candor will acquit me of the inconsistency of invading what I have fought and bled to defend." If Franks had delivered his order in a manner that was haughty, imperious, or insolent, then he was not without fault, Arnold added. But the matter lay between the sergeant and the major, and he did not propose to intervene.[11]

Although in this exchange Arnold had combined reasonableness with firmness, Matlack never forgave him: he harried him in both press and Council. The *Pennsylvania Packet* carried an anonymous article on November 12, 1778 in which the writer condemned the secret agreement between Arnold and Gideon Olmsted respecting Arnold's half interest in the sale of the *Active* and her cargo; the anonymous author was later discovered to be Matlack. On November 14, the *Packet* published a communication from one who signed himself, "A Militia Man." Presumably written by William Matlack, but probably by Timothy, the letter commented acidly on the barber incident. Though willing to serve when needed, Matlack objected to being called upon "out of mere parade, to stand at the door of any man, however great." Furthermore, he whined, "at the whim and caprice of any of his suite to be ordered on the most menial services, piques my pride and hurts my feelings most sensibly. . . ." He could not believe "that the commanding officer views himself as exposed to any real danger in this city. From a public enemy there can be none. From Tories, if such there be amongst us, he has nothing to fear, for they are all remarkably fond of him. The Whigs, to a man, are sensible of his great merit and former services and would risk their lives in his defence." [12]

The implication in his remark about Arnold's relations with Tories was grossly unfair but typical of the atmosphere of growing suspicion and tension that existed within the city. General John Cadwalader, an officer who bowed to none in his patriotism, testified in a letter to General Greene on December 5 that Arnold "is become very unpopular among the men in power in Congress, and among those of this state in general. Every gentleman, every man who has a liberal way of thinking highly approve his conduct. He has been civil to every gentleman who has taken the oath, intimate with none. The ladies, as well those who have taken an active part (as our low-lived fellows will call it) as those who are good approved whigs, have been visited and treated with the greatest civilities. These are charges too absurd to deserve a serious answer. They may serve the purposes of party or faction, but can never injure the character of a man to whom his country is so much indebted." [13]

Cadwalader put his finger on the crux of the difficulty: the extreme patriot faction did not want an objective attitude on the part of the commander of Philadelphia, or, for that matter, anyone else. As Reed declared scornfully, in a letter of November 4 to Greene, "New characters are emerging from obscurity like insects after a storm. Treason, disaffection to the interests of America and even assistance to the British interest is called openly only error of judgment, which candour and liberality of sentiment will overlook." Hence the Council of Pennsylvania, with Reed and Matlack beating the drums of persecution, proceeded to ferret out twenty-three collaborators and hanged two of them notwithstanding the action of the jury in recommending clemency and the drafting of petitions of mercy to which many patriots put their signatures.[14]

Though scarcely charitable, Reed's sentiments are understandable; he spoke for those patriots who had sacrificed much for the cause and who had had all they could tolerate from active or "concealed" Tories. He himself had been a soldier, but most of the Council were civilians, and, as has been so aptly remarked, "War hath no fury like a non-combatant." Men were Whigs or they were enemies of the nation; and, if enemies, everything they had done or said in the past could be used against them. Now was the time for all good patriots to rally to their country. The currency was tobogganing to but a fraction of its original value, there was fear that the French alliance might merely signify exchanging King George for King Louis, and too many people were wondering if the war was worth the sacrifice of so much that they had enjoyed as part of the Empire. Confronted with such conditions, the extreme patriots decided on a rigorous policy of "no compromise." So far as the duration of the Revolution was concerned, Reed's was the voice of the future. He hated Tories of whatever complexion, a feeling shared by George Washington himself. By displaying liberality, Arnold had made a fatal mistake; in Reed's eyes he was virtually declaring himself a Tory-lover despite the fact that at this time he was merely a soldier trying to remain aloof from political feuds.[15]

Arnold presently became so disgusted with the prevailing party strife that he welcomed the possibility of quitting Pennsylvania altogether for New York. When General Schuyler remarked in a letter that New York wished to give him some mark of approbation for his services in that state, Arnold, on November 30, thought of securing a large estate either on the frontiers or on lands confiscated from the Loyalists. The property belonging to Major Philip Skene, who had assisted Burgoyne, looked attractive to him, all thirty-four thousand acres of it, while a New York Congressman had mentioned the forfeited estates of the Johnsons along the Mohawk River. Arnold had an idea of forming a settlement consisting of officers and soldiers who had served under him. John Jay of New York, now president of Congress, liked the shape of Arnold's project, as did the entire New York delegation, which jointly solicited Governor George Clinton of New York to do his utmost to secure the assistance of the legislature. Jay, in writing privately to Clinton about Arnold, expressed a wish that the legislature "may recollect the services he has rendered to his country, and the value of such a citizen to any State that may gain him. . . . I have no doubt but that generosity to Arnold will be justice to the State." Unfortunately difficulties in accomplishing the project proved greater than anticipated, and it was dropped.[16]

While the result of this development was still pending, Arnold set out for Poughkeepsie on February 3, 1779 in order to consult with Schuyler about it. Though regretful at leaving Peggy, he was relieved to be out of Philadelphia. As recently as January 21, Matlack, acting for the Council, had revived the affair of the wagons in addressing a series of questions to Arnold. The latter replied that he failed to understand the reason for Matlack's letter since the facts were already available to them. He told the Council, moreover, that he was ready at any time to answer for his conduct to Congress or to General Washington, to whom alone he was accountable. Reed, who was now president of the Council, then called on Congress for justice, expressed the hope that it would detain Arnold, and requested that he be prohibited from exercising further command in the city until the charges against him were examined. Before the Council met to draw up its complaints in a formal resolution, Arnold left for Poughkeepsie. On the next day, a courier caught up with him at Bristol and handed him a copy of the Council's charges. Copies were also delivered to the governors of all the states and to the press.[17]

Instead of returning at once, Arnold chose to continue on to Washington's headquarters at Middlebrook. Consultation with the commander-in-chief convinced him he should have recourse to a court-martial. On February 8, he explained in a letter to Schuyler that he had been presented with "a number of charges against me for maladministration while commanding in the city. This cruel and villainous proceeding is the more aggravating as my intention of leaving the city has been publicly known for a month past. I have wrote to Congress requesting a court martial to inquire into my conduct. This with the excessive badness of the road, to my great mortification, will oblige me to return to Philadelphia and deprives me of the pleasure of seeing you for the present." Even so, there were compensations in going back: he would see Peggy again. "Heavens!" he exclaimed in a letter of the same date to her, "what must I have suffered had I continued my journey—the loss of happiness for a few dirty acres. I can almost bless the villainous roads, and more *villainous men,* who oblige me to return." [18]

Arnold, however, could not conceal his bitterness at the Council's treatment of him. To Peggy he confessed that he was almost as tired of human nature as he was of his journey. Ignoring his own dubious money ventures, he added, "I daily discover so much baseness and ingratitude among mankind that I almost blush at being of the same species, and could quit the stage without regret was it not for some gentle, generous souls like my dear Peggy, who still retain the lively impression of their Maker's image, and who, with smiles of benignity and goodness, make all happy around them. Let me beg of you not to suffer the rude attacks on me to give you one moment's uneasiness; they can do me no injury." But contrary to Arnold's assurance to Peggy, the attacks could do him a good deal of injury, and he was scarcely so unrealistic as to deceive himself on this score. If indeed he failed to recognize the measure of his enemies' strength, he was soon to discover it. The Council of Pennsylvania was a band of single-minded, vindictive patriots bent on ruining the commander of Philadelphia.[19]

· XVIII ·

Arnold at Bay

"**I** THINK all the world are running mad," exclaimed Elizabeth Tilghman to her cousin, Betsy Shippen Burd. "What demon has possessed the people with respect to General Arnold, he is certainly much abused; ungrateful monsters, to attack a character that has been looked up to, in more instances than one, since this war commenced." Well might she be perplexed, for the attack of the Council of Pennsylvania was far more serious than Arnold or any of his friends anticipated. If its virulence won for him considerable sympathy within the army and among certain of the more liberal-minded of the people, there were still many Philadelphians who were delighted to see the arrogant general cut down to size. In vain did Major Matthew Clarkson, one of his aides, publish a plea for people to suspend judgment on an absent man accused by authorities who unjustly published and circulated their charges before trial. In vain did Arnold himself issue a similar plea from the army camp. The extremists among the patriots in Philadelphia and the anti-militarists on the Council had found a common meeting-ground in their hatred of the commander of the city.[1]

The charges against him were eight in number. First, he had given a pass to the *Charming Nancy* without knowledge of the Pennsylvania authorities or of the commander-in-chief. Second, he had shut up shops and stores "so as even to prevent officers of the army from purchasing, while he privately made considerable purchases for his own benefit, as is alleged and believed." Third, he had imposed "menial offices upon the sons of freemen of this State, when called forth . . . to perform militia duty." Fourth, he had interposed in the case of the *Active* "by an illegal and unworthy purchase of the suit, at a low and inadequate price . . . to which may, in some degree, be ascribed the delay of justice . . . and the dispute in which the State may probably be involved with Congress hereupon." Fifth, he had appropriated wagons of the state for the transportation of private property. Sixth, he wrote a letter recommending a person to cross into the enemy's lines and had Clarkson sign it when such power of recommendation, by resolution, had been given expressly by Congress to the Council of Pennsylvania. Seventh, he had made "an indecent and disrespectful refusal" to explain the transaction respecting the wagons. Eighth, he had manifested "discouragement and neglect . . . to civil, military and other characters who have adhered to the cause of their country . . . with an entire different conduct towards those of another character. . . ." To underline its disapproval of Arnold, the Council concluded, "And if this command has been, as is generally believed, supported by an expense of four or five thousand pounds per annum to the United States, we freely declare we shall very unwillingly pay any share of expenses thus incurred." [2]

Though well aware that it was on delicate ground, and apprehensive lest it antagonize the powerful Council, the committee of Congress to which the charges were committed tried to be fair and delivered a clear and forthright report on March 17, 1779. It considered the first charge (giving a pass to the *Charming Nancy*), the second (closing the shops and stores), the third (imposing menial offices on the sons of freemen), and the fifth (appropriating the wagons) to be charges triable only in a court-martial. The fourth charge (cutting in on the prize money of the *Active*) was declared an offense triable only in a common law court. The committee regarded the sixth charge (giving a letter of recommendation), the seventh (indecently refusing to explain about the wagons), and the eighth (favoring Loyalists) as offenses neither triable in a court-martial or common law court nor subject to any punishment other than the displeasure of Congress.

Though the committee repeatedly pressed the Council for evidence, it received satisfaction only for the fifth charge (appropriating the wagons) and the seventh (refusing to explain about the wagons). Accordingly, after several fruitless applications for evidence, and after waiting for three weeks, the committee formulated a number of resolutions. It declared that with respect to the first and second charges (issuing a pass to the *Charming Nancy* and profiting from closing the shops and stores), there was not only no evidence to prove these but the charges were fully explained by Arnold and the appearance they carried of criminality was completely obviated by unquestionable evidence. As for the third charge (imposing menial duties), this should be transmitted to General Washington for action according to martial law. The fourth charge (securing part of the *Active* prize money) was pronounced of a civil nature and, together with the eighth charge (favoring Loyalists), was dismissed for lack of evidence. The committee resolved that the fifth charge (appropriating the wagons) should, like the third, be transmitted to the commander-in-chief for action according to martial law. The sixth charge (sending a letter of recommendation) was deemed neither a violation of the Congressional resolution nor a usurpation of authority. About the seventh charge (refusing in an indecent and disrespectful manner to explain about the wagons) the committee had very positive opinions. It declared that the letter, if not expressed in terms of perfect civility, "is not exprest in terms of indignity." In the committee's judgment, "the after conduct of the said Executive Council towards the said General and the unexampled measures they took to obtain satisfaction, totally and absolutely preclude all right to concessions or acknowledgments." [3]

The committee had done all it could for Arnold, and if its report by no means exonerated him, neither did it truckle to Pennsylvania. Heartened by this support, Arnold sent a letter to Congress begging an immediate decision. He complained that he was compelled to endure calumnies and misrepresentations circulated daily by people who considered themselves secure while the issue remained undetermined. And indeed he had had to withstand a great deal of abuse on the streets and in the press, particularly from Timothy Matlack. This indefatigable and relentless enemy threw the John Brown charges at him again in the *Pennsylvania Packet* for February 27, 1779. When Arnold retorted on March 4 to this "envy and malice" by pointing out that Congress, after investigation, had regarded Brown's charges as cruel and groundless, Matlack declared on March 6 that although Brown may have been somewhat too inclusive, he—Matlack—often wondered, on meeting Arnold's coach in the streets and observing his manner of living, how the general could afford these riches unless they flowed from the plunder of Montreal. [4]

In plain language, Pennsylvania was out to "get" Arnold and to assert the supremacy of civil over military authority. Joseph Reed had sent a letter to the Pennsylvania delegates on January 30 requesting them to ask a roll call for the record on any question "which may affect the authority or reputation of this Council, and more especially in the case of Gen. Arnold, . . . that in our correspondence with our sister states we may have an opportunity to shew them how far their delegates in Congress do or do not manifest a disposition to support the authority of civil government, and more especially in the execution of the resolves of Congress." Aware of the formidable power of Pennsylvania, and anxious to preserve unanimity and harmony so far as possible, Congress decided that its committee should now confer with a joint committee of the General Assembly and the Council of Pennsylvania. The committees came up with a number of resolutions clearly designed to show the Pennsylvania authorities that Congress held them in great respect. One of the resolutions, aimed at Arnold, supported Pennsylvania's right to object to disrespectful and indecent behavior by any officer to the civil authority of the state. Congress passed these resolutions and then voted that the commander-in-chief be directed to appoint a court-martial to consider the first (the *Charming Nancy* pass), second (shop closures), third (imposition of menial duties), and fifth (appropriation of the wagons) charges against Arnold.[5]

The situation was extraordinary. Congress had virtually ignored the report of its own committee in deference to Pennsylvania. Francis Lewis of New York wrote Governor George Clinton, before the Congressional committee delivered its report, that "animosities run high, between Genl. Arnold and the executive branch of this State, in so much, that I fear it may form parties in the Congress, and thereby injure the public weal. . . ." Lewis's fear was partially realized, too, for the more intensively the original committee studied the charges and corresponded with the Council, the more it deplored the hypersensitivity of the Council. Committee requests for additional evidence provoked the Council to such irritation that the committee confessed itself unhappy to find that it had "excited emotions of so singular a nature." "Be assured," the committee told the Council through its aristocratic chairman, William Paca of Maryland, who was distinguished for his sense of justice and fair play, "we did not mean to wound your feelings in any degree, much less to such an extreme." At the same time the Congressional committee stood its ground. It resented imputations that its members had had private interviews with Arnold, and it challenged the Council to prove the allegation. "You seem to have taken up an idea," Paca added, "that we consider you as parties and complainants prosecuting before Congress the charges contained in your printed proceedings: we never considered you in that light; we consider you merely as accusers possessed of evidence to prove a publick offense. . . . Our conduct is by no means opposed to what should be observed by grand inquests: for altho' we deny, that we took the *ex parte* examination in favour of the party accused . . . yet we say, it is the right of the party accused to have an examination of his witnesses by the grand inquest before whom he is charged. . . . We wish for your own sakes you had spared your solemn protestation: it is no proof of dignity of conduct." [6]

The reason for Congress's taking no action on the report of its own committee is clear enough: it was reluctant to dispute further with Pennsylvania, particularly on such a high-voltage subject as the Arnold case. It realized that in such a critical period a rupture between itself and Pennsylvania could have tragic consequences for the country. The graceful way out, therefore, was to let its committee and the Pennsylvania joint committee work out a solution. But the debate that ensued in Congress when that solution was proposed, namely to refer the first, second, third, and fifth charges to a court-martial, touched off considerable acrimony. Thomas Burke of North Carolina declared that the Council of Pennsylvania had acted in a "waspish, peevish and childish" manner, a remark for which he was called to order. [7]

Though Arnold naturally did not take kindly to having been made a sacrifice to national unity, he tried to control his indignation. Writing to Congress on April 14, he said, "If Congress have been induced to take this action for the public good, and to avoid a breach with this state, however hard my case may be and however I am injured as an individual, I will suffer with pleasure until a court-martial can have an opportunity of doing me justice by acquitting me of these charges a second time." He also wrote to Washington entreating him to fix an early date for the trial. [8]

Had Arnold not been more guilty in certain respects than even the Council suspected, one would have more sympathy for him; that body objected so strenuously when Washington, on April 20, set the trial for May 1 that the commander-in-chief had to assure the members on April 27 that he did not view them "in the light of a party in the prosecution." In reality they were exactly that, and one can understand Arnold's explosion at the delay, with the trial being deferred at the Council's request until June 1 and even July 1 until witnesses could be summoned and the

Council could assemble all its evidence. Arnold growled that Reed was employing "every artifice to delay the proceedings of a court-martial, as it is his interest that the affair should remain in the dark." On the other hand, Reed contended that Majors Clarkson and Franks, who had been called as witnesses and had been assigned to posts in the south, had absented themselves designedly.[9]

Arnold, however, suffered more excruciatingly than anyone realized. He felt persecuted by the Council, and Congress seemed to be leaning over backward to assist the Council. Mortally injured in his pride, he wrote Washington wildly on May 5:

> If your Excellency thinks me criminal, for heaven's sake let me be immediately tried and, if found guilty, executed. I want no favour; I ask only justice. If this is denied me by your Excellency, I have nowhere to seek it but from the candid public, before whom I shall be under the necessity of laying the whole matter. Let me beg of you, Sir, to consider that a set of artful, unprincipled men in office may misrepresent the most innocent actions and, by raising the public clamour against your Excellency, place you in the same situation I am in. Having made every sacrifice of fortune and blood, and become a cripple in the service of my country, I little expected to meet the ungrateful returns I have received from my countrymen; but as Congress have stamped ingratitude as a current coin, I must take it. I wish your Excellency, for your long and eminent service, may not be paid in the same coin. I have nothing left but the little reputation I have gained in the army. Delay in the present case is worse than death, and when it is considered that the President and council have had three months to produce the evidence, I cannot suppose the ordering a court-martial to determine the matter immediately, is the least precipitating it. I entreat that the court may be ordered to sit as soon as possible.[10]

Calming himself, he subsequently wrote with more restraint. On May 14, he told Washington that he was relieved to learn the trial had been set for June 1. He mentioned again the cruel situation he was in because of the reflection on his character, and he stated his wish to rejoin the army "as soon as my wounds will permit." The commander-in-chief accordingly wrote Reed that Arnold was pressing for "a speedy trial" and "has a right to expect from me, as a piece of justice, that his fate may be decided, as soon as it can be done consistently with a full and fair investigation." He also pointed out to Arnold on the same day that his own situation was "truly delicate and embarrassing." While he wished for Arnold's sake to bring the affair to a speedy conclusion, "the pointed representations of the State, on the subject of witnesses seem to leave me no choice." Arnold replied on May 18 that he was "extremely sorry" that his situation was causing the commander-in-chief such embarrassment but that the Council had had several months in which to muster its evidence. Finally, when everything appeared ready, the movements of the British caused postponement of the trial until after the campaigning season. Not again until December 23, 1779 did court hearings open at Morristown, New Jersey.[11]

The board consisted of three brigadiers, eight colonels, and Major General Robert Howe of North Carolina as president. Of the three brigadiers, Henry Knox of Massachusetts, Mordecai Gist of Maryland, and William Maxwell of New Jersey, at least one entertained no favorable opinion of Arnold, though the latter may not have realized this. It was Maxwell who, following Arnold's defeat on Lake Champlain, had written the critical letter to Governor Livingston of New Jersey in which he alluded to Arnold as "our evil genius to the north." Arnold, however, did not challenge his position on the court-martial board. The prosecutor was John Laurance, judge advocate general of the army, while the defense was undertaken by Arnold himself. Important witnesses included the Matlacks, Major Franks, and John Mitchell, the deputy quartermaster general. The court met off and on until January 26, when it finally adjourned, five days after Arnold defended his position in a vigorous speech in which he examined not only the four charges that Congress had referred to a court-martial but all of the original eight preferred by the Council of Pennsylvania.[12]

In the blue and buff uniform of the Continental Line, and wearing the epaulettes of a major general and the sword knots presented him by Washington, Arnold opened his defense with a review of his military career. As he explained to the court, leaning on a cane to favor the leg wounded at Quebec and Saratoga, "When one is charged with practices which his soul abhors and which conscious innocence tell him he has never committed, an honest indignation will draw from him expressions in his own favour which on other occasions might be ascribed to an ostentatious turn of mind." He then proceeded to read copies of Washington's letters testifying to his courage and ability, and he dwelt on the action of Congress in acknowledging with thanks and the award of a horse his services at Ridgefield. Having established, on paper at least, his favorable past, he considered the charges of the Council, whose proceedings against him constituted, in his opinion, "a vile prostitution of power."[13]

As to the first charge, the matter of a pass to the *Charming Nancy,* Arnold declared that he sympathized with the owners' intention of saving both ship and cargo for the citizens of the United States and that he did what he could to assist its accomplishment. Naturally in this statement Arnold did not feel impelled to inform the court that he had subsequently acquired a substantial share in the ownership of the vessel. He ridiculed the Council's assertion that the pass was given without Washington's knowledge. As if, he pointed out, the commander-in-chief were in need of such assistance from Pennsylvania! "The general," he said bitingly, "is invested with power, and he possesses spirit to check and to punish every instance of disrespect shewn to his authority; but he will not prostitute his power by exerting it upon a trifling occasion; far less will he pervert it when no occasion is given at all."

The second charge, that of the closed shops, he dismissed with scorn. He had closed them on Congressional order and with the full cognizance of Reed himself; and he called on Reed to prove the allegation that he had made purchases to his own advantage. Confident that his accusers could not lay their hands on the secret agreement with James Mease and William West to share in the purchase and subsequent sale of commodities beyond what the army could use, he pronounced the charge false. Had it been true, he contended, he would "stand confessed . . . the vilest of men; . . . stigmatized with indelible disgrace, the disgrace of having abused an appointment of high trust and importance to accomplish the meanest and most unworthy purposes. The blood I have spent in defence of my country [he was forever alluding to his sufferings] will be insufficient to obliterate the stain." But the charge was true, at least in part, and his affirmation of honorable innocence was an example of consummate hypocrisy.

The third charge, imposing menial duties upon the sons of freemen, Arnold construed as an attempt by the Council to turn the militia against him. To this, he said, "My ambition is to deserve the good opinion of the militia of these states, not only because I respect their character and their exertions but because their confidence in me may (as I flatter myself it has hitherto been) prove beneficial to the general cause of America. But having no local politics to bias my voice or my conduct, I leave it to others to wriggle themselves into a temporary popularity by assassinating the reputation of innocent persons and endeavouring to render odious, a principle the maintenance of which is essential to the good discipline of the militia and consequently to the safety of these states." These were interesting statements and to a point true. Arnold had a way of winning the confidence of militia, and he handled them in the field with extraordinary skill and effectiveness. On the other hand, none appreciated more than did he the weakness of poorly trained militia hurriedly summoned from their homes to do a soldier's job. In his exasperation at the successful withdrawal of British Governor William Tryon to his boats off Compo, Arnold wrote of the American pursuit to General McDougall on April 28, 1777, "Many of the officers and men behaved well. The militia, *as usual*. I wish never to see another of them in action." [14]

The fourth charge, the affair of the *Active,* had been a civil matter, and, as Arnold explained, had been dismissed by the grand jury in April for lack of evidence to support the indictment. Arnold had only good words for the jury and condemnation for the "tyranny" of the Council. Of course he mentioned neither the deal he had induced Olmsted to make with him in exchange for his assistance nor the part he had played in bringing witnesses to testify before the jury that he was innocent of any interest save that of wanting to help out fellow citizens of the same state as himself. [15]

As for appropriating the wagons, the fifth charge, Arnold declared frankly that he had never considered the application for their use as other than a private request. The property conveyed in the wagons was admittedly private, and he fully intended to pay for their hire. At present, he was being sued for £1,100 by his wagon master, Jesse Jordan, who, so Arnold contended, and perhaps with some degree of truth, had been advised by the Council to refrain from accepting his belated pay and, instead, to sue for twice the amount due him. "Is it not very extraordinary," Arnold asked, "that I should be accused and tried before this honourable court for employing public wagons, and at the same time and by the same persons be prosecuted in a civil court of Pennsylvania for employing the same wagons as private property?" [16]

The sixth charge, the recommending letter, though not on the agenda of the board, was explained by Arnold in detail. It was scarcely of this importance, and Congress was justified in throwing it out as of little consequence. While Arnold could have ignored it, his pride refused to let even the slightest imputation remain unchallenged.

In examining the seventh charge, which, though also not on the agenda, he considered important because of its relation to the fifth, he carried the battle to the enemy. Certainly he did not consider his reply to the Council's request for additional information on the wagons as either indecent or disrespectful. But if it seemed disrespectful to the Council, the Council had only itself at fault: ". . . when public bodies of men show themselves actuated by the passions of anger, or envy, and apply their effects to sap the character of an individual and to render his position miserable, they must not think it extraordinary if they are not treated with the deference which they may think their due. It is the dignity with which an office is executed, much more than the name, that can ever secure respect and obedience from a free people; and true dignity consists in exercising power with wisdom, justice, and moderation." This was truth, admirably stated, but it scarcely added to the strength of his position, which was already well buttressed by the favorable sentiment of the Congressional committee.

The last charge, his favoritism to Loyalists and neglect of patriots, greatly angered him, and though Congress had dismissed it, Arnold refused to ignore it. He appealed to the many officers and civil officials whom he had entertained to judge if he was guilty of neglect. As for his attention to Loyalists, "I have paid none but such, as in my situation, was justifiable on the principles of common humanity and politeness. The president and council of Pennsylvania will pardon me, if I cannot divest myself of humanity merely out of complaisance to them." For the president, Joseph Reed, Arnold had nothing but contemptuous words. He, Arnold, had not proposed to his associates in the hour of danger in late 1776 "basely to quit the General and sacrifice the cause of my country to my personal safety, by going over to the enemy and making my peace. I never basked in the sunshine of my General's favour, and courted him to his face, when I was at the same time treating him with the greatest disrespect and vilifying his character when absent. This is more than a ruling member of the council of the state of Pennsylvania can say, as is alleged and believed." The imputation of desertion and back-biting was strong, but Arnold was merely reiterating the common interpretation of Reed's behavior. Washington's adjutant general, and later a general of cavalry, Reed had written scathingly of Washington's generalship to General Charles Lee after the fall of Forts Washington and Lee to the British in the autumn of 1776, and Washington had accidentally intercepted the communication. The breach in the good relations between the two men was never completely repaired; Washington felt that Reed had gone behind his back, as it were, and betrayed his trust. Reed, however, remained a stalwart patriot notwithstanding his criticism of the commander-in-chief; he was no more guilty of trafficking with the enemy than Arnold had been guilty of this eighth charge.[17]

The court-martial delivered its verdict on January 26. On the permit to the *Charming Nancy* the court was of the opinion that Arnold had had no right to issue it, "circumstanced as he was." This was certainly a reasonable judgment. As for closing the shops, he had merely been complying with his instructions, and the court, not knowing of his agreement with Mease and West, acquitted him of making purchases for his own advantage. Of the charge of imposing menial offices upon the sons of freemen he was also acquitted, this time without elaboration; the court quite properly regarded the charge as of no consequence. But on the charge relating to the use of the wagons the court was not so laconic:

> . . . it appears that General Arnold made application to the deputy quartermaster general to supply him with wagons to remove property then in imminent danger from the enemy; that wagons were supplied him . . . on the application which had been drawn from the state of Pennsylvania for the public service; and it also appears that General Arnold intended this application as a private request and that he had no design of employing the wagons otherwise than at his private expense, nor of defrauding the public, nor injuring or impeding the public service, but considering the delicacy attending the high station in which the general acted, and that requests from him might operate as commands, they are of the opinion the request was imprudent and improper and that, therefore, it ought not to have been made. The court, in consequence of their determinations respecting the first and last charge exhibited against Major General Arnold, do sentence him to receive a reprimand from his Excellency the commander-in-chief.[18]

Congress approved of the verdict on February 12, 1780, but it was so inexcusably tardy in notifying Washington to carry out the court's instructions that it was not until April 6 that the commander-in-chief issued his reprimand. In this reprimand Washington could be accused neither of harshness nor of maudlin sympathy: "The Commander in Chief would have been much happier in an occasion of bestowing commendations on an officer who has rendered such distinguished services to his country as Major General Arnold; but in the present case a sense of duty and a regard to candor oblige him to declare, that he considers his conduct in the instance of the permit as peculiarly reprehensible, both in a civil and military view, and in the affair of the waggons as 'Imprudent and improper'." [19]

The sentence has been considered rigorous. Arnold himself was mortified at the action of the court and said to Silas Deane on March 22, "I believe you will be equally surprised with me when you find the court martial have fully acquitted me of the charge of employing public wagons, or defrauding the public, or of injuring or impeding the public service, and in the next sentence say 'as requests from him might operate as commands,' I ought to receive a reprimand. For what? Not for doing wrong, but because I might have done wrong; or rather, because there was a possibility that evil might have followed the good I did." Arnold had a blind spot where self-criticism was concerned. Determined to make out the best case, he may have deluded even himself as to the measure of his guilt. He was indeed fortunate to escape with a reprimand; had the Council of Pennsylvania been better able to substantiate several of its charges, he would have incurred a heavier penalty. The reprimand, however, was sufficiently galling to the man's proud spirit; the public disgrace seemed impossible to bear. Even the Council appeared a regretful Shylock. On February 3, 1780, news of the verdict having reached Philadelphia, the Council wrote Congress a strange letter filled with unction and concern, a letter possibly influenced by critical opinion in the army and among civilians: "We do not think it proper to affect ignorance of what is the subject of public conversation, and the sentence of the court martial tending to impose a mark of reprehension upon General Arnold. We find his sufferings for, and services to, his country so deeply impressed upon our minds as to obliterate every opposing sentiment, and therefore beg leave to request that Congress will be pleased to dispense with the part of the sentence which imposes a public censure, and may most affect the feelings of a brave and gallant officer." [20]

But the Council was too late to prevent the execution of justice, the wheels of which it had set in motion precisely a year before in submitting its complaints to Congress. Its attitude and policy toward Arnold had fallen scarcely short of persecution. It hated the man and the military authority he represented, and it resorted to every device known to politicians to ruin his reputation. In some of its charges it had been childish and cruel, but in others, though the evidence was flimsy, it was closer to the truth than it realized. So vindictive had been the Council that Arnold had long since given up hope of a reconciliation. Indeed it is difficult to resist sympathizing with him notwithstanding one's realization that, as, for example, in the charge of profiting from closing the shops, he was acquitted when he was in reality deeply guilty. But one's inclination to feel any commiseration for the harassed hero is tempered by the knowledge that he was already involved in a far greater crime than any of which he was accused by the Council of Pennsylvania. Within a few days of his wildly emotional letter of May 5, 1779, begging Washington to try him immediately and, if he was found guilty, to execute him, Benedict Arnold had decided on that course of action which culminated in the treasonous West Point conspiracy and national disgrace.[21]

· XIX ·

Treason

WHY DID Arnold commit treason? It is a distortion to contend that, simply because he needed money, he decided to sell out to the British. Motives are subtle, inner things, and, materialist though he was, even Arnold did not act solely on a money motivation. That he could use the money and that he sold himself are true, of course; that he finally received a very substantial sum of the King's gold is equally true. But the traitor's method of enriching oneself holds hazards to life and reputation. As a soldier, Arnold had often put both at stake, for he was by nature a gambler. Now, however, newly and happily married, he had much to live for. If his reputation was in tatters, it was so regarded only by his enemies. What mattered was its status among respectable people, and who at this juncture were more respectable than the British? In his eyes the American civil authorities, whether the Massachusetts General Court, the Continental Congress, or the Council of Pennsylvania, had discredited themselves, and very likely the cause for which he had suffered so much, by their treatment of him. The British, on the other hand, might better appreciate his worth as a soldier. Certainly they were in a position to translate his own estimate of his value to them in terms of hard cash instead of a promissory note or Continental paper money, which was already depreciating toward the point where a cartload of it was hardly sufficient to buy an equivalent amount of potatoes.

Arnold's indignation at the civil authorities burned with unquenchable fury. Massachusetts had betrayed him at Ticonderoga in deference to Connecticut. Inexplicably Congress had sacrificed him in favor of officers inferior in rank, experience, and ability, and only after he had proved his mettle beyond shadow of doubt had Congress grudgingly promoted him and restored his rank. The Council of Pennsylvania, jealous of any military encroachment on civil authority, had made his life a torment, sometimes with good reason, but more often with none. To Arnold his case as expressed in the New York *Royal Gazette* for February 17, 1779, was probably no understatement: "General Arnold heretofore has been styled another Hannibal, but losing a leg in the service of Congress, the latter considering him unfit for any future exercise of his military talents, permit him thus to fall into the unmerciful fangs of the executive council of Pennsylvania." In his letter of May 5 to Washington, Arnold asserted that "a set of artful, unprincipled men in office" might even treat the commander-in-chief as they had himself. The statement appears like the grossest insolence but was typical of Arnold's attitude toward politicians who opposed him. It is beyond denial that he had often been shabbily treated. Unfortunately he lacked the perspicacity and honesty to recognize his own faults, the moral stature to forgive or overlook slights, or the patience to endure persecution. Few of the truly great men of the Revolution escaped criticism and abuse: Franklin and Jefferson, among the politicians; Washington and Greene, among the soldiers. But whereas these refused to quit the game or to change the color of their coats, a number of lesser men succumbed; while a great soldier, Arnold lacked the greatness of character that distinguished these men.[1]

It is possible, too, that Arnold entertained serious doubts about the value of independence in a country whose government was neglectful of its heroes and poisoned by prejudice. With desertion rampant in the army and the recruiting efforts of the states virtually at a standstill, it was well-nigh impossible to build an effective force. Finances, whether state or national, were skidding. Many of the "best" families swung into a neutral or Loyalist position with the apparent disintegration of the great cause. Indeed, with Britain now holding out home rule to America and offering to distinguished Americans high office in the new colonial governments to be created, there were certain Americans who were persuaded that independence was a dubious advantage. Arnold originally favored the political arguments in support of independence, and on the day before he engaged the British in the glorious if disastrous battle off Valcour Island he had written to Gates, "If you have read Price's

pamphlet sent you by Mr. Franklin, I will take the loan of it a favour."
Major Richard Price of England in his *Observations on Civil Liberty*
highly approved the position taken by the Americans before 1775, and his
pamphlet, widely publicized in America, may have formed a subject of
interesting conversation when Arnold had last dined with Gates at the
latter's headquarters at Ticonderoga. This was in October, 1776. At his
trial, to be sure, Arnold said, "I flatter myself the time is not far off, when,
by the glorious establishment of our independence, I shall again return
into the mass of citizens." But this was in January, 1780, eight months
after he had opened negotiations with the British; his concern for independence was now only lip service for the occasion. American government, if for no other reason, may have disqualified itself in his eyes in
terms of efficiency and justice.[2]

The alliance with France has often been suggested as a factor influencing Arnold against continuing with the Americans. He acknowledged as much after the treason; Catholic France was an enemy to the
liberties of mankind and to the Protestant faith. But before the treason
he never admitted such views. In fact, in a letter to Schuyler on March 8,
1777, he welcomed the prospect of France's entering the war when he
said, "The amazing preparations making for war, in France and Spain,
leave little doubt of their hostile intentions against Great Britain. I hope
and believe we shall have the burden of the war taken off our hand, this
summer." On the other hand, Arnold may well have shared the suspicion
that so many people, particularly his fellow New Englanders, entertained
toward France. At any rate, his mistrust of the alliance, if mistrust it he
did, is a distinct possibility, though it is impossible to be sure to what
extent it swayed him.[3]

Another factor—and a very controversial one—was his wife. Most
people were convinced at the time that Peggy Arnold knew nothing
about Arnold's treason, least of all was involved in it. This view persisted
from the time of her astounding demonstrations of hysteria at West
Point until the publication of Carl Van Doren's *Secret History of the
American Revolution* in 1941. This remarkable work, based upon a
thorough study of British Army Headquarters Papers, which have been
made available to the public only in the last quarter century, has established convincingly that not only did she know of the treason but also
participated in it. Yet whether her complicity extended to the point of
influencing Arnold to become a traitor is still unsettled. Van Doren
believed that, at most, she could merely confirm a powerful will like that

of Arnold, who once had angrily announced at a conference during the Saratoga campaign that no man had ever influenced his judgment.[4]

Peggy Shippen Arnold, however, was no ordinary woman. Her career, when she lived in England after the Revolution, revealed a degree of fortitude and devotion present only in a person of strong character. Furthermore, after her husband's death, she manifested sufficient cleverness and business acumen to enable her on limited funds to pay off his debts and provide for her children. Demure and innocent before marriage, she soon evinced a capacity for passion that enthralled the vigorous Arnold. In a letter of September 12, 1780, to a bachelor acquaintance, Major General Robert Howe, he wrote, "Be assured, sir, no sensations can have a comparison with those arising from the reciprocity of concern and mutual felicity existing between a lady of sensibility and a fond husband. I myself had enjoyed a tolerable share of the dissipated joys of life, as well as the scenes of sensual gratification incident to a man of nervous constitution; but, when set in competition with those I have since felt and still enjoy, I consider the time of celibacy in some measure misspent." There were surprising facets indeed to Peggy Arnold, whose character and abilities have been too often underestimated. Perhaps it would have been remarkable if, with her background and her many Loyalist and British friends, she had not encouraged her discontented fiancé to take the decisive step that would bring him both revenge and vindication.[5]

More certain than any of Arnold's reasons for selling himself to the British was his desire for money. His attitude toward money was by no means that of a penny pincher. In his investments he gambled for large stakes and spent his gains lavishly, whether for a battalion for his friend Colonel Lamb, an education for General Warren's children, or a magnificent estate for himself and Peggy. Money afforded him the goods of this world, and these in turn assured him of social prestige and position. How this money was obtained troubled him little; to get it, he often danced a tightrope between what was legal and what was illegal, or at least unethical.

Whatever his attitude, there was no doubt that in the spring of 1779 his financial affairs were in a bad way. On April 25, he had to pay £5,000 hush- and support-money to the other claimants in the *Active* case; and, of course, the case lingered in the courts. Congress found difficulty settling his accounts, which were in fact never straightened out, so it turned them over to the Board of Treasury for more competent investigation. Although undoubtedly he received some income from his illicit trading, resignation of his Philadelphia command had cost him money he could ill afford to lose. His marriage, moreover, was hardly an exercise in economy. Wardrobes for himself and Peggy, new furniture for the estate, one party after another—such expenses ate great holes in his income. In addition, he still had the expense of supporting his sister and his three boys. In 1778, he had sent his sons to Samuel Goodrich's school in Middletown, Connecticut, but in the winter he moved them and Hannah to Philadelphia. Not liking the influence of the capital on the boys, he enrolled them in May, 1779, at a school near Hagerstown, Maryland, run by Bartholomew Booth, to whom he enclosed three hundred dollars and instructions to treat the boys as he would his own and not to spare corrective measures if needed. With all these drains on his income, he had difficulty making good his easy assurance to Edward Shippen that his fortune was sufficiently ample to make both himself and Peggy happy.[6]

Notwithstanding his very real need of money and his consuming interest in it, it is doubtful that the desire for money alone would have induced him to commit treason. His political dislikes were inseparably linked with his financial situation, and his dislikes—a mild word indeed for Arnold's feelings on the subject—were founded, in the last analysis, less upon a mistrust of American political forms and principles than upon an intense personal hatred of those politicians who, in reality or in his fancy, had treated him with gross injustice, disrespect, and contumely. He could never rise above the personal issue, could never recognize that his own deficient ethical standards, his lack of self-control, his vanity, his avarice, and his pride made him painfully vulnerable to his enemies.

His was a pathetic case of insecurity. He had to be first in all things, and in nothing could he be wrong. In the terrible pride of the general was the pride of the boy who had been the daredevil among his friends, the strongest of arm and fleetest of foot. In the officer who sought respectability in wealth and in marriage into one of the first families of Philadelphia was also the highstrung lad who had chafed under the humiliation of a drunken father. All his life he pursued respectability and acceptance by "first families" as a social equal. Unfortunately one of his obsessions was that riches ensured respectability and that the means by which those riches were gained was immaterial. The result was that to obtain respectability as he conceived of it, he constantly resorted to devices that jeopardized his objective and made his honor as a "gentleman" a mockery. At the same time, he fiercely resented any imputation on that honor. "Conscious of the rectitude of my intentions"—how often he employed this very expression or one similar to it, and his sword was ever ready to support his pretensions. Needing money sorely in the spring of 1779, and confronted with public disgrace as a consequence of the enmity of Pennsylvania and the impending court-martial, he looked for reassurance. Where else could it more surely be found than among the British, who would welcome his assistance and pay handsomely for it? And pay handsomely they should: Arnold's trader instinct told him to set his initial price high. The difficult part of the game, which he now entered upon with caution but with cold and deadly calculation, was how to start negotiations with the British. He discovered his "Open Sesame" in Joseph Stansbury.

Stansbury was the proprietor of a glass and china shop on Front Street. A pleasant-mannered little man, and a versifier of a very minor order, Stansbury had taken a firm though quiet stand against independence. Though he welcomed General Howe, helped manage the British general's lottery for poor relief, and served on the city watch commission, the Americans tolerated him after the evacuation, deceived by his taking the oath of allegiance. Somehow Arnold met him and learned to trust him with his great secret. It seems odd that Arnold should have selected Stansbury from the large number of people with Loyalist affinities. He must have had solid assurance from some source that the man was eminently reliable. One theory is that he obtained the information from his wife, who may have learned it from John André during the occupation. This may be a real possibility, for André, despite his brilliance, could be a singularly indiscreet and naïve young man, as was amply evidenced after his capture by the Americans.[7]

Whatever the reason for his trust in Stansbury, Arnold got in touch with the man in early May, 1779. According to Stansbury, Arnold, "after some general conversation, opened his political sentiments respecting the war carrying on between Great Britain and America, declaring his abhorrence of a separation of the latter from the former as a measure that would be ruinous to both." Stansbury disclosed further, in relating this incident after the war, that Arnold "then communicated to me, under a solemn obligation of secrecy, his intention of opening his services to the commander in chief of the British forces in any way that would most effectually restore the former government and destroy the then usurped authority of Congress, either by immediately joining the British army or co-operating on some concealed plan with Sir Henry Clinton." [8]

Stansbury went to New York to communicate personally the information to the British. In this endeavor he was assisted by Jonathan Odell, formerly rector of St. Mary's Church in Burlington, New Jersey, currently a chaplain to a Loyalist regiment, and another versifier of sorts. Odell aided Stansbury in securing a meeting with John André at British Army Headquarters. Though surprised by the revelations of Stansbury, who also disclosed that Arnold was fearful of helping unless the British intended to press the war to a successful conclusion, André preserved an admirable balance between caution born of incredulity and enthusiastic encouragement of the would-be traitor. He assured Stansbury that the British were determined to support the war and expected to have powerful means available to accomplish that end. They would welcome Arnold's help, and if he succeeded in delivering a body of troops into their hands or was instrumental in securing the defeat of a numerous army, he would find the British grateful. With almost prophetic insight, André added, "Shou'd his manifest efforts be foiled and after every zealous attempt, flight be at length necessary the Cause in which he suffers will hold itself bound to indemnify him for his losses and receive him with the honour his conduct deserves." Arrangements were made for both Arnold and André to have copies of the same books on which a communications code should be based. Bailey's *Dictionary* and particularly Blackstone's *Commentaries* were used. Every word in the letters between the two men was to have a code in three digits indicating the page number of the book employed for the word, the line number, and the word number. Letters might also be written in invisible ink. When this was done, "A" was assumed to designate that the process of decoding should be by means of acid; "F," by the heat of a fire. [9]

But André wanted to make doubly certain of secrecy, and in so doing, he revealed that Peggy Shippen Arnold must have been an early and intimate partner of Arnold himself in the treason. "The lady," said André, "might write to me at the same time with one of her intimates. She will guess who I mean, the latter remaining ignorant of interlining and sending the letter. I will write myself to the friend to give occasion for a reply. This will come by a flag of truce, exchanged officer etc., every messenger remaining ignorant of what they are charg'd with. The letters may talk of the Meschianza and other nonsense." Peggy Chew, who had accompanied André to the Meschianza, and who was Peggy Arnold's friend, was to be the dupe. The recipient of André's letters, she was to give her reply to Peggy Arnold for transmission through the lines. Peggy Arnold, in turn, was to transform her friend's letter, by means of interlining and invisible ink, into a communication containing vital information. It was thus not merely as Arnold's wife that King George subsequently settled upon her an annual pension of £500; she had rendered other services, which, in Sir Henry Clinton's words, "were very meritorious." [10]

The treason was thereby launched on a tortuous and hazardous course. Furthermore, despite subsequent allegations that Arnold had been induced by the British to desert, he had instigated the move himself. Though authorized by London to do everything in his power to bring rebel officers back to their allegiance, Clinton took no credit for Arnold's defection. He came over, said Clinton, "without any overtures from me." Arnold called himself "Monk," after General George Monk, the Cromwellian leader, who, following the death of the great Oliver, delivered England into the hands of Charles II. Monk's was successful treason and hence considered patriotism. Arnold chose to think of himself as assuming Monk's role in America; possibly he was ignorant that a noted contemporary of his, Dr. Johnson, the lexicographer and pundit, defined patriotism as "the last refuge of a scoundrel." At Arnold's side stood his ambitious Peggy, perhaps swept away by what she may have believed the romantic and idealistic aspects of such a role to be. Treason? A dark word which success would erase. As an Englishman, Sir John Harrington, had long before observed, ". . . if it prosper, none dare call it treason." General Monk, moreover, had won a dukedom for his efforts. Who could tell what radiant future might therefore open for Arnold, the brilliant soldier of a mistaken Cause, and—by no means incidentally—for his lady as well? [11]

· XX ·

Bargaining in Treason

Arnold's rapprochement with the British was an affair of slow growth, with both parties being guarded in their communications. Clinton could not be justified in revealing his hand until Arnold had given convincing proof of his good faith. Now known variously as "A.G.," "Gustavus," and "Moore," Arnold kept in touch with André, who figured as "John Anderson" in the correspondence, which was forwarded by Stansbury and Odell. Even as Clinton was cautious, so was Arnold. He wanted to be assured of a substantial reward for treason before he made any definite commitments. The initial steps of the treason therefore resembled the early rounds of many a prize fight with both principals feeling each other out.

André wrote Peggy Chew, as he had purposed. He regretted that ill health and duties had obliged him to forego in New York "the pleasing study of what relates to the ladies." His knowledge, however, "that you have every thing from Paris the fountain head" caused him less regret in neglecting her millinery orders. With this allusion to the French alliance, he continued, "I trust I am yet in the memory of the little society of third and fourth Street and even of the *other Peggy* now Mrs. Arnold who will I am sure accept of my best respects and with the rest of the sisterhoods of both streets peruse not disdainfully this page meant as an assurance of my unabated esteem for them." André finished his letter with bits of gossip and good wishes. The letter is undated, though evidently written in May, 1779, and there is no record of its having been sent or received. Still it is possible that it reached Peggy Chew, who passed it on to Peggy Arnold. In any event, there may be some significance to the fact that in a letter in code which Arnold sent André on May 23, he took the trouble to add, "Madam Arnold presents you her particular compliments." Superficially a mere pleasantry, this could also signify that Peggy Arnold recognized and accepted her particular responsibilities in the method of communication.[1]

But getting letters back and forth between Philadelphia and New York was a hazardous business. Odell and Stansbury as intermediaries had their trouble securing messengers. Odell sent a duplicate by a Mrs. Gordon who accompanied a Mrs. Chamier to Philadelphia. Stansbury once relied on two young men for whom Odell sought commissions in the militia. Usually John Rattoon, a vestryman of St. Peters in Amboy, was the courier. At times it would appear that others, unnamed, brought the communications to Stansbury and Odell. Possibly even the mysterious and effective British spy, Ann Bates, was employed. A former schoolmistress in Philadelphia now married to an armorer in the Royal Artillery, she had been given a pass by Arnold in 1778 to go to New York for the purpose of joining her husband. Once there, she was commissioned to bring intelligence concerning Washington's movements in the White Plains area. Later she went to within fifty miles of Philadelphia "to a friend that was in connection with General Arnold." Presently she was sent to Philadelphia itself and returned to André with intelligence concerning American shipping and supplies. Several times she served as a companion for persons going between the lines. Possibly she was the Mrs. Gordon by whom Odell dispatched his duplicate to Stansbury. At any rate, the transmission of the letters involved grave risks: for Stansbury in obtaining messengers, for the messengers themselves should the letters be intercepted, and for both Arnold and Stansbury if the Americans ever suspected the import of the contents.[2]

Arnold was anxious to bring Clinton to terms on the price of treason. On May 23, 1779, he assured André that "As I esteem the interest of America and Great Britain inseparable," Clinton could depend on his "exertions and intelligence." At the same time, he insisted that it would be impossible to co-operate unless there was mutual confidence. As for himself, "I will co-operate when an opportunity offers and as life and every thing is at stake I will expect some certainty: my property here secure and a revenue equivalent to the risk and service done. I cannot promise success; I will deserve it. Inform me what I may expect. Cou'd

I know Sir Henry's intentions he shou'd never be at a loss for intelligence." As a pledge of his good faith, Arnold disclosed a number of secrets concerning American troop movements, French naval dispositions, and the foreign relations of the United States, information of which Clinton was probably already aware through his own agents.[3]

André did not reply until the middle of June; he had accompanied Clinton in the latter's successful thrust against Stony Point on May 31. Ironically it was this move that caused Arnold's court-martial to be postponed for the rest of the campaigning season. When André finally got around to answering Arnold's letter, what he said was of little encouragement to Arnold. Clinton wished to apprise the American general that, although the war would be prosecuted with vigor, "he cannot reveal his intentions as to the present campaign nor can he find the necessity of such a discovery or that a want of a proper degree of confidence is to be inferred from his not making it." Clinton reminded Arnold that it was he himself who originally proposed to assist the British and that he must know in what command he could deliver a telling stroke at a vulnerable point. Through André, Clinton suggested, however, that Arnold "join the Army, accept a command, be surprized, be cut off . . . a compleat service of this nature involving a corps of 5 or 6000 men would be rewarded with twice as many thousand guineas." André proposed that the method could be arranged by his conferring with Arnold. Meanwhile Arnold might exert his influence in procuring the exchange of Burgoyne's army: "It could be urged by none with more propriety, nor would you be sorry to see this act of justice superadded to the shining revolution you may perhaps be instrumental in effecting." With this backward glance at Arnold's glory and a mention of the interview that was to result in the exposure of Arnold's infamy and in his own death, André brought his letter to a close.[4]

Arnold was chagrined and angered by its vagueness. Stansbury wrote Odell that "It was on the evening of the 7th [of July] Mr. Anderson's [André's] favor came to hand, which I immediately delivered to Mrs. Moore [Peggy Arnold]." Expecting to receive a memorandum from Arnold, Stansbury received, instead, a note. In it, according to Stansbury, Arnold declared that "he had carefully examined the letter, and found by the laconic style and little attention paid to his request, that the gentleman appear'd very indifferent respecting the matter." A long talk with Arnold convinced Stansbury that the general was hurt, and also suspicious that Odell knew who he was. Blandly Stansbury denied this, explaining that his friend knew only that "a Mr. Moore was concerned in the business." [5]

This account, which Odell sent on to André, was accompanied by a list of articles desired by Peggy Arnold. She wanted some narrow pale-pink mantua eighteen or twenty-two yards long; one piece of broad pale-pink ribbon; six yards of fine black satinet for shoes; one piece of diaper for napkins; one pair of neat spurs; and one piece of clouting diaper. It is doubtful if this request contained any vital message. Carl Van Doren has remarked that it probably signified only that Peggy remained on good terms with André notwithstanding her husband's disappointment. No attention, moreover, was paid to the list until just before Christmas when Odell notified André that the parcel was ready for delivery.[6]

André was left in no doubt as to Arnold's disappointment; Stansbury communicated Arnold's sentiments directly to André as well as to Odell. Arnold, furthermore, decided to end this shilly-shallying and to set his own value on his services. "I delivered Gustavus [Arnold] your letter," wrote Stansbury; "it is not equal to his expectations. He expects to have your promise that he shall be indemnified for any loss he may sustain in case of detection and whether this contest is finished by sword or treaty that ten thousand pounds shall be engaged him for his services, which shall be faithfully devoted to your interest." As evidence of his continued devotion, he communicated a number of miscellaneous items bearing mainly on the numbers, equipment, and location of the various army commands, particularly that of Sullivan in the Indian country.[7]

André replied deftly to this letter at the end of July. He regretted that any hesitation should still remain as he thought that all had been said "that the prudence with which our liberality must be tempered will admit." Such a sum as Arnold had mentioned required a great deal of accounting for, and could only be warranted by the attainment of real advantages or at least by a generous effort. If Arnold would assume a field command and arrange a meeting with André, the latter was confident that a few minutes of conversation would satisfy both. André also remarked, "Permit me to prescribe a little exertion. It is the procuring an accurate plan of West Point. . . ." [8]

This letter, bearing the first mention of West Point in the negotiations, brought no direct response from Arnold. André learned of his letter's reception from Stansbury. According to the china shop proprietor, Arnold sent for him, showed him the letter, and observed that it contained no reply to the terms mentioned. Furthermore, said Stansbury,

"Tho' he cou'd not doubt your honour yet there was no assurance given that his property in this country should be indemnified from any loss that might attend unfortunate discovery: however sincerely he wished to serve his country in accelerating the settlement of this unhappy contest, yet he shou'd hold himself unjust to his family to hazard his all on the occasion and part with a certainty (potentially at least) for an uncertainty. He hopes to join the army in about three weeks when he will if possible contrive an interview." Arnold, however, did not join the army at that time, and the interview with André had to wait for more than a year. In fact, except for an occasional letter from Stansbury containing information from Arnold, the negotiations languished until the following spring. If the British would not meet Arnold's price, he would try to bridle his impatience until they were more amenable.[9]

Notwithstanding the impasse with Arnold himself, André seems to have thought that something might be accomplished through his wife. He wrote her on August 16, 1779, sending the letter by a Major Giles; it was found among Arnold's papers searched by the sheriff of Philadelphia after the treason plot failed. The letter, André declared, was meant "to solicit your remembrance, and to assure you that my respect for you, and the fair circle in which I had the honour of becoming acquainted with you, remains unimpaired by distance or political broils. It would make me very happy to become useful to you here. You know the Mesquianza made me a complete milliner. Should you not have received supplies for your fullest equipment from that department, I shall be glad to enter into the whole detail of capwire, needles, gauze, &c., and, to the best of my abilities, render you in these trifles services from which I hope you would infer a zeal to be further employed." [10]

Peggy Arnold took her time replying and then was cautiously noncommittal. On October 13, she presented "her best respects to Capt. André, is much obliged to him for his very polite and friendly offer of being serviceable to her. Major Giles was so obliging as to promise to procure what trifles Mrs. Arnold wanted in the millinery way, or she would with pleasure have accepted of it. Mrs. Arnold begs leave to assure Captain André that her friendship and esteem for him is not impaired by time or accident." That she understood André's "zeal to be further employed" can hardly be doubted, nor can the fact that her profession of good will left the way open for further negotiation. At the same time, the note, so terse and proper, must have conveyed to André an awareness that, for the time being, she sympathized with her husband's position or, at least, refused to differ with him in any negotiations with the British.[11]

Thus ended the early phase of Arnold's treason. Nothing definitive had been achieved, nothing, that is, except that Arnold had fatally compromised the honor of which he talked so elevatedly. Henceforth, too, he was a marked man among the British. Should he again become active against them, they had the evidence which, if revealed to the Americans, could hang him. But André was too shrewd an officer to believe that a man who, of his own volition, sought to become a traitor, would easily relinquish the rewards on which he had set his mind. Stansbury might yet get word to headquarters that Arnold was ready to do something decisive. Arnold, however, had not been a successful trader for nothing; he had stated his price, and if the British refused to meet it exactly, they would have to approach it. Undoubtedly he was not surprised that for treason, even as for merchandise, one must haggle. Meanwhile he would wait, see his court-martial through, and hope that, before long, Sir Henry Clinton would find the price he had set on his treason not beyond the capacity of the British purse. Once he had committed himself, treason was henceforth becoming, above all things, a matter of pounds and pence. One wonders if Arnold in his present mercenary-mindedness ever recalled those heroic days when, heedless of the risk to life, he had led the Kennebec column up the narrow, snow-and-shell-swept streets of Quebec, when he had fought his shattered and smoking hulks against hopeless odds off Valcour Island and Split Rock, when he had stormed Breymann's redoubt at Bemis Heights with a blazing courage that astounded his enemies in both armies. But it is unlikely. He seems to have been preoccupied with working himself into the ironical position of bargaining for sufficient British gold to betray the very people before whom he was bent on clearing his name at his court-martial.

· XXI ·

Uneasy Months

THE NEGOTIATIONS with the British having been broken off, Arnold passed restless and dissatisfied months. He barely escaped personal violence. He suffered humiliation at the verdict of the court-martial. He vainly sought to obtain a naval command. The condition of his finances impelled him not only to appeal again to Congress for a settlement of his accounts but also to seek assistance from the French, and in neither endeavor was he successful. But in all this catalogue of gloomy developments it is likely that, for the time it lasted, the exposure to violence provoked him most.

The incident occurred in the first week of October, 1779. With paper money declining rapidly in value, prices going up, and hardship increasing, many of the less privileged in Philadelphia looked for a scapegoat and found one in the war profiteers. For many merchants and financiers the war presented a magnificent opportunity to enrich themselves, and, in spite of his great services to the country, none took more advantage of the situation than Robert Morris. When a mob of workmen, waterfront rabble and disgruntled militiamen suddenly rose against such profiteers, a number of those so charged, including Morris, fled to the residence of the jurist, James Wilson, where the mob besieged them. In the course of the "Fort Wilson" riot and the accompanying commotions, blood was spilled. Learning of the plight of those at Wilson's, Arnold went to their rescue, but, in doing so, he turned the wrath of the mob against himself.

In short order, he, the would-be rescuer, stood in need of assistance himself. Two men closed in menacingly. But, as one of the Burd family wrote, Arnold "happened to have his pistols and prevented them from hurting him by threatening to fire at them." [1]

Though he escaped being manhandled, the danger was by no means over, and Arnold's rage grew as the ignominy of his position became more evident when men surrounded his own house. Quickly he dashed off a note by a runner, requesting Congress for twenty Continentals and a good officer since "a mob of lawless ruffians" had attacked him in the streets and now threatened his life in his own home for defending himself when attacked. "As there is no protection to be expected of the state for an honest man," he said scornfully, "I am under the necessity of requesting Congress to order me a guard of Continental troops. This request I presume will not be denied to a man who has so often fought and bled in defence of the liberties of his country." [2]

This appeal fell on deaf ears. Although the request was no more extraordinary than the circumstances which had prompted it, Congress declined to become involved in a jurisdictional dispute with Pennsylvania. Curtly it informed Arnold that he should have applied to "the executive authority of the state of Pennsylvania, in whose disposition to protect every honest citizen Congress have full confidence, and highly disapprove the insinuations of every individual to the contrary." Arnold at once expressed regret that Congress had misunderstood his meaning concerning protection. Referring to the Pennsylvania authorities, he said, ". . . their disposition to protect the honest citizens I did not doubt, their abilities I doubted and still have reason to doubt from the fatal consequences of yesterdays commotions." In the end, the authorities were able to quiet the rioters, and Arnold and others were spared the worst effects of something Henry Laurens acknowledged he had long dreaded, "a convulsion among the people." [3]

The court-martial verdict in January, 1780, was no more calculated to soothe Arnold's feelings than was the fact that, because of the verdict and his previous persecution by the Council of Pennsylvania, he was, as General Charles Lee observed, "served up as a constant dish of scandal to the breakfast of every table on the continent . . . in this general rage for abuse." In Arnold's mind the malice of his enemies knew no bounds. At the same time, he chafed at his inactivity and at the condition of his finances, which were declining with the deteriorating currency. Naturally others were as badly affected as himself, but his extravagant manner of

living, which he refused to curb, aggravated his need. Thus it was in all
likelihood a combination of his own restlessness and the depressed state
of his finances that impelled him again to consider a naval venture.[4]

Perhaps with his Lake Champlain experience in mind, Arnold seems to
have had complete confidence in his ability both to obtain and to discharge a naval command. He wrote to Silas Deane on March 22 that he
had proposed to the Board of Admiralty "an expedition which will require three or four hundred land forces to act in conjunction with the
ships; the matter rests with General Washington. If the men can be
spared, and my plan takes place, you will hear from me soon. If it should
not, I propose going to Boston, with the intention to take command of a
private ship." It is possible that Arnold had boosted his own importance
to Deane, for in two letters to Washington, detailed descriptions on
March 6 and 20, he left little doubt that the initiative came from the
Admiralty. On the other hand, he may have originated the idea, suggested it to the Admiralty, and then have had the satisfaction of informing Washington that the Admiralty wished him for the command. Either
course sounds like Arnold. At any rate, he sorely wanted to be with the
expedition, which was to sail the middle of April and be gone for about
two months, presumably to the West Indies. To Washington he said,
"From the injury I have received in my leg, and the great stiffness in my
ankle, my surgeons are of opinion it will not be prudent for me to take
command in the army for some time to come." [5]

His hopes were cruelly dashed. Washington wrote the Board of Admiralty disapproving the removal of the troops from his already weak-
ened army, though he had no objection to Arnold's assuming the
command. In his second letter to Washington, Arnold had requested a
leave of absence for the summer or until his wounds had recovered sufficiently to permit him again to take the field. Though Washington declared
on March 28 that it had been his "wish and expectation" to see Arnold in
the field, he granted the request subject to one condition: if Arnold
wanted to leave on a voyage of his own, he would have to obtain permission from Congress since Washington had ventured in no instance to
grant leaves to any place not within the United States. The point, however, had already become partially academic; five days before Washington wrote Arnold, the Board of Admiralty notified the commander-in-
chief that it had dropped the idea of a naval expedition. Arnold likewise
gave up his privateering notion; perhaps it had been only a notion all
the time. So vanished another money-making scheme.[6]

Meanwhile Arnold hoped for a settlement of his accounts by Congress. The Board of Treasury, to which the accounts had been referred in April, 1779, reported to Congress on October 1, but it had found the accounts so confusing that Congress then gave them to a committee of five. On February 14, 1780, this committee declared it "impracticable" for such a committee as itself to adjust the accounts "with that accuracy and attention which the nature of them demand." Accordingly it urged that they be returned to the Board of Treasury where "the business of liquidating accounts is now carried on in a regular manner." Congress voted the next day to accept the committee's recommendation, and ordered the accounts turned over to the Board. Angrily Arnold protested this move, alleging that the Treasury people were motivated in his case by "private resentment or undue influence." He had had differences with a number of the Board who had now become, so he contended, "parties in the matter and by no means disinterested and proper persons to judge of his accounts and claims." Congress, however, took no steps to change its disposition of the case.[7]

The Board of Treasury made its report to Congress on April 27. It had discovered Arnold's accounts so snarled as to be practically impossible to unravel, but it had done its best to put them in order. It found Arnold indebted to the United States for approximately $70,000. Of this amount, $66,671 was carried on the Canadian account. The balance, £1,000 or $3,333, was a point of controversy. Arnold conceded its existence but alleged that he had paid it to John Halstead, commissary of provisions in the Canadian expedition. Halstead denied ever having received the sum and refused to admit himself as accountable. The Board had therefore insisted that it could not place the sum to Arnold's credit unless he could produce a voucher that would make Halstead accountable. This Arnold could not do, though a search was undertaken in the Treasury Office, where the general said he had deposited the receipt. When it could not be found, Arnold insisted it must have been lost or else one of the commissioners of accounts had stolen it. The Board had then examined the depositions respecting Arnold's allegation. It found no proof that the voucher had ever been lodged in the Treasury and satisfied itself that, if the voucher had ever been there, no commissioner had removed it. The Board therefore refused to credit Arnold with the sum in question, but it declared that he was not precluded from recovering it if he could produce the voucher.

If the Board was niggling in withholding this sum, it could not be accused of being consistently rigid. It conceded to Arnold's credit $51,993, a sum that represented, in the words of the report, "payments and advances made by the General to sundry persons, who if he is credited by them must be charged and accountable to the United States." He was even allowed full value, $2,666, for his sloop *Peggy* which, lying at the island of Orleans near Quebec in January, 1776, had been used as a fireship on May 3, 1776, in a vain attempt to destroy the British fleet. The Board, however, refused to allow full value for the cargo, which had consisted of oats, hay, water hogsheads, fish, miscellaneous provisions, and twenty-five horses then stabled ashore. General Wooster, since deceased, had certified that the *Peggy* had been burned with part of her cargo, presumably the hay and hogsheads as combustibles, while the provisions were used by the army. John Taylor, who had served with the commissary at Quebec, also declared in August, 1779, that there may have been twenty-eight horses, of which total the *Peggy's* captain had brought three to army headquarters near Quebec, where they had been pressed into public service. Taylor believed that all the horses had been thus employed eventually and were not returned. But the Board decided not to credit Arnold with the horses in view of insufficient testimony, and conceded him only $369 on the cargo, which was purported to be worth almost four times that amount. In the final tallying of accounts, the Board stated that Arnold owed the United States a balance in specie of $2,328.[8]

Arnold bitterly assailed the report of the Board. In a letter of May 10, 1780, to Congress, he requested "that honorable body to point out the method of proceeding in appeals from the Board of Treasury, and to be informed when he can be heard on the subject of appeal." Congress at once notified him that he could state his objections to the report in writing. Two days later, submitting a letter and a number of enclosures in behalf of his position, he refused to retract his condemnation of the Treasury. He insisted that, in connection with the missing voucher, someone had been neglectful by accident or design. He was convinced that Elbridge Gerry of Massachusetts, the Congressman who had partially blocked his attempts to aid General Warren's children, had persuaded accountants in the Treasury to juggle the accounts to his prejudice. Furthermore, Congress had ignored his claim for £1,000 as his four-percent charge on the £25,000 which had passed through his hands while acting as his own commissary and quartermaster in Canada; this rate, he asserted, was less than the charge would have been for a person hired specifically for the task of handling the money. He concluded that, all told, the government owed him £2,500 "lawful money," of which £2,000 should be paid in specie or its paper equivalent. But in taking cognizance of his appeal Congress declined to depart from its usual procedure; on May 16, it appointed a committee of three to consider both the appeal and the report of the Board.[9]

The history of the accounts was a tale that reflected little credit on either Arnold or Congress. Whether or not Arnold was guilty of padding them will never be known. It certainly would not have been beyond him, and there were those who were in no doubt that he had falsified them. Furthermore, his accusations against Gerry were unfounded. Gerry himself, in his subsequent career at any rate, was scarcely a model of political rectitude, while, during these weeks, he refused to attend sessions of Congress because of a tiff with that body over parliamentary procedure. On the other hand, his long explanatory letter of May 18 to Congress demolished in a very convincing manner Arnold's allegation that he had given private instructions to the commissioners of accounts, thereby unduly influencing the settlement of Arnold's accounts. Arnold was always quick to accuse, perhaps in this instance with the hope of concealing possible culpability. It must be said, however, that Congress had been unconscionably tardy in getting even this far toward a permanent settlement; four years had elapsed since the Canadian campaign, which was surely time enough to reach a decision that Arnold owed the government money. Nor, in its deliberations, does Congress seem to have taken into consideration the physical and mental strain under which Arnold operated during the campaign, the scarcity of competent quartermaster and commissary officers, the shifting daily demands as situations changed, the difficulty of keeping faithful records in the exigencies of the wilderness march, of the swirling snows at Quebec, of the desperate days of disease and frantic retreat. In its turn, the Board of Treasury, while crediting Arnold with most of the funds, chose to balk on the full amounts submitted for such items as table and forage rations, and horses! [10]

But if the £2,000 in question—£1,000 for the missing voucher and an equal amount for other expenses—exemplifies a certain niggardliness on the part of the government, it also indicates the need that Arnold had for money at this time. He struggled to obtain the amount as if it were several times as large. So hard-pressed was he to meet his obligations that he turned again to the French. The secretary of the French minister, the Chevalier de la Luzerne, was François de Barbé-Marbois. This young man possessed energy, a vivid imagination, and sympathy for the American cause. Years after the Revolution was over, he wrote an account of the Arnold conspiracy which lacked nothing in color and drama. In it he included a version of Washington's reprimand of Arnold that was a gem of courtesy and elegant expression, more laudatory than reproachful, and utterly fictitious; few of Arnold's biographers have neglected to quote this purple passage. Barbé-Marbois also related a story that testified to the measures Arnold took to salvage his finances.[11]

The incident occurred in the winter of 1780 following publication of the verdict of the court-martial. One day, according to Barbé-Marbois, Arnold came to Luzerne and solicited a loan. He felt that if he did not receive immediate and effective assistance he must resign his commission and again become a civilian in order to support his family. Naturally, in his stated opinion, France would not wish to see him out of the army. But if Arnold had hoped to gain money by being almost painfully explicit, Luzerne was a Frenchman with a fine sense of honor and a close-fisted attitude in financial matters; he could not accommodate the American general. Evidently Arnold's regard for the French was not enhanced by the rejection, for after the treason a number of Arnold's letters were found in his wife's apartment in which the character of Luzerne was, as Barbé-Marbois testified, "roughly handled." When the letters were brought to the French minister, the aristocratic Luzerne disdainfully consigned them to the flames without bothering to read them.[12]

Were the incident dependent on Barbé-Marbois's word alone, there would be some reason to suspect it because of his flair for exaggeration and the fact that he was writing a generation later. On the other hand, he was certainly in a position to know the facts. Confirmation of a sort, moreover, was given his account by a report in the *Pennsylvania Packet* for September 30, 1780. This was while the capital was still rocking with the news of the treason. The sheriff's men closed in at once on Arnold's property, seizing, among other things, such papers as survived. The *Packet* reported that certain private letters of Arnold and his family bore "the most sarcastic and contemptuous expressions of the French nation and of an eminent personage of that country, whose hospitality and politeness they were at that time frequently experiencing." If the two accounts are true—and there seems little reason to doubt what is common to both, namely, that Arnold was resentful of his treatment by Luzerne—they may help explain Arnold's alleged suspicions of the alliance with France as a cause of his treason; subsequently, at any rate, he ascribed his defection in part to his distrust of French motives. Possibly his feeling toward

France, articulated with such extraordinary bitterness after his treason, was owing mainly to his realization that, had Luzerne loaned him money to meet his needs in the winter of 1780, he might not have turned again to the British in the spring to supply what neither the French minister nor the Continental Congress was disposed to do.

During these exasperating months, Arnold's personal life remains something of a mystery. His pleasantest experience was probably the birth of his son, Edward, on March 19, 1780, of which he proudly notified Washington. The commander-in-chief and Mrs. Washington joined in their congratulations to Arnold and Peggy on "the late happy event." As for his attitude toward Peggy, there is little reason to suspect that he was different from any affectionate husband, anxious in the closing days of his wife's pregnancy and relieved, proud, and delighted at the successful appearance of their first child.[13]

If there was any rift in the household, the difficulty lay between Peggy and Hannah. With Benedict and Richard at school in Maryland, Hannah remained with the Arnolds to take care of young Henry. She was an outspoken woman, and the time was to come when she would sharply criticize Peggy. A capable, warm-hearted person under a somewhat crusty exterior, very New England-ish and old-maidish, she found Philadelphia worldly and sinful. Now, however, she undoubtedly assumed the burden of the household. If Arnold could share his confidences concerning the past British negotiations only with Peggy, he could at least be sure of Hannah's sympathy and loyalty during the court-martial and the dismal winter days of 1780 until Washington should issue his reprimand and Congress should arrange the long-awaited settlement of accounts. Probably Peggy was no more put out than Hannah at both the reprimand and the failure of Congress to make a definitive statement. But Peggy, and only Peggy among Americans, could have known that, by late spring, Arnold had reached the limit of his patience and resources and had decided to reopen negotiations with the enemy; the British might prove more prompt and generous in their recognition of him than his own people.

· XXII ·

Treason in Full Flower

ARNOLD'S decision to investigate again the advantages which a British connection might hold for him came at a time when the nation was
tottering, and in no institution was weakness so evident as in Congress. It
is possible that the failure of Congress to make a favorable settlement in
his behalf convinced Arnold of both a lack of good faith on the part of
that body and its inability or unwillingness to effect a settlement. Whatever he felt, there was certainly abundant evidence of Congressional incapacity and want of prestige in the closing years of the Revolution.
Financial ruin impended as Congress was forced to turn to the states for
money and supplies, for the states as a whole were notoriously lethargic
in meeting their obligations. As James Madison observed in a letter to
Jefferson, ". . . the situation of Congress has undergone a total change
from what it originally was. Whilst they exercised the indefinite power of
emitting money on the credit of their constituents they had the whole
wealth and resources of the continent within their command, and could
go on with their affairs independently and as they pleased. Since the
resolution passed for shutting the press, this power has been entirely given
up . . . They can neither enlist pay nor feed a single soldier, nor execute
any other purpose but as the means are first put into their hands." [1]

Meanwhile, with Congress thus enfeebled, the state governments generally disposed not to hurry, and a large body of the public apathetic, the
army suffered. In fact, it barely survived the worst winter of the Revolu-

tion, one far more disastrous than that at Valley Forge. Now, in the spring of 1780, it was disintegrating, starving, and penniless, and few officers could have been more alert to the significance of its condition than Arnold. A committee of Congress headed by Arnold's old friend, General Philip Schuyler, now a civilian, reported on May 10 not only that the patience of the soldiers was exhausted but that "Their starving condition, their want of pay, and the variety of hardship they have been driven to sustain, has soured their tempers, and produced a spirit of discontent which begins to display itself under a complexion of the most alarming hue." Officers were "entirely destitute," while the Medical Department was wanting in "those necessaries which are indispensable for the sick," an especially grievous situation "as the army grow more sickly every hour." With so many sick and so few recruits turning up, infantry companies were reduced to an average of fifteen enlisted men while a number of officers, Lord Stirling wrote Washington, were "so naked" that they were "ashamed to come out of their huts." [2]

On May 25, writing to General Robert Howe, Washington considered the situation of the army "melancholy." It was indeed, for at dusk two desperate regiments of the Connecticut Line mutinied and were held in check only by the skill of several officers and the presence of the Pennsylvania Line, which was itself to mutiny the next winter because of many of the same conditions. As if this were not sufficiently discouraging, it was common knowledge that Sir Henry Clinton had laid Charleston, South Carolina, under close siege; on May 30, Washington learned of the fall of that city with the capture of General Benjamin Lincoln and five thousand men. The only salvation seemed to lie in a rejuvenated Congress which would mobilize the human, financial, and physical resources of the nation to a degree never yet attempted. The commander-in-chief expressed himself to one Congressman as "Certain . . . that unless Congress speaks in a more decisive tone; unless they are vested with powers by the several states competent to the great purposes of war, or assume them as a matter of right; and they, and the states respectively, act with more energy than they hitherto have done, that our Cause is lost." [3]

The trend of these developments was hardly lost on the wily Arnold. Early in May, he had an extended conversation in Philadelphia with his friend Schuyler, and appears to have suggested his own name for the command of West Point. On the 25th, he wrote Schuyler inquiring who was to have command on the Hudson. Schuyler replied on June 2 that he had discussed the matter with Washington. The commander-in-chief, said

Schuyler, "expressed himself with regard to you in terms such as the friends who love you could wish. . . . He expressed a desire to do whatever was agreeable to you, dwelt on your abilities, your merits, your sufferings, and on the well-earned claims you have on your country, and intimated that as soon as his arrangements for the campaign should take place that he would properly consider you." So far, so good; but Arnold read with less satisfaction that he would be offered the alternative of "an important post" or a field command. And, indeed, Washington hoped to have Arnold assume command of the left wing of the army, but this Arnold was determined not to accept. He had plans for West Point that would raise his value appreciably in the eyes of the British.[4]

Evidently in May, he renewed his correspondence with the enemy through Stansbury. Now, however, Clinton and André were in South Carolina, and in command at New York was the Hessian general, Wilhelm von Knyphausen, whose aide, Captain George Beckwith, handled the correspondence with "Mr. Moore." The gist of this correspondence was that Arnold was now prepared to undertake a decisive role, that he was concerned about his family's security, that he expected the same indemnification as before, and that he wished to confer with an officer "in whom we can place a mutual confidence." But since neither Knyphausen nor Beckwith thought it proper to make any commitment until Clinton's return, Arnold had to content himself with feeding the British bits of information, including the intelligence that the French and the Americans intended to attack Quebec. This was a false clue which Washington hoped the British would learn, but of its true character Arnold was ignorant. He also informed the British that he intended to make a trip to Connecticut and would be back in Philadelphia about July 4.[5]

His visit to his home state had two objects, to clinch the West Point command and to get rid of his property. He talked with Washington about West Point at Morristown on June 12. After his conference, he wrote to the British the same day that the French expeditionary force was due shortly in Newport and that "Mr. Moore expects to have the command of West Point offered him on his return." It appears that he embroidered what Schuyler had said into something tantamount to a promise from Washington. In a post-treason letter to Joseph Reed in which he vouched for Schuyler's integrity and loyalty, Washington said:

General Schuyler informed me that he had received a letter from Arnold intimating his intention of joining the Army and rendering such services as his leg would permit, adding, that he was incapable of active service; but could discharge the duties of a stationary command without much inconvenience or uneasiness to his leg. I answered that as we had a prospect of an active and vigorous campaign I should be glad of General Arnold's aid and assistance but saw little prospect of his obtaining such a command as appear'd to be the object of his wishes because it was my intention to draw my whole force into the field when we were in circumstances to commence our operations against New York, leaving even West Point to the care of invalids and a small garrison of militia; but if, after his previous declaration, the command of the post, for the reasons he assigned, would be more convenient and agreeable to him than a command in the field, I should readily endulge him.

Precisely what Washington said to Arnold in their conference is not clear, but certainly Arnold assumed that West Point was his.[6]

Nor was his application lacking support from other than Schuyler. On June 22, Congressman Robert Livingston of New York, who was a friend, but as innocent as Schuyler of Arnold's real intentions, wrote Washington that he hoped West Point would be given to Arnold, "whose courage is undoubted, who is the favourite of our militia, and who will agree perfectly with our Governor." Washington alluded to Livingston in his letter to Reed when he said that he had "had it hinted to me by a very respectable character, a member of Congress (not General Schuyler) that a measure of this kind would not be unacceptable to the State most immediately interested in the welfare, and safety of the post." [7]

After conferring with Washington, Arnold paid a quick visit to the Point, sharply criticized its defenses to General Robert Howe, its commander, sent an appraisal of the defenses to Clinton, then went on to Hartford. In May, he had petitioned the Assembly in behalf of himself and Israel Putnam to be admitted to the "benefits and advantages" granted the Connecticut Line of the Continental Army by acts of the previous year. These acts were designed to pay to both officers and men an allowance sufficient to make up what was lost through the fall of the currency. The Assembly voted that his wages should be adjusted with the balance to be drawn from the Treasurer, who should give him state securities for the amount of the order. The settlement was to be effected in four annual installments starting in June, 1782. Having no time to spare in discussing the exact amount owed him, he authorized Titus Hosmer of Middletown, an able, patriotic lawyer, to act as his agent; he also gave Hosmer a retainer of $1,000 to persuade the state to intercede with Pennsylvania in behalf of the Connecticut participants in the *Active* case. He then went to New Haven by way of Middletown. While at New Haven, he tried to induce Enoch Brown of Boston to buy his house for £1,000, though the original cost of the entire estate was £1,800. The house, however, was still in Arnold's name when he went over to the British, and thus became a total loss to him with its confiscation by the state.[8]

Back in Philadelphia by early July, Arnold feverishly renewed his quest with the British. Had he known at the time, he might have been chagrined to learn that, while he had been away, information supplied by him to the British had caused Clinton and Knyphausen to withdraw from a hitherto successful invasion of New Jersey. Arnold's letter of June 12 was clearly the source alluded to in Clinton's report to William Eden in London, "Immediately on my arrival from the southward [his capture of Charleston] I received from such authority as I should have risked an action upon, intelligence that the French fleet and 6000 troops were expected at Rhode Island." At the same time, Clinton's activity in the field had delayed the treason correspondence, and Arnold grew peremptory on July 15 as he received no answer to his letters. He wanted assurance of £10,000 in the event of loss of property and £100 per annum in lieu of the pay and emoluments he would be giving up. He added, "If I point out a plan of cooperation by which Sir Henry shall possess himself of West Point, the garrison, &c. &c. &c. twenty thousand pounds sterling I think will be a cheap purchase for an object of so much importance. At the same time I request a thousand pounds to be paid my agent—I expect a full and explicit answer. The 20th I set off for West Point." [9]

Arnold probably left for the Point shortly after July 21. Washington had informed Congressman Livingston on June 29 that as soon as arrangements could be effected, he would bring the present commander, General Robert Howe, into the line and would let Arnold have the post if operations of the campaign permitted the Point's being placed under an officer of such high rank. Carl Van Doren has observed that Livingston could hardly have failed to inform his friend Arnold of this conditional agreement and that "the sanguine Arnold took it as a promise." [10]

But if Arnold hoped his departure for West Point would stir the cautious British to meet his terms, he also hoped to use it to squeeze money from Congress. Hence, on July 17, after reminding Congress that he was owed nearly four years' pay, he asked for an advance of four months' pay in order to purchase field equipment. In his request he did not mention that his was to be a garrison post; had he done so, Congress would likely have been less generous. On the 20th, Congress accepted the Board of Treasury's report and authorized an advance of $25,000 to Arnold "on account of his pay; and for which he is to be accountable." With American money in his pocket and high hopes of wringing his price from the British, Arnold then left Philadelphia forever.[11]

He also left matters of communication in a state of confusion. Now operating as Arnold's principal agent and messenger between Philadelphia and New York was the Quaker, Samuel Wallis. A native of Maryland, and a landowner recently interested in the Indian country in northwestern Pennsylvania, he is said to have offered General John Sullivan a map that would lead the general's punitive expedition against the Six Nations astray, and he is known to have performed certain hush-hush services for Sir William Howe during the occupation of Philadelphia. Losing faith in Stansbury for no very good reason, unless his own impatience could qualify, Arnold found Wallis a more amenable go-between. Stansbury, however, was not excluded, and both he and Odell retained André's confidence. Also continuing in the role of messenger was John Rattoon. With Arnold off for West Point, communication between him and the British proved more difficult, and delivery of correspondence fell weeks behind. Stansbury wrote Odell on August 14, "Mr. Moore commands at West Point but things are so poorly arranged that your last important dispatches are yet in *her* [Peggy's] hands, no unquestionable carrier being yet to be met with. When you have opened your communication on the spot, these delays will be avoided." Meanwhile Arnold continued to send information to Peggy. Though this was in the guise of newsy, chatty letters, he had no doubt that she would get the intelligence into the hands of Stansbury or Wallis. It is fascinating to conjecture in what ways the transmission was effected without rousing suspicion. Certainly, however, it is increasingly evident that the romantic Peggy played an important role in her husband's treason.[12]

Soon after arriving in the north, Arnold had an encounter with Washington that shook him profoundly. Several years after the treason, the commander-in-chief recalled meeting Arnold on July 31 while the army was crossing the Hudson River at King's Ferry; Clinton's movement up the Sound toward Rhode Island had been the signal for Washington to start concentrating his forces near New York. As Washington related the incident, "I was going to see the last detachment over, and met Arnold, who asked me if I had thought of anything for him. I told him he was going to have the command of the light troops, which was a post of honour, and which his rank entitled him to. Upon this information his countenance changed and he appeared to be quite fallen; and instead of thanking me, or expressing any pleasure at the appointment, never opened his mouth." [13]

The shock indeed must have been considerable to Arnold, who saw his well-spun web of treachery suddenly in danger. It is possible, of course, that in his recollection Washington was drawing in part on his imagination, fed by the hatred he felt for the man who had betrayed his trust. Douglas Freeman, Washington's biographer, points out that in this instance Washington's memory was certainly faulty since he could not have tendered the superior but less arduous command of the left wing to Arnold and then have changed it to the inferior and more arduous command of the Light Infantry. Nor was it likely in any event that he offered the Light Infantry to Arnold, for he had previously promised it to Lafayette as a reward for his work in behalf of the United States while in France. What probably happened is that he again offered the left wing to Arnold, and Arnold was speechless at being confronted with the prospect when he thought West Point was already his.[14]

His apprehension deepened when, on the very next day, August 1, Washington announced in general orders from Peekskill that the left wing was to be commanded by Major General Arnold! Quickly Arnold hobbled over to Washington's headquarters and protested his physical inability to discharge such a responsible command. One wonders what thoughts must have crossed the mind of the grave-faced commander-in-chief, immaculate in his blue and buff, as he listened to the confession of weakness from this most redoubtable of fighters and a man who possessed an almost pathological love of action. But if Washington considered the request at all strange, he kept his own counsel.[15]

By the same token, what indeed were Arnold's thoughts? Though not a sentimental man, it is likely that, as a soldier, he must have realized that he was voluntarily relinquishing the finest military opportunity of his American career. As commander of the left wing, he would have been serving for the first time in a responsible position with the main army and with only Washington himself above him. True, the Continental Army was pitifully weak, but, such as it was, three divisions would have been his, under distinguished officers like Robert Howe, McDougall, and Steuben. His counterpart on the right wing would have been Greene, who was friendly to him. But Arnold's brusque rejection of the left wing and his insistence on the West Point command would certainly seem to indicate that he had no lingering doubts of the advantage of the British connection in reputation and fortune.

As a consequence of his importunities, he received the West Point command on August 3. Actually West Point was but the core of his jurisdiction. The Point's dependencies from Fishkill to King's Ferry were also his. So, too, were the infantry and cavalry units on the east side of the river clear down to the enemy's lines, as well as the forts at Stony Point and Verplanck's Point. Joyfully Arnold accepted his triumph, and, by August 5, he had established his headquarters at the Robinson house on the bank opposite, and two miles southeast of, West Point. Set among many fine orchards and flower gardens, this large wooden structure, which fire destroyed in 1892, had belonged to a one-time friend of Washington and now a Loyalist, Colonel Beverly Robinson. It had been General Robert Howe's residence before Arnold's appointment and was the quarters which Arnold planned to have his beloved Peggy share with him until the conspiracy was consummated with the British capture of West Point.[16]

Now in command, Arnold presently added to his official family. In need of another aide to assist Major David Franks, he asked Schuyler's former secretary, Lieutenant Colonel Richard Varick, to serve on his staff. Varick's duties, Arnold wrote him on August 5, would take up only part of his time and would leave him considerable leisure to pursue his legal studies. As an added inducement, said Arnold, "I expect Mrs. Arnold will soon be with me." Eagerly Varick accepted on the 7th, expressing his particular pleasure that Mrs. Arnold would be present. He promised that by the 13th he would report at headquarters.[17]

Ten days after Varick arrived, Arnold sent Franks to bring Peggy up from Philadelphia. Carefully Arnold specified the route and accommodations in a letter to Peggy. Six nights she should spend on the way, coming via Bristol, Trenton, Brunswick, Newark, Paramus, and Kakiat, with no single day's journey extending beyond twenty-eight miles. On the seventh day, she should arrive at the Point. He begged her not to make the stages so long as to fatigue herself or the baby, and he proposed alternative stops. He explained that a feather bed in a light wagon would make an easy seat and that the wagon would be cooler and pleasanter on smooth roads than a closed carriage. In the meantime, he awaited with ill-concealed passion the arrival of what Franks, writing from Philadelphia on August 28, described as "the greatest treasure you have." [18]

While Franks was off to Philadelphia to fetch his wife, and Varick was discovering to his disappointment that administrative and secretarial duties allowed him little time for his legal studies, Arnold learned that Clinton had at last agreed to his price. In a letter of July 24 which did not reach Arnold until precisely a month later, André declared that if Arnold would surrender West Point with all its artillery and stores and three thousand men to boot, he would be paid the sum of £20,000. This indeed was vindication of Arnold's refusal through these long, uncertain months to treat for less. It was now up to him to keep his part of the bargain— and so much remained to be done, including an augmentation of the garrison, now sadly short of the three thousand mentioned, and an inter- view with André to work out the details of the final steps of the treason.[19]

Writing his acceptance on the 30th, Arnold sent it back by William Heron of Redding, Connecticut, hitherto a patriotic member of the Assembly, who asked for a pass to New York on the 29th, ostensibly to recover money owed him. Heron proved an unreliable messenger, for, though he went to New York and subsequently became an agent for the British, he never delivered the letter. But the British were not long in ignorance of the nature of Arnold's response. On September 3, he wrote another letter and gave it to one Mary McCarthy who was the wife of a soldier of the British 9th Regiment now a prisoner. Mary was then not only issued a pass to enter the British lines with her two children but was also rowed down the river by a lieutenant and a detail of soldiers under a flag of truce. In his letter Arnold sought an interview with—as Varick later testified his commander had told him when dictating the missive— "a person in New York whose fictitious name was John Anderson, to establish a line of intelligence of the enemy's movements." [20]

All unknowingly Varick had thus innocently participated in the trea- sonous correspondence, which, however, was to last for only a few more weeks. Soon autumn would appear in the valley, blighting flower and leaf with frosty breath, and as if to meet it, plowing the river waters from the south, would come the *Vulture,* British man-of-war, with its fateful passenger aboard. But Major John André, alias John Anderson, could hardly be expected to know that the real price of Arnold's treachery was to be John André's own life.

· XXIII ·

Growing Menace to West Point

THE PRINCIPAL problem in the latter stages of the great conspiracy was one of communication, and Arnold's efforts to expose American spies in New York to the British and, at the same time, to secure some spy whom he could trust led him into a disagreement with both Lafayette and Robert Howe. When he requested from the former the names of the intelligence agents whom the Frenchman employed in New York, Lafayette refused to divulge them; his pledge of secrecy to them would not permit him to take even the new commander of the Hudson into such a confidence. Lafayette, however, seems not to have regarded Arnold's request as in any way extraordinary, as indeed it was not for one in Arnold's position.[1]

Similarly, on August 5, Arnold wrote to General Howe, whom he had just succeeded in command, stating that since the safety of the post depended in good measure on intelligence of the enemy's movements, and since Howe had been successful in his choice of agents, he must request their names. But Howe felt as honor-bound to silence as had Lafayette, and refused to comply. Miffed, Arnold persisted for a time, but Howe remained obdurate. Had Howe requested his agents to be more specific, and had he himself been of a less trusting nature, he might have uncovered the treason sooner than it was revealed, for his agents were following a spoor of a most suspicious aspect. On September 26, following Arnold's flight, Howe wrote Washington, "Some time since, if your Ex-

cellency recalls, I hinted to you that one of my emissaries had found that
a general officer high up was in compact with the enemy. I also mentioned it to General Greene, and though I could not credit it, yet the
information was so reiterated upon me that it induced me to hesitate and
gave me concern. Little did I think Arnold was the man. . . ." [2]

Very likely it was Arnold's search for a reliable agent that led him to
renew an acquaintance with Joshua Hett Smith, whom he had first encountered while commandant of Philadelphia. Smith was a Whig landholder of considerable education, and had formerly been active in the
New York militia and in provincial politics. In Charleston in 1778, he had
married a South Carolinian and had there met Howe, who, when subsequently commander at West Point, used Smith as a receiving and transmitting agent for his New York spies. Howe, moreover, recommended him
to Arnold as a trustworthy person who could be of valuable service. Soon
after seeing Smith, Arnold pressed him to give him the names of Howe's
agents, and Smith assured Arnold he would visit him and supply him
with the information. In addition, he told Arnold that Peggy would be
welcome to stay at his house if she should come north. Arnold thanked
him for these civilities, but had to be wary; Varick disliked Smith.
Joshua was the brother of William Smith, chief justice of New York and
a pronounced Loyalist now with Sir Henry Clinton. Also suspicious of
Smith was Colonel John Lamb, Arnold's old Quebec comrade, whose
wife is said to have been related to Smith. Joshua seems to have been
something of a Paul Pry, a garrulous busybody eager to share in great
affairs but lacking in the decisiveness of character needed to carry them
to a conclusion. He was to figure prominently and suspiciously in the
climax of the conspiracy. [3]

In the meantime, Arnold looked to his private affairs. When word
reached him that Titus Hosmer had died, he asked Caleb Bull in mid-
August to represent him at Hartford, to convert the back pay due him by
Connecticut into specie or sterling bills as soon as his accounts were adjusted, and to get new lawyers to speed up the *Active* case. He also tried
unsuccessfully to find a buyer for his New Haven property. He became
wildly angry when he learned of the reply of Congress to a memorial
from the general officers requesting an increase in their pay. Congress
rejected any increase but reaffirmed its position of May, 1778, namely, in
view of the depreciation of the currency, to grant seven years' half pay
and eleven hundred acres to major generals after the war. Bitterly Arnold
impugned Congress in a letter to General Parsons of the Connecticut

Line, and to both Parsons and Greene he suggested that the army send a monster committee to Congress to set forth the officers' claims and to request immediate justice. Naturally Arnold had his own particular reasons for wishing a settlement hastened; time was running out on the value of any promise Congress might make him. Quicker returns, however, even if of a very petty nature, were available in his ability to sell for cash pork, salt, wine, and rum issued him from the commissary. These stores he kept in a room which he permitted none but his servant and his housekeeper to enter. Varick soon grew disgusted at this greediness, as had Franks before him, but Arnold blandly explained that his unsettled account included back rations and that he would sell such rations as were not consumed.[4]

While he lined his pockets with this small change, he was endeavoring to discover a go-between for messages between himself and André. He cast on Colonel Elisha Sheldon, who commanded a cavalry outpost near Salem and North Castle. Arnold told Sheldon of a person in New York with whom he hoped to open a regular channel of intelligence. André, as John Anderson, then wrote to Sheldon on September 7, asking his indulgence in permitting a meeting between himself and a friend, "Mr. G[ustavus].," at twelve o'clock on September 11 at Dobbs Ferry. "Should I not be allowed to go," André added, "the officer who is to command the escort between whom and myself no distinction need be made can speak on the affair." Sheldon forwarded the letter to Arnold with the comment that he had never heard of John Anderson before opening the letter. Disturbed lest Sheldon become suspicious because of André's allusions to an officer, which would indicate official British sanction of Anderson's visit, Arnold pretended in an acknowledgment to Sheldon that his letter sent by Mary McCarthy had been intercepted and that the John Anderson of the letter might not be his real agent; in any event, he intended to go to Dobbs Ferry to meet the flag of truce.[5]

That Arnold was annoyed at the complications which seemed to have risen goes without saying. To André he wrote as "Gustavus" on September 10, maintaining the fictitious possibility that his letter of September 3 had been intercepted since he could not suppose that André would be so imprudent as to trust a British officer to come on what was presumably a private and commercial matter. André must come himself, or send some person in whom he had confidence, to Sheldon's headquarters, but he was not to hint to Sheldon what his real intentions were. Arnold advised

André to follow the plan of getting into the American lines by stealth; once he was there, Arnold assured him, he would be safe.[6]

Notwithstanding the confusion, Arnold intended to barge downriver to Dobbs Ferry in the event that André kept the appointment. As a precaution, he wrote Washington in a letter dated "Dobbs's Ferry, September 11," that he was "here this morning . . . to establish signals to be observed in case the enemy come up the river; to give some directions respecting the guard-boats, and to have a beacon fixed upon the mountain about five miles south of King's Ferry, which will be necessary to alarm the country. . . ." Unfortunately for him and the success of his plan, guardboats from the British sloop-of-war *Vulture* were patrolling the river, and one of them, evidently not apprised that Arnold's barge was coming to meet the flag, fired on the barge and chased Arnold over to the west bank; he nearly lost his life. Meanwhile, on the eastern shore, André waited for Arnold with Colonel Beverly Robinson as his companion. Neither Arnold nor André would take the lead in crossing the river under a flag of truce, with the result that both went back to their respective headquarters, leaving behind them their best chance to transact their business.[7]

Back at Robinson House, Arnold prepared for the next move. To the outpost commander at North Castle, Major Benjamin Tallmadge, a friend and Yale classmate of Nathan Hale, he wrote that if one John Anderson from New York should come to the lines, Tallmadge should send him up under escort and, if possible, accompany him. Lieutenant Colonel John Jameson, who had replaced Sheldon at Lower Salem, was also notified. Arnold then drew up a number of documents relative to the fortifications and the number of men in his command, now 3,086, to be given to André. On September 15, he wrote that if there were any objections to André's coming by land, despite the fact that he would receive protection from Tallmadge and Jameson, "I will send a person [Smith] in whom you may confide, by water to meet you at Dobbs's Ferry on Wednesday the 20th Inst between 11 and 12 o'clock at night, who will conduct you to a place of safety, where I will meet you. It will be necessary for you to be disguised. . . . If I do not hear from you before you may depend upon the person being punctual at the place before mentioned." In a few sentences veiled with commercial terminology he indicated the strength of Washington's forces and of his own command.[8]

The same day, Arnold received a note from the commander-in-chief containing vital information. "I shall be at Peekskill on Sunday evening

[September 17], on my way to Hartford to meet the French Admiral and General," Washington wrote. "You will be pleased to send down a guard of a captain and 50 at that time, and direct the Qr. Master to endeavour to have a nights forage for about forty horses. You will keep this to yourself, as I want to make my journey a secret." But it was soon no secret, at least not to the British, for Arnold at once dashed off the following to André: "General Washington will be at King's Ferry Sunday evening next on his way to Hartford, where he is to meet the French Admiral and General and will lodge at Peak's Kill." Having thus afforded the British the opportunity of capturing Washington during the river crossing should they be able to take advantage of the information, Arnold could turn to Peggy and his young son and enjoy their companionship.[9]

They had arrived on Thursday, the 14th, at Smith's house at Haverstraw on the west bank of the Hudson, and Arnold went to meet them. It was therefore no coincidence that he could write his letter of the 15th to André in which he mentioned that a person would come to meet André at Dobbs Ferry; a conference with Smith, and perhaps with Peggy, had obviously been held. Arnold was overjoyed to have Peggy with him again, and not simply as a fellow conspirator. After weeks of separation, their reunion had the elements of a honeymoon but one spiced with knowledge of the dangerous game they were playing. No one except Arnold himself, furthermore, could have been more aware that the success of the conspiracy had hinged on the West Point assignment. Recently at a dinner party at Robert Morris's house in Philadelphia, a friend of the Arnolds had congratulated Peggy on Arnold's having been appointed to a more honorable command than West Point. Presumably this was an allusion to the left wing of the army. The effect of the information on the startled girl was to bring on, as Morris testified, "hysteric fits. Efforts were made to convince her that the general had been selected for a preferable station. These explanations, however, to the astonishment of all present produced no effect."[10]

But now they were together and could talk of many things. There was the concert given by the Chevalier de la Luzerne which she had attended, and if her remarks on him and others present were as feline in nature as were her comments on him in a letter to Arnold, they must have been most entertaining. They could whisper, too, of the conspiracy: of Stansbury, Odell, and Wallis; of Clinton and André; of Washington's trip to Hartford and the bare possibility that the British would intercept him on the river. Possibly they also chatted of the gathering in New York of a powerful British squadron under Admiral Rodney and the loading of transports with troops said to be bound for the South but actually destined for the highlands of the Hudson. The hours were becoming fewer, and soon the great conspiracy would culminate in the thunder of British naval guns and a swift surprise assault by overwhelming numbers of redcoats. Arnold probably explained to Peggy that, to facilitate this, he had sent out several hundred men on firewood and guard details, thereby preventing the defenses from being finished and weakening the garrison. Despite his applications for teams to use in repairing the great chain stretched across the Hudson to block the passage of British warships, teams and supplies were not available, and the supports of the chain continued to deteriorate; as early as June, he had been convinced that a heavily laden ship, riding a strong wind and tide, could break the links.[11]

It is likely that Arnold dared not chide Peggy too seriously on the contents of a letter Hannah had sent him. Peggy's youth and love of gaiety must have stirred the older woman to bitterness. Of West Point, Hannah said, "As you have neither purling streams nor sighing swains at West Point, 'tis no place for me; nor do I think Mrs. Arnold will be long pleased with it, though I expect it may be rendered dear to her for a few hours by the presence of a certain chancellor; who, by the by, is a dangerous companion for a particular lady in the absence of her husband." The chancellor alluded to was Robert R. Livingston, a family friend, about whose attentions, added Hannah, "I could say more than prudence will permit. I could tell you of frequent private assignations and of numberless *billets doux,* if I had an inclination to make mischief. But as I am of a very peaceable temper I'll not mention a syllable of the matter." [12]

In these waspish comments Hannah's suspicion and jealousy are clear. Still there is nothing further to substantiate her gossip, and Peggy Shippen Arnold, with her marriage to Arnold and her prettiness, her moods and her hysterics, was a prime subject for catty tongues. Had there been anything real to Hannah's charge, one can be sure that others besides herself would probably have known of it and would certainly have talked. Arnold knew his loyal but lonely sister too well to make an issue of her tales. Presently, moreover, as if in atonement for her revelations to her brother, Hannah wrote a warmly affectionate letter to Peggy describing how sorely she and young Harry missed her.[13]

Sunday noon, September 17, while Arnold was dining with his family, with the Smiths who had arrived for the weekend, and with his aides and officers from West Point, a messenger arrived with two letters from

Beverly Robinson, who, on Saturday, had come upriver on the *Vulture* to an anchorage off Tellers Point. One letter was to be forwarded to General Putnam; the other was addressed to Arnold. Robinson said that if Putnam had returned to Connecticut, "I beg my letter [to Putnam] may be returned to me; and in that case I am persuaded (from the humane and generous characters you bear) that could I be so happy as to see you, you would readily grant me the same request I should make to him but for prudential reasons I dare not explain the matter further until I have some assurances that it shall be secret if not granted." [14]

Skimming through the letter, Arnold pocketed it with a brief remark that Robinson wanted to see him. At once, Colonel Lamb, who was in charge of the principal defenses at West Point, protested that to grant Robinson an interview would invite suspicion of an improper correspondence; Robinson should address communications concerning his private affairs to the governor of the state. Believing that General Washington would bear him out, Lamb persuaded Arnold to agree to speak to the commander-in-chief about the matter when next he saw him. Lamb was so in earnest that Arnold saw no point in arguing the case. [15]

Later that day, Arnold joined Washington at Smith's house, where the general had stopped for dinner, and accompanied him across the river to Peekskill. On arriving, he mentioned the Robinson letter. The reply he received could have left no doubt in Arnold's mind; he was not to hold an interview with Robinson, and he was to notify him by letter that he should get in touch with the civil authorities. Arnold wrote as directed, but, under the urging of Varick, who thought the answer too friendly in tone, he revised the letter. Unbeknownst to Varick, however, he sent along another letter as well, one in which he said that he would dispatch a person to Dobbs Ferry or to the *Vulture* on Wednesday night, September 20, with a boat and a flag of truce. Robinson could depend on the man's secrecy and honor. Meanwhile the *Vulture* should remain where she was. Arnold enclosed with his private letter to Robinson a letter for "a gentleman in New York from one in the country." To that gentleman in New York, André, Arnold sent copies of his communications of September 10 and 15, the one requesting André to come to Sheldon, the other proposing a meeting on September 20 at Dobbs Ferry. André would thereby realize that the earlier letters had been authentic. The main difference from the original plan was that Arnold might now send a man at night to the *Vulture*. [16]

The afternoon that Arnold crossed the river with Washington he is said to have had an uncomfortable moment with Lafayette. Though the story is based on a Lafayette reminiscence—and at times the Frenchman had a vivid imagination—it could well have happened. For weeks, Washington and the French leaders had hoped that the Comte de Guichen, in command of the French West Indies fleet, would bring the fleet northward or send enough of it to give Admiral de Ternay at Newport an advantage in strength over the British. In that event, Ternay or Guichen, moving in from the sea, and Washington and Rochambeau, attacking by land, could try out Washington's plan for an assault on New York. Of late, Washington had lost hope of Guichen's coming, had dismissed most of his militia, and was now on his way to Hartford to discuss the deteriorating war situation with Rochambeau. Rumor that Admiral Rodney had arrived instead of Guichen was discouraging to all, but Lafayette clung to a faint hope that Guichen might still appear. Since Lafayette knew that Arnold sent flags of truce to New York and had his own agents there, the Frenchman turned to Arnold in the boat and said, "Since you have communication with the enemy, you must ascertain as soon as possible what has became of Guichen." Startled, Arnold burst out, "What do you mean?" Before Lafayette could explain, the boat landed, and the conversation took another turn. The shock of misinterpretation, however, must have put spurs to Arnold's desire to speed the plot to a finish.[17]

He could have been hardly less eager than Clinton and André. According to Lord George Germain after the conspiracy, Clinton contemplated waiting until Washington, from Kingsbridge, and the French, from Long Island, where they were to have been landed by their fleet, had attacked New York. Said Clinton, "General Arnold surrendering himself, the forts and garrisons, at this instant, would have given every advantage which could have been desired: Mr. Washington must have instantly retired from King's bridge, and the French troops upon Long Island would have been consequently left unsupported, and probably would have fallen into our hands. The consequent advantage of so great an event I need not explain." Faced with an absence of an Allied offensive, Clinton would still have found possession of West Point invaluable in permitting him to hold the Hudson, thereby splitting the colonies. With the arrival of Rodney's powerful squadron on September 14, he need not fear the French naval threat. Hence, on the 19th, he readied ships and men for a dash up the river as soon as André could work out with Arnold the details of the surrender of West Point.[18]

André's task was unmistakably a hazardous one. Realizing this, Clinton cautioned him not to put on a disguise or to enter the American lines. Though Clinton may have been loath to let André go, the one officer in the army for whom the querulous, grumpy general had any warm feeling, there can be little doubt that both officers had understood that André was to be the contact man. Clinton later vowed that Arnold had originally sought the interview with André, but the record is against him. In the middle of June, 1779, when writing to Arnold of how he could surrender a force to the British, André had said, "The method wou'd be arranged by my meeting you as flag of truce or otherwise as soon as you can come near us." Certainly what André had to do came as no surprise to him.[19]

Nor is there convincing evidence that André went to the *Vulture* (ominous name!) with trepidation and foreboding. Strong doubt, however, has been cast on the old story that on his last night in New York he attended a banquet given in his honor at Jacobus Kip's residence by officers who knew of his new duty, and that in the pleasures of food, wine, and good fellowship, he had sung the song "How Stands the Glass Around?," supposedly rendered by the ill-fated General James Wolfe to his staff on the eve of his assault on Quebec. The only known activity of André's the day before he departed was his visit, in Clinton's company, to Madame Riedesel, the lively little wife of the German general who had shared in Burgoyne's unfortuate expedition. It is unlikely that the healthy-minded André saw in this visit any portent. What is more probable is that, in his youthful zeal, he was buoyed up by the patriotic adventure itself and the distinct possibility of promotion. He later remarked that he sought military glory, a goal that seemed far more substantial and awakened more enthusiasm in the eighteenth century than in our era. He also considered the thanks of his general and the approbation of his King "a rich reward for such an undertaking." No fears, then, no backward glances troubled his composure as, on Wednesday, September 20, the young officer shook hands with his commander and left New York for his rendezvous with the American general who contended that he could best serve his country by betraying it.[20]

· XXIV ·

The Meeting with André

THE *VULTURE,* Captain Andrew Sutherland and Colonel Beverly Robinson aboard, swung at her moorings off Tellers Point, about fourteen air miles from Arnold's headquarters. Those on her had an unrestricted view of King's Ferry and the forts at Stony Point and Verplanck's Point, approximately six miles to the north above Haverstraw Bay. At seven o'clock in the evening of September 20, a small boat grated against her hull, and up the gangway nimbly climbed Major John André in the brilliant scarlet of the British Army. After a warm handclasp, Sutherland led him and Robinson to his cabin.

Tonight was the night, and both André and Sutherland had stories to tell. André said that he bore letters from Clinton to Sutherland and Robinson. In his letter to the former, Clinton ordered Sutherland to bring the *Vulture* down to Dobbs Ferry, the place where André was to have met Arnold. At the outset, therefore, André had disobeyed his superior by leaving Dobbs Ferry to be his own messenger to the *Vulture.* As for Sutherland, he related an incident of the day that disturbed him acutely. Several Americans had raised a white flag from some rocks ashore, and he and Robinson, thinking Arnold might be trying to communicate with them, sent out a boat. When the craft was within range, the Americans fired on it, forcing it to return to the *Vulture.*[1]

What to do now that André had arrived was a serious question. Clinton's orders for André to wait for the *Vulture* at Dobbs Ferry and for

Sutherland to bring the man-of-war there had been explicit. At the same time, Arnold had clearly indicated that he might send a person aboard that night. After discussing the situation, the officers decided to remain at the anchorage in the event that the visitor should arrive. For hours, André walked the deck in anxious suspense, talking now with Robinson, now with Sutherland. When the false dawn arrived, with still no word from Arnold, André had to make another decision. To leave now might upset the whole conspiracy, while to absent himself longer from New York might excite suspicion in that quarter among American agents. He therefore compromised by pleading so bad a cold and a return of a recent stomach disorder that Robinson and Sutherland insisted on his remaining aboard until he was better. He wrote to Clinton that he hoped to get back to New York on the morrow. In another letter, however, one that presumably neither Robinson nor Sutherland saw, he said, "This is the second excursion I have made without an ostensible reason, and Colonel Robinson both times of the party. A third would infallibly fix suspicions. I have therefore thought it best to remain here on pretence of sickness, as my inclosed letter will feign, and try further expedients." [2]

One of the expedients was a letter of protest on September 21 from Sutherland to Arnold at the firing on the flag of truce. The letter was in André's hand and countersigned by "John Anderson, Secretary." Arnold could thereby be in no doubt that André was aboard the *Vulture*. This letter, together with one to Arnold from Robinson expressing the latter's disappointment at not seeing the messenger at the appointed time and his anxiety to conclude the business, was sent to Arnold under a flag of truce. Arnold received the missives in the afternoon and, while at Verplanck's Point, briefly spoke to Colonel James Livingston concerning the firing on the *Vulture's* boat the day before. Livingston, who had commanded one of the French-Canadian contingents during the assault on Quebec, thought Arnold "a good deal reserved" on this first day of autumn, 1780.[3]

Arnold had occasion to be both reserved and concerned, for the final details were not easy to arrange. To make the atmosphere more tense, Franks, who had had enough of Arnold's rudeness, was thoroughly disgruntled at having failed, the previous weekend, to obtain a transfer to the staff of one of the French generals, while Varick, on Sunday afternoon, had quarreled with Smith after Arnold had gone off to meet Washington. Despising and distrusting Smith, who had expressed his opinion that America could have made an honorable peace with the Carlisle

Commission in 1778, which the British government had sent to America to offer virtual home rule, Varick burst into sound and fury. But Smith, to Varick's disappointment, remained distressingly unruffled. He left the next day to take his family to Fishkill, presumably to get them out of the way should Arnold wish to meet André at his house.[4]

Arnold's arrangements with Smith entailed careful planning. The idea of Smith's removing his family to Fishkill had evidently been worked out with Smith—and possibly Peggy—when Peggy had first arrived at Smith's house from Philadelphia. It was necessary, furthermore, to notify Smith that he was to go to Dobbs Ferry or to the *Vulture* on the 20th. Hence Arnold gave him a pass of that date which read, "Permission is given to Joshua Smith, Esquire, a gentleman, Mr. John Anderson, who is with him, and his two servants, to pass and repass the guards near King's Ferry at all times." Arnold also gave Smith an order for a light boat to be drawn from Major Kierse, the quartermaster at King's Ferry.[5]

The success of the conspiracy now hinged in large measure upon Smith. Just how much he knew of Arnold's design is something of a mystery. The record of his trial and the narrative he subsequently wrote are at odds on many points, and the difference undoubtedly can be accounted for by the fact that the one was a record of his fight for life and the other was an attempt to convince the British, to whom he later fled, that he was a true Loyalist. When it suited him, Smith could embroider with convincing sincerity and consummate skill so intricate a pattern of allegations and denials that truth and fiction became practically indistinguishable. From contradictions in the two accounts, however, it is reasonably clear that he knew nothing of the real purpose of André's visit but that he thought the visit might involve the discussion of propositions that could serve as the basis for a satisfactory peace. In any event, he was hardly so naïve as to believe that an affair attended by so much risk could be simply of a commercial nature.[6]

Smith proved so frail a reed for Arnold to lean on that, though he had Arnold's order on the afternoon of the 20th, he procured neither boat nor boatmen; hence, on the 21st, Arnold intended to leave as little as possible to chance or to Smith. Disappointed that André was not already at Smith's house waiting for him, he went downriver to Verplanck's Point, where, from Colonel Livingston, he received Sutherland's message from the *Vulture* concerning the firing on her flag of truce. Crossing over almost at once to Stony Point, he questioned Major Kierse about the boat he had commissioned Smith to obtain. Learning that no boat was at hand, he ordered his barge upriver to bring one down and asked Kierse to see that it reached that part of Haverstraw Creek nearest Smith's house as soon as possible.

Afterward, he rode from Stony Point to Smith's, arriving in time to put weight behind Smith's attempt to persuade Samuel Colquhoun, one of his tenants, to go down the river that night. When Colquhoun protested his reluctance and fatigue, since he had been up much of the previous night, Arnold appealed to his patriotism. This proving futile, Arnold rasped out a threat to view him as a Tory. Intimidated, the man agreed, as did his brother, Joseph Colquhoun, when confronted with the Arnold technique. Presently Smith sent his Negro servant to the landing, and the man returned with a note from Kierse that the boat was ready. At that, Joseph protested to Arnold that neither he nor his brother wanted to go. But when Arnold threatened to put both men under arrest, they sullenly agreed to go with Smith to the boat.

While Arnold, accompanied by Smith's Negro servant with a spare horse for André, trotted down the river road to a spot opposite the *Vulture,* Smith rowed with muffled oars to the man-of-war, lying six miles away. In the event that an American guardboat hailed him, he had a new pass that Arnold had made out in the morning: "Permission is given to Joshua Smith, Esq., to go to Dobb's Ferry with three men and a boy with a flag to carrry some letters of a private nature for gentlemen in New York and to return immediately." Arnold had added as an "N.B." that Smith "has permission to go at such hours and times as the tide and his business suits." [7]

Smith carried a letter to Robinson. "This," wrote Arnold, "will be delivered to you by Mr. Smith who will conduct you to a place of safety. Neither Mr. Smith or any other person shall be acquainted with your proposals. If they (which I doubt not) are of such a nature that I can officially take notice of them, I shall do it with pleasure. If not, you shall be permitted to return immediately. I take it for granted Colonel Robinson will not propose anything that is not for the interest of the United States as well as himself." The letter, so couched, was sufficient to convince any American guardboat officer that the trip was legitimate. Arnold had also given Smith a scrap of paper on which nothing more was written than "Gustavus to John Anderson." André could henceforth be in no doubt, if still he was, that "Gustavus" was Arnold and that Arnold was waiting ashore to see him. André, moreover, had soon to make up his mind since, hard on the hour of midnight, Smith's boat entered the loom of the *Vulture* and the watch hoarsely ordered it alongside. The officer of the deck, evidently not apprised that the ship might have a visitor, gave Smith the rough side of his tongue until Captain Sutherland sent word that Smith was to come aboard. A few moments later, he was closeted in the captain's cabin.[8]

The decision on the *Vulture* was momentous. That André should go ashore rather than that Arnold should come to the *Vulture* had been clearly understood. In no way did Arnold order André to meet him; nor could he have done so by any authority real or fancied. The interview, moreover, had been at André's own suggestion. André also understood that if it was too late for Smith to return him to the *Vulture* when the interview was over, Smith was to lodge him until the next night in a safe place. In the matter of attire, Sutherland suggested that André not wear his regimental coat, and offered him clothes of his own. But remembering Clinton's instructions, André refused; he accepted only a large blue watchcoat, or surtout, which, flapping open, scarcely concealed the scarlet regimentals. Just before leaving, Robinson observed that, since Smith's boat was so large for the two men handling it, one of the *Vulture's* boats should tow it. Both André and Smith objected to this as inconsistent with the character of a flag of truce despite the fact that the boat was actually not displaying one. Then, between twelve and one o'clock, the boat moved over the dark water toward the rendezvous with Arnold. Wisdom after an event may be easy to achieve, but it does seem extraordinary that Sutherland did not order out a ship's boat to hover at a safe distance offshore, ready to ensure André's safe return.[9]

After a row of two miles to the west side of the river, about six miles below Stony Point, the boat grated on the shore. Presently, said Samuel Colquhoun, "I heard the noise of a man at a bank above, and Mr. Smith went up and returned immediately; and the person we brought on shore went up, and Mr. Smith stayed with us." What transpired in that place where, according to Smith, Arnold was "hid among firs," is another of the mysteries of the case. What, indeed, were the thoughts of the traitorous American hero and the ardent young English officer? The compelling factor of time, however, must have kept their attention on the subject. Naturally they discussed Arnold's reward; at least Arnold subsequently wrote to Clinton that they had, and there seems no good reason to doubt that he wanted the money issue settled. And, of course, they went over the details of the surrender. Although it seems that the essential elements could surely have been covered within the two hours they were together, they were still deep in conversation when Smith interrupted them at four o'clock to inform them that dawn was not far off.[10]

The question of what to do with André now became of paramount importance. Smith later claimed that Arnold came down to the boat and tried to persuade the Colquhouns to row André back to the *Vulture*. The brothers, on the other hand, asserted that they saw neither Arnold nor André after the latter had stepped ashore without their knowing his identity. In fact, Samuel declared that it was Smith who tried to get them to row André back and that they refused because of fatigue and the approach of daylight; at this point, said Samuel, Smith told them they could do as they thought best.[11]

It is unlikely that Arnold, proficient in methods of intimidation, would have let the men leave had there not been unfinished business to transact with André; and on the chance that he would not be able to complete the negotiations, he had brought along a spare horse. Thus, while Smith left with the Colquhouns for Haverstraw Creek, he and André rode to Smith's house where the Englishman was to remain concealed until nightfall. On the way, to André's surprise, they were hailed and passed by an American sentry. André had therefore entered the American lines contrary to his own expectations and to Clinton's instructions. None could have known better than himself the increasing peril of his situation.[12]

Both men soon discovered that the situation was becoming not only more perilous but more complicated as well. While they conferred upstairs in Smith's handsome two-storied stone house with its wooden wings, and while Smith, who had returned, had breakfast prepared, the distant boom of a heavy gun resounded across the river, followed by another and still another. Startled, both men sprang to a window. What they saw must have set their hearts to hammering with the detonations: cannon on Tellers Point were firing on the *Vulture*.[13]

For some time the presence of the sloop-of-war had angered Colonel Livingston, who had applied vainly to Arnold for cannon. The very night that Arnold and André met on the west bank of the Hudson, Livingston was busy on the east bank mounting a four-pounder and a howitzer borrowed from Colonel Lamb at West Point. Scoffing at Livingston, Lamb said, "Firing at a ship with a four pounder, is in my opinion, a waste of powder; as the damage she will sustain, is not equal to the expense." But Lamb was wrong. Robinson, aboard the *Vulture,* wrote Clinton that the Americans "began a very hot fire on us . . . which continued two hours . . . but luckily their magazine blew up." Furthermore, "tho' every exertion was made to get the ship out of their reach sooner, six shot hulled us, one between wind and water. Many others struck the sails, rigging, and boats on deck. Two shells hit us, one full on the quarterdeck, another near the main shrouds. Captain Sutherland is the only person hurt, and he very slightly on the nose by a splinter." The effect of this shelling was that between eight and nine o'clock the *Vulture* dropped downriver out of range.[14]

Arnold now realized that he must change his plans to get André back to the British. Until the *Vulture* departed, the water route had appeared

Head Quarters Robinsons
House Sep.ʳ 22ᵈ.1780

Pamet Mr. John Anderson to pass the
Guard to the White Plains, or below
if he Chuses. He being on Public
Business by my Direction

B. Arnold M Genl

ARNOLD'S PASS TO MAJOR ANDRÉ

the likely one, but now the land route seemed more feasible. To cover both possibilities, Arnold scribbled two passes for Smith, heading them as from Robinson House. One gave him permission to go by boat with three men and a flag to Dobbs Ferry and return; the other authorized him to pass the guards to White Plains and return. With the latter contingency in mind, Arnold inscribed the following pass for André: "Permit Mr. John Anderson to pass the guard to the White Plains or below, if he chooses, he being on public business by my direction." [15]

Though André accepted the pass, he still believed that somehow he was to be returned to the *Vulture*. When Arnold gave him the plans of West Point and expressed a wish that, in the event of interception, André would destroy them, the Englishman replied that of course he would do so, "as when I went into the boat I should have them tied about with a string and a stone." Arnold did not argue the point since time alone would reveal which plan would have to be adopted; certainly he did not order André to return by land.[16]

Why Arnold ever insisted that André take the papers and why André accepted them will likely never be known. There were six documents, all but one in Arnold's handwriting. While they might have been useful to Clinton, the latter had excellent intelligence reports from his own agents concerning the fort. He later remarked that both Arnold and André could not have helped knowing that the documents "were not wanted for my information." One theory is that they were given to André or exacted by him as a pledge of fidelity since he was already mistrustful at having been led into the American lines and was suspicious of betrayal. But Arnold had been at work for days preparing the papers to give to André and had brought them along with him for that purpose. Did he want to demonstrate to Clinton beyond the shadow of a doubt that he had come over completely to the British and that the fortress could be taken? After all, hesitation or a false military move on Clinton's part might spoil the game, thus depriving Arnold of the full value due him for his treason and making of that treason but an empty gesture. Money and reputation were at stake, and Arnold was not one to scoff at either.[17]

Arnold left by ten o'clock for Stony Point to return to Robinson House, and Smith accompanied him to the barge. André said that before Arnold departed, "some mention had been made of my crossing the river, and going by another route; but, I objected much against it, and thought it was settled that in the way I came I was also to return." En route to Stony Point, however, Arnold must have talked over the matter with Smith; presumably he left the decision to Smith's discretion. They must also have discussed the question of a disguise for André, which would indubitably be necessary if the land route were chosen. What else they considered is only conjecture, but it is clear that Arnold placed much faith in Smith—had to, perhaps, because there was no one else to trust. Still, he had carefully gone over in his own mind the pros and cons of both routes. The historian of the conspiracy is therefore undoubtedly correct in his surmise that, given the hazards of American gunboats on the river on the first night after the firing on the *Vulture*—gunboats whose officers would surely hesitate to let a British officer slip by them regardless of his pass—Arnold was convinced that the land route was no more dangerous than that by water.[18]

While Arnold went upriver in his barge, probably thinking the conspiracy on its way to happy fulfillment, Smith returned to André, who was growing impatient to be on his way. Smith's indecisiveness was effectively demonstrated by the delay. If he had resolved to take André to the *Vulture,* which returned to her station later in the day, he could perhaps have done so after dark; but he made no attempt. True, it might have been the ague from which he suffered that impelled him not to spend the night hours on the river; at least, this was Smith's own contention. The historian Justin Winsor, however, seems to have called the turn a century afterward when he said, "The fact probably was, that, after the cannonading of the morning, Smith had no desire to risk himself on the river in a boat." Instead, therefore, of making arrangements to go to the *Vulture,* Smith chose the land route, but, whereas he might have been helping André through the day to put dangerous miles behind him, he waited until late in the afternoon to start. André, still expecting to return by water, then learned that Smith "to my great mortification persisted in his determination of carrying me by the other route." [19]

The land route required a change of clothing. So far as Smith knew, or pretended to know, André was only a merchant masquerading as an officer, though to believe this, after he had been on the *Vulture* and had seen André together with Robinson and Sutherland, would have strained the credulity of a less intelligent man than Smith—and, while Smith's character has been impugned, his intelligence has not. Perhaps Arnold should have told him who André really was, in which case, Smith, with the Loyalist propensities which he professed at the moment, might have made a real effort to get André to the *Vulture* that night; furthermore, no disguise would have been needed. On the other hand, Arnold may have refused to divulge André's identity for fear that the shifty Smith would tell all to the Americans. His mind made up to go by land, Smith gave André a beaver hat and one of his coats, a purple or brown garment trimmed with worn gold lace and buttonholes bound in vellum. André wore his own nankeen smallclothes, his shiny white-topped boots, and his blue watchcoat with its heavy cape. By putting off his regimentals, André disobeyed another of Clinton's injunctions. Finally, when the sun began to set, Smith, accompanied by his Negro servant, started out with André, the latter on the horse that Arnold had left behind.

Their course caused the usually convivial André to fall silent and reserved. They rode to Stony Point and crossed at King's Ferry; and wherever they went, Smith talked. In fact, Smith, strangely jocular, was a veritable chatterbox, carrying on extended conversations with officers at Stony Point and with Livingston at Verplanck's Point. To all, Smith said that he was bound for Robinson House. When Livingston, who had studied law with Judge William Smith, invited him to remain for supper or at least for a drink of grog, Smith declined, explaining that he was with a gentleman on urgent business who was anxious to move on. Livingston subsequently declared that he did not see Smith's companion because darkness had fallen and the gentleman had ridden on ahead. Afterward, Smith and André headed downriver, André still concerned but, in Smith's opinion, more cheerful.[20]

Between eight and nine o'clock a hoarse challenge brought them to a sudden stop, and Captain Ebenezer Boyd, in command of a patrol of New York militia, strode forward and demanded their credentials. Smith at once produced Arnold's pass and informed Boyd of their intention to go to White Plains to gather intelligence for the general. When Smith boldly inquired the best route, Boyd told them the safest way was via North Castle since British partisans infested the Tarrytown road. At the same time, Boyd, who became inquisitive and almost officiously solicitous, insisted that they remain the night at a neighboring house. Though unwilling, André submitted when Smith, fearful of detection, refused to move on. Accordingly the two slept in the same bed, Smith's slumbers disturbed by André, who constantly tossed and turned and sighed.[21]

The next morning, Saturday, September 23, André's mood lightened; this was the day of his return. They were up before sunrise and rode more than a half-dozen miles to a point near Pine's Bridge across the Croton River, where they stopped at a farmhouse for breakfast. André was now communicative and gay, but not for long; at breakfast Smith shocked him by telling him that henceforth he was on his own. It is difficult to ascribe Smith's reason for not going farther to any motive but fear. The area beyond the Croton was the so-called "Neutral Ground," the zone between the American and British lines frequented by partisans of both sides. These partisans were the American "Skinners" and the British "Cowboys." Of the two, the "Cowboys" confined their activities largely to robbing American farmers of their livestock to sell to the British. The "Skinners," on the other hand, despoiled friend and foe alike, his person as well as his animals; hence, the name "Skinners." Smith was known to many of the latter, and, with his acquaintance with them and with his pass, could probably have got André safely through to the British. Had the "Cowboys" intercepted them, André would have had nothing to fear and could have spared Smith from molestation. But Smith, who knew the roads, let André, who knew them not, start out for White Plains by himself.[22]

While Smith therefore turned back at the Croton River to report to Arnold, André rode on. Naturally of a cheerful disposition, he may have consoled himself that he was well rid of a prying character like Smith, that Arnold's pass would protect him, and that he had not far to go to be among friends. Moreover, he may have seen himself winning honor and fame within a week not only by securing general recognition of his dangerous exploit but also by personally leading one of the assault columns against West Point. But it is possible, too, that this happy contemplation, if indeed he pursued it, was clouded by the realization that, short as was his distance, he had fifteen miles to cover before he could be certain of safety. He was still in a dangerous country, he had shed his regimentals, and between his stockings and his feet lay the documents Arnold had given him. In all these respects he had acted contrary to his general's instructions. He had disobeyed for the good of the Cause, to be sure, but, in doing so, he had hazarded his honor and his life. Though he may have been cheerful after passing the Croton, it could not have been for long as he entered this "No Man's Land" of ruined farms and dismal woods.[23]

· XXV ·

Debacle

THE GREAT conspiracy burst into the open between nine and ten o'clock that Saturday morning. André had had phenomenally good luck near Tarrytown when he passed an American officer whom he knew, Colonel Samuel B. Webb. An officer in the 3d Connecticut Regiment, Webb had been a prisoner since December, 1777, and was now on parole. Though Webb stared hard at him, André was not stopped. But hardly had he caught his breath when his good fortune ran out after he crossed a rude bridge over a brook barely a half mile north of Tarrytown. A group of seven young militiamen on a strictly volunteer basis had banded together to stop all British sympathizers and rob them. While four kept watch for cavalry units of either army, three lay in wait on the south side of the bridge. These three were John Paulding, Isaac Van Wart, and David Williams. It was André's white-topped boots that seem to have convinced the trio to stop him. As his horse stepped off the bridge, the three leaped out of the bushes, and Paulding, his musket ready, challenged him.[1]

At this point, André appears to have shown himself wanting in the calmness and dissimulation that might have carried him through the predicament; espionage was simply not his dish. He answered the challenge by expressing the hope that the men belonged to his party. Asked what party he meant, he replied, "The lower party." When Paulding acknowledged that this was indeed their party, he exclaimed, "Thank God, I am once more among friends!" And observing a British army coat on Paulding, he declared that he was a British officer. To his dismay, however, Paulding now told him that they were Americans, and ordered him to dismount. At this, André flourished Arnold's pass, but Paulding, who was the only literate one of the trio, waved it aside; André's admission had made them suspicious. Said Paulding later, "Had he pulled out General Arnold's pass first, I should have let him go."

There is some doubt that, even then, they would have kept him had they not discovered the documents; they were looking for loot, not evidence of treason. They robbed him of his watch and the little money he had, and, disappointed at not finding more, they decided he must have valuables concealed on his person. Taking him under a tree, they made him strip. At first, he threatened them with Arnold's displeasure; when this failed to impress them, he tried to bribe them. But the papers that Paulding and Williams found when they ripped off his boots and stockings evidently awakened a sentiment deeper than cupidity, at least in Paulding. With the other two concurring, he made up his mind to turn André over to Lieutenant Colonel John Jameson at North Castle. These three bushwhackers were unsavory characters bent on a type of enterprise condemned by both armies. Still, the best that can be said of them is enough: they may have saved the republic that Saturday morning.

Colonel Jameson was probably far from happy with the new responsibility that Paulding gave him. To begin with, Jameson was comparatively new to his post, having succeeded Sheldon when the latter had been arrested on spurious charges brought by Dr. Darius Stoddard, an army surgeon. Jameson, moreover, was an officer who possessed neither energy nor much intelligence. Since he knew Arnold was expecting a John Anderson from New York, he sent him to Arnold together with a letter explaining the capture and discovery of the papers. That he should not at once have become suspicions of Arnold seems extraordinary; it is doubtful that the more intelligent Sheldon would have made the same mistake. Fortunately Major Benjamin Tallmadge, more skilled at espionage, returned from patrol. At his vigorous intercession, Jameson grudgingly ordered André brought back to his quarters. Though Jameson insisted that his letter to Arnold go through, he sent the captured documents to Washington, who was on the way back from Hartford.[2]

Along with the letter and the documents, which were dispatched in their different directions late on Sunday, went a letter from André to Washington. André confessed who he was and explained that his purpose was to meet a person who was to give him intelligence. He emphasized that against his "stipulation" and his "intention," and "without . . . knowledge beforehand" he was led into the American lines. "Thus become prisoner," he added, "I had to concert my escape." André hit the nail squarely when he admitted that he was "too little accustomed to duplicity to have succeeded." [3]

Meanwhile Arnold, the individual—next to André—most affected by these developments, continued in ignorance of them until Monday, but the interim was far from pleasant. Incensed at what they considered Arnold's avarice as embodied in a commercial transaction with New York people effected through Smith, his aides, Varick and Franks, begged Peggy to exert her influence to break up the intimacy between her husband and Smith. Their resentment broke out again, very hotly this time, at dinner on Saturday, September 23, when Smith returned to tell Arnold that André was clear of the American lines. Both Smith and Lamb were guests, as Arnold, his family, and his aides sat down. When a servant presently informed Peggy of a shortage of butter, Arnold exclaimed, "Bless me, I had forgot the olive oil I bought in Philadelphia. It will do very well with salt fish." After the servant brought the oil, Arnold said that it had cost eighty Continental dollars. Smith then sarcastically remarked that what Arnold really meant was that it had cost eighty cents. This tart comment on the low value of the dollar infuriated Varick, who retorted, "That is not true, Mr. Smith." At this point, the salt fish and the olive oil were forgotten as tempers exploded all around the table. Varick and Smith loosed verbal thunderbolts at each other, with Franks joining Varick and Arnold opposing Franks. The scene soon became so stormy that Peggy cried out sharply, begging them to stop their quarreling. Varick, who was not well, excused himself at once and went to his room, then used as the office at Robinson House. The meal ended in a sullen silence.

With dinner over and Smith on his way to Fishkill, Varick was soon joined by Franks. While the two angry aides considered what they should do now, Arnold clumped into the room, and the storm blew up again. Arnold declared that if he asked even the devil himself to dinner, the gentlemen of his family should be civil to him. To this Franks retorted that if Smith had not been at Arnold's table, he would have hurled a bottle at his head, and that henceforth he would treat him as a rascal. Though Varick interposed by acknowledging that he was at fault for the entire altercation, Franks shook his head. He told Arnold bluntly that he was tired of having the general view every point of his conduct with a prejudiced eye, and he begged to be relieved as an aide. On that note of passion he left the room. Varick sought immediately to cover Franks's abrupt departure by telling Arnold that he was sure Smith was a rascal, a scoundrel, and a spy. He and Franks, he said earnestly, were anxious to preserve Arnold's reputation. Arnold replied, according to Varick, "that he was willing to be advised by the gentlemen of his family but, by God, would not be dictated to by them; that he thought he possessed as much prudence as the gentlemen of his family." Later that evening, when Varick went to him and also asked to be relieved of his duties as an aide, Arnold had cooled off. Blandly he assured Varick that he was quite right about Smith; he promised, too, that he would have nothing more to do with the man! [4]

Sunday was an uneasy day. Though he had no idea that André had been taken, that a messenger with the incriminating documents was on his way to Washington, and that Robinson was writing to Clinton at having heard nothing of André since the young officer's departure from the *Vulture*, Arnold had moments of concern. Smith declared later that Arnold had approved of what he, Smith, had done with André, but Arnold knew too well the dangerous nature of those miles of country through which André had had to pass to feel completely at ease until he learned that the major had reached New York. By now, however, André must certainly have returned to Clinton, and by Monday, a message to that effect, one possibly containing important instructions from Clinton, might arrive. Man of action that Arnold was, he probably found the hours of that Sabbath painfully slow in passing. And—no help to his peace of mind—relations continued strained between himself and the feverish Varick, who kept to his bed a good part of the time, while Franks, who had served him for years, nursed his anger over in Newburgh. Peggy's nerves, moreover, were taut because of the disagreeable scene of the previous day and undoubtedly because of the suspense about André as well.

But eventually the hours passed and Monday arrived, September 25, the most tragic day of Arnold's stormy life. Washington had spent the night in Fishkill at the residence of a Dr. McKnight, with whom Smith also dined, neither Washington nor Smith knowing as yet of André's capture. In the morning, the general informed his staff that they would ride the ten or fifteen miles to Robinson House before breakfast (how his staff hated this customary pre-breakfast exercise!). He sent Colonel Alexander Hamilton ahead to Robinson House to escort the baggage and to advise the Arnolds that the commander-in-chief and his officers would presently arrive for breakfast. But while riding up the river road at a brisk pace, Washington turned into a side road. When Lafayette at once protested that he had taken the wrong road, Washington smilingly replied, "I know that all you young men are in love with Mrs. Arnold." Since they obviously wished to get to her residence as soon as possible, he continued, they were at liberty to do so but he must postpone that honor as he intended to inspect two redoubts on the river bank. Though the officers declined to leave him, Major James McHenry, Lafayette's aide, and Captain Samuel Shaw, General Knox's aide, were sent galloping ahead to tell Peggy not to wait for the commander-in-chief, who would be delayed for a few minutes.[5]

The two young men arrived even before Hamilton to find Arnold already at the table. Courteously he asked them to have breakfast with him, an invitation the hungry officers were only too glad to accept. While they were eating, Lieutenant Solomon Allen from Colonel Jameson's command arrived with letters which he handed to Arnold. Opening one of them, Arnold read that a John Anderson had been captured with a passport signed in his name and with papers containing valuable information concerning the West Point defenses. The papers, Jameson said, had been sent on to General Washington.[6]

For a moment the blood thudded in Arnold's ears as the full significance of the letter burst upon him. McHenry distinctly observed an "embarrassment" on Arnold's face, but it was gone in a flash as the general's self-possession reasserted itself. Certainly he needed every bit of his self-control with Washington on the way. If Jameson's messenger had reached the commander-in-chief with the documents, he was indeed lost; even if the messenger had not caught up with Washington, it was only a question of time before he would do so. In any event, Arnold could not, with safety, refuse to divulge to Washington the contents of Jameson's letter to him. What had to be done must be done now; the need for action was never more urgent.[7]

With a muttered injunction to Lieutenant Allen to remain silent about André's seizure, Arnold excused himself and went upstairs to Peggy. Whatever he wished to disclose to her was cut short two minutes later as Franks, back from Newburgh, knocked at the door to tell them that the commander-in-chief's servant had arrived and announced that General Washington was near at hand. The sudden terror that stabbed at Peggy must have been almost intolerable, but Arnold, who was desperately fond of her, had no time to console her; the anguish he felt at leaving her was lost in the more pressing need to save his own life. That she fainted or was too stunned to speak is likely. At any rate, there appear to have been none of those extreme manifestations of hysteria in which she was soon to take refuge, but only the silence of fear and desolation.

Abruptly leaving his wife, Arnold hobbled downstairs, threw his cloak over his shoulders, and ordered his horse saddled. Curtly he instructed Franks to tell General Washington that he was going over to West Point and would return in about an hour. It was now about ten o'clock. Then he spurred his horse by a short cut over a hill ("Traitor's Hill") and down a steep declivity ("Arnold's Path") to the landing. Leaping aboard his barge, he bade the oarsmen row hard for the *Vulture* off Tellers Point since he must soon be back to meet General Washington.[8]

Barely thirty minutes after Arnold's departure, Washington arrived at Robinson House. Franks told him that Arnold had been summoned to West Point but expected to be back in an hour. Mrs. Arnold, he added, was ill, as was Varick. Washington at once put the embarrassed Franks at ease and, asking him to order breakfast, told him that the party would go over to West Point and meet Arnold there. After the meal, leaving Hamilton at Robinson House, Washington, Lafayette, and Knox were rowed over to the Point. A two-hour inspection of the defenses revealed them to be in a condition of neglect that shocked Washington. When he inquired about Arnold, Colonel Lamb replied that Arnold had not been there this day. Puzzled and disturbed, Washington recrossed the river to Robinson House. As he recorded in his diary, "The impropriety of his [Arnold's] conduct when he knew I was to be there, struck me very forcibly, and my mind misgave me; but I had not the least idea of the real cause."[9]

He was not long in the dark. Shortly after he entered the room set aside for his use, Hamilton appeared with a packet received from Colonel Jameson; these were the papers captured on André and André's letter to Washington. As the commander-in-chief read, the terrible, incredible truth sank home: the brave and gallant Arnold had sold out to the enemy. Even in the shock of revelation, however, Washington retained the presence of mind for which he was so celebrated. Instantly he ordered Hamilton and McHenry to try to catch Arnold before he reached the *Vulture.* The two quickly armed themselves, saddled up, and spurred away. If, thanks to them, American guardboats or shore batteries could

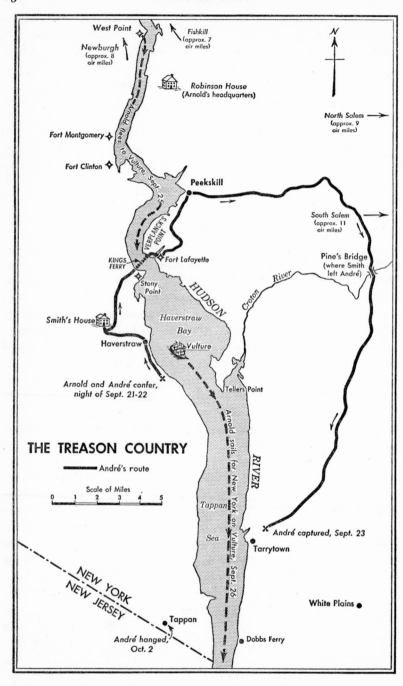

West Point

Newburgh
(approx. 8
air miles)

Fishkill
(approx. 7
air miles)

N

Robinson House
(Arnold's headquarters)

North Salem
(approx. 9
air miles)

Fort Montgomery

Fort Clinton

Peekskill

South Salem
(approx. 11
air miles)

to Vulture, Sept. 25

VERPLANCK'S POINT

KINGS FERRY

Fort Lafayette

Pine's Bridge
(where Smith
left André)

Stony Point

HUDSON

Croton River

Smith's House

Haverstraw Bay

Haverstraw

Vulture

Arnold and André confer,
night of Sept. 21-22

Tellers Point

THE TREASON COUNTRY

—— André's route

Scale of Miles
0 1 2 3 4 5

Arnold sails for New York on Vulture, Sept. 26

RIVER

Tappan

Sea

André captured, Sept. 23

Tarrytown

NEW YORK
NEW JERSEY

White Plains

Tappan

Dobbs Ferry

André hanged,
Oct. 2

have halted Arnold's barge, they would have achieved one of the great triumphs of the war.

But Arnold was fully alert to the danger of pursuit and forced his crew to put their backs into the work of rowing. The penalty of being intercepted was simply too dreadful to contemplate. When he passed Verplanck's Point, he tied a white handkerchief to the flagstaff. If horsemen had not arrived there with the news of his treachery, the handkerchief would protect him from American gunboats and shore batteries as well as against any force the British had on the river. It was also designed to convince his oarsmen that this was a legitimate mission, but should they have other ideas, he would not hesitate to use his pistols. At last the flying barge came within range of the *Vulture's* guns, and much of Arnold's tenseness left him. He now informed the coxswain, Corporal James Larvey, that he was joining the British and that if the coxswain would come along, he would try to get him a good position. To this, Larvey replied that he would be damned if he fought on both sides. Soon Arnold was on deck, stiffly shaking hands with Robinson and Sutherland. He tersely explained the situation involving André's capture which brought him aboard and requested, successfully, that his bargemen be detained as prisoners, hardly a charitable act. All this was a sorry end to his hopes and aspirations.[10]

Meanwhile, back at West Point, Arnold's flight had effects on Washington and Peggy that were profoundly different but none the less interesting. Prepared by McHenry, who had hurried into his dressing room to look for a brace of pistols, Lafayette found Washington deeply troubled. "Whom can we trust now?" the general asked sadly of Lafayette and Knox. But his self-control was so firm that he could sit down to dinner late that afternoon and converse as if nothing had happened.[11]

Following dinner, he first talked with the ill Varick to learn what he could of Arnold's behavior, then obliged Peggy by calling on her at her request. The visit was a painful experience, for, about an hour after he had left for the Point, she had gone into hysterics which persisted throughout the day. Having made tea for Varick in his illness the day before, Peggy, with Washington away, dashed toward his room in her morning gown, her hair disheveled. Suddenly Varick heard a shriek, and, rushing upstairs, he met her, raving. She grasped him by the hand and cried, "Colonel Varick, have you ordered my child to be killed?" Then she fell to her knees and begged him to spare her baby. While Franks hurried to aid him in raising her up and she struggled to free herself, Dr. Eustis, the headquarters surgeon, was called. With his assistance they got the hysterical girl to her room. Later she burst into tears and told Varick she had no friends left here. When he assured her that Arnold would soon be back with General Washington, she cried, "No, General Arnold will never return, he is gone, he is gone forever; there, there, there," she wailed, waving her hand toward the ceiling, "the spirits have carried [him] up there." Now, Washington having returned, she asked to see him, declaring that a hot iron rested on her head and none but he could remove it. But when the general appeared, she refused to believe it was he. Even when Washington himself gently assured her, she exclaimed, "No, that is not General Washington; that is the man who was a-going to assist Colonel Varick in killing my child." Without another word, Washington left the room. As Lafayette, who, with Hamilton, deeply sympathized with her, remarked, "She looked on us as murderers. . . ." [12]

That Arnold was gone was certain; Hamilton and McHenry failed by a margin of hours to overtake their prey. Instead, when they reached Verplanck's Point, a flag boat arrived from the *Vulture* with a letter from Arnold to Washington:

On board the Vulture, 25 September, 1780

Sir; The heart which is conscious of its own rectitude, cannot attempt to palliate a step which the world may censure as wrong; I have ever acted from a principle of love to my country, since the commencement of the present unhappy contest between Great Britain and the Colonies; the same principle of love to my country actuates my present conduct, however it may appear inconsistent to the world, who very seldom judge right of any man's actions.

I have no favor to ask for myself. I have too often experienced the ingratitude of my country to attempt it; but, from the known humanity of your Excellency, I am induced to ask your protection for Mrs. Arnold from every insult and injury that a mistaken vengeance of my country may expose her to. It ought to fall only on me; she is as good and as innocent as an angel, and is incapable of doing wrong. I beg she may be permitted to return to her friends in Philadelphia, or to come to me, as she may choose; from your Excellency I have no fears on her account, but she may suffer from the mistaken fury of the country.

I have to request that the enclosed letter may be delivered to Mrs. Arnold, and she be permitted to write to me.

I have also to ask that my clothes and baggage, which are of little consequence, may be sent to me; if required, their value shall be paid in money. I have the honor to be with great regard and esteem, your Excellency's most obedient humble servant.

Benedict Arnold

N.B. In justice to the gentlemen of my family, Colonel Varick and Major Franks, I think myself in honor bound to declare that they, as well as Joshua

Smith, Esq., (who I know is suspected) are totally ignorant of any transactions of mine, that they had reason to believe were injurious to the public.[13]

The letter is written in a bold, clear hand with few words crossed out, which could indicate a conviction of purpose that admitted of no doubt. "The heart which is conscious of its own rectitude"—this expression, so common in Arnold's letters, was probably never more true than in the present instance. Though under no illusions of how Americans might view his behavior, he was not afraid to oppose public opinion. He believed that whatever he did was right, and therefore justified. Though different in motivation, his conviction had something of the consuming sincerity and ruthless self-righteousness of the social reformer or the religious zealot. But an awareness of the censure that his infamy would evoke also pervades the letter, pervades it so thoroughly, in fact, that it suggests a qualification to his conviction; momentarily—but momentarily only—a struggle seems to have gone on within him between his sincerity and a sense of guilt. Furthermore, writing aboard the *Vulture,* secure from the wrath of his former friends and companions-in-arms, he took upon himself the onus of the affair. Any man with a trace of decency would not hesitate to protect his family, but a thoroughgoing scoundrel would have let Varick, Franks, and Smith work out their fate as best they could. Though Arnold's perfidy is clear enough, he was not entirely lost to honor.

Not only did Washington respect Arnold's wishes in regard to his wife, who recovered her reason the following day, but the commander-in-chief's gallant young officers fell all over themselves in their sympathy for her and in their conviction of her innocence. This was particularly true of Hamilton and Lafayette, whom she received in her bedroom on the morning of September 27 for the purpose of soliciting their help with General Washington in securing a pass to Philadelphia. Hamilton almost wept over her plight in a letter to his own beloved, Elizabeth Schuyler, General Schuyler's daughter. The aid of the officers, however, was not needed, for Washington, ever the gentleman, sent her on her way before sunset with Franks as her escort. In our more suspicious and less gallant age, she would not have fared so lightly even if innocent, which she decidedly was not.[14]

The one man who seems not to have been convinced that she was "as innocent as an angel" was also accused of treason in his lifetime, a man whose numerous affairs with ladies of all degrees of station gave him at least a passing acquaintance with the potentialities of Peggy's sex. This exception was Aaron Burr, who, in July, 1782, married Theodosia Prevost, at whose house in Paramus Peggy stopped for the second night en route to Philadelphia. According to Burr, "The frantic scenes of West Point were renewed, and continued so long as strangers were present. Mrs. Prevost was known as the wife of a British officer, and connected with the royalists. In her, therefore, Mrs. Arnold could confide. As soon as they were left alone Mrs. Arnold became tranquillized, and assured Mrs. Prevost that she was heartily sick of the theatrics she was exhibiting. She stated that she had corresponded with the British commander—that she was disgusted with the American cause and those who had the management of public affairs—and that through great persuasion and unceasing perseverance, she had ultimately brought the general into an arrangement to surrender West Point to the British." [15]

For this story Burr has been calumniated for over a century by numerous people. Admittedly, it came many-handed to light: Matthew Davis, Burr's biographer, related what Burr had said that Theodosia Prevost had said that Peggy Arnold had said. The Shippen family, ignoring Burr's strange decency in not relating his tale until long after both Arnold and Peggy were dead, countered Burr's allegations with their family tradition. According to the tradition, the unprincipled Burr, who had been brought up by the uncle of Peggy's father, became Peggy's escort from Paramus to Philadelphia, and "on the way he made love to this afflicted lady, thinking to take advantage of her just feelings of indignation toward her husband, to help him in his infamous design. Yet this is the fact, if our tradition be true. And indignantly repelled, he treasured up his revenge, and left a story behind him worthy of his false and malignant heart. . . ." [16]

Traditions die hard, but, in addition to the fact that it was Franks, not Burr, who escorted Peggy all the way to Philadelphia, the tradition of her innocence has suffered a body blow from the disclosures in the Clinton Papers. It is unlikely that Peggy played the major role that Burr assigned her in the West Point conspiracy, but that she was aware of what was going on and at least helped to transmit the treasonous correspondence can hardly be doubted. Whether she was play-acting at West Point cannot be determined for a certainty. She was evidently of a type prone to hysteria induced by shock and possibly by morbid contemplation. At Robert Morris's house, when she learned that Arnold had been given command of the left wing of the army, she had honestly lost control of herself. At West Point, however, the sympathetic presentation of her own innocence seems to have been extraordinarily well conceived rather than just to have happened; witness the timing of her loss of reason after Washington left for West Point, her protestations of friendlessness to the lonely Varick, the alleged threat to her baby by the commander-in-chief himself, her alluring dishevelment, and her bedroom receptions for the admiring young officers. Varick admitted, years afterward, that he thought she had been putting on an act, but he made the admission at a time when he was well past young manhood and when Peggy's youthful beauty and charms had faded in his memory. On the whole, therefore, it would seem that the alleged scandal-mongering of Aaron Burr—liar, libertine, possible traitor, a man more able and dangerous than Arnold— was nearer the truth than the opinions of his contemporaries or the considered judgments of biographers and historians have allowed.[17]

With Arnold off to New York on the 26th and Peggy on her way to Philadelphia on the 27th, American attention focused on two objects, the strengthening of West Point and the trial of Major John André; and though in New York, Arnold found himself involved in the fate of that young officer. The first object was soon taken care of. Washington put the loyal but ailing Alexander McDougall in command until Arthur St. Clair could arrive to assume command. Meanwhile the details ordered out by Arnold were recalled, units of the main army drawn close to the Point in the event of attack, and the defenses vigorously repaired. By the 28th, Washington considered West Point secure enough for him to go to Tappan, where he had sent Smith and André, whom Tallmadge had brought to him on the 26th. All was now set for the trial of André.

The trial was a tragically simple undertaking. The board, of which General Nathanael Greene was president, examined the papers found on André, read a statement prepared by him, and asked questions. They also studied letters from Beverly Robinson and Clinton explaining that André had gone up with a flag at Arnold's request and received a pass from him to return by land. Clinton, moreover, enclosed with his letter one that Arnold had written to him on his arrival in New York via the *Vulture* on September 26. Arnold said of André, "This officer cannot . . . fail of being immediately sent to New York, as he was invited to a conversation with me, for which I sent him a flag of truce, and finally gave him passports for his safe return to Your Excellency; all of which I had then a right to do, being in the actual service of America, under the orders of General Washington, and commanding general at West Point and its dependencies." [18]

The decision of the board was aided by André's own admissions. The officers seem not to have been concerned whether or not André came at Arnold's request and acted under his orders in entering the American lines and subsequently donning a disguise to return by land. After all, André as a British officer engaged in helping an American general commit treason was hardly subject to the latter's jurisdiction. There was indeed no question that André had entered the lines and left them under an assumed name, in a disguise, and with papers containing vital intelligence. The board, however, was interested in determining if André thought he had come ashore under the sanction of a flag of truce, the keystone of the British efforts to support his defense. When this very question was put to André, his reply, in the language of the court minute, was, "It was impossible for him to suppose he came on shore under that sanction, and [he] added, that if he came ashore [under a flag of truce] he certainly might have returned under it." The candor of this reply was in keeping with his behavior in writing his letter of confession to Washington. His was a fine nature, but he was surprisingly naïve for an officer in his position. Nor should it be forgotten that while he elicits one's sympathy as a victim of the conspiracy, he had been, as Clinton's adjutant general, an important functionary in the co-ordination of secret intelligence and a partner to many plans to induce American officers to renounce their allegiance to the United States. The board condemned him as a spy and considered that, in accordance with "the law and usage of nations," he should die.[19]

Grim though the verdict of the board, their personal feelings were otherwise. André's charm and gracious manners had captivated the generals. Tears dimmed more eyes than Greene's at the signing of the report. Lafayette described the trial as "one of the most painful duties he had to perform." Summing up what was undoubtedly the unofficial opinion of the board, Baron von Steuben growled, "It is not possible to save him. He put us to no proof, but in an open, manly manner, confessed every thing but a premeditated desire to deceive. Would to God the wretch who drew him to death could have suffered in his place." [20]

Though Washington approved the verdict of the board and ordered André to be executed in the afternoon of October 1, desperate last efforts by Clinton impelled him to postpone the execution until mid-day, October 2. Clinton wrote that he doubted that the court possessed full information of the circumstances on which they had based their judgment. Accordingly he proposed sending Lieutenant General James Robertson with

Lieutenant Governor Andrew Elliott and Chief Justice William Smith (Joshua's brother) to Dobbs Ferry. Washington directed Greene to meet Robertson as an individual but not to permit the two civilians to land. In the conversation between the two generals, Robertson went over the same ground as before. When he mentioned Arnold's statement that André had come under a flag of truce, Greene told him the Americans believed André rather than Arnold. Robertson reported to Clinton that Greene suggested an exchange of André for Arnold but that, at this interjection, he answered with a look that "threw Greene into confusion."[21]

Washington would have been delighted to get Arnold back for André had it been possible. Hamilton, Lafayette, and Major Harry Lee were especially keen for it, while Hamilton went so far as to write a letter to the British making that proposition. At any rate, Lieutenant Colonel John Simcoe of the Queen's Rangers, a friend of André, recorded in his journal that "Amongst some letters which passed on this unfortunate event, a paper was slid in without signature, but in the hand writing of Hamilton, Washington's secretary, saying that the only way to save André was to give up Arnold." Subsequent research by historians would seem to confirm Simcoe.[22]

The last recourse, therefore, lay with Clinton, not with Washington; if he surrendered Arnold, he could save André. Captain Aaron Ogden, on instructions from Lafayette, mentioned to the officer commanding the British detachment at Paulus Hook (Jersey City) that the exchange of Arnold for André would be welcomed by the Americans. At once the officer left for New York but returned two hours later and informed Ogden of Clinton's reply "that a deserter was never given up." Part of Clinton's duty was to persuade as many Americans as possible—and the more prominent, the better—to come over to the British. From the humane point of view, it was regrettable that André had to pay with his life for Arnold's treason, but his capture was no excuse for Clinton's giving up Arnold, whose chief offense in British eyes was not in returning to the British fold but in ever having taken up arms against the King.[23]

Presently time ran out. The gibbet awaited spies, and Washington, despite André's plea to be shot, saw no reason to change the method of execution. Hamilton thought him hard, and André won the ardent sympathy and generous friendship of most of the younger American officers, notably Tallmadge. Bravely, to the solemn beat of the drum and the wail of the fife, André marched to the place where he was to die. He showed emotion only when he sighted the gibbet itself, for he had hoped to the last to die by a firing squad. Instantly composing himself, however, he adjusted the rope about his neck and tied the handkerchief over his eyes, lifting the latter only to call on those present to observe that he died a brave man. Then the wagon which he had mounted moved quickly from under him, and his body swung violently to and fro. He expired with scarcely a struggle, while many of the thousand spectators, military and civilian, wept audibly at his passing.[24]

ANDRÉ'S PORTRAIT OF HIMSELF, OCT. 1, 1780

Although Washington thought André "more unfortunate than criminal," he could not have helped thinking the reverse true of Arnold, particularly as he gazed at the two letters from the traitor that reached his desk less than two hours after André's death. In one of them Arnold formally resigned his commission from Congress but assured Washington "that my attachment to the true interest of my country is invariable, and that I am actuated by the same principle, which has ever been the governing rule of my conduct in this unhappy contest." [25]

The other letter—as expressive of Clinton's as of Arnold's feelings and certainly not written without Clinton's knowledge—was of a less pacific nature. From a note of appreciation of Washington's kindness to Peggy, Arnold moved to a review of the conspiratorial meeting with André for which he took upon himself the full responsibility. He insisted that André ought not to be made the victim for acts that he himself had authorized as commanding officer in that area. But if André should be held responsible, "I shall think myself bound by every tie of duty and honor to retaliate on such unhappy persons of your army as may fall within my power, that the respect due to flags, and to the law of nations, may be better understood and observed." Furthermore, until now Sir Henry Clinton had shown clemency to forty South Carolinians who deserved to die; should André be executed, there might ensue "a scene of blood at which humanity will revolt." Finally, said Arnold, "Suffer me to entreat your Excellency, for your own and the honor of humanity, and the love you have of justice, that you suffer not an unjust sentence to touch the life of Major André. But if this warning should be disregarded, and he suffer, I call Heaven and earth to witness, that your Excellency will be justly answerable for the torrent of blood that may be spilt in consequence." [26]

The content might be Clinton's, but the language was Arnold's, menacing and truculent, and somehow revolting after the exquisite courtesy and bright courage of the young officer whose body was just being interred on the spot on which it had been cut down.

· XXVI ·

Attempts at Influence and Vindication

A RNOLD could not have expected a hero's welcome in New York, and
he received none. The curious naturally dogged his footsteps. High officers
in the army and many important Loyalists treated him politely but re-
servedly. Only Clinton and Judge William Smith showed him any real
friendship. Had André's life been spared, the situation would undoubtedly
have been different, but there were few who did not associate his escape
with André's death. The younger officers, with whom André had been
immensely popular, could not tolerate him, and their attitude seriously
affected his subsequent efforts to raise a military unit. Six weeks after his
arrival, an observer remarked, "General Arnold is a very unpopular character in the British army, nor can all the patronage he meets with from
the commander-in-chief procure him respectability. The subaltern officers
have conceived such an aversion to him, that they unanimously refused to
serve under his command, and the detachment he is to lead was, on this
account, officered from the Loyal American corps." Such treatment, coming from people from whom he had hoped to secure recognition, must
have cut him sorely.[1]

Presently Peggy joined him. After a miserable journey with Franks, she
found Philadelphia decidedly hostile to her, and the press suspicious that
she was not altogether guiltless. This feeling was based in part on the
sheriff's discovery, when he seized Arnold's papers, that André had written Peggy on August 16, 1779 suggesting that he would be glad to pur-

chase millinery supplies for her in New York. A fallacious belief that this letter had opened the way to Arnold's negotiations with André helped raise popular clamor for her banishment. Finally, on October 27, 1781, the Executive Council, considering her continued residence in the city dangerous to the public safety, ordered her to leave within fourteen days. The Shippen family and their friends fought the order hard, and when they failed, their grief and anger were great. "We tried every means to prevail on the Council to permit her to stay among us, and not to compel her to go to that infernal villain her husband in New York," lamented her sister's husband, Edward Burd, to his father, Colonel James Burd. "If she could have staid Mr. Shippen would not have wished her ever to be united to him again. . . . I cannot bear the idea of her re-union. The sacrifice was an immense one at her being married to him at all. It is much more so to be obliged, against her will, to go to the arms of a man who appears to be so very black." [2]

But the laws of the Medes and the Persians were never more immutable than this order of the Executive Council of Pennsylvania. Peggy simply had to leave whether she wanted to or not, and a grieving Edward Shippen accompanied his daughter and her infant son as far as Paulus Hook. She arrived in New York on November 14, and Arnold took her to the residence he had rented adjacent to Sir Henry Clinton's headquarters. Probably she felt not too lonely since Arnold was delighted to have her with him again and many of the British officers had been guests at her father's house during the occupation of Philadelphia. A Loyalist woman, a Mrs. Rebecca Shoemaker, wrote to her daughter in Philadelphia and, mentioning the arrival of a Captain Lloyd of the Guards and his wife, said, "Peggy Arnold is not so much admired here for her beauty as one might have expected. All allow she has great sweetness in her countenance, but wants animation, sprightliness, and that fire in her eyes which was so captivating in Capt. Lloyd's wife. But notwithstanding she does not possess that life and animation that some do, they have met with every attention indeed, much more than they could have promised themselves, and the very genteel appointment which he (Gen. A) holds in the service, joined to a very large present, (which I am told he has received,) is fully sufficient for every demand in genteel life." [3]

The appointment and emolument alluded to by Mrs. Shoemaker were part of the rewards of treason, and Arnold had been in New York barely more than three weeks—and only a little more than a fortnight after André's death—before he pressed Clinton regarding the money due him.

He told Clinton that though André, according to orders, had promised him only £6,000, the major had expressed little doubt that Clinton would accede to Arnold's request for £10,000. No amount of money, Arnold insisted, would have been sufficient inducement for him to endure the danger and anxiety he had experienced—nothing but zeal to serve the King and "the common cause." Arnold, therefore, "with the greatest cheerfulness" submitted the matter to Clinton, having full confidence that the latter would not think the claim unreasonable "when you consider the sacrifices I have made, and that the sum is a trifling object to the public though of consequence to me, who have a large family that look up to me for support and protection." [4]

There can be little doubt that pecuniarily Arnold made a good thing of crime. Within twelve days of his letter to Clinton, Sir Henry paid him off handsomely. Arnold received the £6,000 that Clinton had commissioned André to offer, plus £315 expense money. The £6,000 alone would have a modern purchasing power of approximately $55,000, which is probably on the conservative side. This, however, was not all Arnold received. As a cavalry colonel on the regular establishment, his pay started immediately at £450 a year and continued after the war at half that amount for as long as he lived. Serving now as a Provincial brigadier general, he drew an additional £200 until peace was signed. Of the capital sum received, Arnold's London broker invested £5,000 with the bankers of the Court for £7,000 in consolidated annuities at four per cent. [5]

But even these compensatory awards were far from the whole story. On March 19, 1782, the King issued a warrant to his paymaster of pensions that "Our will and pleasure is, and we do hereby direct, authorize and command, that an annuity or yearly pension of five hundred pounds be established and paid by you unto Margaret Arnold, wife of our trusty and well beloved brigadier general, Benedict Arnold, to commence from the day of the date hereof, and continue during our pleasure. . . ." In view of the revelations in the Clinton Papers, it becomes increasingly clear that Peggy had earned her pension by aiding and abetting the treason of her husband. As Clinton himself observed—and who should know better?—she had performed "services" which were "very meritorious." One is reminded, in this connection, of Dr. Johnson's definition of a pension: "In England, it is generally understood to mean pay given to a state hireling for treason to his country." [6]

Provision was also made for the children. Each of Arnold's five surviving children by Peggy received a pension of £100 that netted £80 annually. Likewise his three sons by Margaret Mansfield were rewarded by being given commissions in the British army, Benedict on November 30, 1780 when he was still twelve years old, and Richard and Henry in October, 1781, when they were twelve and nine respectively. After the war, these lads received half pay which continued as long as they lived, except for Benedict, who naturally qualified for full pay when he went on active duty against the French in the 1790's. The total of the three half-pay pensions amounted to £225, no bagatelle as an aid to their father in rearing them. Years after the war, when Peggy had borne all her children, the British government was paying to the Arnold family annual pensions amounting to £1,450, or about $14,000 in modern purchasing power. Finally, in 1798, Arnold received, in grants to himself and his family, 13,400 acres from among the Canadian waste lands of the Crown reserved for American Loyalists. Thus, with the pensions to the children and Peggy, his own war pay and subsequent pension, the £6,000 given to him outright, and the grant of lands, Arnold had truly made crime pay. The Crown was nowhere near so generous to those other Americans who had lost their fortunes and their homes because of their loyalty to the King, many of them serving in his armies through all the long, heart-breaking years of war.[7]

Though the British were willing to pay well for treason, Arnold sought to justify his behavior almost at once after coming to New York. His efforts were embodied in two addresses, one "To the Inhabitants of America," inscribed on October 7 and printed by the *Royal Gazette* on October 11; the other, "A Proclamation to the Officers and Soldiers of the Continental Army," dated October 20 and printed by the *Royal Gazette* on October 25. In drawing up these papers, Arnold had the help of Judge William Smith. Even before word of André's death reached New York, Arnold was hard at work making extensive notes which he brought to Smith, who then drafted the copy and returned it to Arnold for revision. Arnold was with him when the news of André's hanging arrived, and Smith recorded in his diary that Arnold was "vastly disconcerted and retires on the chariot coming for him from General Robertson."[8]

The address, "To the Inhabitants of America," echoed Loyalist opinion, though some Loyalists were critical of it. Arnold set forth the motives which allegedly induced him to join the British; this was for the benefit of his countrymen who lacked the ability or opportunity to detect "the artifices by which they are duped." As to "that class of men who are criminally protracting the war from sinister views, at the expense of the public interest, I prefer their enmity to their applause." These were "the usurpers in the revolted provinces," the Congress. The allusion is interesting, because Arnold had never before expressed antagonism toward Congress in principle.

Somehow Arnold had to justify his becoming a rebel in the first place. As he explained, "When I quitted domestic happiness for the perils of the field, I conceived the rights of my country in danger, and that duty and honor called me to her defence—a redress of grievances was my only object and aim; however, I acquiesced in a step which I thought precipitate, the Declaration of Independence; to justify the measure many plausible reasons were urged, which could no longer exist, when Great Britain with the open arms of a parent offered to embrace us as children, and grant the wished for redress." The first part of his statement is true enough, but there is no evidence in surviving correspondence that he thought the Declaration precipitate; in fact, at his court-martial in 1780, he had thought the establishment of independence "glorious." Nor is there on record any statement that he disapproved of the rejection of the British peace terms in 1778. Said Arnold, "I had my suspicions of some imperfections in our councils, on proposals prior to the Parliamentary Commission of 1778, but . . . I continued to be guided in the negligent confidence of a soldier. But the whole world saw, and all America confessed, the overtures of the second Commission exceeded our wishes and expectations." This last sentence was unadulterated Judge Smith rather than Arnold.

The key to the justification was the alliance with France. Americans, said Arnold,

have been duped by a virtuous credulity, in the incautious moments of intemperate passion, to give up their fidelity to serve a nation counting both the will and the power to protect us, and aiming at the destruction both of the Mother Country and the provinces. . . . In the firm persuasion, therefore, that the private judgment of any individual citizen of this country is as free from all conventional restraints since, as before the insidious offers of France, I preferred those from Great Britain, thinking it infinitely wiser and safer to cast my confidence upon her justice and generosity, than to trust a monarchy too feeble to establish your independency, so perilous to her distant dominions, the enemy of the Protestant faith, and fraudulently avowing an affection for the liberties of mankind, while she holds her native sons in vassalage and chains.

That Arnold disliked a number of Frenchmen was true, and he was especially annoyed at Luzerne for having refused to advance him money in Philadelphia. Perhaps, too, it was only a little step from disliking a few Frenchmen to distrusting France. But again there is no surviving record of his antipathy for the alliance before his treason.

With no little guile he affected to be frank. He had determined to surrender his command to the British for the good of his country since he was anxious "to accomplish an event of decisive importance, and to prevent, as much as possible in the execution of it, the effusion of blood." Naturally he did not mention that he received a recompense for his treachery. He testified to his fellow soldiers and citizens that he found "solid ground to rely upon the clemency of our Sovereign, and abundant conviction that it is the generous intention of Great Britain, not only to have the rights and privileges of the colonies unimpaired, together with their perpetual exemption from taxation, but to superadd such further benefits as may consist with the common prosperity of the Empire. In short, I fought for much less than the parent country is as willing to grant to her colonies, as they can be to receive or enjoy." What neither Arnold nor Judge Smith and other Loyalists of his ilk perceived was that although the colonies would probably at one time have accepted the British offers had the offers not been so late, they would not now be denied their independence.

Finally Arnold considered the timing of his change of heart, remarking, "Some may think I continued in the struggle of those unhappy days too long, and others that I quitted it too soon." To the first, the Loyalists, he lamely admitted that "I did not see with their eyes, nor perhaps had so favorable a situation to look from, and that to one common master I am willing to stand or fall." Even Judge Smith must have blushed at this distortion. As for those who thought he gave up too soon, they were divided into the "candid" and the "censurers." "In behalf of the candid . . . some of whom I believe serve blindly but honestly in the ranks I have left, I pray God to give them all the lights requisite to their own safety before it is too late." From this pious invocation he turned to dip his pen in venom. For the "censurers, whose enmity to me originates in their hatred to the principles, by which I am now led to devote my life to the reunion of the British Empire, as the best and only means to dry up the streams of misery that have deluged this country, they may be assured that, conscious of the rectitude of my intentions [that invincible self-righteousness!] I shall treat their malice and calumnies with contempt and neglect." [9]

Filled with the zeal of the newly converted, he moved from this general address to a proclamation directed "To the Officers and Soldiers of the

Continental Army who have the real Interest of their Country at Heart, and who are determined to be no longer the Tools and Dupes of Congress, or of France." Sir Henry Clinton had authorized him to raise a body of cavalry and infantry. Every noncom and private would be given a bounty of three guineas, while the commissioned officers would be nominated by himself. With infinite satisfaction he embraced "this opportunity of advancing men whose valor I have witnessed, and whose principles are favorable to an union with Britain and true American liberty." Announcing a scheme of liberal pay and recognition, which must appeal to those who had suffered "every distress of want, of pain, hunger and nakedness, from the neglect, contempt and corruption of Congress," he said that he wanted a chosen band of Americans to help "share in the glory of rescuing our native country from the grasping hand of France as well as from the ambitious and interested views of a desperate party among ourselves who, in listening to French overtures, and rejecting those from Great Britain, have brought the colonies to the very brink of destruction."

He harped continually on their destitution, their loss of liberty in the very act of trying to obtain it, and the menace of France. Though William Smith must have prompted him repeatedly, Arnold probably now believed what he wrote, particularly in regard to France. "What is America," he asked, "but a land of widows, beggars, and orphans?—and should the parent nation cease her exertion to deliver you, what security remains to you for the enjoyment of the consolations of that religion for which your fathers braved the ocean, the heathen, and the wilderness? Do you know that the eye which guides this pen lately saw your mean and profligate Congress at mass for the soul of a Roman Catholic in purgatory, and participating in the rites of a church against whose anti-Christian corruptions your pious ancestors would have witnessed with their blood?" This last was an allusion to the funeral, the previous May, of the Spanish representative in Philadelphia, Don Juan de Mirailles, which Arnold attended; again, no record of his opposition at that time has been found. In fact, Arnold had shown the utmost courtesy and attention to Mirailles personally, and to his wife, for which the latter, in her widowhood, expressed her deep appreciation. The appeal to religious intolerance, however, might have been effective had France not given ample evidence of her support in money, supplies, and men, thus blunting the anti-Catholicism of New England in particular. It would seem a little incongruous for Arnold to be speaking in the spirit of John Calvin if it were not for the fact that, before he became an Episcopalian following his marriage, he had been a Presbyterian, while William Smith was already one. Arnold closed by promising "the most affectionate welcome and attention to all who are disposed to join me in the measures necessary to close the scene of our afflictions" which must continue to increase until people had the wisdom to be "contented with the liberality of the parent country, who still offers her protection, with the immediate restoration of our ancient privileges, civil and sacred, and a perpetual exemption from all taxes, but such as shall think fit to impose on ourselves." [10]

Eight days later, October 28, Arnold sent to Lord George Germain a letter and a paper entitled, "The Present State of the American Rebel Army, Navy, and Finances." This had actually been composed three weeks before. Arnold reported the size and condition of the various American armies, the wave of officer resignations because of dissatisfaction and a sense of the futility of the struggle, the feebleness of the navy, and the lack of public monies. Arnold proposed in his letter that Washington might be agreeable to accepting a title. Soldiers and officers might be won over by payment of their arrears, by half pay for seven and one-half years at the end of the war, and by generous promises of land. Probably drawing on his own experience, Arnold was so certain of the efficacy of bribes in inducing desertion that he said he could raise a force of between two and three thousand former rebels. In fact, the British should make extensive use of Loyalist troops. Naturally a large British army, in which he expressed his hope to serve as a major general, would furnish the real muscle for an offensive. This offensive should preferably take the form of an operation against the American posts in the highlands of the Hudson or, leaving a sufficient force to garrison New York, the British could move into the Chesapeake area and seize Baltimore. With Maryland and Virginia overawed, and British governments established there, the army could then proceed against Pennsylvania, New Jersey, and New York. [11]

The letter was a curious compound of folly and reasonable military judgment. The idea that Washington would submit for a title is almost comical and reveals Arnold's abysmal ignorance of his former commander-in-chief. But the military operation against the highlands was entirely feasible except for Arnold's failure to take note of two important factors: Clinton's extraordinary caution at locking horns with Washington and his almost pathological fear for New York. Arnold had not yet experienced the frustration that sickened the younger British officers at their chief's timidity and that drove prominent Loyalists like Judge

Thomas Jones into a frenzy. The suggestion of moving south also had its merits, and it should be pointed out that Arnold was opposed to a force marching into Virginia from South Carolina. Instead, unlike Cornwallis's campaign the following year, South Carolina should be held in strength and the Chesapeake area opened as a separate theater of action. Though this conception did not originate with Arnold, his articulation of it undoubtedly encouraged Clinton to believe in, and eventually to exploit, its possibilities.

But if this latest epistolary activity had any positive effect, his efforts to justify himself to his countrymen and to induce them to desert to the British proved disappointing. A mere handful changed sides. As Washington so aptly remarked to Rochambeau, ". . . traitors are the growth of every country and in a revolution of the present nature, it is more to be wondered at, that the catalogue is so small than that there have been found a few." And as soon as the treason was discovered, Lafayette dashed off a note by the first mail, also to Rochambeau, explaining that "This is the first example of treason in our armies—an extraordinary thing in this kind of revolution. . . ." Washington was correct that the catalogue was small, but Lafayette erred in saying that Arnold was the first traitor in the army. On the other hand, Lafayette was right in one sense: Arnold's was the first instance of treason by an officer of his stature.[12]

Count Vergennes, the French foreign minister, admitted that "A crime so atrocious was too enormous to be thought of as finding many imitators," but he put his finger on a fundamental weakness when he said in the same breath, "It is less the example that I dread than the motives on which the treason was based, for, they can flourish in a country where jealousy is somehow the essence of government." This weakness among Americans the British sought to exploit, and Andrew Elliot, the New York Loyalist, wrote to London, "The jealousy amongst them is at present rather more than even the event might naturally produce." But Vergennes need not have feared, while Elliot was indulging in wishful thinking. What neither Arnold nor the British perceived was that the treason had an effect contrary to what they anticipated. The treason shocked the country into a semblance of unity. While factiousness could not be eradicated, even among patriots, henceforth people could not be lukewarm or indefinite in their affiliations. Arnold had raised the issue of difference above the level of political parties. From now on, to be a Tory in politics was to be an enemy.[13]

The denunciation of Arnold by his countrymen remains without parallel in American history; none has been so universally and deeply execrated. Said the *New Jersey Gazette* in commenting on André's hanging, "It is ardently to be wished . . . that General Arnold, that most abandoned and infamous traitor and intended betrayer of the just and glorious cause of America, should share a like fate." But this was mild. He was hanged or burned in effigy in Boston, Providence, Philadelphia, and scores of smaller places. Nowhere, however, did feeling run higher than in his home state of Connecticut, where his effigy suffered particularly humiliating treatment in New Milford, Middletown, and New Haven. In the last place, scene of his civilian rise to prominence, his effigy, seated, was given two faces, symbolic of his conduct, while he held a letter in his right hand from Beelzebub telling him that, having done all the mischief he could, he must go hang himself. Behind him stood the devil himself in black robes shaking a purse at Arnold's left ear, while in his Sable Majesty's right hand was a pitchfork poised to drive Arnold into hell as a reward for the crimes his thirst for gold had led him to commit. After being dragged through the streets, the effigy was first hanged, then committed to the flames. Childish, perhaps, but not the dangerous temper of the participants. The name of Arnold was so hated that a Norwich mob stormed into the local cemetery and destroyed his father's tombstone because it bore the same name as the traitor. General von Steuben even persuaded one Private Jonathan Arnold of the Connecticut Line to change his name to Steuben, a transformation which the General Assembly heartily endorsed.[14]

The treason, moreover, brought out a rash of criticisms of Arnold's former conduct. Adjutant General Alexander Scammel said that Arnold's "conduct and sufferings at the northward, has in the eyes of the Army and his country covered a series of base, grovelling, dirty, scandalous and rascally peculation and fraud; and the Army and the country [ever] indulgent and partial to an officer who has suffered in the common cause, wished to cover his faults, and we were even afraid to examine too closely, for fear of discovering some of his rascality." Samuel Huntington wrote Governor Trumbull of Connecticut that "many of his scandalous transactions are brought to light that were before concealed." Mad Anthony Wayne went further than any when he snapped that Arnold "never possessed either fortitude or personal bravery—he was naturally a coward and never went in the way of danger but stimulated by liquor even to intoxication." This charge, absurd though it was, and coming from a good but overrated soldier, is indicative of the feverish sentiment of the times.[15]

It remained for Washington to have the most bitter word for the traitor. Not quite a fortnight after André's death, he wrote an affectionate letter to his young friend, Lieutenant Colonel John Laurens. After remarking that André's capture was caused in part by "An unaccountable deprivation of presence of mind in a man of first abilities," he said, "André has met his fate, and with that fortitude which was to be expected from an accomplished man, and gallant officer. But I am mistaken if at *this time,* Arnold is undergoing the torments of a mental Hell. He wants feeling! From some traits of his character which have lately come to my knowledge, he seems to have been so hackneyed in villainy, and so lost to all sense of honor and shame that while his faculties will enable him to continue his sordid pursuits there will be no time for remorse." [16]

Though Washington was seeing Arnold as completely evil, a condition beyond the capacity of any human being, he seems to have been correct at least in part. There is nothing substantial to indicate that at this time Arnold had any regrets for his conduct. If he felt any, they were that the conspiracy fell through. Furthermore, André was scarcely cold in his grave before Arnold was dunning Clinton for his reward, writing his propaganda articles with Judge Smith, and trying to raise troops; he thus appears to have had little time for remorse even had he possessed the inclination.

But Arnold believed what he did was right (he would not have been Arnold otherwise!), and what was right for him was right for the country. Let Washington call his appeal to the Continental Army an "unparalleled piece of assurance." Let Washington say of his address to the American people, "I am at a loss which to admire most, the confidence of Arnold in publishing, or the folly of the enemy in supposing that a production signed by so infamous a character will have any weight with the people of these states, or any influence upon our affairs abroad." In Arnold's opinion, those who differed from him were either stupidly misguided wretches or knaves. They were the traitors, not he! He had returned to his King, whilst they continued to defy him. One cannot read the addresses he composed with Judge Smith's assistance without marveling at the man's egocentricity. He had completely justified himself in his own eyes, if not in those of his countrymen. Henceforth, moreover, he would translate his new faith into military action, endeavoring to wield his sword as vigorously for Britain as he had for America, and zealously advancing the fame and fortune of Benedict Arnold.[17]

· XXVII ·

The Virginia and New London
Expeditions

WHILE Arnold sought by his publications "to work upon the distrust
he has spread to all parts of the continent," as one Englishman expressed
it, he busied himself also in trying to form his American Legion and in
planning a raid into the South. Entreated by Cornwallis to make a diversion in his favor, Clinton took advantage of the appearance of Admiral
Rodney's squadron to send General Leslie to the Chesapeake in mid-
October. Leslie had scarcely arrived, however, before a dispatch in Cornwallis's name reached him, begging him to sail to Cape Fear. With
Clinton's approval, he complied, for Cornwallis had had to fall back on
Winnsborough, South Carolina, his plans for an invasion of North Carolina ruined by the mountaineers who killed or captured a thousand troops
under Major Patrick Ferguson at King's Mountain. Still trying to help
Cornwallis, Clinton proposed to send Arnold to the Chesapeake with
orders to make his base of operations at Portsmouth, which commanded
the mouths of the Elizabeth and James rivers, to destroy what American
shipping he could, and to impede navigation.[1]

Before leaving for the West Indies, that old seadog, Admiral Rodney,
had spent some time with Arnold and evidently found much in common
with him. Both were men of energy and military imagination, and both
were lovers of money (Rodney's seizure of the wealthy Dutch island of

St. Eustatius in February, 1781, and his appropriation of private as well as public property constituted an example of buccaneering that Henry Morgan himself would have envied). Rodney wrote Germain from the West Indies in December, "Believe me, my Lord, this man Arnold, with whom I had many conferences, will do more towards the suppressing the rebellion than all our generals put together." But, he added as a sober afterthought, "Jealousy, my Lord, unless commands from home signifies his Majesty's pleasure, will prevent Arnold being long employed to advantage." [2]

It was not only jealousy that was sowing antagonism. The Honorable George Damier, who later appeared in Virginia as a gentleman-volunteer, told Germain in mid-October that Arnold spoke "handsomely" of Washington and his officers, Gates excepted. Futhermore, he "does not scruple to mention the inactivity of our army at certain periods in former campaigns, and in this he very strongly expressed his astonishment upon his arrival at our not having attacked the French upon their disembarking at Rhode Island." British officers, including Clinton, were scarcely disposed to appreciate praise of the enemy or such criticisms of their own army. [3]

Clinton himself was less jealous of Arnold than fearful that something might go wrong in Arnold's first venture under the old flag. Hence, on December 14, he wrote Arnold, "Having sent Lieutenant Colonels [Thomas] Dundas and [John] Simcoe, officers of great experience and much in my confidence, with you, I am to desire that you will always consult these gentlemen previous to your undertaking any operation of consequence." Humiliating as this injunction must have been to him, Arnold was spared a greater humiliation in not knowing that, to both Dundas and Simcoe, Clinton issued "a blank dormant commission which is only to be made use of in case of the death or incapacity of Brigadier General Arnold to execute the duties of the command which is entrusted to his direction. You are upon no account to make known that you are possessed of such a commission, or open the same, except in the cases above mentioned; and if this should not happen, you are to transmit this commission to me unopened." [4]

Before Arnold left, he barely escaped being the victim of a kidnapping plot contrived by Major "Light Horse Harry" Lee with the knowledge and encouragement of Washington, who promised ample rewards for its success. Washington enjoined Lee, however, that Arnold must be brought back alive since he aimed to make a public example of him. Lee engaged two men, chief of whom was powerful Sergeant John Champe of his cavalry. Champe, whom Lee described to Washington as "a very promising youth of uncommon taciturnity and invincible perseverance," was to desert, join Arnold's corps, and "insinuate" himself into some position near Arnold. A glory-seeker in his own right, Champe deserted on October 20, successfully answered questions thrown at him on the 23d by the British adjutant-general's office, and, meeting Arnold "accidentally on the street," told the story of his desertion to Arnold, who invited him to become a member of the American Legion.

As Lee related the tale years later, developments from this point on were nothing short of hair-raising. Champe carefully studied Arnold's habits. He discovered that after coming home about midnight, but before going to bed, Arnold used to visit the garden, presumably to answer a call of nature. Champe presently worked out a scheme based on this nocturnal visit. He planned to seize Arnold at that time, gag him, and carry him into an adjoining alley. Carefully he removed palings of the fence between the garden and the alley and then replaced them so that he could reach the alley with ease. Once there, he and his companion were to place themselves under Arnold's shoulders and bear him through unfrequented streets to one of the wharves on the Hudson, where a third associate was to be ready with a boat. Should they be questioned on the way to the wharf, they were to represent Arnold as a drunken soldier whom they were taking to the guardhouse. After they reached the boat, they were to head for Hoboken, where Lee was to be waiting in the woods with a detail of dragoons.

Champe, however, encountered an obstacle which he did not anticipate. Before darkness fell on the very day the kidnapping was to occur, his unit was ordered aboard its transports; and Lee waited in vain through the long night. Champe sailed with the rest for Virginia, his native state, and served with the enemy for some time before he found an opportunity to desert to the Americans. It is doubtful that Arnold ever realized how near he had come to being made a victim of Washington's wrath.[5]

Arnold left New York on December 21 with 1,600 men, half of them British regulars and Hessians; the other half, Loyalists. He was no sooner clear of Sandy Hook than to his dismay the weather turned nasty with snow and wind. Presently a wild winter gale set in, and he bucked high seas all the way. He feared, and with reason, for Simcoe's horses; half of them were dead by the time the wallowing transports and men-of-war were sighted off the Chesapeake capes on the last of the old year. Without waiting for all his scattered fleet to gather, he pushed up the James River. His boats beaten off by militia at Burwell's Ferry on January 2, 1781, he put his sick and battered men and animals ashore at Westover on January 4, and in the afternoon drove on to Richmond with 800 men.

The march was surprisingly easy. When his attempted landing at Burwell's Ferry had been opposed, he had, rather naïvely, expressed his surprise to observe the hostile manner of the people under arms ashore. Prepared now for resistance, Arnold encountered none as he entered the town which Scottish factors had made a great trading center. After establishing his headquarters at the City Tavern on Main Street, he proceeded with his work of destruction. First, however, he offered to spare the town if Governor Jefferson would consent to let the British ships remove the stores, particularly the tobacco, without molestation. At Jefferson's refusal, Arnold set fire to the warehouses. A great deal of private property was plundered, public buildings and private dwellings were burned, and official records were destroyed. But this was not all. Arnold had dispatched Simcoe several miles beyond Richmond on a similar raid. The cannon foundry at Westham was razed, the powder magazine emptied, and tons of gunpowder and small arms thrown into the river. The torch was applied to warehouses and mills and to the clothing depot at Chesterfield. Arnold now slowly retired to Portsmouth, destroying as he went and encountering only scattered and ineffective opposition on his way.[6]

Back in Portsmouth, Arnold fortified it in compliance with his orders, but grew increasingly morose. As early as January 23, he complained to Clinton that "A life of inaction will be prejudicial to my health." He was not unaware, moreover, of the angry Virginia militia swarming in force under their own generals and Baron von Steuben, and he realized that if Continentals should arrive to stiffen them and if the French secured command of the sea, he would be trapped at Portsmouth. As Sir John Fortescue, the British Army historian, has observed, after mentioning that Arnold could be trusted to do well in the field, "Clinton, by setting him down permanently in isolation with a mere handful of men, was giving him as a hostage to fortune, for the British squadron on the coast was little if at all superior to the French." [7]

And indeed his downfall was being contrived. Jefferson had set a price of 5,000 guineas for his capture, while riflemen sharpened their shooting eye by firing at a mark carved to represent Arnold's head. Whenever Arnold ventured afield, he stood in real danger, but his iron nerve never faltered. Still, far more dangerous than any individual attempt was a

move by Washington to capture what Robert Morris described to a
Baltimore friend as "that rascal Arnold with a ragamuffin banditti."
Barely out of Richmond before Arnold marched in, Richard Henry Lee
wrote Washington that a single powerful warship with a frigate or two
could destroy Arnold and his collection of sloops and brigs. Washington
realized this himself, and while, in mid-February, he assigned Lafayette
and 1,200 Continentals to Virginia with orders to hang Arnold summarily
if the Frenchman caught the traitor, he also tried to persuade the French
to co-operate by sending a fleet and troops. It was not alone the desire to
catch Arnold, the traitor, that prompted this maneuver; Washingon saw
Arnold, the British general, as being able not only to ravage Virginia but
also to act as the northern arm of a pincers movement—of which Cornwallis was the southern arm—which might eventually squeeze General
Nathanael Greene and the little Southern Army into disaster.[8]

When Arnold's treason was discovered in time to prevent a national
catastrophe, Washington thought that Providence had interposed in
America's favor; now it suddenly seemed that Providence was again being
kind, for a great storm scattered and half wrecked the British fleet.
Admiral Destouches, who had succeeded Admiral Ternay in command of
the French fleet, could now put to sea from Rhode Island. But Destouches
was wary of committing the bulk of his fleet in such weather. True, a
small French squadron came safely through the storm that damaged the
British, but, after looking in at the Chesapeake, soon returned. Destouches
took his own good time to prepare his ships—weeks, in fact—but, on
March 8, he finally sailed for the Chesapeake with 1,200 regulars. Admiral
Arbuthnot, his British counterpart, warned that "the blow meditating
against General Arnold is of a deadly aspect," and got his own squadron
under way. The fleets were about equal, but Destouches had a thirty-six-
hour start.[9]

Meanwhile Arnold maintained his precarious position with cool self-
possession. Though unaware of the approach of Destouches, he knew the
French could reach the Chesapeake if they wanted to—had not the small
but powerful squadron that had returned to Rhode Island kept his own
flotilla bottled up temporarily? Furthermore, Steuben's militia hung on
his outskirts, and Lafayette was at Yorktown awaiting the arrival of his
Continentals from Annapolis. Probably, too, he suspected that General
Wayne might join Lafayette and Steuben as soon as he replenished the
ranks of the Pennsylvania Line which had mutinied in January; this
mutiny, of which Arnold had said at the time that he was glad to hear,

had resulted in the discharge of hundreds of veterans. If besieged by all these forces, Arnold would give a good account of himself and try to hold out until the British Navy could save him. If forced to capitulate, he might have taken his own life. At any rate, Rochambeau wrote Washington that he had heard Arnold had said he would never be taken alive. In miniature, the situation, as one historian has observed, resembled that in which Cornwallis found himself several months later, but in the latter's case the question of personal survival hardly existed.[10]

The entire problem now became one of sea power. As Washington remarked, all hopes and plans for taking Arnold depended largely on the ability of the French to "block up Arnold in the Bay." The French tried, but Arbuthnot engaged Destouches so heavily on March 16 off the Virginia capes that though the British suffered greater losses, the French admiral decided to return to Rhode Island. Arnold was thereby saved from an ignominious end. His salvation was further secured ten days later when transports bearing strong reinforcements of 2,000 troops arrived with General William Phillips in command. Phillips, who had been Burgoyne's artillery chief and who ranked Arnold, now took command of the entire force, a sharp blow to Arnold's pride.[11]

While subordinate to Phillips in the latter's maneuvers with Steuben and Lafayette during April, Arnold energetically participated in the destruction or capture of vast stores of war material, and for a brief period actually commanded the army. Phillips fell ill in early May and died on the 12th. Unfortunately for whatever aspirations Arnold may have entertained of being chief indefinitely, the arrival of Cornwallis at Petersburg on May 20 put an end to them. Still Cornwallis's arrival was no surprise; for several days Arnold had known he was on his way from Wilmington, to which point he had originally retreated after his Pyrrhic victory over Greene at Guilford Courthouse in mid-March. But if the appearance of the genial, handsome Lord Charles was hard for Arnold, it made for easier stomachs in the officers' mess. Dundas had written Clinton on the day of Phillips's death that although Arnold's "abilities and inclination" were never in question, "there are many officers who must wish some other general had this command." Rodney had been uncannily accurate in his prediction of the jealousy that would hamper Arnold. Henceforth, the officers had Cornwallis, and, fair general though he was, he led them to disaster at Yorktown. Meanwhile Arnold was recalled to New York with his American Legion, arriving there by June 10.[12]

Judge Thomas Jones, that honest but dyspeptic-minded old Loyalist

who despised Clinton in almost the same degree that he hated Judge
William Smith—the general for his supineness and his acceptance of the
advice that Smith allegedly gave him, had a mixed opinion of Arnold.
If he considered Arnold "a man of spirit, courage, decision, and resolu-
tion," he also thought him avaricious. He said that, on this occasion,
Arnold returned to New York "as rich as a nabob, with the plunder of
Virginia." This was in line with opinion in certain military quarters in
New York that Arnold's "love of money, his ruling passion, has been very
conspicuous in Virginia." [13]

How much of this comment originated in envy and how much was true
are points difficult to establish. That Arnold shared in the prize money is
certain, but, in accepting it, he was but following the custom of the day.
As Carl Van Doren has pointed out, prize money was considered as part
of a soldier's pay; Wayne's seizure of Stony Point in 1779 netted the
assault force the sum of $144,000 from the proceeds of the captured mili-
tary stores that were sold, the manner and proportion of the distribution
effected according to the decision of the commander-in-chief.[14]

The question of the division of the Virginia prize money was a complicated one. The army and the navy usually posted conflicting claims, and
this time was no exception. On the way to Virginia, Arnold and Captain
Thomas Symonds, representing the navy, had agreed verbally at Symonds's suggestion that whatever was taken as a prize while they were acting together should be equally divided. In a petition to the King, Thomas
Charles Williams, Arnold's agent for the army, contended that when the
expedition was over, the navy refused to comply. The case went before
the vice-admiralty court of New York, which ruled the agreement valid.
Half the proceeds were then given to the navy, while the other half remained with the court for the Crown pending the King's pleasure. In
March, 1782, the King answered Williams's petition, ordering that one-
eighth of the amount awarded to the Crown be given to Arnold and the
remainder divided among the officers and soldiers of his expedition "as
had been done on former occasions." [15]

The decision was not accepted without opposition. Several naval officers, including Symonds, objected strenuously to his petitioning the King
for the amount deposited in the court, said to consist of £10,341; they
contended that they had aided ashore as well as at sea. Faced with such
men looking for a two-way cut, Arnold wrote for information to Sir
George Collier, who, with General Edward Matthews, had devastated
the Chesapeake region in 1779. Collier replied that, on that expedition,

he and Matthews had divided one-eighth of the total prize money between themselves, while the army and navy had divided the remainder,
which was distributed in a manner customary to the respective services.
Arnold sent Collier's letter to the government in support of his position.[16]

It will probably never be known precisely how much Arnold realized,
but there is at least one figure on record, £2,068, of which most came
from the one-eighth portion of the £10,341 in question. There were also
fees due him on the prize money he claimed for the American Legion,
possibly £30 or £40, and Arnold was never one to turn up his nose at
"small change." Furthermore, he rarely failed to try to collect every penny
due him; for expenses allegedly contracted in connection with the prize
money, he charged Williams's estate in the amount of £177. 18. 4¼.
While it is unlikely that Arnold sent to New York a sloop loaded with
livestock and provisions for a present to Peggy, as Judge Jones claimed,
the Virginia expedition had clearly added to his fortune. Arnold, however, considered the expedition a personal disappointment financially and
militarily.[17]

That summer of 1781 continued disappointing to him, his dissatisfaction relieved only by the birth of a second son to Peggy on August 28,
whom they named James Robertson. Arnold had little luck in filling up
his Legion, while Clinton's indecisiveness and lack of enterprise discouraged him. He hoped in vain that Clinton would make a vigorous
effort to take West Point. Though Clinton dismissed the idea, mainly on
the ground that Arnold underestimated American strength, the British
commander-in-chief had entertained the prospect of a destructive raid on
Philadelphia, only to have it spoiled by Cornwallis's reluctance to send
reinforcements from Virginia and by the delayed arrival of Hessian regiments from Bremen. That Arnold would have had a command in this expedition is highly likely, and what a sense of vindication he would have
enjoyed had he been able to enter in force the city that had brought him
such humiliation! But, instead, he presently found himself given command
of an expedition to New London, Connecticut, a venture designed to di-
vert Franco-American attention from Cornwallis, who had maneuvered
himself into a trap at Yorktown. No convincing evidence has been discovered that, as has been often claimed, the expedition was made at his
suggestion, but he may well have proposed it.[18]

Arnold sailed on this tragic enterprise on September 4, the very day
that the French troops marched through Philadelphia on their way to
Yorktown. He had with him about 1,700 men. Anchoring on the Long

Island side of the Sound opposite New London on the afternoon of the 5th, he had his fleet of warships and transports under way again about seven in the evening. His expectations of landing by midnight were disappointed when the wind shifted to the north. Not until nine o'clock in the morning of September 6 were the transports able to beat into the mouth of the Thames, and not until an hour later were the troops put ashore.

The troops arrived in two divisions. The one on the New London side, which was under Arnold's direct command, consisted of the 38th Regiment, the Loyal Americans (Colonel Beverly Robinson's outfit), the American Legion Refugees (Arnold's own), and a small detachment of Hessian Light Infantry. The division on the Groton side of the river, which was under the command of Lieutenant Colonel Edmund Eyre, was composed of the 40th and 54th Regiments, a battalion of New Jersey Volunteers, a company of Hessians, and a battery of artillery. Of the regulars, the 40th had achieved a particularly notable record. It had occupied key positions in the battle of Long Island and the storming of Fort Washington, fought a good part of Washington's entire army at Princeton, participated at the Brandywine, and held the Chew House at Germantown, the defense of which figured prominently in the American defeat. These, then, were real veterans.[19]

Arnold's division had little trouble. Though the Americans had fired alarm guns and Lieutenant Colonel William Ledyard, who commanded the few troops in the area, had sent messengers galloping to towns near by for assistance, Arnold easily took New London. Most of the guns of Fort Trumbull, like those of Singapore in 1941, faced only toward the water, and the fort soon fell to the force that Arnold threw at it from the rear. Spiking their guns, the garrison managed to escape to boats and rowed for Fort Griswold on the Groton side. Meanwhile Arnold himself seized the town after but slight opposition. Then, quickly ascending the hill behind the town where the old burial ground lay, he studied the situation.

What he saw impelled him to alter a previous decision. Part of the objective of the expedition was the destruction of the fleet of privateers and merchantmen that had made New London their home port. Soon after the British arrived, many of these vessels cracked on sail and headed for Norwich. Misinformed by local Loyalists as to the strength of Fort Griswold, Arnold had sent a messenger to Colonel Eyre after Fort Trumbull fell, ordering him to take Griswold as soon as possible lest these ships

flee past its guns unhindered. Now, surveying the scene from the burial
ground, Arnold discovered Fort Griswold to be much stronger than he
had been led to believe, and perceived that its garrison was increased by
those escaping from Fort Trumbull. He saw, too, that the ships were
making their way to safety despite the fire from British guns hastily emplaced along the riverside. Taking in these developments at a glance,
Arnold immediately dispatched an officer to Eyre to countermand the
attack on Fort Griswold. Unfortunately the officer arrived after the attack
had started, and the result of his lateness was a tragedy of the war that
deepened Arnold's infamy in the eyes of his former countrymen.

The defense of Griswold was in the capable hands of Colonel Ledyard,
who had directed its construction. The fort, a square with flankers, had
walls of stone about ten to twelve feet high on the lower side, surrounded
by a ditch, surmounted by pickets projecting twelve feet, and topped by a
parapet with embrasures, a firing platform for cannon, and a shooting
step for small arms. Including one hundred farmers and artisans who had
come in since the alarm was given and the escaped garrison from Trumbull, Ledyard had about one hundred and fifty men to oppose the eight
hundred under Colonel Eyre now forming for the attack. Coolness itself,
Ledyard evidently had complete confidence in the strength of his fort and
the spirit of his militia to repulse Eyre's assault. He may also have been
encouraged by a promise given him by an American colonel to assist him
with several hundred militia; the colonel was unable to make good his
promise, was court-martialed in consequence after the battle, but was
acquitted.[20]

Before sending his troops forward, Eyre ordered Ledyard to surrender.
This order he dispatched by Captain George Beckwith, General Knyphausen's adjutant with whom Arnold had had treasonous correspondence
while André was away with Clinton in South Carolina; Beckwith, a
Loyalist from New Jersey, eventually became a lieutenant general in the
British Army during the Napoleonic wars. When Ledyard peremptorily
rejected Eyre's demands, Beckwith signaled for the assault to start.

Both the attack and the defense were waged with the greatest intrepidity. Moving up from three sides, the British mounted on their comrades' backs to wrench away the pickets. Meanwhile the Americans
enfiladed part of their position with cannon and threw hot shot at them.
The British losses were severe, but they maintained the lodgment they had
made until a sufficient number of troops had gathered for them to burst
through the embrasures at the bayonet's point. The defenders now

grasped spears and boarding pikes, which they handled effectively. Colonel Eyre had been mortally wounded early in the assault. Major William Montgomery, who took over the assault column, received a mortal wound from a pike. Several company officers were likewise killed or wounded. The command now devolved on Major Stephen Bromfield, who, with Beckwith, finally succeeded in carrying the fort.

It was at this juncture that sheer horror ensued. The Americans had lost a half dozen killed and about a score wounded; the British, about forty killed and over one hundred wounded. Ledyard, seeing the futility of further resistance now that his men were surrounded, ordered them to throw down their arms. But the British, their blood up, continued firing. Suddenly either Bromfield or Beckwith called out, "Who commands this garrison?" Handing his sword to the officer, Ledyard answered, "I did, sir, but you do now." An instant later, Ledyard fell dead, run through the body with his own weapon. The combatant narrators are divided as to whether the odium belonged to Bromfield or Beckwith. After carefully sifting the evidence, examining Ledyard's torn clothing in a Hartford museum, and reconstructing the scene, the historian of the battle, William Harris, concluded that while the guilty one might have been Beckwith, who conceived the flag and himself insulted when Ledyard rejected the surrender demand, it would have been difficult for either officer to commit the murder because of the position he would have had to assume to receive the colonel's sword. Harris felt that an aide or subaltern standing near by was probably responsible. However that may be, the soldiers continued firing and bayoneting for some time before their officers could get control of them. By that time, eighty-eight Americans were dead and thirty-five wounded. Resolving to blow up the powder magazine, Bromfield ordered the fort evacuated. The American wounded were then placed in a heavy ammunition wagon, which was drawn out of the fort by the redcoats. In the descent of the hill, the British, unable to hold back the wagon, let go of it; it tore down the hill, gathering momentum all the time, crashed into a tree, and scattered the shrieking wounded over a wide area.[21]

While these horrible events were occurring, Arnold was at his work of devastation in New London. He destroyed a dozen ships, an immense quantity of European and West Indian goods, many cannon, and warehouses. His troops also plundered and set fire to shops, stores, and private dwellings. In the course of this military and civilian destruction, the wind shifted and spread the flames rapidly through a considerable section of the town. Even the house of a Loyalist with whom Arnold dined, James Tilley, was consumed; in fact, one hundred and forty houses in New London and Groton were left in ashes. Finally Arnold re-embarked, to the great relief of the stricken communities. On September 8, off Plum Island, he sent in his report to Clinton. Sir Henry complimented him on his "very spirited conduct" but lamented the heavy loss in officers and men, who numbered forty-eight killed and one hundred and forty-five wounded. One of General Heath's spies in New York reported the British as saying that if Arnold retained his command, "they will be able to make but few more expeditions." The defenders of Fort Griswold had thus not died alone.[22]

Arnold's responsibility for that dreadful September day was divided. Regardless of the caprices of the wind, he was directly responsible for what happened in New London. For the slaughter at Fort Griswold, however, he had no direct responsibiliity since he was on the other side of the river; true, he had ordered the attack, but he had also rescinded it. Still his name was identified with the massacre, and, of course, as commanding officer of the expedition, though not present at the scene of battle, the ultimate responsibility was his. On the other hand, as General Heath, who commanded the Eastern and Northern Departments in Washington's absence at Yorktown, wrote in his diary several days after the tragedy,

> It is not meant to exculpate or to aggravate the conduct of the enemy on this occasion—but two things are to be remembered; first, that in almost all cases the slaughter does but begin when the vanquished give way; . . . secondly, in all attacks by assault, the assailants, between the feelings of danger on the one hand, and resolution to overcome it on the other, have their minds worked up almost to a point of fury and madness, which those who are assailed, from a confidence in their works, do not feel; and that consequently when a place is carried, and the assailed submit, the assailants cannot instantaneously curb their fury to reason, and in this interval, many are slain in a way which a cool by-stander would call wanton and barbarous, and even the perpetrators themselves, when their rage subsided, would condemn.[23]

Regardless of anything that can be said in explanation of Arnold's role, the fact remains that he was in command of the expedition and was held responsible for the massacre by his former countrymen. Andrew Ward of Guilford wondered that the command should ever have been vested "in the hands of a madman," while Governor Trumbull fumed to Washington about "the infamous Arnold." Undoubtedly what many Americans thought could not be printed. They were particularly outraged that he should have ravaged his native state, and, moreover, a community but a few miles from his birthplace. There seemed in this enterprise an element almost of sacrilege. Though he probably regarded this task solely as his duty and manifested far less personal animus than would have been the case had he raided Philadelphia, the destruction of life and property placed the seal on his infamy in the eyes of Americans. Clinton would have been better advised to have chosen another officer; Arnold, to have declined the command. Had war in the field continued much longer, the New London raid, which was utterly futile in diverting Allied attention from Cornwallis, would have stirred the country to fiercer resistance. As it was, there were people who, remembering the fire and slaughter of that September 6, considered the terms given Lord Cornwallis when he surrendered Yorktown in October as erring grossly on the side of leniency.[24]

· XXVIII ·

A New Start in England and New Brunswick

ALTHOUGH the surrender of Cornwallis at Yorktown signified to Lord North in London that all was indeed over, Arnold was by no means so certain, and he requested permission to leave for England with the intention of presenting his point of view. Clinton told him on November 5, 1781 that when the French fleet had gone and a ship was available, he would be glad to comply with Arnold's wishes. Arnold was so delighted that he must have talked freely, for that same day Mrs. Shoemaker, whom he knew, recorded in her diary, "Gen. Arnold and family go home in the next convoy." There followed a hasty packing, then a tedious wait while a fleet assembled, and finally the departure on December 15. Cornwallis and Arnold sailed on the same warship, the *Robuste*. Peggy and her family, said Mrs. Shoemaker, went "in a private ship as more agreeable for her than a man of war, yet not safe for him. They give for the cabin 300 guineas and then took in what company they chose, chiefly military, I believe. I do not hear of any females but her maids." Hannah Arnold remained in New Haven to which she had gone with Henry after her brother's treason, and with her were the two older boys, who, although holding commissions in the British Army, had not left Connecticut since returning from their school in Maryland in 1780.[1]

But if Arnold in a fleet of one hundred sail had little to fear from

French cruisers or American privateers, he barely escaped disaster from a storm. The *Robuste* was pummeled so severely when eleven days out of New York that she nearly went down. Though surviving, she suffered such damage that she steered to the West Indies for repairs, while Arnold transferred to the *Edward* and Cornwallis to the *Greyhound*. England, even in the grip of winter, must have been doubly welcome to the storm-tossed exiles.

What kind of reception Arnold and Peggy expected to receive can only be conjectured. That Peggy was apprehensive is likely; after all, she was a nervous girl far from home for the first time and the wife of a traitor to a cause that had many friends in England. It is doubtful, however, that Arnold himself was greatly troubled. Though he had brought only himself back to the King, his failure to surrender West Point and its garrison had not occurred for lack of trying. If, afterward, he had not covered himself with glory under British colors, again it was not his fault. Rodney's prediction had been only too accurate; jealousy and suspicion had prevented Arnold's being given the kind of command that might have afforded him the opportunity to achieve as startling feats of arms as he had effected while an American. Now, nearing England's shores, he must have suspected that he was likely to encounter similar obstacles. Still he had a letter of recommendation from Clinton to Germain, and he hoped to persuade the latter that the war was not lost.

The actual reception given him was mixed. The Whig newspapers and the friends of America criticized him. There is a story that he was hissed at a theater, and another that a member of Parliament wanted to move that the House of Commons be cleared unless Arnold withdrew but relented on Arnold's promise not to come again. It is difficult to credit some of the tales, but there was undoubtedly considerable feeling toward him. What was chiefly important to him, however, was that people who mattered should accept him, and many of them did. Germain treated him with respect, while Sir Guy Carleton gave him his arm on his introduction to the Court, and Sir Walter Stirling presented him. The King was both kind and considerate, and wanted his views. In fact, Benjamin Franklin wrote to America from Paris, "We hear much of audiences given to Arnold, and his being present at councils." The King's brother and the Prince of Wales walked with him in the public gardens. As for Peggy, whose beauty was greatly admired, it was said the Queen liked her so much that she wished the Court ladies to pay the young woman a great deal of attention. Such recognition must have been cherished by the two exiles, who presently took a house in Portman Square.[2]

It was in 1782, not long after his reception by the King, that at His Majesty's request Arnold drew up his "Thoughts on the American War." For this paper Arnold may have depended on notes that William Smith had given him on December 10, 1781, "notes," as Smith wrote in his diary under that date, "for answers to questions that may be put to him [Arnold]." The paper, which projected a plan to bring the colonies back into allegiance, is a compound of common sense and nonsense. Arnold declared that originally Britain had been deceived as to the strength of the malcontents in America but that now a great majority of Americans were averse to a separation. If Arnold had said that in the beginning this last was so, he would have been more nearly correct. Most Americans, he contended, could not express their dissatisfaction with the United States because they were excluded from the elections. Still, conditions were favorable for a change. The farmer groaned under his taxes, Congress was bankrupt, the Continental Army was rife with desertion and mutiny, with the French having gone home the Americans were as unable to attempt any great enterprise as before the French had arrived, and the separatist negotiations of Vermont with the commanding officer in Canada excited apprehension throughout the land. Arnold conjectured that unless the French helped reduce New York in the spring of 1782 Congress would move to seek an accommodation with the British.

Though his conjecture was wide of the mark, his knowledge of the specific hazards and grievances of the Americans was pretty accurate, and he set forth a plan to meet the situation. Delicately criticizing "the inactivity and misdirection" of the King's arms, he pointed out that no attempt had been made to set up civil authority "where the usurpation had been beaten down," and that, consequently, many Loyalists had failed to rise in support of the Crown. One of the first measures must therefore be to set up a civil government where the King's troops were successful. Increased efforts should be made to detach Vermont and to take the Hudson forts in the spring since many New Yorkers "and a very great proportion of the country between them and the Connecticut River are known to be very favorably inclined to the reunion." With a solid appreciation of sea power, he insisted that the navy must establish a superiority by March or April along the coast in order to confine any French reinforcements to their place of debarkation for the defense of their ships.

He considered a new peace commission "indispensably necessary," one composed of men of rank who should be "rather statesmen than soldiers." "Perplexed as the Congress must be under the growing uneasiness of the people," he declared, "neither affection to the French, nor a republican attachment, nor even the aims of ambition, would prevent them from listening to overtures that were decisive and irreversable." The commission should be appointed with power to come to a final agreement with any or all of the colonies whether the matter concerned be "civil, commercial, military, or ecclesiastical." Furthermore, the commission should have power to appoint officers from governors downward so that when the members returned to England they would leave behind them a government "established upon such a plan as, all things considered, may appear to be expedient." Of course, concluded Arnold, his suggestions were based "upon the supposition that Great Britain has such an interest in her colonies, as is worth fostering for the common good. It will be melancholy if the discovery should be made too late."[3]

On the whole, the plan made about as much sense as any the British government had heretofore projected, which is not saying much, to be sure. The main difficulty was its timing. Despite the appalling conditions in the new republic and the spinelessness of Congress in the closing years of the war, the Americans would never consent to a reunion. Neither the King, who was favorable to continuing the conflict, nor Arnold could or would realize this—the King, because he wanted the colonies back as part of the Empire and because he feared, if they were lost, the diminution of his political and personal prestige; Arnold, because British acknowledgment of defeat would be a personal disaster. Had some plan like Arnold's been offered early in the war, a reunion might well have been achieved. Many of the men who signed the Declaration of Independence hesitated long before committing themselves to a separation, and there were thousands of Americans who initially regarded their "patriotism" as a defense of their rights as Englishmen rather than an endeavor to found a new nation. The times had moved ahead of Arnold and his King. Wiser men in England saw that the struggle with the former colonies was about played out, and the peace treaty of 1783 wrought the downfall of any hopes Arnold entertained of a triumphant return to America.

Not long after the war, a movement started with the object of erecting a monument in Westminster Abbey to the memory of André, and Arnold's interest in the movement was keen. Presently a monument was raised in the south aisle of the Abbey with the following inscription on the panel: "Sacred to the memory of Major John André, who, raised by his merit, at an early period of life, to the rank of Adjutant-General of the British forces in America, and, employed in an important but hazardous enterprise, fell a sacrifice to his zeal for his King and Country, on the 2d of October, 1780, aged twenty-nine, universally beloved and esteemed by the army in which he served, and lamented even by his foes. His gracious Sovereign, King George III, has caused this monument to be erected." A visit to the Abbey is always popular with Americans newly arrived in London, and one of the points of greatest interest is André's monument, which became more meaningful after his body was removed from its rude grave in America in 1821 and reinterred in the Abbey. A Loyalist, Peter Van Schaack, had a singular experience soon after the dedication of the monument. His biographer wrote, "In one of Mr. Van Schaack's visits to the Abbey, some time after Arnold's treason, his musings were interrupted by the entrance of a gentleman, accompanied by a lady. It was General Arnold and the lady was doubtless Mrs. Arnold. They passed to the cenotaph of Major André, where they stood and conversed together. What a spectacle! The traitor Arnold in Westminster Abbey, at the tomb of André, deliberately perusing the monumental inscription, which will transmit to future ages his own infamy." Was Arnold merely perusing or was he envying aloud the respect and honor in which André was held? In any event, he presently changed his motto from *"Mihi gloria sursum"* (translated by the Arnold family as "Through glory yielded to me") to *"Nil desperandum"* ("Never despair").[4]

In 1785, Arnold soon felt the need of making further provision for his family. Lacking employment, he sought to recover in sterling from the British government the losses he had incurred by coming over to the King. Accordingly he submitted to the commissioners on Loyalist claims a memorial in which modesty found little place. Making the best possible case for himself, he asserted in the third person that, conceiving the British peace proposals of 1778 to be "just and equitable he used his endeavours and influence to have them accepted," a palpable falsehood. Then, seeing the American government determined on a separation, he had resorted to the negotiations with Clinton that ended in his flight. To support his statement of negotiations, he appended a certificate from Stansbury, who was freed after his arrest, fled to New York and then to London, and ended his career in an insurance company back in New York. Arnold mentioned in his memorial that the real and personal property forfeited in Pennsylvania and Connecticut was worth "at a moderate computation"

the sum of £16,125, all of which had been confiscated and sold by authorization of the legislatures.[5]

Included in an extensive list of claims were several items that reveal the
money-grabbing propensities of the memorialist. He described in detail his
real estate in Philadelphia and Connecticut. Mount Pleasant he estimated
as being worth £5,000, which was £1,000 more than it had been ap-
praised at in September, 1784, by Richard Footman and Tench Coxe.
Naturally Arnold neglected to inform the commissioners that Peggy's
father had bought back the estate for him after the confiscation, nor
could the commissioners know that in July of this year, 1785, he was to
notify Judge Shippen through Peggy that since American lands appeared
to be falling in value, Shippen was to sell for as much as he could get.
The New Haven property Arnold estimated at £1,800, which was
£1,200 less than he declared it cost him and £800 more than he was
willing to sell it for in the summer of 1780; though, to do him justice, he
had said in 1780 that he would have preferred not to sell even for
£2,000.[6]

Claims for service were even more extraordinary. He estimated lands
promised by Congress as worth £5,000 and the life half-pay for his dis-
ability (allegedly promised by Congress and the states and commuted to
ten-years pay) at £4,050. Though his public accounts had never been
settled, he claimed a total of £2,731 from Congress and £1,125 from
Connecticut. The most fantastic claim, however, was involved in his statement that "in consequence of his loyalty and engagements with Sir Henry
Clinton he refused the command of the American Army in South Carolina offered him . . . by Washington which was afterwards given to . . .
Greene who (the memorialist is informed) has been rewarded by the
states of the Carolinas and Virginia with the sum of £20,000 sterling for
his services which would probably have been given to the memorialist had
he accepted the command." In the first place, Arnold was never offered
command of the Southern Department and, secondly, he was misinformed
concerning the sum; while South Carolina voted Greene a substantial
emolument, Greene spent most of it keeping his army in the field.

Arnold himself eventually realized that his claims were outrageous.
On April 26, 1786, he asked that his papers be returned, explaining that
he had received from Clinton compensation for the loss of his personal
estate and that his wife had acquired her pension. Although, in his
opinion, these rewards were "not a full compensation for the loss of my
real estate, for risks run, and services rendered, yet I have upon duly con-

sidering the great expense which I shall probably incur, by remaining in London to prosecute a further claim, the loss of time, and difficulty attending it, thought proper to withdraw my claim for any further compensation." [7]

It is likely that part of his reason for not wishing to linger was his desire to be off on a new venture. He was buying and equipping a brig, the *Lord Middleton,* with the idea of taking up his prewar occupation of merchant and master mariner. This time he intended to establish his business at the new Loyalist settlement of St. John, New Brunswick, and he went about that summer readying the brig with eager zeal. The venture meant an end to his terrible restlessness, and it held a promise of great rewards which he felt he needed for his growing family.

His family, however, was not as large as it would have been had death not cut down two children soon after they appeared. These were Margaret, born in January, 1783, and George, born in March, 1784. Fortunately another child, Sophia Matilda, born in London, July 28, 1785, survived, and she was to become very dear indeed to Arnold. Thus it is understandable that Arnold, with a young family of two sons and one daughter, should feel impelled to increase his fortune.

Leaving Peggy and the children in London, Arnold sailed in October, 1785, and, after a voyage of five weeks, arrived at Halifax on November 19. His sudden appearance startled a number of the citizens there. Sampson S. Blowers, a Loyalist and now attorney general of Nova Scotia, wrote of Arnold's arrival to Ward Chipman, also a Loyalist, a Harvard graduate like Blowers, and now starting a distinguished legal and political career in New Brunswick. "Will you believe," Blowers exclaimed incredulously, "General Arnold is here from England, in a brig of his own, as he says, reconnoitering the country. He is bound for your city, which he will of course prefer to Halifax, and settle with you. Give you joy of the acquisition." [8]

Arnold found St. John a young, bustling, lumbering-and-fishing town, only six months previously having received its charter, and having been formed by the union of Parr Town and Carleton on opposite sides of the harbor. Much of the city, particularly the Parr Town area, had been built up by thousands of Loyalists from many of the former American colonies, the first of whom had arrived in force in May, 1783. With a fine eye for its trading possibilities, Arnold bought a lot on Main Street in Lower Cove, built a store, and took as his partner, Munson Hayt. This man had been a Loyalist and had served as a lieutenant with the duty of quarter-

master in the Prince of Wales's American Volunteers; Arnold had probably known him in New York. Arnold's hopes of a quick prosperity,
however, received a sharp jolt when his brig went down in a storm. The
next May, anxious to replace her, he bought from another Loyalist,
Nehemiah Beckwith, a vessel still on the stocks at Mangerville to which
he gave the name, *Lord Sheffield*. Shortly afterward, with Hayt in charge
of the business at St. John, Arnold left for the West Indies in his new
ship.[9]

It was probably during this winter of separation from Peggy that
Arnold formed a liaison that resulted in the birth of an illegitimate son,
called John Sage. Who the woman was in the case has remained a
mystery. Arnold was unpopular in St. John, and it seems that if people
who disliked him had known the identity of his mistress, their whispers
would have echoed down the years. The secret was so well kept that it
suggests a conspiracy of silence. Was she a lady of "station"? Some have
speculated that she was Jacataqua, the sachem of Swan Island, thereby
confusing Arnold with Aaron Burr, while one reputable biographer has
actually placed the birth of the boy as occurring between 1775 and 1777.
Arnold himself cleared up the matter of the date. In providing for John
Sage in his will, Arnold mentioned the lad as being "about fourteen years
of age." Since Arnold signed his will on August 30, 1800, the boy must
have been born in late 1786.[10]

Possibly it was Arnold's preoccupation with his inamorata as well as
his concern over his business following the loss of his ship that accounted
for the long interval between his letters which so distressed Peggy, who
had been ill much of the time since the birth of Sophia. In a pathetic
communication to her father in March, 1786, she admitted her "most unhappy state of suspense respecting the General" and her further unhappiness at being "separated from, and anxious for the fate of the best of
husbands." So far as is known, this was Arnold's only lapse while married
to Peggy. He confessed the affair to her and presumably won her for-
giveness.[11]

Arnold's voyage to the West Indies ended in England in order to fetch
Peggy and the children to New Brunswick. He returned with them in July,
1787, and bought a house at the corner of King and Canterbury Streets.
He also sent for his older sons, who came downeast with Hannah. Occasionally, however, Hannah returned to New Haven; in fact, she was there
in 1792 attending to some business for her brother. Eventually she went
to live permanently with Richard and Henry in Canada. What Peggy

thought of the new start in New Brunswick was probably colored by its relative proximity to Philadelphia and her family, whom she intended to visit in the near future. As for Hannah, the good woman never really felt at home anywhere outside of New Haven.[12]

Meanwhile Arnold sedulously developed his business. He established trading stations at St. John, Campobello Island, and Fredericton, the capital, a raw wilderness town settled by Loyalists in 1783 and linked with the outside world only by the St. John River. Arnold liked Fredericton so much that he bought three lots on what is now Waterloo Row and enough other lots for elbow room so that his holdings totaled twelve acres. He even lived there off and on for a period of two years in a house that he purchased from Peter Clements, formerly a Loyalist captain in the King's American Regiment.[13]

But Arnold did not find this life in New Brunswick a smooth existence. His trading ventures in lumber and provisions were not so successful as he had hoped. Men with whom he did business borrowed money from him which they had difficulty in repaying or entered his name as security for debts which they contracted without his knowledge or consent. Though he had at least one other vessel besides the *Sheffield* in operation, the *George,* insurance rates and the intense competition cut his profits markedly. Furthermore, he had lost little of his old arrogance, and people hated him for it and distrusted him for his record of betrayal in the war. Captain John Shackford, who had been on the march to Quebec with him and was taken prisoner in the assault, once loaded a ship for him at Campobello under Arnold's personal direction. Shackford said later of this experience, "I did not make myself known to him, but frequently . . . I sat upon the ship's deck, [and] watched the movements of my old commander, who had carried us through everything, and for whose skill and courage I retained my former admiration, despite his treason. But when I thought of what he had been and the despised man he then was, tears would come, and I could not help it." [14]

Popular disapproval of him steadily increased. In 1788, he sailed to England with a cargo. This was disappointing to Peggy, who had hoped to go to Philadelphia before this, but the birth of a son, George, on September 5, 1787, and Arnold's trip to England caused a postponement. While Arnold was away, he accepted the advice of friends in England and insured a warehouse in Lower Cove for £1,000, the stock for £4,000, and the stock in his store on King Street for £1,000. He returned from England to find that on July 11 fire had destroyed the warehouse and its contents and that Henry, who had been sleeping there, nearly perished. At once Arnold moved to recover damages. Rumors that he had set the fire himself, however, so impressed the insurance underwriters that the companies sought to escape liability. Eventually they were forced to pay, but the rumors persisted. Possibly it was this rising ill feeling that he encountered in St. John which impelled him, in early 1789, to rent his house for £50 per annum and live in Fredericton.[15]

A year later, friction having developed between himself and Munson Hayt, their partnership ended in a lawsuit and mutual recrimination. Hayt alleged that, on May 7, 1787, Arnold and his family had robbed him of £400 and subsequently of £300. But Hayt did not stop here. As he acknowledged in a legal plea in 1790, he "did speak, assert, publish, and proclaim with a loud voice in the hearing of divers of His Majesty's faithful subjects" that "You [Arnold] burnt your own store" and that "it is not in my power to blacken your character for it is as black as it can be." Arnold at once brought suit for slander against Hayt. He retained as counsel the solicitor general, Ward Chipman, and the distinguished attorney general, Jonathan Bliss, who had been a native of Springfield, a Harvard graduate of the class of 1763, a former member of the General Court of Massachusetts, and brother-in-law to the famous Fisher Ames of that state. Hayt employed a skillful lawyer, Elias Hardy.

The suit was tried before Justice Isaac Allen, a native of Trenton, New Jersey, and now on the bench of the Supreme Court of the province. The trial revealed Hayt to have misjudged his man. Unpopular as Arnold was, he was not one to submit to such defamation, however strong the sentiment in favor of Hayt. Arnold produced documentary evidence in the form of signed promissory notes to prove Hayt indebted to him for nearly £2,000. After enumerating and producing the specific notes, Arnold contended in his declaration that Hayt "not regarding his said several promises and undertakings so made as aforesaid but contriving and fraudulently intending craftily and subtly to deceive and defraud . . . hath not yet paid him the said several sums of money . . . and hath hitherto altogether refused and still doth refuse. . . ." Quite clearly, it had been Arnold's desire to collect from Hayt that had induced the latter—"falsely and maliciously," according to Arnold in his replication— to counter with his allegations. Furthermore, that Arnold had personally burned the store was impossible since he was then in England. Naturally Henry's presence in the building at the time and Arnold's taking out the insurance policies when he did seemed suspicious factors, but nothing was proven to make Arnold legally culpable. The verdict was delivered in his favor, but instead of the £5,000 damages for which he had sued, Judge Allen awarded him two shillings and sixpence.[16]

Meanwhile Peggy had made her long-anticipated visit to Philadelphia. On June 30, 1788, she wrote to her father of her happiness at the prospect of seeing him and her mother again. "Yet," she added, "my pleasure will not be unaccompanied by pain; as when I leave you, I shall probably bid you adieu forever." In August, 1788, she told her sister, Betsy Burd, "I feel great regret at leaving the General alone, and much perplexed with business, but as he strongly urges a measure that will be productive of so much happiness to me, I think there can be no impropriety in taking the step." Then Arnold's business trip to England intervened, during which the fire occurred, so that not until the fall of 1789 was Peggy able to sail for New York with the baby. The trip nearly brought disaster. As Edward Burd wrote to a friend in mid-November, "We have received an account of Mrs. Arnold's arrival at New York tho' no letters have been received from her. The vessel she came in, the papers say run ashore, but I suppose must have got off, or she would not have been in New York." Apprehensions eventually vanished, for, by early December, Peggy had joined her family.[17]

Her reception in Philadelphia was of a mixed quality. While her family rejoiced to see her again, there were some people, even including former friends of hers, who treated her with coldness and neglect. On the other hand, others showed her every mark of attention as if to compensate for criticisms from individuals and the press. She left Philadelphia for St. John on April 26, 1790, never to see her old home again. Implicated though she was in the perfidy of her husband, of which her presence in Philadelphia had been an uncomfortable reminder to many Americans, there is pathos in her letter to Burd's wife on July 5, 1790. Remarking upon the difficulty of knowing what contributes to happiness in this life, she said, "I had hoped that by paying my beloved friends a last visit, I should insure to myself some portion of it, but I find it far otherwise. The affectionate attention of my friends has greatly increased my love for them, and of course my regret at this cruel dreadful separation. I shall never forget my dear, my beloved sister, your tender and affectionate behavior to me, and that of my more than brother, Mr. Burd, who has endeared himself extremely to me." [18]

With Peggy back in St. John, Arnold now began to think of breaking up their home in New Brunswick and returning to England. Unfortunately for Peggy, he could not go as soon as she wished. In the letter of July 5 to her sister, she had also said, "From the present appearance of things there is great reason to apprehend a disappointment in our going home this fall. For my own part, I have given up every hope of going. There has been a succession of disappointments and mortifications in collecting our debts ever since my return home—but I will not begin to relate grievances, but for a time endeavor to shake off that gloom that has taken possession of me, and for which I have too much cause." [19]

It was not only from a man like Hayt that Arnold could not collect his debts. Peggy's own brother had touched up Arnold for a loan of £750 which he could not repay. In a flash of the same generosity that had impelled him, on one occasion, to help Colonel Lamb raise an artillery regiment and, on another, to relieve the destitution of General Warren's children, Arnold relinquished all claim on the money for himself but asked that it be settled on Peggy and her children for their sole use. Peggy's father then stepped in and pledged security for repayment, remarking of his son, "If he does not discharge the debt in my lifetime, you may rest assured I will make such a provision in my will, that it shall be paid out of such parts of my estate as I shall allot for the use of him or his family." [20]

The year 1791 was a time of almost unmitigated wretchedness and hard work. Hayt had once spoken of Arnold to a friend as "that greatest of all possible villains," and many of the people of St. John, where Arnold had again resumed residence, seemed to agree with him. Regardless of Arnold's victory in the slander suit, they believed him guilty and hated him. The collection of debts is never calculated to make one popular, and Arnold's efforts to wipe the slate clean before he left for England roused antagonism. Nor did his arrogance endear him to his fellow citizens. Finally a mob gathered, marched on his home, and burned an effigy of him in front of his door. The classic touch of irony to the menacing occasion was that these former Loyalists labeled their effigy "Traitor!" They might have done more had not the riot act been read to them and troops been called out. [21]

While Peggy lived in terror that summer, Arnold worked furiously to rid himself of his property. Since it was impossible to dispose of much of it privately without lingering in the city longer than he cared to, he advertised in the *Royal Gazette* for September 6, 1791, that an auction of household goods would take place at his house on the 22d. He purposed to sell such items, among many others, as "excellent Feather beds," "a set of elegant cabriole chairs covered with blue damask, sopha and curtains to correspond," "an Easy & Sedan chair," "an elegant desert set of Wedgewood Gilt Ware," "a Terrestrial Globe," "a double wheel Jack," and "a Lady's elegant Saddle and Bridle." From the type and quality of many of the items in the advertisement, it is clear that Arnold lived well in New Brunswick. In the same advertisement, moreover, he offered to sell other property "on very easy terms" at an auction on September 12. This property included 16½ lots of land in the St. John area, one thousand acres elsewhere, two wharves, a house, and the seasoned frame of a 300-ton ship. Still unable to find purchasers for all his property, either in St. John or Fredericton, Arnold gave a power-of-attorney to Jonathan Bliss and Ebenezer Putnam on September 30. Not until the new year, however, was he at last able to take Peggy and the children back to England.[22]

If Peggy, as she watched the shores of New Brunswick recede, felt a prayerful relief, Arnold considered the departure with a relief that was more angry than devout. He was still angry as, wretched with an attack of gout, he wrote Bliss from London on February 26, 1792, "We had a very rough and disagreeable voyage home, but our reception has been very pleasant, and our friends more than attentive since our arrival. The little property that we have saved from the hands of a *lawless ruffian mob* and *more unprincipled* judges in New Brunswick is perfectly safe here, as well as our *persons from insult,* and tho we feel and regret the absence of the friends we had there, we find London *full as pleasant!* and I cannot help viewing your great city as a shipwreck from which I have escaped." Scarcely more welcome among Canadians than he would have been among Americans, Arnold felt himself truly an alien, and he never again landed on the shores of continental North America.[23]

· XXIX ·

Last Ventures and Death

THE LAST years of Arnold's life saw no interruption in the long catalogue of frustration and tumultuous activity. They were years signalized
by renewed efforts to find a suitable military appointment, by commercial
and privateering activities in the West Indies, by a constant struggle to
provide adequately for his wife and family, and by a duel when his honor
was impugned in the House of Lords. In none of these engagements did
he enjoy the measure of success he sought, though in the duel he vindi-
cated himself to the satisfaction of the witnesses present. The difficulty he
encountered in these twilight years was owing in large part to his love
of extravagant living, to his addiction to attractive but hazardous investments, and to the inability or refusal of men of important position to
recognize his military merits.

He was back in England but a few weeks when he fought his duel with
James Maitland, Earl of Lauderdale. After leaving America in 1781,
Arnold rarely, if ever, alluded to his treason. This did not necessarily
signify that he regretted it; rather that he recognized it as a subject to be
avoided since it had brought unhappiness to his wife and marked out his
family for an undesirable notoriety. But if he did not wish the matter discussed in private, neither did he tolerate disparaging remarks in public
concerning it. On May 31, 1792, with the cabinet worried lest England
become infested with the virus that had produced a new form of government and a new society in France, the King issued a proclamation against

seditious meetings. The proclamation was hotly debated in the House of Lords, where members charged the government with inconsistency, moving as it had from reform to the suppression of its discussion. In England, reform was becoming identified with revolution, and even people gathering for prayer meeting were suspected of holding revolutionary assemblies. To be a Whig in the reactionary 1790's was to lay oneself open to the charge of being a radical or a Jacobin, even as today in America to be a liberal is to invite the label of Communist. On this occasion, none was more eloquent in denunciation of the government than Lauderdale, of whom the *Parliamentary History* reported, "The Earl at length took notice of the camp at Bagshot, which he said the noble Duke (of Richmond), who had been so strenuous for reform, was appointed to command, to overawe the people, and destroy their endeavors to obtain a reform. He declared he was glad the Duke was to command the camp. If *apostacy* could justify promotion, he was the most fit person for that command, *General Arnold excepted.*" [1]

Lauderdale stirred up a hornet's nest. Challenged at once by Richmond to explain or send his second, Lauderdale replied that the expression applied only to the Duke's public conduct, not his character. Arnold likewise bristled at the slight and demanded an apology. When Lauderdale refused to give one, Lord Edward Hawke, whom Peggy later described as "a most respectable peer and our particular friend," volunteered to act as Arnold's second. Lauderdale then chose as his second a great and brilliant friend of America during the Revolution, Charles James Fox. Hawk and Fox accordingly arranged a meeting for their principals at Kilburn Wells, just outside London. The time was set for seven o'clock, Sunday morning, July 1. [2]

While Peggy, who had been ill for a week, strove to suppress her feelings "lest," as she confessed, "I should unman the General," Arnold went to meet his opponent. The principals agreed to fire when Fox gave the word. At Fox's signal, Arnold alone discharged his pistol, but the shot went wild. Bracing himself to receive his opponent's fire, he felt his cheeks blush with shame as Lauderdale refused to respond. Hawk called on the Earl to fire, as did Arnold himself. But Lauderdale still declined, saying that he had not meant to wound Arnold's feelings in his address and that Arnold might fire again if he wished. Both Arnold and Hawk declared this to be impossible and insisted that he fire or retract what he had said in the Lords. When Lauderdale refused to do either, Arnold demanded that he fire; again the Earl would not be swayed. At this impasse,

Fox conferred with Lauderdale and subsequently with Hawke. The principals then walked toward each other, and Lauderdale admitted that he had not meant to asperse Arnold's character or hurt his pride, and expressed his regret that anyone should have been injured by what he had said. Arnold acknowledged his acceptance of this statement as an apology if the seconds would agree, which they did.

Arnold now hastily returned to Peggy, who was nearly beside herself with grief. The relief and joy she felt were undoubtedly important factors in her quick recovery from illness. Soon she proudly wrote her father that "It has been highly gratifying to find the General's conduct so much applauded, which it has been universally, and particularly by a number of the first characters in the kingdom, who have called upon him in consequence of it. Nor," she added with an interesting flash of self-pride, "am I displeased at the great commendations bestowed on my own conduct upon this trying occasion." [3]

Possibly endeavoring to cash in on the favorable publicity that attended his conduct, Arnold now sought a position from the government, preferably military, but, in any event, lucrative. Since Clinton was back in England nursing his grievances over the course of the American war and the approval given his rival, Cornwallis, Arnold requested him on July 23 to speak in his behalf to the prime minister, William Pitt the younger. Clinton wrote back in August, promising only to do his best. When no action was forthcoming from Sir Henry, Arnold followed up with letters in October, November, and December, reciting his services, his desires, and his needs. Peggy even interceded herself. Writing Clinton in mid-November, she lamented her inability to educate her numerous family in a style equal to what the earlier part of her life had promised. As a mother, she was therefore deeply interested in her husband's application. Clinton in his slow, cautious way then communicated with Pitt and recommended Arnold. The government, however, took no steps to recognize with employment the man whose treason in England's behalf had shaken two continents a decade before. [4]

Rebuffed, Arnold bought a ship in 1793 and turned to trade again. "I expect to embark in about a fortnight for the West Indies, to remain there five or six months," he wrote Jonathan Bliss in early February, 1794; "I shall visit the different islands—Barbados, Dominico, Grenada." His "fortnight" was somewhat extended, for, on March 19, he informed Bliss again that, "as the wind is now fair," he was about to sail. But with French privateers making the Channel hazardous, he let himself be persuaded by Peggy—now pregnant again—to go overland to Falmouth and wait for his ship to come around from London. Once he had arrived, however, he became impatient and sailed on another vessel for St. Kitts, leaving his own to follow. This was indeed fortunate for him since his own ship was captured by the French only a few days after she had left Falmouth.[5]

While waiting at a waterfront tavern in Falmouth, Arnold had an unusual and unpleasant reminder of his past. A storm-shattered ship bound for America from Greenwich put into port for repairs bearing Charles Maurice de Talleyrand, later the great minister of Napoleon and now a refugee from the persecution of the Jacobin government in France. Quite by chance Talleyrand dined in the same tavern where Arnold was lodged, and their meeting was, in Talleyrand's words, "a rather striking incident."

The innkeeper at whose place I had my meals [he explained] informed me that one of his lodgers was an American general. Thereupon, I expressed the desire of seeing that gentleman, and, shortly after, I was introduced to him. After the usual exchange of greetings, I put to him several questions concerning his country, but, from the first, it seemed to me that my inquiries annoyed him. Having several times vainly endeavoured to renew the conversation, which he always allowed to drop, I ventured to request from him some letters of introduction to his friends in America.

"No," he replied, and after a few moments of silence, noticing my surprise, he added, "I am perhaps the only American who cannot give you letters for his own country . . . all the relations I had there are now broken . . . I must never return to the States."

He dared not tell me his name. It was General Arnold. I must confess that I felt much pity for him, for which political puritans will perhaps blame me, but with which I do not reproach myself, for I witnessed his agony.

This is the only recorded occasion of Arnold's ever mentioning his former country after his arrival in England. If he never praised her, neither did he condemn her, as did so many disgruntled, unhappy Loyalists. Evidently he had tried to bury the memories of former years, and the encounter with the brilliant, probing Talleyrand was a painful experience.[6]

After trading for a while in St. Kitts, he sailed for Pointe-à-Pitre, Guadeloupe, an old stamping ground, with £5,000 to buy sugar. Almost at once he found himself in trouble. The French planters of the West Indies had become so alarmed at the Negro revolt on the island of Haiti in 1791 and at the subsequent spread of revolutionary propaganda to the other islands that they appealed to the British for protection. Accordingly, in early 1794, British forces acquired control of the French islands. The radical Jacobin government in Paris sent out in April a squadron with troop transports that slipped through Lord Howe's blockade, reached the West Indies safely, and recovered Pointe-à-Pitre. Leader of the French was a Jacobin mulatto named Victor Hugues. A ruthless, efficient ruler, he proclaimed freedom for the slaves, executed 1,200 Royalists, and eventually caused the British catastrophic loss of life and prestige.

Arnold headed straight for Guadeloupe after first notifying Peggy. She dashed off a frantic letter to Richard Arnold in August, saying, "I am now in a state of most extreme misery, from the report of your father's being a prisoner to the French. . . . It is contradicted by some gentlemen lately from St. Kitts, but your father's last letter to me, being of the first of June, wherein he says he shall set off the next day for Point-a-Peter, makes it but too probable, as the French took possession of that place the 4th of June. We are in hourly expectation of its recapture, till I hear of which I shall not know a moment's peace of mind." Fortunately the poor woman, assailed with a bilious complaint ever since the birth of her latest child, William Fitch Arnold, on June 25, 1794, was in ignorance of the precise nature of the danger to her husband.[7]

That danger, moreover, was great. At first thinking the tall ships in the harbor British, he learned too late that they were French. Escape impossible, he boldly landed, declaring that he was John Anderson (fateful name!) and that he was an American here to buy a cargo. But the French evidently suspected him of being English, even if they did not know that he was a retired British officer, for they placed him with other captives aboard a prison ship. Since they permitted him to take a certain amount of personal property with him, he concealed the money in his effects.

Arnold had lost none of his courage and craft. When a British fleet under Sir John Jervis, later Earl St. Vincent, arrived to blockade the French, Arnold determined to reach it. And when a sentry informed him that Hugues had learned his real identity and intended to hang him, he moved quickly. With the aid of a few gold pieces strategically scattered among the guards, he laid his plans. Securing an empty cask, he hid his treasure in it, together with a letter explaining whose it was. With darkness falling and the tide at the turn, he eased the cask into the sea. Then when all was still save the tramp of the watch overhead, he lowered himself from a cabin window by means of a rope to a rude raft of planks that had been prepared. This he propelled by means of his hands through

the shark-ridden water to a small boat moored not far away. Clambering
aboard, he picked up the oars. It was now but a few minutes after midnight, the morning of June 30, and the British fleet lay near the horizon.
But Arnold was not discouraged. Muffling the oarlocks, probably with
strips of his clothing, he rowed for those distant ships. Near at hand lay
the dark hulls of the French squadron, through which he picked his way
with the utmost care. Once a guardboat hailed him, and when he gave no
reply, chased him. Arnold, however, darted in and out among the anchored ships, eluding his pursuers in the darkness. Still, it had been touch-
and-go for a while, and he did not breathe freely until four o'clock that
morning, when he reached the *Boyne,* flagship of Admiral Jervis. Later
he even recovered the cask, which drifted ashore in an area below Pointe-
à-Pitre occupied by a British landing force.[8]

Though Arnold was pressing his middle fifties, the outbreak of war in
the West Indies had a rejuvenating effect on him. And the British had
need of his services, for, throughout the islands, the French, the Negro
insurrections, and the deadly yellow fever claimed 40,000 British lives in
three years before Pitt ordered the French West Indies evacuated. Had
the British renounced slavery, the blacks might have become their friends,
but the government refused to take the step. Consequently, while the
words have a strange appearance coming from Arnold's pen, they were
nevertheless true when he wrote Bliss from St. Pierre in Martinique that
war was now "carried on with a brutality unknown to former times, and
very little to the honor of humanity or the cause of freedom." [9]

His part in the hostilities was a mixed contribution. He served as a gentleman volunteer to Sir Charles Grey, the general in command, as an ex-
pediter in the organization and operation of the supply service, and as an
agent, representing the interests of the West Indian planters and merchants. As always, when danger was imminent, he was lavish with energy
and devices. To his great disappointment, he could not get far with Grey,
who, though appreciative of the aid he rendered, coldly refused even to
consider his request to be made the senior brigadier on the strength of his
American career. Still, he performed useful services, of which the government was eventually to take notice.[10]

The time came when he was anxious to return to England. Though he
had prospered while in the Indies, he had also, as he admitted to Bliss,
lost a great deal of money. Besides, it was humiliating to be treated so
cavalierly by the military. On the other hand, he was immensely gratified
by the fact that his decision in 1795 to leave evoked a resolution from the

standing committee of West Indies planters and merchants which was presented to Arnold by Gilbert Franklin, the chairman. The resolution was a real tribute. After thanking him, the committee declared "that they are fully sensible of his services in the West Indies, and feel themselves particularly obliged by his exertions, at the request of the commander-in-chief, which were attended, with such beneficial effects, in covering the retreat of the troops at Guadeloupe, and they cannot refrain from expressing their concern at his having quitted the Islands at a time when their safety is in the utmost hazard, and they beg leave to assure him it would give them the most entire satisfaction to find he was again in a situation to render further service to his Majesty in that part of the world." To Arnold such approbation was a rare experience, and he responded in a fitting letter of thanks. He had plans, moreover, that he intended to submit for ending the war in the West Indies if the government would listen.[11]

He returned to England in the summer of 1795, and Peggy exclaimed to Bliss, "I have, thank God, got him safe home." He found Peggy "very much an invalid, but as her disorder is in a great measure nervous, I hope she will soon get the better of it." He was pleased with the progress of Edward, James, and George at school, and relieved that the difficulty with Henry was over. Henry was something of a trial to him, lively and endearing, but also stubborn and irresponsible. In 1791, a friend of Arnold's, James Adair, had put up security for him when, as Adair remarked, Henry had "by youthful vivacity been led into some indiscretion in point of expense." Arnold refunded Adair but could do little about his son's propensity for getting into debt (an old Arnold custom) even when Henry came to the West Indies while Arnold himself was there. Arnold at last became thoroughly exasperated. "If my obstinate and imprudent son would [use?] his own interest and common prudence and economy," he burst out to Josiah Blakesley from his headquarters in St. Pierre, "I would in a short time put him in a very line to make a fortune. I want an assistant very much, but until I can trust him with money and be assured that he will not squander it away and think himself above giving an account of it, I will treat him as a stranger and not as a son. I wish to God he would have a little sense and prudence and determine to reform. . . . Pray give my love to Harry. I expect a letter from him when he has an apology." Eventually Henry made his peace with Arnold, but whether he changed his ways is not known.[12]

But to Arnold's pride and interest in his family was soon added tragedy.

His oldest son by Peggy Mansfield, Ben, was returned to England in 1795 after two years of imprisonment in France, then was sent out almost at once as an artillery officer to the West Indies. Severely wounded in the leg during a skirmish with maroons, those half Negro–half Indian savages of the Jamaican hills, he refused to have the limb amputated, and died of a gangrenous fever on October 24, 1795, at Iron Shore on the north coast of the island. "I have recently received the melancholy information of the death of my oldest son in Jamaica," wrote Arnold to Bliss. "I have the consolation to hear that he was much respected and beloved by the officers of his acquaintance. Major General Walpole was his particular friend . . . and Lord Balcarres had promised him further promotion. His death . . . is much regretted by them, and is a heavy stroke on me. . . ." Fond of all his children, Arnold had a further consolation when Sir Grenville Temple returned from the West Indies and presented him with his son's sword.[13]

Arnold now encountered a host of obstacles to his desires. Having agreed to the merchants' and planters' request to go out to the West Indies if his terms were complied with, he was anxious to depart. The ministry, however, so Peggy informed Bliss, were eager to send him but could not meet his conditions. These were that he go either as second-in-command of the main expedition or as head of a separate force. In view of the tradition-ridden War Office, the reason she gave for the ministry's rejection of him made sense, namely, "they were fearful of putting him over the heads of so many old general officers." Undoubtedly the ministry also considered that the higher army commands usually went to officers with some claims to aristocratic lineage, that Arnold had been a mere colonial, and that as a traitor he was intensely disliked by most of the opposition Whigs, regarded with little favor by many of the Tories, and detested by the officers of the army. Although Arnold did not stand a chance of securing the kind of appointment he wanted, Peggy could still point out with pardonable pride, ". . . it is universally acknowledged, that had his advice been followed, we should now be in possession of Guadeloupe, and the necessity of sending such a force as is now going, prevented."[14]

Foiled in this endeavor, Arnold tried again in 1796. He devised a plan of action against the Spanish West Indies which he communicated to Lord Cornwallis, now a family friend, who submitted it to Pitt, the prime minister. Arnold pledged himself to begin operations with a force of five thousand, under protection of a covering fleet, and he undertook to raise so formidable a body of "natives, creoles, and people of colour" that no force the Spaniards possessed in that area would be able to prevent the liberation of the islands from Spanish rule. The plan was no worse—in fact, better—in its general formulation than a number of plans that the British developed in the dreadful West Indies campaign. The government, however, rejected it.[15]

Arnold made three successive attempts in as many years to obtain military employment. In 1797, with England fearful of invasion and part of her fleet flying the red flag of mutiny, Arnold thought that surely there would be a place for him. He therefore applied to Lord Spencer, who was Lord Privy Seal, to be employed as the latter saw fit; Spencer had nothing for him. The next year, the threat of invasion increasing, he offered his services to the Duke of York; that good-natured, mulish incompetent who ruled at the War Office shrugged the offer aside. His soldier's pride all but broken, Arnold tried once more in 1799, this time to Lord Liverpool in hopes that he could find a place in a corps reportedly being raised for the defense of London; Liverpool referred him to the Duke of York. With this rebuff, Arnold gave up. Brokenly he told Peggy that the army had denied him a chance even to seek a soldier's death.[16]

Still Arnold had the satisfaction of receiving in a substantial form recognition of his services in the Revolution and on the island of Guadeloupe. As a half-pay officer of a former Loyalist regiment, he was entitled to wastelands belonging to the Crown in Upper Canada. Accordingly, on April 13, 1798, he applied to His Majesty's Council in Upper Canada for lands for himself and his family: 5,000 acres in his own name, 1,200 for his wife and each of his five children by her, and 1,200 for his illegitimate son, John Sage. Since Richard and Henry had already received their grants as half-pay officers, his claim totaled 13,400 acres. He requested, however, that he and his family be exempted from the usual residence requirement. The secretary for the Home Department, the Duke of Portland, granted his request and issued an order to Peter Russell, president of His Majesty's Council in Upper Canada, supporting Arnold's petition and exempting him from residence "in consequence of his late gallant and meretorious services in Guadeloupe." [17]

This was not the end of the wastelands affair. The Duke's office instituted a policy of demanding a fee of $7\frac{1}{2}$ d. per acre and charged Arnold that rate on his lands with the exception of the 5,000 acres granted to him personally. Arnold protested vigorously that this meant a payment from him of £235 in addition to the £50 expenses that it had cost his agent to apply for the grant. He contended that the Council had mistaken the Duke's order and intentions since the fee had never been demanded before the date of his memorial. "This grant," he declared, "was made to me in consequence of my having raised a regiment, and served during the war. The regiment cost me upwards of £6,000 sterling, more than I have ever received from [the] government for all my losses and sacrifices." Manifestly he had chosen to forget the liberal financial settlement that Sir Henry Clinton had made with him as part of the reward of his treason. He considered the lands as having been promised him as early as 1798 when he had spoken privately with the Duke, who urged him to submit his memorial. The grant, furthermore, was, in his opinion, "a *fair* and *dear* purchase by my services, which [the] government cannot in justice deprive me of, or refuse on the usual condition of grants." Evidently the Duke of Portland, who was noted for his forgetfulness and monumental irresolution, realized that he had made an error, for his office agreed to Arnold's requests, namely to notify the Council of Upper Canada that the new requirements should not apply to Arnold's grant and to permit Richard and Henry to locate the lands for him. But the time was now already midsummer of 1800, and Arnold's concern for his lands was primarily for their value to his family, not to himself.[18]

He was now so ill that he seems almost to have sensed the little space of time left him, and consequently threw himself into privateering in a last frenzied attempt to make money quickly. Yet in this financial venture he was no more successful than he had ever been since returning from Canada. His captains appear to have despoiled him of about £50,000. One of them cut out an enemy merchant convoy, but, instead of seeing his prizes into port, he let them go off unprotected; they were recaptured. On February 4, 1801, the *Ferret* sent in a Spanish prize worth £20,000, most of which was immediately claimed by creditors. A Swedish skipper sued for detention of his ship and cargo, and though an admiralty court threw out his claim two years after Arnold's death, the expenses to the Arnolds were great. What to do with another privateer, the *Earl Spencer,* sorely troubled Arnold. Said Peggy to their son Edward on January 14, 1801, "He has no encouragement to fit her out again, and yet I suppose there never was a vessel better calculated for that purpose. But he is, at present, in the most harassed wretched state that I have ever seen him. Disappointed in his highly raised expectations, harassed by the sailors who are loudly demanding their prize-money, when in fact their advances have greatly exceeded anything that is due to them, and wishing still to do something, without the health or power of acting, he knows not which way to turn himself." What business acumen or good luck Arnold may once have possessed, he seems to have lost. Though privateering was a legitimate business in those days, for Arnold it had become, in Peggy's words, an "unfortunate speculation." [19]

These last years were indeed unhappy for Arnold. He had no military present or future, he incurred heavy financial losses, and he grieved at the misfortunes that assailed his family. Peggy was a semi-invalid. Though he had moved her into a new house at Gloucester Place in Portman Square, he had continually to take her away for months at a time, now to Chigwell for the country air, now to Cheltenham for the waters. Notwithstanding these trials, his affection for her, as she admitted to her father, "was unbounded." To make matters worse, his daughter, Sophia, suffered a paralytic stroke in early 1800 that left both parents despairing of her life. Eventually she recovered, but only after months at Brighton in care of Ann and Sarah Fitch, dear friends to the Arnolds.[20]

In their melancholy situation, they derived some consolation from their friendships with a number of former Loyalists, above all the Fitches. Samuel Fitch, whose uncle, Nathan Whiting, had presented Arnold for membership in the Masonic Lodge in New Haven, had been advocate general to the admiralty court in Boston, and had fled with his wife and family to London. The Arnolds soon became attached to them, particularly to the children: Ann, a year older than Peggy; Sarah, a year younger; and William, who was so beloved that Arnold and Peggy named their own son after him. There were also Nathaniel and Anne Middleton, William Vassal, who had been high sheriff of Middlesex County in Massachusetts, and Daniel and Sarah Coxe—Coxe had been a member of the governor's council in New Jersey. Only Vassal, who owned a sugar plantation in Jamaica, had salvaged much from the wreck of his fortunes. Though Coxe did well in London for a time, his wastrel of a son gambled the family into destitution. It was a fairly close-knit group of Loyalists, drawn together by their common tragedy, and, except for the younger Fitches, living saddened and embittered lives. Peggy seems to have mixed more with the group than Arnold. After all, his own lot had been decidedly different, and none was likely to forget it. Moreover, he never lost heart as did so many of the Loyalists who made their new home in London, painfully aware of their poverty, their exile, and their colonial origins.[21]

In addition to friendships, there was consolation for Arnold in observing the progress of his sons. George and William were doing well at school, and Lord Cornwallis was soon to see that George entered the Royal Military Academy. James, who had been stationed at Gibraltar, was sent to Malta as second engineer in the conduct of the siege. Edward, who left for military service in Bengal in June of 1800, went under the personal patronage of Cornwallis, who was very loyal to the Arnolds. But the departure of Edward, who was the favorite son, sorely distressed both Arnold and Peggy. As the latter told her sister, "My darling Edward leaves . . . to try his fortune in the East. His death could scarcely be a more severe stroke." Neither parent was to see him again.[22]

During the early months of 1801, Arnold steadily declined in health. An asthmatic cough that had developed since his return from the tropics troubled him by day and made his nights such a misery that he had barely more than two hours of sleep. One leg was fearfully swollen, presumably with gout, while the other, the one wounded at Quebec and Bemis Heights, throbbed so acutely that he never ventured to walk without a cane. His once-firm flesh became flabby; his face, deeply seamed and sallow in complexion; his broad, powerful shoulders, stooped and bony. Only the rasping voice and the pale eyes, occasionally flashing with their old fire, revealed the indomitable will and driving energy that once were his. Certainly this was no longer the bustling, successful Colonial merchant, the brilliant American soldier of whose exploits his country could be proud, or even the confident exile. This was a ruined man, hated by the land of his nativity, despised, ignored, or forgotten by the country of his new allegiance, and ravaged by ill health.

Despite his last valiant efforts to provide for his family, he was also a financial failure whose debts subsequently placed an almost intolerable burden on his wife. Yet that shrewd and devoted lady, dying of cancer within three years of her husband and living in the most straitened circumstances, succeeded in paying off his obligations and in discharging at least part of the provisions of his will, which he made out with generous recognition of Hannah and all his children in August, 1800, before his finances completely collapsed. If Peggy had had the management of his investments, she and Arnold might have ended their days in comfort instead of despair. As it was, she called the turn accurately when she observed in 1794, "There seems to be a cruel fatality attending all his exertions." No doubt moralists have ever since derived satisfaction in pointing to Arnold's last years as evidence of a retributive Justice.[23]

The end came in June, 1801. He and Peggy had recently spent a week with the Fitch sisters at Galleywood, near Chelmsford, and intended to return after taking care of some unfinished business in London. His nerves, which had been pretty thoroughly shattered, had quieted while in the country, and Peggy was anxious to get him back to Galleywood as

soon as possible. But, on June 8, he fell seriously ill. Physicians now diagnosed his gout as dropsy, his throat became so inflamed that he could not
swallow, and his asthma threatened to choke him. On the 10th, he went
into delirium. The legend exists that before he died he asked to be clothed
in his old Continental uniform and begged God to forgive him for ever
putting on another. This makes a pleasant sentiment by which to remem-
ber him, and there is, to be sure, the possibility that he made such a request. If he did so, however, it must have been in his delirium, and the
people at his bedside, Peggy, the Daniel Coxes, and the Fitch sisters—all
of them Loyalists—would have been the last persons to mention the incident. In his few rational moments, said Peggy, he kept imploring blessings
on her and the children. Finally, at half past six on Sunday morning,
June 12, "after great suffering, he expired . . . without a groan." [24]

In that exciting era, which saw Napoleon redrawing the map of Europe
and England desperately striving through her fleet and her money to
oppose him, Arnold was all but forgotten. The newspapers made only a
brief recognition of his death. The *Times* on June 16 and the *Morning
Post* on June 17 merely mentioned his passing, though, two days later,
the anti-government *Post* commented, "Poor General Arnold has departed this world without notice; a sorry reflection this for the Pitts and
the Portlands and other turncoats." The *European Magazine,* in its issue
for July, 1801, described him as "a person much noticed during the
American War," while the *Gentleman's Magazine,* after announcing his
demise, declared that "Seven mourning coaches and four state carriages
formed the [funeral] cavalcade." [25]

But the *Gentleman's Magazine* erred in saying that Arnold was interred
at Brompton. Recent research has revealed that he was buried at St.
Mary's, in Battersea, where, three years later, his beloved Peggy joined
him. Once a fashionable little church in a pleasant neighborhood on the
south bank of the Thames, St. Mary's is now a dingy, forlorn-looking
brick structure surrounded, except on the river side, by factories, a flour
mill, and slum dwellings. Even the ragged, knowing little children who
slip stealthily inside and christen their dolls over the pink-marble baptis-
mal font, who shout for the vicar when a stranger arrives, and who be-
seech the visitor for pennies and gum, do not realize that their church
shelters in its crypt the remains of America's greatest traitor. In fact,
they have not the slightest idea that there ever was a man named Benedict
Arnold.

· XXX ·

The Summing Up

A STUDY of Arnold's life leaves one curious about the answer to three questions. What happened to his family? How does he compare with other American generals then and since? Where is his place among American traitors? The answer to the first of these is relatively simple, though there are many blanks still to be filled in with respect to the details of their lives.

Whatever one may think of Peggy Shippen Arnold, the romantic bride of an ambitious officer, there is little reason for disagreement on the nature of her character in the later years of her life. An adoring wife and a devoted mother, she held her family together by affection and attention. Nor can one say that she was less dutiful toward Arnold's sons by his former wife than toward her own children; her letters to Margaret Mansfield's boys were models of what a mother's communications—let alone a stepmother's!—should be to her sons. At the same time, as Arnold's executrix, she faced a disagreeable financial situation with unflinching courage. She told Edward that "there is but little probability of any thing being saved to the family, out of the wreck. I fear not even the furniture, as the debts amount to upwards of £5,000." Even so, she managed to pay practically all of Arnold's ascertainable debts by Spartan living and astute management of his investments, and succeeded in seeing her own children, except for Sophia and William, started in their careers. Furthermore, she continued to maintain a lively interest in them and their welfare through the months of cancerous agony that mercifully terminated in her death on August 24, 1803, when she was but forty-four years of age.[1]

As for Arnold's first family, both Richard and Henry, the surviving sons, married and had a number of children. Richard wedded Margaret, daughter of Samuel Weatherhead of Augusta in Upper Canada, in December, 1804, while Henry married Hannah, daughter of Richard Ten Eyck of New York, in December, 1796. They have descendants living in Canada today. Both men became merchants and owned considerable real estate in Canada by virtue of the lands granted them by the British government. Though they made their permanent homes in Canada, Henry died in New York in 1826; Richard lived until 1847. Of the two, Henry was the favorite of Hannah Arnold, the general's sister. Both the nephews, however, looked after her until her death at Henry's home in Montigue, Canada, in 1803.

Arnold's surviving children by Peggy Shippen included four sons and one daughter. Edward Shippen Arnold went to India under the patronage of Lord Cornwallis, becoming an officer in the 6th Bengal Cavalry and, later, paymaster at Muttra. Unlike his father's case, there was no question concerning the care and honesty with which he handled his accounts. Subsequently, having accumulated a small fortune through private business, he became noted for his charity and his devotion to religion. He died prematurely at Dinapore in December, 1813. George, the third son, joined Edward in India and also became a cavalry officer, holding the rank of lieutenant colonel in the 2d Bengal Cavalry at the time of his death in 1828. Unlike Edward, George married, the girl being Anne Martinez Brown by whom he had several children.

James Robertson Arnold, the second son and the one who most resembled his father in appearance, had a distinguished career. An officer in the Royal Engineers, he saw action at Malta, in Egypt, and in the West Indies. For leading a brave and successful assault upon a fort in Surinam, he received a mention in dispatches, a public purse, and a wound in the leg. Later he was stationed for two years in Bermuda and given command of the Engineers in Nova Scotia and New Brunswick from 1818 to 1823. While on this last command, he visited his father's house in St. John and reportedly wept like a child when he entered it. He wanted to visit his mother's family in the United States, but, believing he would be insulted because of his father, he never went there. When William IV became King, he made James an aide. Subsequently James was created a knight of the Hanoverian Guelphic Order and a knight of the Crescent, and was promoted to lieutenant general. In March, 1807, he married Virginia, daughter of Bartlett Goodrich of Saling Grove, Isle of Wight. He died without issue in London, December, 1854.

William Fitch Arnold wandered less distantly from England than any of his brothers. He was a captain in the 19th Royal Lancers, married Elizabeth, daughter of Captain Alexander Ruddock, R.N., of Tobago, and established himself as a country gentleman at Little Messenden Abbey in Buckinghamshire, where he served as Justice of the Peace for that county until his death in 1846. He had two sons and four daughters. One of his sons, William Trail Arnold, was a captain in the 4th Foot, went to the Crimea in the war against Russia, and, on May 8, 1855, suffered a mortal wound in an assault upon one of the defenses of Sebastopol. The old Arnold energy in battle was evidently still potent, for the commander-in-chief, Lord Raglan, commended William posthumously for his spirited manner. The other son, Edward Gladwin Arnold, became a clergyman and married Lady Charlotte Georgiana, eldest daughter of the Marquis of Cholmondely. One of William Fitch Arnold's daughters, Georgiana Phipps Arnold, married the Reverend John Stephenson. Of this union was born Major General Theodore Stephenson, C.B., who served in the British Army in World War One and died in 1928.

Arnold's daughter, Sophia Matilda, especially beloved by all the family, seemed ill prepared for life because of her weak constitution and the loss of her parents on whom she was extraordinarily dependent. At Edward's request, she sailed to join him in India, where, with George's help, he took care of her. A friend and fellow officer of Edward's was Pownall Phipps who had previously married the daughter of a French nobleman. His wife lately deceased, he became deeply attached to Sophia, while she fell in love with him. Yet it was probably more out of pity that Phipps married her in 1813; Sophia, seriously ill, believed herself dying and expressed a deathbed wish to become his wife. The marriage, however, must have spurred Sophia to live longer, for she recovered to bear Phipps five children before she finally died of tuberculosis at Sunbury, England, in 1828. Both she and Phipps were very religious and lived happily together. She enjoyed a reputation for unusual beauty of face and character.

It is interesting to observe the military and religious propensities among Arnold's children. All his sons by both wives were soldiers at one time or another, several serving with distinction. All of them, particularly Edward and James among Peggy's children, were genuinely religious, but their

Christianity was not simply of a devotional nature; they also resorted to good works as a testimony of their faith. Edward was especially remarkable for his generosity and unobtrusive charity. Sophia, too, believed in a practical kind of Christianity that helped endear her to people wherever she lived. They could not have drawn this religious interest from their parents. Arnold was singularly silent on the question of religion in his private life. While he moved from the Presbyterianism of his youth to Episcopalianism after his marriage, there is little evidence that his was other than a nominal faith. Though Peggy was a sincere Christian, her faith was hardly of the devout, evangelical character that distinguished that of Edward and Sophia. Possibly the tragedy of the parents' lives impelled the children to think in deeper and more devotional terms than most of their contemporaries. Neither in their religion nor in their vocations were they likely to forget that the principal reason for which their father was remembered was for an act abhorrent to most people.

That act, however, should in no way prevent his being given his proper place in the military history of the United States. He had to his credit a number of solid accomplishments, among the more important being the march to Quebec, the maintenance of the siege of that city, the battles of Valcour Island and Split Rock (strictly speaking, naval rather than military encounters), the pursuit of Tryon from Danbury, the relief of Fort Stanwix, and his part in the Saratoga battles. From these activities it is possible to compare Arnold with other American general officers both during and since the Revolution. Naturally all such comparisons are somewhat invidious, often purely speculative, and never completely satisfactory; even so, the conclusions with respect to Arnold may not be out of line.

The outstanding American leaders who survived the Revolution were Washington, Greene, Schuyler, Wayne, Morgan, and Arnold. Washington's fame in the field rests largely on the brilliant Trenton-Princeton campaign and the joint operation with the French Army and Navy that ended with the surrender of Cornwallis at Yorktown. He made dreadful mistakes in the New York campaign of 1776, while bad luck and superior British numbers and leadership defeated him in the Pennsylvania campaign of 1777. His greatest contribution to the war was his unshakable faith, powerful will, and incorruptible character. It was in the first and last of these qualities that Arnold was so lamentably lacking. Without Washington the Revolution would have collapsed in the field; he was its sustaining force.

Greene, Schuyler, and Wayne were lesser lights, particularly Wayne. The Pennsylvanian had dash and aggressiveness that resembled those very facets in Arnold. But Wayne, though performing notably at Monmouth, at Stony Point, and in Virginia with Lafayette and Steuben, had not the vision, the magnetic, personal appeal, or the furious effectiveness of Arnold. Greene, on the other hand, excelled in strategic conception, in a quality of tenacious patience hardly exceeded even in Washington, and in the ability to work well with officers, whether his subordinates, his equals, or his superiors. These last two attributes found their antithesis in Arnold; patience was not his long suit, and he was a touchy officer to work for or with, or to command. As for Schuyler, while overcautious for the supreme command of the Northern Army when that force took the offensive in Canada, he nevertheless proved his mettle in organizing the lake defenses in 1776 and in personally supervising the measures that slowed Burgoyne to a crawl in 1777. The Saratoga victories might well have been his had he not been removed for political reasons in favor of Gates, whose chief abilities lay in the field of administration. On the field of battle, however, Arnold was infinitely superior to either Schuyler or Gates.[2]

Arnold was easily the outstanding battlefield officer of the Revolution. His nearest American rival was not Wayne but Morgan, and though neither Arnold nor Morgan liked the other, they enjoyed a mutual respect, grudging though it might be on occasion. Both were able, resourceful, courageous fighters who fought to win. The giant ex-teamster, furthermore, could work with the little former apothecary. They were together on the wilderness march, in the Quebec assault, and at Freeman's Farm and Bemis Heights. But although Morgan, by excellent judgment and great good luck, later fashioned a little jewel of an action in destroying Colonel Banastre Tarleton's army at Cowpens, his hesitation at the storming of Quebec may have cost the Americans the city; Arnold was not the hesitating kind. Morgan, moreover, lost control over his riflemen at Freeman's Farm, when, though repelling the British attack, he let his men be hopelessly scattered, and wept like a child; it is difficult to imagine the resourceful Arnold ever letting himself be caught in Morgan's plight or taking out his fury and despair in impotent tears.

Few men have displayed sounder judgment in the analysis of military abilities than Sir John Fortescue, the historian of the British Army. Nicely summing up Arnold's peculiar capacities, he said, "To boundless energy and enterprise he united quick insight into a situation, sound strategic instinct, audacity of movement, wealth of resource, a swift and unerring eye in action, great personal daring, and true magic of leadership." The inscription on the monument to Arnold's wounded leg on the field of Bemis Heights is no exaggeration if applied to battlefield performance: "In memory of the most brilliant soldier of the Continental Army, who was desperately wounded on this spot, the sally port, Burgoyne's Great Western Redoubt, 7th October, 1777, winning for his countrymen the decisive battle of the American Revolution and for himself the rank of Major General." [3]

The qualities that made Arnold so effective a leader in the face of enemy fire were reflected in leaders of other wars. Sherman had them in the Union Army, as did Stonewall Jackson and John Bell Hood of the Confederacy. If Sherman, moreover, had his march through Georgia, Arnold had his through Maine; and the obstacles of nature that Arnold encountered proved fully as stubborn as the Confederate opposition to Sherman. Jackson's consuming preference for independent command, as in the Shenandoah Valley, and his ability to deliver hammer strokes, as at the Second Bull Run and at Chancellorsville, possessed, like Hood's furious assaults on Little Round Top at Gettysburg and against the Union center at Chickamauga, a peculiarly Arnoldian flavor. In World War Two, Douglas MacArthur was chiefly distinguished for his organizational and strategical genius, but, in World War One, as a division commander, he displayed the kind of courage, dash, and imagination that reminds one of Arnold. Moreover, what critics of both men often failed to perceive was that their accomplishments actually exceeded the notoriety attending them.

The officer of World War Two who most closely resembled the battlefield Arnold was General George Patton. Both these followers of fine fashions in clothes and weapons loved the offensive, took great risks with calculation, hit swiftly and hard, and preferred the slam-bang of contact to the semi-academic cerebrations of staff work. Utterly courageous, each would have welcomed a soldier's death. In temperament there was a surprising similarity, for both were high-strung, impulsive, trigger-tongued, and irascible. Each even had his man-striking incident: Patton, the private in Sicily; Arnold, the captain at Bemis Heights. Both were beloved and hated by their troops, Arnold winning perhaps the greater degree of affection, which, however, turned to bitter detestation after his treason. In integrity of character the comparison ends; Patton was an honest man.

Great soldier that he was, Arnold had his limitations, and the limitations were probably less those of training (he was an amateur like most of the American generals of the Revolution) than those of character and temperament. He was no gifted, painstaking organizer like the Union's George McClellan, no master of strategy like Greene, Ulysses S. Grant, or MacArthur, no tactical genius like Robert E. Lee or Jackson. Although he possessed all of these abilities in varying degrees, he was lamentably deficient in those qualities that made Washington, George C. Marshall, and Dwight D. Eisenhower strikingly successful as soldier-statesmen (Arnold's relations with Congress, the Executive Council of Pennsylvania, and many fellow officers were usually dreadful).

Arnold's forte lay in a sphere now generally outmoded by the changes of methods and communications in warfare except on the platoon, company, or battalion-commander level, or occasionally in the divisional-commander status if one can judge by General William Dean's activity in the early days of the Korean War. This sphere was that of personal leadership in the forefront of battle, a position usually least effective nowadays in terms of leadership for an officer of Arnold's standing. In this preference, Arnold was like Gustavus Adolphus at Lützen and the young Napoleon at the bridge of Lodi, or, for that matter, like Howe at Bunker Hill and Burgoyne at Bemis Heights. Though Benjamin Rush may have been correct in reporting a remark of Arnold's that he had no courage until he was fifteen years old, there was certainly no doubt of his courage as a mature man. The love of conflict, of will against will, of personal participation in the melée was like a fever in Arnold's blood. The hardship and challenge of battle brought forth all the glowing magic of his leadership, and his troops would follow him anywhere. As an old veteran said of him, "A bloody fellow he was. He didn't care for nothing; he'd ride right in. It was 'Come on, boys!' 'twasn't 'Go, boys!' . . . there wasn't any waste timber in him. He was a stern looking man but kind to his soldiers." [4]

Despite his forte, it is likely that in all of our wars since the Revolution, with the possible exception of World War One, which was not a war of movement, Arnold would have been a great corps or army commander. It is most unlikely that he would have been effective with the supreme field direction like Grant or Lee, Pershing or Bradley, while Eisenhower's task as a coordinator of coalitions would have been simply beyond him. On the other hand, he could easily have been another Patton, and, with an understanding officer like Lee as his superior, he might have fallen not too far short of Stonewall Jackson. In any event, he had no peer among his contemporaries, American or British, on the field of battle.[5]

Where Arnold stands among American traitors depends upon the motive, the circumstances of the treason, and the status of the country at the time. Ethically Arnold was wrong by almost any standard, and even success would not have justified him. What, then, was his motive? And here the problem is lifted out of its purely historical frame into that of contemporary interest and importance. What goes on in a man's soul that influences him to repudiate his friends, his country, his own sacrifices? The desire for money? Certainly it was an important motive with Arnold but not, by any means, the only one. Though it is a question whether he would have become a turncoat had the British not met his price, he had already become one in his heart. The scripture on this point is severe but not unjust. Arnold was so outraged by his treatment by the politicians of his country that the basis of his loyalty was affected even before he opened negotiations with Clinton. That basis was his own self-esteem which Congress had cruelly injured by its inexplicable slights and Pennsylvania by its only partially warranted persecution. Had he been less sensitive about his "honor," his consciousness of "rectitude," it is possible that he would not have stooped to treason to obtain money, always a weakness with him.

Arnold had a peculiar nature. Utterly egocentric, he demanded that his moral standards be accepted, while, at the same time, he objected if people resented his breaking theirs. His arrogance and his unwillingness or inability to forgive prevented him from ever surmounting the personal issue. Given his fierce pride and a consuming sense of grievance, the addition of a catalytic agent like the need of money created an explosion. Any intellectual conviction, such as a belated appreciation of the worth of British rule or an antagonism toward the French alliance—both of which may have existed even if not recorded—was subordinate to the emotional revulsion. Why he should have permitted himself to become so personally oriented is another question, one which will probably never be satisfactorily explained. The answer, in all likelihood, involves a matter of the influences of his childhood and of his civilian and military careers, his glandular structure, and the nature of his psyche. But here one is among intangibles that elude precise analysis and conclusion.

That Arnold was a traitor does not admit of doubt. The United States as a nation existed in fact and in law, and he had taken an oath of allegiance to it. Notwithstanding his oath, he conspired against his country, attempted to deliver a post of the utmost importance and a portion of the nation's military forces into the hands of the enemy, and went over to the enemy himself and offered his services. By any definition Arnold had committed treason of a gross nature, one, moreover, in a time of great national jeopardy.

When the founding fathers defined treason in article III, section 3 of the Constitution, they avoided the generality of the English concept. The Constitution explicitly says, "Treason against the United States shall consist only in levying war against them, or in adhering to their enemies, giving them aid and comfort. No person shall be convicted of treason unless on the testimony of two witnesses to the same overt act, or on confession in open court." The limits are narrower and more sharply defined than in 1780, but, had they existed then, Arnold would still have been flagrantly guilty.

He was not, however, the first or only American traitor of the Revolution. The doubtful honor of being first belonged to Dr. Benjamin Church, who studied medicine in London, married an English wife, and returned to Boston, where he became active among the Whigs. He served on the committee of safety and was made director and chief physician of the army hospital for Washington's forces besieging Boston. Presently he was revealed to be one of General Thomas Gage's paid informers, a mistress having burdened him with debt which only connivance with the enemy enabled him to pay off. Ironically, the carelessness of the same woman led to the discovery of letters which exposed Church for the traitor he was. Imprisoned during the war, he went as an exile to the West Indies in 1782 and was lost at sea. Yet, however mercenary his motive, the magnitude of his offense scarcely compared with Arnold's. Also early in the field of treachery was William Demont, adjutant to the commander of Fort Washington, who deserted to the British in 1776 with the plans of the fortress. Likewise reprehensible was the conduct of a Lieutenant Zedivitz who was cashiered for treasonable correspondence with British Governor Tryon after the battle of White Plains. Dr. Edward Bancroft, Franklin's trusted secretary in France, has often been considered a traitor. Secretly a Loyalist to begin with, he was a master spy, to be sure, but not strictly a traitor. Regardless of others, Arnold was the one responsible for giving to treason that peculiarly obnoxious connotation which still persists for Americans.[6]

On the other hand, was Arnold more a traitor than Aaron Burr, or Clement Vallandigham, the Copperhead leader in the Civil War, or Mildred Gillars ("Axis Sally") in World War Two? And what of that group of Americans who are so persuaded of the superior merits of communism as to transmit vital information to the Soviet Union—are they less traitorous than Arnold? Concretely, was Arnold's unsuccessful attempt to betray West Point worse treason than the Rosenbergs' successful enterprise in relaying atomic secrets to Moscow?

Aaron Burr has succeeded even to the present in keeping people uncertain whether or not he was guilty of treason. Discredited by the tragic duel with Alexander Hamilton, Burr sought to restore his fortunes and to find fame in the Louisiana territory lately acquired from France. Historians are divided as to whether he aimed merely to set up an empire in Mexico or whether his objective also involved the secession of a portion of Louisiana including New Orleans. Certainly at one point he discussed with the British minister to the United States the possibility of creating with British naval help an independent state between Louisiana and Mexico. He also intrigued with General James Wilkinson, Arnold's old enemy, who, though the American commanding officer in the southwest, was simultaneously in the pay of Spain. The conspiracy was far more complex than Arnold's, and was further complicated by Burr's positive gift for deception. Eventually, when the time for action arrived, Wilkinson doublecrossed Burr by revealing what he knew to President Jefferson.

Captured and brought to Richmond, Virginia, Burr was tried before the famous Justice John Marshall. Jefferson and Marshall were bitter enemies, and Jefferson wanted Burr convicted of treason. In one of the most famous trials in American history Marshall could not find Burr guilty of treason according to the definition of the Constitution. He had conspired to overthrow the authority of the United States in part of her territory but had not levied war against her. Furthermore he had not aided her enemies since at the time the country was at peace with both England and Spain. Had two witnesses to his alleged treason come forward to testify, Burr might have fared badly, but Wilkinson alone was present. Though he was a more devious-minded person than Arnold, grossly scandalous in his private life and fully as venal, Burr was not a general officer of the United States commanding a post of great strategic importance who conspired to sell it and himself to an enemy in time of war. By such measurements, Arnold's offense was more odious.

More dangerous than Burr was Vallandigham. As leader of the powerful Copperhead movement during the Civil War, that group of Northerners, particularly in the Middle West, who favored the South, Vallandigham worked until 1864 to nullify the Northern war effort. His training as a minister, a lawyer, an editor, and a Congressman stood him in good stead in his obstructionism, and there is little doubt that he was sincere in his pro-slavery, pro-Southern affinities. Adapting his tactics to the changing war situation, he played up the dreadful casualties and the defeatism in the North; warned what the Emancipation Proclamation would mean to white labor; opposed conscription, pointing out that the provision by which a draftee could escape service by paying $300 made the draft a poor man's institution; and criticized Lincoln's policy of establishing martial law in non-rebellious areas, authorizing wholesale arrests, and suspending *habeas corpus*. Finally he made a speech in Ohio contrary to the order of General Ambrose Burnside prohibiting declarations of sympathy for the enemy. Burnside at once ordered a midnight arrest and had him tried before a military court which sentenced him to imprisonment for the duration of hostilities.

Vallandigham's case was a delicate one for the Federal government, for his criticisms had been warmly supported by various groups. Furthermore, his arrest on an order for which no legal basis really existed provoked a roar of protest from thousands of people not normally sympathetic with him but who were concerned about the issue of civil liberties. Skillfully Lincoln let off the pressure not by overruling the verdict of the military court but by altering the sentence. Even as a judge in the winter of 1953 thought it might be a good idea to deport a collection of convicted Communists to the Soviet, so Lincoln believed deportation the remedy for Vallandigham. The latter, therefore, was soon hustled over the border into the Confederacy, where, his power gone, he was less than welcome.

Both Arnold and Vallandigham were dangerous men. That either would have succeeded in accomplishing his country's defeat is unlikely, but both jeopardized the security of the nation while it was at war. As between the two, however, there can be little question of whose was the greater guilt. Vallandigham acted on principles to which he firmly held; Arnold was actuated mainly by personal grievance and greed. Vallandigham proclaimed his opposition from the beginning; Arnold changed sides in the course of the war. Vallandigham was a civilian; Arnold had taken an oath as a general officer to support the government and wore the uniform of his country while he connived at her overthrow.

World War Two turned up a curious assortment of American traitors among a sadly considerable number, radio traitors, people who assisted saboteurs, and traitors within the armed forces. The two best-known radio traitors were women. One was Mildred Gillars ("Axis Sally"), a confused, lonely, rather silly woman who left America during the depression and found love and work in Hitler's Reich. The other was Iva Ikuko Toguri d'Aquino (one of six women known as "Tokyo Rose"), who discovered in Japan a more agreeable haven than California during the war. Another traitor, personally more formidable, was a husky German-American Fascist named Max Stephan, who succored a Nazi officer landed from a submarine. All these were convicted of treason and received long prison terms. As compared with Arnold, all made no bones about their hopes for an enemy victory, all were civilians, and none was so dangerous to the nation's security.

More like Arnold was one of the most criminal traitors of the war, Lieutenant Martin Monti. Among the too numerous traitors in the armed forces, this man's career was the most amazing. After receiving his wings, he became a P-38 pilot and was sent to India in 1944. In October, he turned up in Italy, stole a photographically equipped P-38, and flew over to the Germans near Milan. Though the Nazis at first thought him a spy and shipped him to Germany as a prisoner, he convinced the authorities that he really wanted to help them. In return, they put him on the radio, where he met Mildred Gillars, who allegedly said she would have nothing to do with him since he was a traitor! Later he joined a propaganda detail of Heinrich Himmler's SS troops. When the war ended, and the Army caught up with him, he convinced a military court that curiosity had impelled him to steal the plane, that the Germans shot him down and imprisoned him, and that the Underground helped him don for protection the SS uniform in which he had been captured. The court was merciful; he was stripped of his commission and given fifteen years of imprisonment, a sentence he started to serve on September 30, 1945. Subsequently, family and political pressure induced the Army to review his case, and what he had done was attributed to his youth and headstrong temper. Hence, thanks to special dispensation from President Truman, his sentence was commuted provided he re-entered the Army as a private. He agreed in February, 1946. Unfortunately for him, the Department of Justice continued to work on his case, discovered the extent of his activities after leaving the American lines in the stolen plane, and brought him to trial again. Thus confronted, Monti confessed to treason on twenty-one counts. He received a sentence this time of twenty-five years and a fine of $10,000.

The treason of Monti and Arnold had more in common than that of the others and Arnold. Both were officers, both went over to the enemy, and both then assisted the enemy; both, moreover, were adventurers and deceivers. But here their major points of similarity cease. Monti seems to have possessed a consuming hatred of communism and of Soviet Russia, which, in his mind, was the real enemy of the United States. He regarded Nazi Germany as a defender of the West, and considered that the United States had committed a terrible mistake in fighting her. As motivation, Arnold could lay claim to no such degree of fanatical hatred of France before his treason; if he had felt as deeply toward her as Monti did toward Russia, he could scarcely have suppressed it so that no whisper of it was heard until after he had gone over to the British. Arnold, furthermore, possessed rank, authority, and trust far exceeding that of Monti; his responsibility and guilt were therefore correspondingly greater. Nor did Monti literally sell himself as did Arnold. Yet at heart both men were of the same stripe, reckless, shallow, fickle, domineering, and antagonistic toward most of their fellow officers. Psychiatrists declared Monti sane and above average in intelligence, but possessed of traits of paranoia. Perhaps, had psychiatry existed in the eighteenth century, a nearly identical diagnosis might have been given of Arnold.[7]

Still, if the Martin Montis are a hazard, even more dangerous are those people so convinced of the blessings of communism that they labor in behalf of the Soviet Union in complete disregard of their responsibilities and allegiance as citizens of this nation. The fact that technically the United States and the Soviet are at peace has served as a useful cloak to their activities. On the other hand, although the Constitution requires an overt act to be treason and the existence of a declared enemy to which adherence or aid and comfort may be given, the evidence produced during the recent trials under the Smith Act indicates with startling clarity how far Communists have gone in seditious conspiracy without actually crossing the borderline of overtness. Furthermore one has only to consider the activities of Julius and Ethel Rosenberg to see of what people are capable who, strictly by the Constitution, are not traitors.

The Rosenbergs were charged with conspiracy in stealing atomic secrets and transmitting these secrets to the Russians. Technically they were not traitors since their offense did not come within the purview of the Constitutional definition of treason. But although their arraignment was for espionage, their activities were in effect traitorous. They had prevailed upon Ethel's brother, David Greenglass, a machinist at Los Alamos, to send them drawings and such other information as he could obtain. They arranged a meeting between Greenglass and the courier for the spy ring, Harry Gold, who had also relayed information from the British scientist-spy, Emil Fuchs, to the chief Russian in the set-up, the Soviet vice consul in New York. Of their guilt there could be no doubt. They had labored with heart and mind in behalf of communism in general and the Soviet Union in particular. Evidently to them the Soviet appeared to be a humanitarian form of government and to hold in its destiny the hope of the world. Certainly it would seem that their motives were haloed with a kind of mushy idealism, and this, at any rate, lifted them above the level of personal rancor and avarice which animated Arnold, though he professed afterward to have long observed the superior merits of British to American government. In other respects, the differences that existed between Arnold and civilians like Burr, Vallandigham, and the World War Two group also existed between Arnold and the Rosenbergs. Unlike them, he was a general officer in a position of great trust who sought to betray that trust coldly and deliberately, and for great mercenary gain. False though the gods of the Rosenbergs and deplorable as was their offense (worse, indeed, than murder in the opinion of the judge who tried their case), Arnold's treachery, if easier to understand, is harder to forgive.

Arnold is a convenient point of reference when treason is mentioned, and his name has been invoked in damning terms from the trial of André to the treason trials of the present day. Though patriotic orators and schoolbooks have frequently painted him as a villain of the blackest dye, he has not been lacking defenders among historians, biographers, and novelists. They have in no way defended his treason, but they have pointed out that his intense feeling of grievance was not without justification. In this they have been correct. If ever there was a maligned and maltreated officer of the army, it was Arnold, a victim of politics and politicians, military and civilian—but a victim, too, of his own defects in character and personality. A number of writers, however, have evinced such admiration of his achievements and indulged in such unqualified denunciation of his political and military critics that they have virtually become his apologists.

Arnold needs and deserves no apologist if his crime is viewed in the light of the whole man. He was a brilliant and daring soldier who accomplished a great deal of good for the young republic, probably even saving it. He was also a proud, imperious, avaricious individual who hungered after power and glory and high social standing, a man who saw in every slight a blemish upon his honor. Some of those slights were justified, many were not; but Arnold refused to distinguish between them. He was infallible in his own eyes, and his consciousness of his own rectitude seems to have evoked no inner revulsion of a significant nature at breaking faith with his country. That he was subsequently neither very successful in military and business ventures nor happy except in his domestic life may invite those so inclined to point a moral even if it does not adorn the tale. But that he ever suffered remorse is unlikely, which seems to be true of most traitors. He was his own standard. If no American traitor has ever rendered such valuable service to his country, no treason has ever matched his in perfidy.

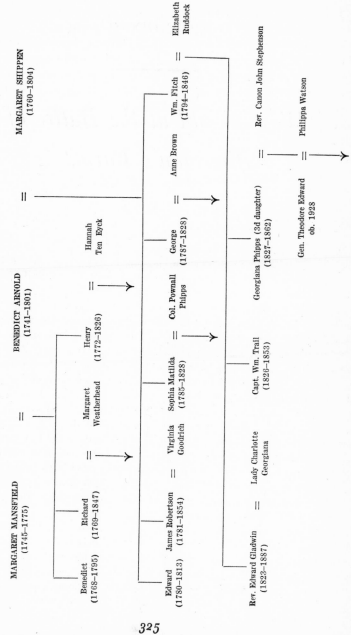

The Arnold Family

MARGARET MANSFIELD (1745–1775) == BENEDICT ARNOLD (1741–1801) == MARGARET SHIPPEN (1760–1804)

Benedict (1768–1795)

Richard (1769–1847) == Margaret Weatherhead

Henry (1772–1826) == Hannah Ten Eyck

Elizabeth Ruddock == Wm. Fitch (1794–1846)

Edward (1780–1813)

James Robertson (1781–1854) == Virginia Goodrich

Sophia Matilda (1785–1828) == Col. Pownall Phipps

George (1787–1829) == Anne Brown

Rev. Edward Gladwin (1823–1887) == Lady Charlotte Georgiana

Capt. Wm. Trail (1826–1853)

Georgiana Phipps (3d daughter) (1827–1862) == Rev. Canon John Stephenson

Gen. Theodore Edward ob. 1928 == Philippa Watson

APPENDIX II

Was Arnold at the Battle of Freeman's Farm?

Arnold was chiefly responsible for checking Burgoyne's advance at Freeman's Farm, September 19, 1777, but writers have spilled a great deal of ink trying to prove that he was not on the field of battle. Wilkinson in his memoirs declared that "not a single general officer was on the field of battle the 19th Sept. until the evening, when General Learned was ordered out." Congressman Robert R. Livingston, brother of Colonel Henry Brockholst Livingston, who had been one of Schuyler's young admirers and who was actively engaged on the 19th, wrote a letter in behalf of his brother to Washington on January 14, 1778. In this letter he said, "I take the liberty to inclose to your excellency an extract of a letter to him, written under General Arnold's directions, by a gentleman of his family [staff], he being unable to hold the pen himself. After a warm recommendation of his conduct, both in the camp and in the field, and giving him and his regiment a full share of the honor of the battle of the 19th of September *(in which General Arnold, not being present, writes only from the reports of those who were)*, he adds: [herein follows a description of Colonel Livingston's gallant part in the action of October 7]." Thus from Wilkinson, a Gates man, and from Congressman Livingston, whose brother was friendly to Arnold, there are two very definite statements of Arnold's absence.[1]

The point of view does not lack for support. A contemporary historian, the Reverend William Gordon, wrote that "Arnold's division was out in the action, but he himself did not lead them; he remained in camp the whole time." Later historians, notably George Bancroft (who relied largely on Wilkinson and Livingston), James Austin Stevens, and Edward Channing, considered the evidence in favor of Arnold's absence from the field. So, too, has Lynn Montross, historian of the Continental Congress and its army. Samuel Patterson, biographer of Gates, leaves it an open question. The implication of these authorities is, of course, obvious: that Arnold had no part in the victorious contest, the glory of which must go chiefly to Horatio Gates, of whose abilities Bancroft had some doubts and Channing none.[2]

But, naturally, there is another side to the argument, the main sources of which are two of Schuyler's former officers, his military secretary, Colonel Richard Varick, and Colonel Henry Brockholst Livingston, the same officer in whose behalf his brother, Robert, later wrote to Washington. Of Arnold, Livingston wrote Schuyler on September 23, "He is the life and soul of the troops. Believe me, Sir, to him alone is due the honor of our late victory." With trouble breaking out between Arnold and Gates following the battle, Livingston informed Schuyler that, to induce Arnold to remain with the army, "General Poor proposed an address from the general officers and colonels of his division, returning him thanks for his services, and particularly for his conduct during the late action, and requesting him to stay." Varick had written his former chief in similar terms on the 22d. "Arnold," he said, "has all the credit of the action." Varick further declared, after Burgoyne's surrender, "During Burgoyne's stay here [Albany] he gave Arnold great credit for his bravery and his military abilities; especially in the action of the 19th, whenever he speaks of him, and once in the presence of Gates."[3]

If neither of these officers mentioned in so many words that Arnold was actually in the field, they certainly testified to an activity of great value, and there were others who were more explicit. Brigadier General Philip Van Cortlandt, then a colonel, said that while marching toward the enemy he received his orders from Arnold. Brigadier General Enoch Poor, who had chaired the court-martial board in Hazen's trial and had sought Arnold's arrest for his behavior toward the board, wrote the day after the battle, "Arnold rushed into the thickest of the fight with his usual recklessness, and at times acted like a madman. I did not see him once, but S. [Poor's friend, Colonel Alexander Scammel] told me this morning that he did not seem inclined to lead alone, but as a prominent object among the enemy showed itself, he would seize the nearest rifle-gun and take deliberate aim." Very shortly, according to Livingston, Poor was drawing up his petition to persuade Arnold to remain.[4]

Further testimony is also available. Ebenezer Wakefield, who served in Dearborn's light infantry, declared that Arnold was active on the field of battle. Chaplain Smith, who was present, said distinctly that Arnold commanded the troops. Charles Neilson, whose father served as guide to the American forces during the battle, described graphically Arnold's riding up to Gates from the battle with a request for reinforcements after Phillips's arrival to support Burgoyne; Wilkinson, he said, was completely mistaken in his remarks on Arnold. Additional evidence comes from the Vermont council of safety, which was informed within a matter of hours by a Major Cochran, riding express from Gates's headquarters and returning with Major General Lincoln, that "General Arnold with his division attacked a division of Burgoyne, in which General Arnold gained the ground, when the enemy were reinforced by the main body, when General Arnold was obliged to retreat, but being reinforced, recovered his own so that the ground remained 8 o'clock yesterday divided between them." [5]

Similarly, Joshua Pell, Jr., an officer in Burgoyne's army, wrote in his diary of Arnold's advance in force on the British right at half past five in the afternoon, a comment not out of line, except in time, with Colonel John Marshall's statement in his biography of Washington that "about four o'clock Arnold, with nine continental regiments and Morgan's corps, was completely engaged with the whole right wing of the British army." Between the publication of Marshall's first edition and the appearance of his revised, abbreviated edition, Wilkinson had published his memoirs. Doubtless recognizing the controversial nature of his statement in view of Wilkinson's remarks, Marshall, then chief justice, omitted in the revised edition his original statement but declared, "The accounts of the day stated that the Americans were commanded by General Arnold." [6]

Other authorities also assert that Arnold was by no means inactive that day. Max von Eelking in his study of General Riedesel, which was based on the Brunswicker's letters and journals, speaks of American deserters telling that Arnold had commanded the troops in action. Charles Stedman in his contemporary history of the Revolution stated that "The enemy were led to the battle by General Arnold, who distinguished himself in an extraordinary manner." Another contemporary historian, the Italian, C. G. Botta, who is reputed to have been acquainted with many of the foreign officers serving in the war, said that in this contest Arnold "encouraged his men by voice and example." Later historians supporting Arnold's presence include Benson J. Lossing, biographer of Schuyler; John Fiske and Woodrow Wilson, among the general historians; Henry B. Dawson, Colonel Henry Carrington, and General Francis V. Greene, military historians of the Revolution; John W. Fortescue, historian of the British Army; Hoffman Nickerson and Christopher Ward, whose accounts of the situation are brilliant examples of historical analysis. [7]

Arnold himself, however, has a word on the subject. In the course of his altercation with Gates, which was presently to develop, he told his commanding general, ". . . you desired me to send Colonel Morgan and the light infantry and support them. I obeyed your orders, and before the action was over, I found it necessary to send out the whole of my division to support this attack." Gates never denied this activity, but Wilkinson declared the statement to be "incorrect in fact, as the orders went in detail from headquarters." Wilkinson would perhaps have been well advised to let his comment stand as it was, but he added the words, "though it is not known what conversation passed between the generals," thereby begging the entire question and vitiating the strength of his criticism. [8]

The conflict of witnesses leads of necessity to an evaluation of them. Wilkinson, as deputy adjutant general of the army, was presumably in a position to know what was going on. But Wilkinson published his memoirs in 1816, when Arnold's treason was still fresh in the popular mind. Wilkinson was a Gates man at the time of the battle, violently anti-Schuyler and hostile to Arnold, whom he, as well as his commander, seems to have regarded as the leader of the Schuyler faction now that Schuyler himself was absent. In the course of his life, Wilkinson, having started his career as a medical student, became a leading general in the army of the republic. He also became a liar, a moral coward, a corrupt politician, and the next thing to a traitor to his country, attempting to separate Kentucky from the United States and ally it with Spain, and succeeding in making a good deal of money in the effort. Constantly in trouble with army authorities, he was subsequently court-martialed for his implication in Aaron Burr's conspiracy but was acquitted, perhaps because, thoroughly frightened, he had hastened to betray his own accomplice, Burr, to the government. His was an unsavory character, and a large part of his memoirs constitutes a case of special pleading for reinstatement in the good graces of his countrymen. In this endeavor he failed, and the country was well rid of a real scoundrel when he went to Mexico to live out his final years. The statements of such a man are to be accepted with the utmost reservation.

The other chief witnesses, Varick and Livingston, were as enthusiastic for Arnold and Schuyler as Wilkinson was for Gates, but in this case of prejudice *versus* prejudice their characters stand closer scrutiny than Wilkinson's. Continuing on Arnold's staff until the treason, Varick faced a great deal of criticism and suspicion when that tragedy occurred. Even so, Washington was sufficiently impressed with his honesty and loyalty to make him recording secretary for the headquarters papers of the Continental Army. After the war, Varick helped codify the statutes of New York City, and became speaker of the assembly, attorney general, and mayor of New York City. He was a founder of the American Bible Society and president of the New York Society of the Cincinnati. His friend, Livingston, enjoyed a legal career of even greater eminence. A classmate of Madison at Princeton, Livingston became a judge of the supreme court of New York and was subsequently appointed by Jefferson to the supreme court of the United States. It is possible that these officers were lying in their letters to Schuyler, though Schuyler was not one to surround himself with sycophants and would not have expected untruths of his friends. On the other hand, it is by no means unlikely that they were telling the truth. Certainly by any test of character their word is to be preferred to Wilkinson's.

As for the credibility of other pro-Arnold witnesses, Van Cortlandt, no friend to Arnold, had no axe to grind in admitting that Arnold had given him orders. Neilson may have confused fact and tradition, but his account in other respects is too accurate for his statements in this respect to be arbitrarily dismissed as the mere crotchet of a local historian; after all, the battle was fought on his father's farm where he was brought up. Wakefield and Smith believed what their eyes told them, though, of course, they may have been deceived; a soldier's view of an action is usually pretty constricted. Pell's remark concerning Arnold's advance may have been an allusion to Arnold's division rather than to Arnold himself. On the other hand, though Riedesel's statement that Arnold commanded the troops might be attributed to the free-wheeling editorship of Max von Eelking, who occasionally introduced extraneous bits of information, General Poor's comments on Arnold, together with his action in approving a petition that Arnold remain with the army and in thanking him for his conduct in the battle, are less easily disposed of. Though not on the field, Poor would certainly have learned what occurred there. As between the two contemporary historians, Stedman and Gordon, the former, though a Loyalist officer, wrote a far more careful and honest history than Gordon. Apart from the fact that Gordon's friendship with Gates hardly qualified him as a completely unprejudiced chronicler, Gordon's work has been revealed, thanks to critical examination by a competent historical scholar, as consisting in large part of an immense plagiarism of Edmund Burke's *Annual Register*. In general, Stedman is the more reliable authority.[9]

The most puzzling feature of the testimony that Arnold was not present in the field is the letter from Robert Livingston, which would seem to confirm Wilkinson's original statement that no general officer was present until General Learned's appearance. On the other hand, if one compares it with the letter by Henry Brockholst Livingston, in whose behalf it was written, one can see that there need be no discrepancy. Though highly praising Arnold's part in the battle, H. B. Livingston does not mention that Arnold was present on the field of battle, that is, actively leading his troops. Nor does Arnold's own statement of his role necessarily indicate that he was up where the fighting was going on. To that extent, therefore, Wilkinson may be correct, and so also may be the remark in Robert Livingston's letter. But if one accepts as fact that Arnold was not present in the fighting area, which may be unfair to Arnold, is one compelled to conclude with the pro-Gates people that therefore Arnold had nothing to do with the battle and that the glory of repulsing Burgoyne belongs solely to Gates?

By no means. The testimony of Livingston and Varick, honorable men, is too strong to the contrary. They lauded Arnold, as did Poor in the petition, for his part in the battle. Van Cortlandt said that he received orders from Arnold. Arnold declared that he gave orders, and although Wilkinson contended that orders came from headquarters, he admitted that Arnold and Gates were engaged in secret conversation. All this can but signify that Arnold was serving in a command capacity, actively directing his division, Wilkinson to the contrary. He may have remained at Gates's headquarters two miles back of the lines all the time, and though this seems improbable, we know that he was there near the close of the action when he requested reinforcements. It is more likely, however, that he stayed for most of the battle at his own headquarters north and west of where Gates took station. His headquarters was invisible from Gates's position, as was most of the battlefield because of a dense forest. Hence Wilkinson, who was reminded by Gates that his own position was near his commanding officer, was certainly unable to perceive what Arnold was doing. But that Arnold took an active role cannot in reason be doubted.

It is very easy for one's view of Arnold as a soldier to be a one-sided view. One tends to think of him as always giving his troops the kind of fierce, reckless, personal leadership so evident in the second battle on Bemis Heights when he had no direct command; and that he had given evidence of preferring this type of leadership was amply clear. On the other hand, his division on September 19 was the largest body of troops he had ever directed, it was impossible for him to be in all places at once, and naturally he was dependent on the reports of his regimental commanders for the details of developments on their fronts. Possessing, as a Frenchman wrote of him, "what is called the *sage militaire,*" Arnold could exercise restraint and guile, as at Fort Stanwix, and assume active direction of an operation without insisting on being in the field personally leading the advance guard; this capacity he had demonstrated from time to time during the march to Quebec and the conduct of the siege. In the battle of Freeman's Farm, September 19, he appears to have rendered this directorial type of leadership; in fact, the nature of the battle, with regiments committed one by one, would indicate that this type was employed. Though he loved the personal type, may have used it occasionally in the afternoon, and would surely have resorted to it in the closing stages of the battle had Gates not recalled him, his critics have forgotten, or never discerned, that in leadership Arnold was an extraordinarily versatile officer.[10]

In the last analysis, apart from the fact that it is practically impossible to conceive of an officer with a battle record and a fiery nature like Benedict Arnold's taking no role in the four to five hours of furious fighting that hot afternoon, it is an aspersion on Gates's own leadership to assume that he would deprive the army all that time of Arnold's abilities; after all, no serious rift had yet developed between them. Gates, it is true, was no ball of fire as a general. Gross overestimation of the numbers and capacities of his own troops and failure to heed the advice of officers who knew the country better than he did cost him the battle of Camden in 1780, a contest from which he permitted himself almost immediately to be swept from the field by fugitives without attempting to return and which, according to General Nathanael Greene, should never have been fought. He also missed an opportunity of hitting Burgoyne perhaps a fatal blow by letting his right wing lie idle when Phillips and Riedesel stripped the British left to save Burgoyne in the center. Though this was not necessarily an error since, by keeping the right wing where it was, he blocked the one road by which the British could advance their artillery in the event of a British victory, he committed a gross mistake in refusing Arnold the direction of Learned's troops; for want of proper liaison work by Gates's staff, Learned missed his objective entirely, the British center.

Still, Gates was no fool. He possessed both military and political insight and knew this was one of the crucial battles of the war. Favoring a holding action, he presently found himself fighting a battle increasingly offensive in character. In these circumstances it was hardly likely that he would rob Arnold's division of the man most capable of directing that attack, their own commander. Henry B. Dawson, a military historian of the most meticulous judgment, has declared, "in falsifying history for the purpose of robbing General Arnold of his hard-earned fame, he [Wilkinson] at the same time impeached the military character of General Gates, in maintaining that an action of this importance, where the destiny of the country and of the great principles on which the parties had taken issue was involved, was intrusted to the individual caprices of colonels of regiments, without the controlling superintendence of a general officer; and 'was fought by the general concert and zealous cooperation of the corps engaged, and sustained more by individual courage than discipline.' " As Trevelyan remarked, in respect to Wilkinson's "impudent falsehood" that Arnold took no part in the battle, "One might as well demand evidence to prove that Nelson was in the sea fight off Cape St. Vincent." [11]

On the basis, therefore, of available evidence and reasonable probability, the conclusion seems inescapable that on September 19 Arnold was in active command of his division except for the closing minutes of the action, that he was chiefly instrumental in repulsing Burgoyne, and that Gates alone prevented him from delivering the blow that might have finished the British general.

APPENDIX III

Did Arnold Offer to Give
Himself Up for André?

There is a story that Arnold made such an offer, one discovered by Winthrop Sargent, André's biographer. After Arnold arrived in England, a Welshman named Robert Morris, secretary of the Bill of Rights Society, was so indignant at Arnold's reception by the Court that he wrote a scathing denunciation in the *General Advertiser* for February 9, 1782. Among his remarks was one that Arnold made no suggestion of surrendering himself for André. Captain James Battersby of the 29th Foot, an officer in Burgoyne's army in America, replied in the *Morning Herald* that he believed Arnold had made such an offer. He was in New York at the time of Arnold's flight there, he said, and it was reported in, and believed by, the garrison that Arnold had suggested to Clinton that he should be allowed to give himself up for André. According to Battersby, Clinton replied, "Your proposal, sir, does you great honour; but if André was my own brother, I could not agree to it." Scoffing at Battersby's tale, Morris tried through the press to insult Arnold to a duel. Though unsuccessful in this objective, he had roused Battersby to such a point that the captain challenged him. Only at the eleventh hour, after their seconds had been chosen, did the two men reconcile their differences. Morris himself later admitted that Burgoyne had said of the altercation, " . . . it was just like two gentlemen quarreling for a common whore." [1]

The story is interesting. Either Battersby knew what he was talking about or else rumor had duped him. Certainly he believed so strongly in Arnold's offer that he did not hesitate to fight a duel when his word was challenged. Rumors are probably nowhere so prevalent or so convincing as in an army, and no rumor is quite so persuasive as one that a man wishes to believe. Honorable men would have wanted Arnold to make the offer to surrender himself for André; at the same time, they would have recognized that Clinton as an honorable man whose duty as a King's officer was to deal in the dishonor of his enemies could not allow Arnold to return. That Arnold possessed the courage to give himself up can scarcely be doubted, but that he actually offered to do so implies a degree of remorse, of self-disgust, even of idealism that is out of line with his behavior. Realist though he was, he could scarcely be expected to see that nothing to which he would subsequently turn his hand would succeed and that he might as well retrieve part of his honor and reputation by sacrificing himself. He was a gambler; if one move failed, he tried another, and wasted little energy in vain regrets. While it is possible that Battersby was telling the truth, it is likely that he was the victim of rumor.

APPENDIX IV

The Last Will and Testament of Benedict Arnold

I, Benedict Arnold of the City of London being of sound Mind and Memory do make and constitute this my last Will and Testament in manner following.

Imprimis. It is my Will that all my Just Debts and Funeral Expenses be first paid; the latter I request may be only decent but by no means attended with any expense that can possibly be avoided.

Item. I give to my Sister, Hannah Arnold Forty pounds Sterling per annum during her natural Life to be paid to her annually out of Interest of such Monies or Income of such Estate as I may die possessed of, provided she shall and does give up to my Heirs or Executors all Obligations that she may have against me; and also does relinquish all Claims against my Estate, except for the Annuity before mentioned.

Item. I give and bequeath to my sons Richard and Henry all sums of Money that they are in any wise Indebted to me; and having in the course of the last and present year written to them to Draw Bills of Exchange upon me in London for the following Sums of Money, Viz; One hundred and eighty pounds Sterling (to make up a sum of three hundred pounds, part of which I have paid to them) to enable them to Build and Stock their farm in Canada. Also two hundred and thirty pounds Sterling to enable them to pay two protested Bills; as also three hundred and sixty pounds Sterling to enable them to pay all their Debts due in January 1801, to the total amount, adding these sums, of Seven hundred and seventy pounds Sterling. I give and bequeath the before mentioned Sums of Money to my Sons, Richard and Henry equally; and it is my Will and Pleasure that these Bills of Exchange for the before mentioned Sums be honored by my

Executors, and paid out of the Estate I may die possessed of.

Item. I Give Devise and Bequeath to my Beloved Wife her Heirs, Executors and Administrators all my Estate both *Real* and *Personal* that I may die possessed of, after paying my Debts and Legacies as before and herein after mentioned, for her own use and benefit during her continuing a Widow and to be disposed of among *all* my Children at her Death, as she may think proper, not doubting her doing them all equal justice. But should she Marry again, Then it is in that case, my Will and Pleasure that all my property shall be divided among my Children upon her second Marriage, and in that case, I hereby Give, Devise and Bequeath all my Estate both Real and Personal that I may have, or die possessed of to my Children to be divided among them in such equal proportions as my beloved Wife shall think Just and Proper, consideration being had to those Sums of Money that they have already received and that have been Expended upon them for their Education, &c. And Consideration being also had to their respective Ages and Situations in Life, not doubting that she will do them *all equal Justice* as she knows *it is* and has always been my intention (as my affection has been equally divided among them) to make an equal provision for them all.

Item. I give, devise and bequeath to John Sage, now in Canada, living with my Sons there (being about 14 years of age) Twelve hundred Acres of Land, being part of a Grant of thirteen thousand four hundred Acres of Land made to me as an Half Pay Officer for myself and Family by Order of the Duke of Portland, by his Letter directed to Peter Russell Esqr. President of the Council in Upper Canada, dated the 12th of June 1798, which said 1200 Acres of Land I give to him to be located altogether in one place out of the before mentioned Grant as my Executors may judge equal and fair. I also do here by give and bequeath to the said John Sage twenty pounds per annum to be paid to my Sons Richard and Henry for his use for Board Cloathing and Education until he shall be of the Age of Twenty one Years to be paid out of the Estate I may die possessed of—I also give and bequeath to the said John Sage, fifty pounds to be paid to him when he shall attain the age of twenty one Years.

I do hereby Constitute and Appoint my Beloved Wife Sole Executrix to this my last Will and Testament. And in case my Wife should Marry again or die Intestate, I do hereby Constitute and Appoint Miss Ann Fitch and Miss Sarah Fitch of Devonshire Street, Joint Trustees to manage my Estate, and carry this my Will in Execution, and they are hereby authorized (should it be necessary) to Sell any part of my Real Estate for that purpose, and to give receipts to the Purchasers for the Purchase Money which shall be considered as good and valid.

But should my Wife die Intestate, I do hereby give, devise and bequeath to all my Children all my Estate both Real and Personal, that I may die possessed of after paying my Legacies, &c. Viz. The whole to be divided into twelve equal shares; and to Sophia I give four shares; to William I give two shares; to George

I give two shares; and to Richard, Henry, Edward and James, I give each one share, and I do hereby Appoint the before named Trustees to see the same carried into Execution.

And I do hereby Constitute and Appoint my Beloved Wife Sole Executrix to this my last Will and Testament.

In Witness whereof I have hereunto set my hand and seal in London this 30th day of August in the year of our Lord One Thousand eight hundred.

BENEDICT ARNOLD. (Seal.)

Signed, Sealed, and Published by Brigadier General Benedict Arnold as his Last Will and Testament in the presence of us who subscribe our names as Witnesses hereof and in his Presence, and in the Presence of each other.

HARRIET NEWPORT
ANN PRINCE
WILLIAM YOUNG

Notes

N.B. The spelling in quotations in the text has frequently been changed from the eighteenth-century varieties to conform to current usage.

ABBREVIATIONS

Repository Titles:

BM = British Museum, London, England
HSP = Historical Society of Pennsylvania, Philadelphia
LC = Library of Congress, Washington, D.C.
NBM = New Brunswick Museum, St. John, N.B., Canada
NYHS = New York Historical Society, New York City
NYPL = New York Public Library, New York City
PRO = Public Record Office, London, England
WLCL = W. L. Clements Library, Ann Arbor

Item Titles:

A.A. = *American Archives*
A.O. = Papers in Audit Office, Public Record Office
C.O. = Papers in Colonial Office, Public Record Office
H.C.A. = Papers in High Court of Admiralty, Public Record Office
P.M.H.B. = *Pennsylvania Magazine of History and Biography*
T. = Papers in Treasury Office, Public Record Office

Chapter I

FROM GLORY TO INFAMY

1 Arnold, *Arnold,* 198. The quotation is probably apocryphal, but it is likely that he uttered something similar. See Livingston to Schuyler, Sept. 23, 1777, in *Schuyler Paps.* (NYPL); Bolton, *The Private Soldier under Washington,* 244.

Chapter II

YOUTH

1 Deane, Drowne, and Hubbard, *Arnold Genealogy;* Arnold, *Rhode Island,* I, 565; Arnold, *Arnold,* 16–17; Decker, *Arnold,* 1–2.

2   *Ibid.*, 3–4; Arnold, *Arnold*, 17–18; Caulkins, *Norwich*, 276, 306, 409, 410; *Vital Records of Norwich*, I, 153; Arnold, *Arnold Memorial*, 105.

3   Hannah Arnold to Dr. Cogswell (about 1752) in *Biddle Coll.* (HSP.)

4   *Mag. of Hist.*, III, 258; Arnold, *Arnold*, 23–4; Caulkins, *Norwich*, 410.

5   Evidence of the firm's development can be seen in the fact that an invoice of drugs for one year alone brought in by a single ship amounted in value to £8,000, while in the same year that the Lathrops took on Arnold as an apprentice, they also accepted another, one Solomon Smith, who later set up an apothecary shop in Hartford. Arnold was greatly impressed by the variety of stock carried by the Lathrops and imitated it when he had his own shop. See *ibid.*, 326; Bronson, *Waterbury*, 325.

6   For Arnold's enlistments and the desertion notice, see *Muster Rolls of the New York Provincial Troops, 1755–64, New York Hist. Soc. Coll.*, XXIV, 96, 176, 324, 522–3; see also Decker, *Arnold*, 15–16, 473–4; Sparks, *Arnold*, 6–7.

7   *Waterman Family*, I, 123–4.

8   For the elder Arnold's drunkenness and warrant for his arrest (May 26, 1760), issued by Justice of the Peace Isaac Huntington, see *Miscell. Paps.* (HSP.)

Chapter III

Druggist and Merchant

1   *New Haven Colony Hist. Soc. Paps.*, III, 113. Arnold's drug store sign may still be seen in the New Haven Colony Historical Society.

2   Advertisement in the New Haven Colony Historical Society.

3   Miller, *Origins of the American Revolution*, 373–5.

4   Caulkins, *Norwich*, 412–3; Decker, *Arnold*, 20–1; Arnold, *Arnold*, 27–8.

5   *Ibid.*, 30–2; Decker, *Arnold*, 25–6.

6   For a detailed account of the situation in New Haven, see Gipson, *Jared Ingersoll*, 30–2.

7   For the Boles affair, see *Connecticut Gazette* for Feb. 7, 14, 21, 1766; *Jared Ingersoll Record Book*, II, 89; *New Haven Town Records*, IV, 489–90; Sherman's order for Arnold's arrest in New Haven Colony Historical Society; Decker, *Arnold*, 26–9; Arnold, *Arnold*, 30; Gipson, *Ingersoll*, 233–6; Boardman, *Sherman*, 92; Boutell, *Sherman*, 44.

8   Beardsley, *Johnson*, 60; Gipson, *Ingersoll*, 252–7; Schlesinger, *Colonial Merchants*, 56 ff.; Stuart, *Trumbull*, 119–24; Arnold's indenture in *New Haven Col. Hist. Soc. Paps.*, IX, 412 and note.

9   Correspondence in Decker, *Arnold*, 31–3; letter in Maryland Historical Society, dated April 21, 1768; letter in ms. division of Massachusetts Historical Society, dated March 26, 1768; Longman's power of attorney to Lintot, July 7, 1766, and clerk's affidavit *re* Arnold's indebtedness for books (£398) in *Miscell. Paps.* (HSP); Sellers, *Arnold*, 11–12.

10 For information concerning Arnold's Masonic connections, I am chiefly indebted to Mr. Chauncey H. Clements, 33° A.·. A.·. Scottish Rite, Northern Masonic Jurisdiction. Colonel James R. Case of Bethel, Connecticut, has also been most helpful. Naturally I assume responsibility for all statements.

11 Occasionally he ordered supplies of these stockings from Paul Revere. See Forbes, *Paul Revere and the World He Lived In,* 310.

12 *Mag. of Hist.,* III, 259; for Arnold's progeny, see Arnold, *Arnold Memorial,* 132.

13 For Arnold's commercial transactions, see Atwater, *New Haven,* 43; Arnold's *Minute Book* (June-August, 1768) and his *Waste Book* (April, 1773–March, 1780) in New Haven Colony Historical Society.

14 For value and description of the house, see schedule accompanying Arnold's claim submitted to the commissioners appointed by Parliament, in PRO, A.O. 13/96, f. 799; see also Arnold, *Arnold,* 34, and account of house in scrapbook of New Haven Colony Historical Society, which has a fireplace and fan window from the house; for Mansfield's rum orders see Arnold's *Waste Book, passim.*

15 Ms. letter to McKenzie and Campbell, Jan. 7, 1771 (see also copy of letter on obverse) in New Haven Colony Historical Society; ms. letter, dated Jan., 1771, in *Biddle Coll.* (HSP).

16 Arnold to Peggy, May 28, 1766, in *ibid.;* Arnold to Peggy, Aug. 8 and 13, 1768, and Oct. 5, 1773, in *Dreer Coll., Gen'ls of the Revolution,* I (HSP).

Chapter IV

The Call to Arms

1 Arnold to Douglas, June 9, 1770, in *Dreer Coll., Gen'ls of the Rev.,* I (HSP).

2 For the Peters troubles, see Peters, *Connecticut,* 262–9; Clark, *Connecticut,* 93–4; Zeichner, *Connecticut's Years of Controversy,* 175, 326 n. 22; Peters's letters in *Connecticut Journal and Newsboy,* Oct. 21, 1774. The attitude of the clergy in general is examined in Baldwin, *The New England Clergy and the American Revolution.*

3 Zeichner, *Connecticut's Years of Controversy,* 176–7.

4 Atwater, *New Haven,* 40, 650.

5 *Ibid.,* 42.

6 *Ibid.,* 42, 650; Gipson, *Ingersoll,* 337–8; Boardman, *Sherman,* 127–8; Sellers, *Arnold,* 21–3.

7 *A.A.,* 4th ser., II, 383–4; *Conn. Hist. Soc. Coll.,* II, 215–7.

8 Atwater, *New Haven,* 650.

9 For Parsons's meeting with Arnold and his subsequent activities in Hartford, see *Conn. Hist. Soc. Coll.,* I, 181–2.

10 Pell, *Ethan Allen,* 75, 77.

11 See John Brown in *Dictionary of American Biography;* James Easton in Appleton's *Cyclopedia of American Biography;* Oliver Arnold in *National Cyclopedia of American Biography;* Brown's letter in *A.A.,* 4th ser., II, 244; Mott's account in *Conn. Hist. Soc. Coll.,* I, 167–71.

12 Arnold's plan is in *A.A.,* 4th ser., II, 450. For authorization, see *ibid.,* II, 485, 748–9; *Cont. Cong. Paps.* (LC), 162, I, f. 1; *Journals of Each Provincial Congress of Massachusetts,* 527, 529, 530–2, 534, 695 ff. See also *Conn. Hist. Soc. Coll.,* I, 171.

13 Pell, *Ethan Allen,* 83; Smith, *Struggle for the Fourteenth Colony,* I, 110–40; Ward, *War of the Revolution,* I, 67; *A.A.,* 4th Ser., II, 558–9. The command question is discussed in full in French, *Taking of Ticonderoga,* 28–68 *passim.* See also Mott's letter in *Conn. Hist. Soc. Coll.,* I, 171–2; Allen's letter to the Albany committee and Arnold's report to the Mass. committee of safety in *A.A.,* 4th ser., II, 557, 606, 734; Allen's account in his *Narrative;* Goodhue, *Shoreham,* 14.

Chapter V

THE DISPUTED COMMAND AT TICONDEROGA

1 *A.A.,* 4th ser., II, 559–60.

2 For Arnold's difficulties, see *ibid.,* II, 557; "Arnold's Memo. Book," in *P.M.H.B.,* VIII, 366–7; *Conn. Hist. Soc. Coll.,* II, 247.

3 *A.A.,* 4th ser., II, 585; Pell, *Ethan Allen,* 95.

4 For the St. Johns venture, see Arnold's letters in *A.A.,* 4th ser., II, 645–6, 686, 693–4; "Arnold's Memo. Book," in *P.M.H.B.,* VIII, 367–8.

5 *Minutes of the Albany Committee of Correspondence, 1775–1778,* I, 59; *A.A.,* 4th ser., II, 645–6, 693–4, 714–5.

6 *Ibid.,* II, 585, 645, 694.

7 *Ibid.,* II, 733.

8 *Ibid.,* II, 734–5; *Cont. Cong. Jour.,* II, 56.

9 Pell, *Ethan Allen,* 107; *A.A.,* 4th ser., II, 848, 958, 976.

10 *Ibid.,* II, 735, 957–8; "Arnold's Memo. Book," in *P.M.H.B.,* VIII, 373.

11 *Ibid.,* VIII, 373; *A.A.,* 4th ser., II, 1087.

12 *Ibid.,* II, 1086–7.

13 For Arnold's plan, see *ibid.,* II, 976–7.

14 *Ibid.,* II, 1382–3; *Cont. Cong. Jour.,* II, 73–4. For the perplexity of Congress concerning what to do about Canada, see Lawson, "Canada and the Articles of Confederation," in *Amer. Hist. Rev.,* LVIII, 40–3; Ward, *War of the Revolution,* I, 138–9; Smith, *Struggle for the Fourteenth Colony,* I, 166–82, 231–43.

15 *Conn. Hist. Soc. Coll.,* II, 247; *A.A.,* 4th ser., II, 905, 1407–8.

16 Report of committee and Arnold's resignation in *ibid.*, II, 1596, 1598–9. See also "Arnold's Memo. Book," in *P.M.H.B.*, VIII, 374.

17 *Ibid.*, VIII, 376; accounts of Mott and Spooner in *A.A.*, 4th ser., II, 1592–3, 1597.

18 Parsons to Joseph Trumbull, June 2, 1775, in *Conn. Hist. Soc. Coll.*, I, 182; Barnabas Deane to Silas Deane, June 1, 1775, in *ibid.*, 247; *A.A.*, 4th ser., II, 1088.

19 *Ibid.*, III, 952; Fitzpatrick, *Writings of Washington*, IV, 46; French, *First Year of the American Revolution*, 422–4.

20 Arnold's report to Congress in *Cont. Cong. Paps.* (LC), 162, I, f. 20.

Chapter VI

THE WILDERNESS MARCH

1 Arnold, *Arnold*, 47–8; entry for June 23, 1775, in Arnold's *Waste Book*.

2 Arnold to James Price, July 25, 1775, in *Emmett Coll.*, 8036 (NYPL); Hannah to Silas Deane, Feb. 1, 1776, in *Conn. Hist. Soc. Coll.*, II, 356–8.

3 *A.A.*, 4th ser., III, 298, 313, 344; *Conn. Hist. Soc. Coll.*, II, 354; *Cont. Cong. Jour.*, IV, 77–8.

4 For Montreal campaign, see Smith, *Struggle for the Fourteenth Colony*, I, 336–491; Ward, *War of the Revolution*, I, 150–62; Montross, *Rag, Tag and Bobtail*, 61–6; Wallace, *Appeal to Arms*, 67–72.

5 Fitzpatrick, *Writings of Washington*, III, 438.

6 Smith, *Arnold's March*, 75–6.

7 *Historical Mag.*, I, 372; Patterson, *Gates*, 56.

8 Smith, *Struggle for the Fourteenth Colony*, I, 511; Graham, *Morgan*, 67; Henry's journal in Roberts, *March to Quebec*, 301–2.

9 Oswald performed valuable service during the war, particularly at Monmouth. He gained promotion to a lieutenant colonelcy but was ranked by juniors, another blunder by Congress. Resigning, he became a printer. When the French Revolution broke out, he was in England. Crossing to France, he joined the army and commanded a regiment under General Dumouriez at the battle of Jemappe. Subsequently he returned to New York and died in a yellow fever epidemic.

10 Journals of Squier and Melvin in Roberts, *March to Quebec*, 619, 435.

11 Fobes's journal in *ibid.*, 581; Arnold to Tracy, Sept. 28, 1775, in *ibid.*, 68.

12 Arnold to Washington, Sept. 25, 1775, in *A.A.*, 4th ser., III, 960; Smith, *Struggle for the Fourteenth Colony*, I, 525.

13 Report of Colburn's scouts and Arnold's letter of Sept. 25 to Washington in *A.A.*, 4th ser., III, 960–2. The possible part taken by Natanis in the expedition is fully exploited in that excellent novel by Kenneth Roberts, *Arundel*.

14 For accounts of the Burr-Jacataqua story, see Coffin, *Kennebec, Cradle of Americans,* 110–19; Codman, *Arnold's Expedition,* 42–3, 116, 178–9.

15 Arnold to Washington, Sept. 25, 1775, in *A.A.,* 4th ser., III, 960–1; Washington to Morgan, Oct. 4, 1775, in Fitzpatrick, *Writings of Washington,* IV, 2–3; Graham, *Morgan,* 61–2.

16 For the McCormick affair, see Arnold to Washington, Sept. 25, 1775, in *A.A.,* 4th ser., III, 960–1; Arnold to Washington, Sept. 27, 1775, in Roberts, *March to Quebec,* 67; journals of Dearborn, Meigs, Senter, Thayer, Melvin, Haskell, Stocking, Fobes, and Squier in *ibid.,* 132, 175, 199, 249, 436, 474, 547, 581, 620; Codman, *Arnold's Expedition,* 43.

17 Arnold to Washington, Sept. 25, 1775 in A.A., 4th ser., III, 960; Haskell's journal in Roberts, *March to Quebec,* 474.

18 Thayer's journal in *ibid.,* 250.

19 Journals of Arnold and Senter in *ibid.,* 48, 202–3.

20 Journals of Fobes, Senter, and Arnold in *ibid.,* 582, 205, 50.

21 Arnold to Manir, Schuyler, Steele, and Washington, Oct. 13, 1775 in *ibid.,* 69–73; Washington to Arnold, Sept. 14, 1775 in Fitzpatrick, *Writings of Washington,* III, 491.

22 For mention of the council of war, see journals of Arnold, Dearborn, Meigs, and Morison in Roberts, *March to Quebec,* 55, 136, 179, 516. The scene I hereafter describe is, of course, an imaginative reconstruction but, in my opinion, plausible.

23 The decisions of the council of war are in Arnold's journal in *ibid.,* 55–6; Arnold to Washington, Oct. 27, 1775 in *ibid.,* 78.

24 Accounts of the Enos council of war are in the journals of Senter and Thayer in *ibid.,* 209–13, 256–8; an analysis of Enos's position and an account of his trial are given by the Rev. H. E. Hayden, an Enos descendant, in *ibid.,* 631–48; Arnold to Washington, Nov. 8, 1775 in *ibid.,* 85; Washington to Arnold, Dec. 5, 1775 in Fitzpatrick, *Writings of Washington,* IV, 149.

25 Henry's journal in Roberts, *March to Quebec,* 337–8.

26 For Arnold's activities on Oct. 27, 1775, see his journal in *ibid.,* 58–9.

27 *Ibid.,* 59–61.

28 For relations between the Indians and the column, see the journals of Arnold, Dearborn, Senter, Henry, Melvin, Haskell, Fobes, and Pierce in *ibid.,* 61, 215, 220–1 (Senter's account of Arnold's speech to the Indians), 313–5, 317, 344–5, 440–1, 478–9, 584 (Fobes's mention of the young Indian who saved several companies), 670; Arnold to Washington, Nov. 8, 1775, and to Schuyler (probably), Nov. 27, 1775 in *ibid.,* 85, 98.

29 See Arnold to Schuyler (probably), Nov. 27, 1775 in *ibid.,* 99. For a sample of extreme criticism of the march, see Leacock, *Montreal,* 122–3.

30 Journals of Henry and Stocking in Roberts, *March to Quebec,* 347–8, 552; Hannah Arnold to Arnold, June, 1775 in Arnold, *Arnold,* 48; Washington to Arnold, Dec. 5, and to Schuyler, Dec. 5, 1775 in Fitzpatrick, *Writings of*

Washington, IV, 148, 147; Schuyler to Washington, Dec. 9, 1775 in *A.A.,* 4th ser., IV, 226.

31 Arnold to Gregory (probably), Nov. 1, to Montgomery, Nov. 8 and 14, to Washington, Nov. 8 and 14, 1775, in Roberts, *March to Quebec,* 80–6; Smith, *Struggle for the Fourteenth Colony,* II, 9–16, 20–2.

Chapter VII

THE QUEBEC ASSAULT

1 Thayer's journal in Roberts, *March to Quebec,* 264.
2 Arnold to Montgomery, Nov. 14, 1775, and to Washington, Nov. 20, 1775, in *ibid.,* 87, 93; journals of Meigs, Senter, and Thayer in *ibid.,* 182, 225, 264.
3 Arnold to Montgomery, Nov. 14, 1775, and to Schuyler (probably), Nov. 27, 1775, in *ibid.,* 87, 99; journals of Henry and Fobes in *ibid.,* 352–3, 587; *A.A.,* 4th ser., III, 1723; Graham, *Morgan,* 85–6; Smith, *Struggle for the Fourteenth Colony,* II, 25–6, 573–5.
4 Arnold to Cramahé, Nov. 15, 1775, in Roberts, *March to Quebec,* 88–9; Smith, *Struggle for the Fourteenth Colony,* II, 30.
5 Graham, *Morgan,* 88; Henry's journal in Roberts, *March to Quebec,* 356.
6 Journals of Senter, Thayer, Henry, Haskell, Stocking, and Pierce in *ibid.,* 226, 265–6, 360–1, 481, 560, 679–80; Arnold to Montgomery and Washington, Nov. 20, 1775, in *ibid.,* 90–5.
7 See Arnold's letters, and journals of Dearborn, Meigs, Senter, Thayer, Henry, Haskell, and Pierce in *ibid.,* 90–102, 144, 185, 227, 269–71, 363, 481–2, 688.
8 See sketch of Montgomery in *Dictionary of American Biography;* Montgomery to Schuyler, Dec. 5, 1775, in *A.A.,* 4th ser., IV, 189.
9 Journals of Thayer and Pierce in Roberts, *March to Quebec,* 269–70, 271, 689; Arnold's letter of Dec. 2, 1775, in *Biddle Paps.* (HSP).
10 Roberts, *March to Quebec,* 96; *A.A.,* 4th ser., III, 204; *Canadian Archives Report for 1918,* 422; Codman, *Arnold's Expedition,* 188–90; Lossing, *Schuyler,* I, 486.
11 For the incident with the officers, see journals of Meigs, Senter, Henry, Stocking, Fobes, and Pierce, and Mr. Roberts's comment in *March to Quebec,* 187, 231, 374, 561, 589, 698–9, 429; *Montgomery to Schuyler,* Dec. 26, 1775, in *A.A.,* 4th ser., IV, 464–5; Ward, *War of the Revolution,* I, 188.
12 Journals of Fobes and Henry in Roberts, *March to Quebec,* 590, 376–7.
13 For Arnold's wound, see *ibid.,* 108, 233–4. For the Quebec assault, see the journals, and Arnold's letters of Dec. 31, 1775, and Jan. 2, 1776, in *ibid.,* 102–6; Arnold's letters of Jan. 6 and 14, 1776, in *A.A.,* 4th ser., IV, 589, 674; Carleton's report in *ibid.,* 4th ser., IV, 656; casualty lists in *ibid.,* 4th ser., IV, 675 and Roberts, *March to Quebec,* 27–40; "Morgan's Auto-

biography," in *Historical Mag.*, 2d ser., IX, 379–80; Barnfare's letter in *ibid.*, 2d ser., VI, 249–50; *Cont. Cong. Jour.*, IV, 82–4; Smith, *Struggle for the Fourteenth Colony*, II, 111–47; *Codman's Expedition*, 212–49; French, *First Year of the American Revolution*, 614–20; Ward, *War of the Revolution*, I, 191–5; Graham, *Morgan*, 93–107; Bradley, *Dorchester*, 124–32; Wood, *The Father of British Canada*, 107–21.

14 Arnold to Wooster, Dec. 31, 1775, and Senter's journal in Roberts, *March to Quebec*, 102–3, 234–5.

15 Arnold to Wooster, Jan. 2, 1776, and to Hannah (probably), Jan. 6, 1776, in *ibid.*, 105, 109.

Chapter VIII

Withdrawal from Canada

1 Schuyler to Washington, Jan. 13, 1776, in *A.A.*, 4th ser., IV, 666; Washington to Schuyler, Jan. 18, 1776, in Fitzpatrick, *Writings of Washington*, IV, 254.

2 For Wooster's communications and his relations with Arnold, Schuyler, and Washington, see *ibid.*, IV, 254, 278, 453 n.; *A.A.*, 4th ser., IV, 796–7, 870, 1001–4, 1132–3, 1470, 1493. Washington's letter to Reed is in Fitzpatrick, *Writings of Washington*, IV, 298.

3 "Richard Smith, Diary," in *Letters of Members of Cont. Cong.*, I, 302, 304, 307; *Cont. Cong. Jour.*, IV, 47 (Congress did not learn of the Quebec disaster until Jan. 17, 1776); Arnold to Hancock, Feb. 12, 1776, in *A.A.*, 4th ser., IV, 1017; Washington to Arnold, Jan. 27, 1776, in Fitzpatrick, *Writings of Washington*, IV, 281–3; Arnold to Washington, Feb. 27, 1776, in *A.A.*, 4th ser., IV, 1513.

4 Arnold to Hancock, Feb. 1, 1776, in *ibid.*, IV, 907–8; Brown to his wife, March 15, 1776, in Smith, *Pittsfield*, I, 259.

5 Brown's petition is in *A.A.*, 4th ser., I, 1219–20. See also Arnold, *Arnold*, 103.

6 The reaction of the Canadians to American paper money had been predicted by a Scot before the campaign began. See Lawson, "Canada and the Articles of Confederation," in *Amer. Hist. Rev.*, LVIII, 46 and n. 38.

7 Arnold to Schuyler, April 20, 1776, in *A.A.*, 4th ser., V, 1098–1100.

8 Carroll, *Journal*, 30 n.

9 For the Cedars and the cartel, see especially *A.A.*, 4th ser., VI, 389, 576, 587, 588, 591, 595–7 (Arnold's letters to the commissioners and copy of cartel), 598, 599, 748, 757, 769, 924, 928, 5th ser., I, 159, 160, 162, 163, 358, 655, 748, 801, 1571, 1594; *Cont. Cong. Jour.*, V, 446, 454, 468, 475, 534, 601; Fitzpatrick, *Writings of Washington*, V, 108, 109, 113, 118, 130, 147, 279–81, 297 n., 322 n., 465; Jones, *Campaign for the Conquest of Canada*, 54–65; Smith, *Struggle for the Fourteenth Colony*, II, 365–80. For

a pretty complete bibliography of the affair, see *ibid.*, II, 369 n. 19.

10 *A.A.*, 4th ser., VI, 649.

11 Washington's opinion of Sullivan is in Fitzpatrick, *Writings of Washington*, V, 152; Arnold to Sullivan, June 13, 1776, in *Sullivan Paps. (New Hampshire Hist. Soc. Colls.*, XIII), I, 237–8.

12 *A.A.*, 4th ser., VI, 925, 977, 1104–5, 5th ser., I, 165; *Sullivan Paps. (New Hampshire Hist. Soc. Colls.*, XIII), I, 252–3; Wilkinson, *Memoirs*, I, 49–54.

13 *Ibid.*, I, 54–5.

Chapter IX

Summer of Controversy

1 Germain to Burgoyne, Aug. 23, 1776, in *Stopford-Sackville MSS.* (Hist. MSS. Com. Repts.), II, 39. Arnold was a man who made many enemies, among them Dr. Lewis Beebe, a Yale classmate of John Brown, a physician who later entered the ministry and was subsequently unfrocked for liberal ideas. Beebe, no model of modesty, detested the arrogant Arnold and seems to have held him responsible for the failure of the Canadian expedition. On July 9, he wrote of Arnold in his journal in language that Arnold himself might have envied, "I heartily wish some person would try an experiment upon him, (viz) to make the sun shine thro' his head with an ounce ball; and then see whether the rays come in a direct or oblique direction." See Beebe's journal in *P.M.H.B.*, LIX, 342.

2 Arnold to Chase, May 15, 1776, in *A.A.*, 4th ser., VI, 80–1.

3 Arnold to the commissioners, June 2, 1776, in *ibid.*, 5th ser., I, 165; Arnold to Schuyler, June 6 and 10, 1776 in *ibid.*, 4th ser., VI, 925, 977.

4 Arnold to Sullivan, June 13, 1776, in *Sullivan Paps. (New Hampshire Hist. Soc. Colls.*, XIII), I, 238.

5. Arnold to Schuyler, June 13, 1776, in *A.A.*, 4th ser., VI, 1038.

6 *Ibid.*, 4th ser., VI, 1105, 5th ser., I, 538.

7 *Ibid.*, 5th ser., I, 1274; Arnold, *Arnold*, 100; Arnold's protest is in *A.A.*, 5th ser., I, 1272. The court's statement with respect to Scott is as follows (*ibid.*, 5th ser., I, 1273): "From Major Scott's overstrained zeal to serve as Judge Advocate during the course of the trial; from his own acknowledgment in the face of the Court that he had never furnished Colonel Hazen with any written orders from General Arnold; from his appearing extremely solicitous to give evidence in the cause; from his application to the Court to cross-examine a witness; and lastly, from the purport of the testimony of divers witnesses, proving that the goods were delivered to Major Scott, and, while under his care, conducted in such a disorderly manner that part of them must unavoidably have been damaged or lost previous to their arrival at Chamblee; that Colonel Hazen never had the possession of the

goods, and that he could not possibly have taken them, (granting he had been authorized so to do,) not having sufficient store room; from these concurring circumstances, we beg leave to assure your Honour that we were constrained to believe Major Scott so far interested in the event of Colonel Hazen's trial, as to render his testimony inadmissable."

8   *Ibid.,* 5th ser., I, 1273.

9   *Ibid.,* 5th ser., I, 1273.

10 The court's report is in *ibid.,* 5th ser., I, 1273–4; Gates to Hancock, Sept. 2, 1776, in *ibid.,* 5th ser., I, 1268.

11 Wilkinson, *Memoirs,* I, 48–9.

12 For the Board of War action, see *Cont. Cong. Jour.,* VIII, 382. For two interesting developments (with opposite conclusions) of Arnold's Montreal activities and his conduct before the court, see Arnold, *Arnold* (pro-Arnold), 96 ff. and Decker, *Arnold* (anti-Arnold), 154 ff.; see also the anti-Arnold point of view in Patterson, *Gates,* 90–1.

13 For Easton's activities, see *A.A.,* 4th ser., V, 1234–5; *Cont. Cong. Jour.,* IV, 275, 312–4, V, 489, 619, 623, 624, 626.

14 *Ibid.,* V, 485, 618, 626; *A.A.,* 5th ser., I, 1221, II, 143.

15 Arnold to Washington, June 25, 1776, in *ibid.,* 4th ser., VI, 1108. See the requirements for building a gondola in *ibid.,* 5th ser., I, 236, 745, 746.

16 *Ibid.,* 5th ser., I, 207, 563–4, 649–50, 397; Gates to Hancock, July 29, 1776, in *ibid.,* 5th ser., I, 649; Washington to Gates, Aug. 14, 1776, in Fitzpatrick, *Writings of Washington,* V, 433; Schuyler to Gates, Aug. 3, 1776, in *A.A.,* 5th ser., I, 747.

17 *Ibid.,* 5th ser., I, 397, 826–7, 970, 1002.

18 *Ibid.,* 5th ser., I, 1002–3, 1051, 1073, 1277, 1083, 1217, 1185–7.

19 Chase to Arnold, Aug. 7, 1776 in *ibid.,* 5th ser., I, 810; Arnold to Gates, Sept. 7, 1776, in *ibid.,* 5th ser., II, 354.

Chapter X

ARNOLD'S NAVAL CAREER ON LAKE CHAMPLAIN

1   The gondolas were the *Boston, Connecticut, Jersey, New Haven, New York, Philadelphia, Providence, Spitfire,* and *Success.* As Ward has remarked, accounts usually list only 15 vessels in the battle line instead of 16, omitting the *Success.* General Riedesel, however, mentions 16, as does Richard Varick in a report to the New York Convention, while Bayze Wells distinctly states in his journal for September 11 that during his guard duty the *Success* joined the fleet at about 10:00 A.M. See Ward, *War of the Revolution,* I, 472; Riedesel, *Memoirs,* I, 73; Varick's letter in *A.A.,* 5th ser., II, 1037; Wells's journal in *Conn. Hist. Soc. Colls.,* VII, 277.

2   *A.A.,* 5th ser., II, 481, 835, 860.

3 Arnold to Gates, Sept. 18 and Oct. 7, 1776, in *ibid.*, 5th ser., II, 481, 933. Arnold exaggerated the size of the American forces in the New York area by over four times.

4 *Ibid.*, 5th ser., II, 481, 440, 591, 1015.

5 *Ibid.*, 5th ser., II, 1224. The expression "to leeward" is that of Admiral Mahan, who considered Arnold's judgment sound. He said that "A retreat before square-rigged sailing vessels having a fair wind, by a heterogeneous force like his own, of unequal speeds and batteries, could result only in disaster. . . . Better trust to a steady, well-ordered position, developing the utmost fire. . . . The correctness of Arnold's decision not to chance a retreat was shown in [the results of] the retreat of two days later." Mahan, *Major Operations of the Navies,* 19.

6 For the battles off Valcour and Split Rock, see the reports of Arnold and Waterbury in *A.A.,* 5th ser., II, 1038–9; 1079–80, 1224; the reports of Carleton, Pringle, and Douglas in *ibid.*, 5th ser., II, 1040, 1069, 1178–9; Carleton to Burgoyne, Oct. 13 and 14, 1776, in *Canadian Archives Report for 1885,* 248; Riedesel, *Memoirs,* I, 70–4; Wells's journal in *Conn. Hist. Soc. Colls.,* VII, 283–5; Pell's diary in *Mag. of Amer. Hist.,* II, pt. I, 46; Digby, *Journal,* 153; Pausch, *Journal,* 84; Lossing, *Field-Book of the Revolution,* I, 162–5; Dawson, *Battles of the U.S.,* I, 167–75; Van Tyne, *War of Independence,* 370–5; Ward, *War of the Revolution,* I, 393–7; Mahan, "Naval Campaign of 1776 on Lake Champlain," in *Scribner's Mag.,* XXIII, 147–60; Mahan, *Major Operations of the Navies,* 13–26; Paullin, *The Navy of the American Revolution,* 75–8; Allen, *Naval Hist. of the American Revolution,* I, 161–79; Alden and Westcott, *U.S. Navy,* 18–23; James, *British Navy in Adversity,* 40–1, 429; Arnold, *Arnold,* 105–20; Spears, "Benedict Arnold—Naval Patriot," in *Harper's Mag.,* CVI, 277–81. A spirited and authentic account is also to be found in Kenneth Roberts's great novel, *Rabble in Arms.*

7 Mahan, *Major Operations of the Navies,* 25.

8 For Gates's and Varick's opinions, see *A.A.,* 5th ser., II, 1192, 1080, 1102, III, 527. For British opinions, see *ibid.*, III, 1227; *Stopford-Sackville MSS.* (Hist. MSS. Com. Rep't), II, 46.

9 Maxwell to Livingston, Oct. 20, 1776, in *A.A.,* 5th ser., II, 1143.

Chapter XI

DENIAL OF PROMOTION

1 Arnold to Schuyler, Oct. 12 and 15, 1776, in *A.A.,* 5th ser., II, 1038–9, 1080; Gates to Congress, Nov. 27, 1776, in *ibid.*, 5th ser., III, 875.

2 *Ibid.*, 5th ser., II, 911, III, 1158–9, 1160. The specifications in Brown's petition for Arnold's arrest are as follows:

"1st. For endeavouring to asperse your petitioner's character, in the most infamous manner.

"2d. For unwarrantably degrading and reducing the rank conferred on your petitioner by his (General Arnold's) superior officer, and subjecting your petitioner to serve in an inferiour rank to that which he had been appointed.

"3d. For ungentleman-like conduct in his letter to General Wooster, of the 25th of January last, charging your petitioner with a falsehood, and in a private manner, which is justly chargeable on himself.

"4th. For suffering the small-pox to spread in the camp before Quebeck, and promoting inoculations there in the Continental Army.

"5th. For depriving part of the Army under his command of their usual allowance of provisions ordered by Congress.

"6th. For interfering and countermanding the orders of his superiour officer.

"7th. For plundering the inhabitants of Montreal, in direct violation of a solemn capitulation agreement entered into with them by our late brave and worthy General Montgomery, to the eternal disgrace of the Continental arms.

"8th. For giving unjustifiable, unwarrantable, cruel, and bloody orders, directing whole villages to be destroyed, and the inhabitants thereof put to death by fire and sword, without any distinctions to friend or foe, age or sex.

"9th. For entering into an unwarrantable, unjustifiable, and partial agreement with Captain Forster for the exchange of prisoners taken at The Cedars, without the knowledge, advice, or consent of any officer than those present with him on the spot.

"10th. For ordering inoculation of the Continental Army at Sorel, without the knowledge of, and contrary to the intentions of, the General commanding that Northern Department, by which fatal consequences ensued.

"11th. For great misconduct during his command, from the camp at Cambridge, in the year 1775, until he was superseded by General Montgomery, at Point-aux-Tremble, near Quebec.

"12th. For great misconduct in his command of the Continental fleet in Lake Champlain, which occasioned the loss thereof.

"13th. For disobedience of the orders of his superiour officers, while acting by a commission from the Provincial Congress, sent from that State (Massachusetts) to inspect into his conduct; and also for a treasonable attempt to make his escape with the navigators then at or near Ticonderoga, to the enemy at St. John's, which obliged the then commanding officer of Ticonderoga and its dependencies to issue a positive order to stop or sink the vessels attempting to pass that post, and by force of arms make a prisoner of the said General Arnold, (then a Colonel,) which was accordingly done."

3 *Ibid.,* 5th ser., III, 1042–3.

4 Fitzpatrick, *Writings of Washington,* VI, 366, 374–5; *A.A.,* 5th ser., III, 1217; Stryker, *Battles of Trenton and Princeton,* 59–60. Howard Swiggett has raised the question whether Gates may have withheld Arnold's orders since they were enclosed to Gates in Washington's letter of December 14, received by Gates on the 15th, yet not known to Arnold, who had arrived at the Sun Inn with Gates, until the 17th. Had Gates himself wanted the New England command? See Swiggett, *The Great Man,* 73–4.

5 Greene to Cooke, Dec. 21, 1776, in *A.A.,* 5th ser., III, 1343; Washington to Arnold, Feb. 6 and March 3, 1777, in Fitzpatrick, *Writings to Washington,* VII, 115–6, 233–4.

6 See Oswald to Lamb, Jan. 3 and Feb. 16, 1777, in *Lamb Paps.* (NYHS); Leake, *Lamb,* 150–3.

7 Arnold, *Arnold,* 125–6; *New England Hist. and Gen. Reg.,* II, 75–6, XXVI, 201. It is possible, however, that it was less Betsy's coldness than her mother's determination that prevented the marriage. Legend has it that later when Betsy promised to marry Martin Brimmer, Mrs. Deblois broke up the ceremony.

8 *Cont. Cong. Jour.,* VII, 133.

9 *Ibid.,* VII, 132, 133; Fitzpatrick, *Writings of Washington,* VII, 234 n. 22, 352 n. 32.

10 Washington to Arnold, March 3, and to R. H. Lee, March 6, 1777, in *ibid.,* VII, 234, 251–2.

11 Arnold to Washington, March 14 and 26 in Sparks, *Writings of Washington,* IV, 345–6.

12 Freeman, *Washington,* IV, 394–5; Ward, *War of the Revolution,* I, 423–4; Washington to Arnold, April 3, 1777, in Fitzpatrick, *Writings of Washington,* VII, 352–3.

13 Greene, *Greene,* I, 420; *Sullivan Paps. (New Hampshire Hist. Soc. Colls.,* XIII), I, 403; *Cont. Cong. Jour.,* VIII, 537; Adams, *Familiar Letters,* 276.

Chapter XII

Heroism in Connecticut and Humiliation in Philadelphia

1 Arnold to A. McDougall, April 27 and 28, 1777, in *Cont. Cong. Paps.* (LC), 152, IV, f. 139–40, 145; Hughes to General [McDougall?], April 28, 1777, in *ibid.,* 152, IV, f. 141–2; Dawson, *Battles of the U.S.,* I, 212–20; Moore, *Diary of the American Revolution,* I, 423–8; Lossing, *Field-Book of the Revolution,* I, 407–10; Rockwell, *Ridgefield,* 103–19; Leake, *Lamb,* 157–63.

2 *Cont. Cong. Jour.,* VII, 323.

3 Fitzpatrick, *Writings of Washington,* VIII, 47–8.

4 Arnold to Hancock, May 20, 1777, in *Cont. Cong. Paps.* (LC), 162, I, f. 86; *Cont. Cong. Jour.,* VII, 371, 373. The substance of the handbill was contained in Brown's petition of December 1, 1776, to Gates (*A.A.,* 5th ser., III, 1158–9), but the part that stirred Arnold to action on his own behalf may have been the following: "I appeal to every person of common understanding, whether in a military character or not, that if Gen. Arnold did not know himself guilty of the charges laid against him, he would not have endeavored to bring himself to a trial, to clear up his character, which, had he been able to do, he certainly might have called his impeachers to account for false and malicious charges, and put the saddle upon the other horse; but, very far from this, he has used every possible art to prevent a trial, as if his character was not worth a sixpence." For a detailed account of the Arnold-Brown controversy (from a pro-Brown point of view), see Smith, *Pittsfield,* I, 255–77. See also Stone, *Brant,* II, 116–9.

5 Lee to Jefferson, May 20, 1777, in Ballagh, *Letters of R. H. Lee,* I, 292; Adams to Abigail, May 22, 1777, in Adams, *Familiar Letters,* 276.

6 *Cont. Cong. Jour.,* VII, 372–3, VIII, 382; the complete report is in *Cont. Cong. Paps.* (LC), 147, I, f. 177.

7 Schuyler to Gates, Sept. 8, 1776, in *A.A.,* 5th ser., II, 249.

8 Arnold to Congress, Feb. 12, 1776 in *Cont. Cong. Paps.* (LC), 162, I, f. 64–5; *A.A.,* 5th ser., I, 165, 4th ser., VI, 579–80, 931. See also Van Doren, *Secret History,* 160; Arnold, *Arnold,* 136–7. For difficulties faced by the British government through the desire for private gain on the part of certain officers, see Curtis, *British Army in the Revolution,* 145–7.

9 Arnold, *Arnold,* 137; *Cont. Cong. Jour.,* VIII, 467; Arnold to Congress, July 11, 1777, in *Cont. Cong. Paps.* (LC), 162, I, f. 106.

10 Washington to Congress, July 10, 1777, in Fitzpatrick, *Writings of Washington,* VIII, 377.

11 *Cont. Cong. Jour.,* VIII, 545; Washington to Congress, July 12, 1777, in Fitzpatrick, *Writings of Washington,* VIII, 386.

12 *Ibid.,* VIII, 427; Arnold to Hancock, July 12 and 14, 1777, in *Cont. Cong. Paps.* (LC), 162, I, f. 108, 109; Arnold, *Arnold,* 139.

13 *Cont. Cong. Jour.,* VIII, 623–4; Boardman, *Sherman,* 93 n. 26; Boutell, *Sherman,* 271; Van Doren, *Secret History,* 161–2.

14 Much of the trouble Congress encountered with the flood of foreign officers originated in the zeal of one of its commissioners abroad, Silas Deane. See Burnett, *The Cont. Cong.,* 240–6; Montross, *The Reluctant Rebels,* 204.

15 Burnett, *Letters of Members of Cont. Cong.,* II, 585, 442, 445.

16 *Ibid.,* II, 448.

Chapter XIII

RELIEF OF FORT STANWIX

1 Most historians have favored Schuyler over Gates in their controversy. In fact, Gates suffered at the hands of early historians in particular, who may have been influenced by his involvement in the so-called Conway Cabal against Washington and by his peculiar behavior in the battle of Camden. But Gates has not lacked for partisans in his difficulties with Schuyler, and among his present-day apologists are Lynn Montross *(Rag, Tag and Bobtail),* Samuel Patterson *(Horatio Gates),* and Bernhard Knollenberg *(Washington and the Revolution).* More traditional views may be seen in the works of Hoffman Nickerson *(The Turning Point of the Revolution),* Claude H. Van Tyne *(The War of Independence)* and Benson J. Lossing *(Life and Times of Philip Schuyler).* The Schuyler partisans are usually pro-Arnold; the Gates partisans, always anti-Arnold.

2 Arnold, *Arnold,* 153–4; Lossing, *Schuyler,* II, 288; Fitzpatrick, *Writings of Washington,* IX, 106.

3 Copies of the proclamation and the council of war proceedings are in the *Gates Paps.* (NYHS).

4 Arnold to Gates, Aug. 21 and 23, 1777, and to Schuyler, Aug. 21, 1777, in *ibid.*

5 Stedman, *Origin, Progress and Termination of the American War,* I, 335; Gordon, *Rise, Progress and Establishment of the U.S.,* II, 532–3; Burgoyne, *State of the Expedition from Canada,* app. XLVI; Stone, *Burgoyne's Campaign and St. Leger's Expedition,* 213; Nickerson, *Turning Point of the Revolution,* 271–6; Ward, *War of the Revolution,* II, 488–91.

6 Gansevoort to Gates, Aug. 22, 1777, in *Gates Paps.* (NYHS); Arnold to Gates, Aug. 23, 24, and 28, 1777, in *ibid.*

7 *Ibid.*

Chapter XIV

BATTLE OF FREEMAN'S FARM

1 Morris quoted in Nickerson, *Turning Point of the Revolution,* 282; Clajon's remark is in Patterson, *Gates,* 146; for Wilkinson's comment, see his *Memoirs,* I, 172–3.

2 For Arnold's pre-battle activities, see Varick to Schuyler, Sept. 15, 1777, in *Schuyler Paps.* (NYPL); Irving, *Washington,* III, 239; Arnold, *Arnold,* 166–8; Lossing, *Schuyler,* II, 343; Wilkinson, *Memoirs,* I, 235. For Gates's plan of battle, see *ibid.,* I, 235–6, 240; Patterson, *Gates,* 152–3; Nickerson, *Turning Point of the Revolution,* 306–8.

3 The incident at Gates's headquarters is described in Wilkinson, *Memoirs,* I, 245–6.

Chapter XV

THE QUARREL WITH GATES AND THE BATTLE OF BEMIS HEIGHTS

1 Livingston to Schuyler, Sept. 23, 1777, in *Schuyler Paps.* (NYPL); Arnold, *Arnold,* 180–1; Arnold to Gates, Sept. 22 and 23, 1777, in *Gates Paps.* (NYHS).

2 Gates to Hancock, Sept. 22, 1777, in *Cont. Cong. Paps.* (LC), 154; order to Morgan in Wilkinson, *Memoirs,* I, 254; Arnold to Gates, Sept. 22, 1777, in *Gates Paps.* (NYHS).

3 *Ibid.;* Livingston to Schuyler, Sept. 23, 1777, in *Schuyler Paps.* (NYPL); Arnold, *Arnold,* 180–1; Wilkinson, *Memoirs,* I, 254.

4 Arnold to Gates, Sept. 22, 1777, in *Gates Paps.* (NYHS).

5 For a pro-Gates account of the quarrel, see Patterson, *Gates,* 159–63. For the Livingston letter, see his of Sept. 23, 1777, to Schuyler in *Schuyler Paps.* (NYPL).

6 *Ibid.;* Schuyler to Varick, Sept. 25, 1777, in *ibid.;* Arnold, *Arnold,* 180.

7 Livingston to Schuyler, Sept. 26, 1777, in *Schuyler Paps.* (NYPL); Varick to Schuyler, Sept. 25, 1777, in *ibid.;* Arnold, *Arnold,* 183, 184.

8 Gates's letter to Hancock is in Wilkinson, *Memoirs,* I, 257. See Arnold to Gates, Sept. 23, 1777, in *ibid.,* I, 257–8, and in *Gates Paps.* (NYHS).

9 Livingston to Schuyler, Sept. 24 and 26, 1777, in *Schuyler Paps.* (NYPL); Arnold, *Arnold,* 182, 183–4; Patterson, *Gates,* 161–2.

10 *Ibid.,* 162; Wilkinson, *Memoirs,* I, 258–9, 260; Arnold to Gates, Sept. 27, 1777, in *Gates Paps.* (NYHS): Gates to Arnold, Sept. 28, 1777, in *ibid.*

11 Arnold to Gates, Oct. 1, 1777, in *ibid.*

12 Clinton to Burgoyne, Sept. 27, 1777, in *Clinton Paps.* (WLCL).

13 Wilkinson has a report of the sword incident in his *Memoirs,* I, 273. See also Sparks, *Arnold,* 119.

14 Arnold's meeting with the Connecticut militia was told to Isaac N. Arnold by Senator L. F. S. Foster of Connecticut whose father was adjutant of one of Learned's regiments. See Arnold, *Arnold,* 204. For Livingston's comment, see *ibid.,* 181.

15 For Arnold's suggestion with respect to Fraser, see Stone, *Burgoyne's Campaign and St. Leger's Expedition,* 324–5; Neilson, *Burgoyne's Campaign,* 170–1, 256–7.

16 Wilkinson's comments are in his *Memoirs,* I, 273. Accounts of the battle of October 7 are too numerous to mention here, but a rather complete bibliography, particularly of primary material, is in Winsor, *Narr. and Crit. Hist. of Amer.,* VI, 357–66 *passim.* See also Fortescue, *Hist. of the British Army,* III, 239–40; Greene, *The Revolutionary War,* 123–4; Nickerson, *Turning Point of the Revolution,* 356–68; Patterson, *Gates,* 166–8; Wallace, *Appeal to Arms,* 165–7, 290–1; Montross, *Rag, Tag and Bobtail,* 223–4, 227, 498 *passim;* Ward, *War of the Revolution,* II, 526–31.

17 Stone, *Burgoyne's Campaign and St. Leger's Expedition,* 375, 66.

18 Quoted in Roberts, *March to Quebec,* 127, from a letter sent by Dearborn to Wilkinson at the latter's request but not published by that officer in his *Memoirs.*

19 Wilkinson, *Memoirs,* I, 269.

20 *Ibid.,* I, 273; Gates to Hancock, Oct. 12, 1777, in *Cont. Cong. Paps.* (LC), 154, I, f. 272.

21 Burgoyne to Clinton, Oct. 25, 1777, in *Clinton Paps.* (WLCL). Burgoyne told the House of Commons in 1779 that had not Arnold carried the attack to him, he was confident he would have gained a position that would eventually have put the Americans in his power. See Burgoyne, *State of the Expedition,* 26, 50.

22 *Cont. Cong. Jour.,* IX, 861–2, 981, 870; Fitzpatrick, *Writings of Washington,* X, 326; Burnett, *Letters of Members of Cont. Cong.,* II, 545 n. 2.

Chapter XVI

CONVALESCENCE, THE NEW COMMAND, AND MONEY VENTURES

1 Thacher, *Military Journal,* 103; Brown's comment is in *New England Hist. and Gen. Reg.,* XVIII, 34; Arnold to Congress, Jan. 11, 1778, in *Cont. Cong. Paps.* (LC), 162, I, f. 110.

2 Decker, *Arnold,* 285–8.

3 Atwater, *New Haven,* 651.

4 Dearborn's journal in *Mass. Hist. Soc. Proc.,* 2d ser., III, 113; Washington to Arnold, May 7, 1778, in Sparks, *Writings of Washington,* V, 361; Arnold's oath in the National Archives; for new command, Fitzpatrick, *Writings of Washington,* XI, 466; Washington to Arnold, May 28, 1778, in *ibid.,* XII, 84.

5 *Cont. Cong. Jour.,* XI, 571; Washington to Arnold, June 19, 1778, in Fitzpatrick, *Writings of Washington,* XII, 94–5.

6 *Proceedings of Arnold's Court Martial,* 10.

7 Scharf and Westcott, *Philadelphia,* I, 390; Van Doren, *Secret History,* 169.

8 *Ibid.,* 172; *Cont. Cong. Jour.,* XVIII, 871.

9 *Proceedings of Arnold's Court Martial,* 8, 19, 27; Van Doren, *Secret History,* 172–3.

10 *Ibid.,* 173–5; *Proceedings of Arnold's Court Martial,* 6–9, 15–25, 27–39, 49–50, 52.

11 For *Active* case, see *Cont. Cong. Jour.,* XIII, 86–92, XV, 1194–6; *Penna. Archives,* IX, 33–4, 178–90; Middlebrook, *Maritime Connecticut,* II, 117–8; Carson, "The Case of the Sloop Active," in *P.M.H.B.,* XVI, 385–98.

12 Van Doren, *Secret History,* 175–6; PRO, *A.O.,* 13/96.

13 Middlebrook, *Maritime Connecticut,* II, 97–8; Lincoln, *Naval Records,* 311.
14 *Proceedings of Arnold's Court Martial,* 31; Fitzpatrick, *Writings of Washington,* XII, 161, 269–70; Meng, *Dispatches and Instructions of Gerard,* 160.
15 Sparks, *Arnold,* 127.
16 *Ibid.,* 127–8; Arnold, *Arnold,* 216–21; Frothingham, *Warren,* 542–4; *Cont. Cong. Jour.,* XVII, 581.

Chapter XVII

MARRIAGE TO PEGGY SHIPPEN AND CONTROVERSY WITH PENNSYLVANIA

1 *Cont. Cong. Jour.,* XII, 1001–3; Reed to Greene, Nov. 5, 1778, in *Lee Paps. (N.Y. Hist. Soc. Colls.,* VI), III, 252; *Proceedings of Arnold's Court Martial,* 51.
2 Arnold to Peggy Shippen, Sept. 25, 1778, in Walker, "Margaret Shippen," *P.M.H.B.,* XXV, 30–1.
3 *Ibid.,* XXV, 32.
4 *Ibid.,* XXV, 32; Arnold, *Arnold,* 228.
5 *Ibid.,* 230; Walker, "Margaret Shippen," *P.M.H.B.,* XXV, 36.
6 *Ibid.,* XXV, 32, 35.
7 *Ibid.,* XXV, 35–6.
8 *Ibid.,* XXV, 38.
9 *Ibid.,* XXV 39, 40; Arnold, *Arnold,* 231–2.
10 Arnold to Matlack, Oct. 6, 1778, in *Reed Paps.* (NYHS), V.
11 Arnold to Matlack, Oct. 12, 1778, in *ibid.,* V.
12 *Pennsylvania Packet* for Nov. 12 and 14, 1778.
13 Cadwalader to Greene, Dec. 5, 1778, in *Lee Paps. (N.Y. Hist. Soc. Colls.,* VI), III, 270–1.
14 Reed to Greene, Nov. 4, 1778, in *ibid.,* III, 250; Van Doren, *Secret History,* 179.
15 *Ibid.,* 181–2.
16 Ibid., 182–3; Arnold to Schuyler, Nov. 30, 1778, and Feb. 8, 1779, in *Schuyler Paps.* (NYPL); Sparks, *Arnold,* 134–5; Arnold, *Arnold,* 240–1.
17 *Proceedings of Arnold's Court Martial,* 7 ff., for Arnold-Matlack corr.; *Pennsylvania Packet,* Feb. 23, 1779; Van Doren, *Secret History,* 189–90; Arnold, *Arnold,* 242.
18 Arnold to Schuyler, Feb. 8, 1779, in *Schuyler Paps.* (NYPL); Arnold. to Peggy Shippen, Feb. 8, 1779, in Walker, "Margaret Shippen," *P.M.H.B.,* XXV, 38.
19 *Ibid.,* XXV, 38–9.

Chapter XVIII

ARNOLD AT BAY

1 Elizabeth Tilghman to Betsy Burd, March 13, 1779, in Walker, "Margaret Shippen," *P.M.H.B.*, XXV, 39; *Proceedings of Arnold's Court Martial*, 153–4, for pleas.

2 *Ibid.*, 243–5, for charges.

3 *Cont. Cong. Jour.*, XIII, 188–9, 324–6.

4 *Cont. Cong. Paps.* (LC), 162, I, f. 173–4; *Pennsylvania Packet*, Feb. 27, March 4 and 6, 1779.

5 *Penna. Archives*, 1st ser., VII, 174; *Cont. Cong. Jour.*, XIII, 412–7.

6 Lewis to Clinton, March 8, and Paca to the Penna. Council, March 9, 1779, in Burnett, *Letters of Members of Cont. Cong.*, IV, 92, 93–5; Silverman, "William Paca," in *Maryland Hist. Mag.*, XXXVII, 16–7.

7 *Cont. Cong. Jour.*, XIII, 417.

8 *Proceedings of Arnold's Court Martial*, 53.

9 Fitzpatrick, *Writings of Washington*, XIV, 420, 448; Sparks, *Writings of Washington*, VI, 518–9.

10 Arnold to Washington, May 5, 1779, in *ibid.*, VI, 523.

11 Arnold to Washington, May 14 and 18, 1779, in *ibid.*, VI, 523, 524; Washington to Reed and to Arnold, May 15, 1779, in Fitzpatrick, *Writings of Washington*, XV, 82, 85–6.

12 Maxwell to Livingston, Oct. 20, 1776, in *A.A.*, 5th ser., II, 1143.

13 Arnold's defense is given in detail in *Proceedings of Arnold's Court Martial*, 40–55.

14 Arnold to McDougall, April 28, 1777, in *Cont. Cong. Paps.* (LC), 152, IV, f. 145.

15 *Pennsylvania Packet*, Sept. 30, 1780.

16 For Jesse Jordan, see Van Doren, *Secret History*, 174–5, 188–9.

17 Reed to Lee, Nov. 21, 1776, in *Lee Paps. (New York Hist. Soc. Colls.*, VI), II, 293–4.

18 The court judgment is in *Proceedings of Arnold's Court Martial*, 144–5. Brigadier General Philip Van Cortlandt wrote as follows of the judgment: "General Arnold being under arrest for improper conduct in Philadelphia while he commanded there, I was one of the Court-martial. . . . There were also on that court four officers who had been at Ticonderoga when Colonel Hasen was called on for trial . . . and we were for cashiering Arnold, but were overruled, and he was sentenced to be reprimanded by the Commander-in-Chief. If all the court had known Arnold's conduct as well as myself, how he and his Brigade Major had robbed merchants in Montreal, he would have been dismissed from serving any longer in our

army, for he would have been cashiered. If so, he would never have had the command at West Point, and Major André might have lived until this day." "Van Cortlandt's Autobiography," in *Mag. of Amer. Hist.,* II, 291.

19 *Cont. Cong. Jour.,* XVI, 161–2; General Orders for April 6, 1780, in Fitz-patrick, *Writings of Washington,* XVIII, 225.

20 Arnold to Deane, March 22, 1780, in *Deane Paps. (New York Hist. Soc. Colls.,* XXII), IV, 116; Council of Penna. to Congress, Feb. 3, 1780, in *Proceedings of Arnold's Court Martial,* 168.

21 Van Doren, *Secret History,* 193.

Chapter XIX

TREASON

1 *Royal Gazette* for February 17, 1779.

2 Arnold to Gates, Oct. 10, 1776, in *A.A.,* 5th ser., II, 982.

3 See Arnold's "Address to the Inhabitants of America," in Arnold, *Arnold,* 330–2, for views after his flight to the British; Arnold to Schuyler, March 8, 1777, in *Schuyler Paps.* (NYPL).

4 Van Doren, *Secret History,* 194; Livingston to Schuyler, Sept. 26, 1777, in *Schuyler Paps.* (NYPL) for Arnold's allusion to his judgment.

5 Arnold to Robert Howe, Sept. 12, 1780, in *Washington Paps.* (LC).

6 *Penna. Archives,* 1st ser., IX, 179; corr. between Hannah and Goodrich in Nov., 1778, is in New Haven Hist. Soc.; Arnold's letter of May 25, 1779, to Booth is in Maryland Hall of Records.

7 See Van Doren, *Secret History,* 196–7, for Stansbury; Weyl, *Treason,* 46, for theory that Peggy may have learned of Stansbury from André.

8 Stansbury's statement is in PRO, A.O. 13/96. Though Stansbury certified on March 4, 1784, that Arnold sent for him about the month of June, 1779, his memory was faulty, for André's record of his conversation with Stans-bury was made on May 10. See André's instructions to Stansbury and his note to Clinton, May 10, 1779, in *Clinton Paps.* (WLCL) and Van Doren, *Secret History,* 439–40.

9 *Ibid.,* 439–40.

10 *Ibid.,* 440; Clinton's comments on Peggy are in his record of conversation with William Pitt for Nov. 14, 1792 in *Clinton Paps.* (WLCL); PRO, T. 64/291 for Peggy's pension.

11 Clinton to his sisters, Oct. 4, 1780, in *Clinton Paps.* (WLCL).

Chapter XX

BARGAINING IN TREASON

1 André to Margaret Chew, May (probably), 1779, and Arnold to André,

May 23, 1779, in Van Doren, *Secret History* (containing Arnold-André corr. in *Clinton Paps*. [WLCL]), 440–1, 441–2.

2 For Ann Bates (née Burns), see her petition for financial assistance, March 17, 1785, in PRO, T. 1/611.

3 Arnold to André, May 23, 1779, in Van Doren, *Secret History*, 441–2.

4 André to Arnold, middle of June, 1779, in *ibid.*, 448.

5 Odell to André, July 18, 1779 (reporting Stansbury's communication), in *ibid.*, 450–1.

6 Peggy's list in *ibid.*, 451–2; Van Doren's opinion in *ibid.*, 209; Odell to André, Dec. 21, 1779, in *ibid.*, 457–8.

7 Stansbury to André, July 11, 1779, and Arnold to André, June 18, 1779, in *ibid.*, 449–50, 448–9.

8 André to Arnold, end of July, 1779, in *ibid.*, 453.

9 Stansbury to André, no date but sent in reply to André's communication at the end of July, in *ibid.*, 453–4.

10 André to Peggy Arnold, Aug. 16, 1779, in *ibid.*, 454; Sargent, *André*, 220; Walker, "Margaret Shippen," in *P.M.H.B.*, XXV, 157–9.

11 Peggy Arnold to André, Oct. 13, 1779, in Van Doren, *Secret History*, 455.

Chapter XXI

Uneasy Months

1 Edward Burd to his father, Oct. 9, 1779, in Walker, "Margaret Shippen," *P.M.H.B.*, XXV, 157. For the "Fort Wilson" affair, see *Penna. Archives*, 1st ser., VII, 732, 735, 744; Reed, *Reed*, II, 149–55, 423–8.

2 Arnold to Congress, Oct. 6, 1779, in *Cont. Cong. Paps.* (LC), 162, I, f. 185.

3 *Cont. Cong. Jour.*, XV, 1147; Arnold to Cong., Oct. 6, 1779, in *Cont. Cong. Paps.* (LC), 162, I, f. 187; Laurens to John Adams, Oct. 4, 1779, in *Letters of Members of Cont. Cong.*, IV, 468.

4 *Lee Paps. (New York Hist. Soc. Colls.,* VI), III, 442.

5 Arnold to Deane, March 22, 1780, in *Deane Paps. (New York Hist. Soc. Colls.,* XXII), IV, 116; Arnold to Washington, March 6 and 20, 1780, in Sparks, *Corr. of American Revolution*, II, 411; Fitzpatrick, *Writings of Washington*, XVIII, 114, 173 for dates of letters.

6 Arnold to Washington, March 20, 1780, in *Corr. of American Revolution*, II, 411; Washington to Arnold, March 28, 1780, in Fitzpatrick, *Writings of Washington*, XVIII, 173; Lincoln, *Naval Records*, 138.

7 *Cont. Cong. Jour.*, XV, 1126, 1134, XVI, 166, 168; Sparks, *Writings of Washington*, VI, 530 for Arnold's letter.

8 Report of Board of Treasury is in *Cont. Cong. Jour.*, XVI, 393–6.

9 *Ibid.*, XVII, 418 (Arnold's letter of May 10 to Congress), 428, 433; *Cont. Cong. Paps.*, 136, IV, f. 233–75 for his letter of May 12, 1780, and en-

closures to Congress. The certificates of Wooster and Taylor are included in enclosures.

10 On the question of Arnold's accounts, James Lovell wrote Nathaniel Peabody on Oct. 3, 1780, "Many are *mightily shocked* at the West Point plot: I presume you escaped *that* degree of surprise respecting Arnold's baseness, as you had been *prepared* here on 'the committee for his accounts.'" Burnett, *Letters to Members of Cont. Cong.*, V, 402. For Gerry's letter of May 18, 1780, see *ibid.*, V, 151–4. By far the best account of Arnold's financial difficulties is in Van Doren, *Secret History*, 254–7.

11 Barbé-Marbois, *Complot*, 33–4.

12 *Ibid.*, 39–47, 135–6.

13 Washington to Arnold, March 28, 1780, in Fitzpatrick, *Writings of Washington*, XVIII, 174.

Chapter XXII

Treason in Full Flower

1 Madison to Jefferson, May 6, 1780, in Burnett, *Letters of Members of Cont. Cong.*, V, 128–9.

2 *Ibid.*, V, 132–4, for committee's report; Stirling's letter to Washington quoted in Freeman, *Washington*, V, 163–4.

3 Washington to Robert Howe, May 25, 1780, and to Joseph Jones, May 31, 1780, in Fitzpatrick, *Writings of Washington*, XVIII, 413, 453.

4 The Arnold-Schuyler letters are in the *Schuyler Paps.* (NYPL).

5 Van Doren, *Secret History*, 458–60.

6 *Ibid.*, 460; Washington to Reed, Oct. 18, 1780, in Fitzpatrick, *Writings of Washington*, XX, 213–5.

7 Livingston to Washington, June 22, 1780, in Burnett, *Letters of Members of Cont. Cong.*, V, 234; Washington to Reed, Oct. 18, 1780, in Fitzpatrick, *Writings of Washington*, XX, 214.

8 Van Doren, *Secret History*, 267–8; *Conn. Archives*, XVIII, 286–7; Hoadly, *Public Records of State of Conn.*, III, 21, 62-3.

9 Clinton to Eden, Aug. 18 and Sept. 1, 1780, in Stevens, *Facsimiles*, 730; Arnold to Clinton, July 15, 1780, in Van Doren, *Secret History*, 464–5.

10 Washington to Livingston, June 29, 1780, in Fitzpatrick, *Writings of Washington*, XIX, 91; Van Doren, *Secret History*, 275.

11 Arnold to Congress, July 17, 1780, in *Cont. Cong. Paps.* (LC), 162, f. 205; *Cont. Cong. Jour.*, XVII, 649. See *P.M.H.B.*, XXII, 213, for Arnold's Penna. estate profits.

12 Van Doren, *Secret History*, 217–20, 276–80, 467–8 (Arnold's letters to Peggy).

13 For a full account of the incident, see Rush, *Occasional Productions*, 79–85.

14 Freeman, *Washington*, V, 183 n. 33; Hamilton to John Laurens, Oct., 1780,

in Lodge, *Hamilton's Works,* VIII, 19; Washington to St. Clair, Aug. 1, 1780, in Fitzpatrick, *Writings of Washington,* XIX, 295 and n. 96.

15 General Orders for Aug. 1, 1780, in *ibid.,* XIX, 302.

16 *Ibid.,* XIX, 309–10, for the West Point command.

17 *Varick Court of Inquiry,* 82.

18 Arnold's instructions to Peggy are in the *Washington Paps.* (LC) and are quoted in detail in Van Doren, *Secret History,* 305; Arnold to Robert Howe, Sept. 12, 1780, in *Washington Paps.* (LC) for his eagerness to see Peggy; Franks to Arnold, Aug. 28, 1780, in *ibid.*

19 Van Doren, *Secret History,* 281, 287, 466 (André to Arnold, July 24, 1780).

20 *Ibid.,* 296–7, 301; Arnold to Lieutenant Francis Barber, Sept. 4, 1780, in *Washington Paps.* (LC); Hart, *Varick Court of Inquiry,* 124, 171.

Chapter XXIII

Growing Menace to West Point

1 Gottschalk, *Lafayette and the Close of the American Revolution,* 131.

2 Arnold to Robert Howe, Aug. 5, 6, and 16, 1780, in *Washington Paps.* (LC); Howe to Arnold, Aug. 14, and to Washington, Sept. 26, 1780, in *ibid.*

3 Van Doren, *Secret History,* 289; Sparks, *Arnold,* 190; Hart, *Varick Court of Inquiry,* 89–91; Sargent, *André,* 280; Smith to Arnold, Aug. 12, 1780, in *Washington Paps.* (LC). Smith came of a family that had fourteen sons and daughters. See Abbatt, *Crisis of the American Revolution,* 10.

4 *Cont. Cong. Jour.,* XVII, 725–7, 771–3; Arnold to Parsons, Aug. 27, and to Greene, Aug. 23, 1780, in *Washington Paps.* (LC); Hart, *Varick Court of Inquiry,* 135, 154–8, 184–5; Van Doren, *Secret History,* 292–5.

5 The Arnold-Sheldon-André corr. is in Sparks, *Writings of Washington,* VII, 522–4. See also Van Doren, *Secret History,* 471.

6 See corr. in *ibid.,* 471–2.

7 *Ibid.,* 309–10; Arnold to Washington, Sept. 11, 1780, in Sparks, *Writings of Washington,* VII, 524.

8 Arnold to Tallmadge, Sept. 13, 1780, in *ibid.,* VII, 524–5; Arnold to André, Sept. 15, 1780, in Van Doren, *Secret History,* 472.

9 Washington to Arnold, Sept. 14, 1780, in Fitzpatrick, *Writings of Washington,* XX, 48; Arnold to André, Sept. 15, 1780, in Van Doren, *Secret History,* 473.

10 Davis, *Burr's Memoirs,* I, 219–20.

11 *Pennsylvania Packet,* Sept. 30, 1780; *P.M.H.B.,* LX, 380–1, for Peggy's comments; Arnold to Udnay Hay, Aug. 16, 1780, in *Washington Paps.* (LC); Leake, *Lamb,* 251; Van Doren, *Secret History,* 461.

12 Quoted in *ibid.,* 303–4.

13 Hannah Arnold to Peggy, Sept. 10, 1780, in Sparks, *Writings of Washington*, VII, 525.

14 Robinson to Arnold, Sept. 17, 1780, in *ibid.*, VII, 525.

15 Dawson, *Record of Smith Trial*, 103–4.

16 Lodge, *Hamilton's Works*, VIII, 20; Barbé-Marbois, *Complot d'Arnold*, 100–1; Hart, *Varick Court of Inquiry*, 133–4; Sparks, *Writings of Washington*, VII, 526–7, for Arnold's two letters, dated Sept. 18, 1780, to Robinson; Van Doren, *Secret History*, 318–9, 471–2.

17 Gottschalk, *Lafayette and the Close of the American Revolution*, 84–5, 129, 131.

18 Clinton's letter of Oct. 11, 1780, in Sargent, *André*, 256–7; his account of the Arnold affair from his ms. history quoted in *ibid.*, 416–7.

19 Clinton to an unknown correspondent, Oct., 1780, and to his sisters, Oct. 4 and 9, 1780, in Van Doren, *Secret History*, 477, 478; Sutherland to Clinton, Oct. 5, 1780, and André to Arnold, June, 1779, in *ibid.*, 494, 448.

20 *Ibid.*, 323; Sargent, *André*, 268; Stone, *Madam Riedesel's Memoirs*, 179. For André's account of what he sought, see Tallmadge to Sparks, Feb. 17, 1834, in *Mag. of Amer. Hist.*, III, 755–6.

Chapter XXIV

THE MEETING WITH ANDRÉ

1 Clinton's "Narrative," in Van Doren, *Secret History*, 484. The flag-of-truce incident is described in Robinson to Clinton, Sept. 24, 1781, in *ibid.*, 474, and in Sargent, *André*, 279.

2 André's letters of Sept. 21, 1780, are in Van Doren, *Secret History*, 484–5.

3 Sutherland to Arnold, Sept. 21, 1780, in *ibid.*, 473; Hart, *Varick Court of Inquiry*, 98–9.

4 *Ibid.*, 123, 124, 140, 170.

5 Sparks, *Arnold*, 192; Sargent, *André*, 283; Dawson, *Record of Smith Trial*, 116.

6 Smith, *Narrative*, 20–37; Sargent, *André*, 281–2.

7 Dawson, *Record of Smith Trial*, 115; Sargent, *André*, 283.

8 *Ibid.*, 284; Robinson's letter of Sept. 24, quoting Arnold's letter of Sept. 21 to him, is in Van Doren, *Secret History*, 474.

9 *Ibid.*, 474; Clinton's "Narrative," in *ibid.*, 485; André's "Statement," in Sargent, *André*, 349. See also *ibid.*, 288–9.

10 Smith, *Narrative*, 31–2; Dawson, *Record of Smith Trial*, 75–6; Arnold to Clinton, Oct. 18, 1780, in Van Doren, *Secret History*, 480–1, for discussion concerning money.

11 For the part taken by the Colquhoun (sometimes spelled "Cahoon" after

the pronunciation) brothers in the affairs of this night, see Dawson, *Record of Smith Trial*, 6–13; Smith, *Narrative*, 31–2. See also Abbatt, *Crisis of the American Revolution*, 9 n. 2.

12 Smith, *Narrative*, 32; Sparks, *Arnold*, 204–5; Sargent, *André*, 290–1, 349–50 (André's "Statement").

13 Campbell, "Smith's House at Haverstraw," in *Mag. of Amer. Hist.*, V, 21–33.

14 Leake, *Lamb*, 258; Robinson to Clinton, Sept. 24, 1780, in Van Doren, *Secret History*, 475; Dawson, *Record of Smith Trial*, 72. It has been suggested that the *Vulture* returned the fire since, years afterward, balls larger than 4 lbs. were found ashore. See Abbatt, *Crisis of the American Revolution*, 13 n. 5. But Livingston may have used a larger piece than a 4-pounder.

15 The passes are printed in Sargent, *André*, 298.

16 André's "Statement," in *ibid.*, 350.

17 *Ibid.*, 350; Dawson, *André Paps.*, 180–1. The papers given André were six in number:

1. An estimate of the forces at West Point and its dependencies, Sept. 13, 1780; showing a total of 3,086 men of all sorts.

2. An estimate of the number of men necessary to man the works at West Point and its vicinity, showing a total, exclusive of the artillery corps, of 2,438 troops.

3. Artillery orders issued by Major Bauman, Sept. 5, 1780, showing the disposition of that corps in an alarm.

4. Major Bauman's return of the ordnance in the different forts, batteries, etc. at West Point and its dependencies, Sept. 5, 1780, showing the distribution of 100 pieces.

5. Copy of a statement of the condition of affairs submitted by Washington to a Council of War, Sept. 6, 1780.

6. "Remarks on Works at Wt. Point, a Copy to be transmitted to his Excell'y General Washington, Sep'r 1780. . . ." This was a detailed account of the strength and weakness of Forts Arnold, Putnam, Webb, and Wyllys, Redoubts 1–4, and the North and South Redoubts.

18 André's "Statement," in Sargent, *André*, 350; Van Doren, *Secret History*, 337.

19 Smith, *Narrative*, 35; Winsor, *Narr. and Crit. Hist. of Amer.*, VI, 456; André's "Statement," in Sargent, *André*, 350.

20 Dawson, *Record of Smith Trial*, 17–8; Smith, *Narrative*, 38–9.

21 *Ibid.*, 43; Dawson, *Record of Smith Trial*, 43–5; Sargent, *André*, 350.

22 Dawson, *Record of Smith Trial*, 76; Smith, *Narrative*, 43–8; Abbatt, *Crisis of the American Revolution*, 23; Sparks, *Arnold*, 219.

23 For André's aspirations, see Tallmadge to Sparks, Feb. 17, 1834, in *Mag. of Amer. Hist.*, III, 755.

Chapter XXV

DEBACLE

1   For the capture of André, see Dawson, *Record of Smith Trial*, 38, 52, 56; Dawson, *André Paps.*, 1–7; Sargent, *André*, 311–21; Winsor, *Narr. and Crit. Hist. of Amer.*, VI, 466; Abbatt, *Crisis of the American Revolution*, 26–32.

2   For Sheldon's arrest, see Tallmadge to Deane, Oct. 27, 1780, in *Deane Paps., Conn. Hist. Soc. Coll.*, XXIII, 155–6.

3   André to Washington, Sept. 24, 1780, in Sparks, *Writings of Washington*, VII, 531–2.

4   Frank's and Varick's suspicions of Smith, Arnold's table quarrel, and his later altercation with his aides may be found in Hart, *Varick Court of Inquiry*, 98, 126–7, 150, 173–7.

5   Rush, *Occasional Productions*, 82; Dawson, *Record of Smith Trial*, 80; Lafayette, *Memoirs*, 254–5; Moore, *Diary of the American Revolution*, II, 325.

6   Sparks, *Writings of Washington*, VII, 530.

7   See McHenry's letter in Moore, *Diary of the American Revolution*, II, 325.

8   Hart, *Varick Court of Inquiry*, 190.

9   *Ibid.*, 130, 190; Dawson, *André Paps.*, 148; Rush, *Occasional Productions*, 82–3, for Washington's comment.

10   For flight, see Stevens, *Facsimiles*, 739; *Mass. Hist. Soc. Colls.*, 2nd ser., IV, 51–2; *Mass. Hist. Soc. Proc.*, 2nd ser., XII, 346–8; *Mass. Hist. Soc. Colls.* (*Heath Paps.*, III), 7th ser., V, 171–2.

11   Gottschalk, *Lafayette and the Close of the American Revolution*, 137; Lodge, *Hamilton's Works*, VIII, 15–16.

12   For scenes with Peggy, see Hart, *Varick Court of Inquiry*, 131–2, 189–93; Thacher, *Military Journal*, 471–2; Lodge, *Hamilton's Works*, VIII, 16–7, 22–3; Tower, *La Fayette in the American Revolution*, II, 167.

13   Arnold to Washington, Sept. 25, 1780 in Sparks, *Writings of Washington*, VII, 533.

14   Lodge, *Hamilton's Works*, VIII, 16–7; Tower, *La Fayette in the American Revolution*, II, 167.

15   Davis, *Burr's Memoirs*, I, 219.

16   Quoted from the *Shippen Paps.* by Walker, "Margaret Shippen," in *P.M.H.B.*, XXV, 156. See also *ibid.*, XXV, 152–6, 178–90.

17   Varick's admission is in Jones, *New York during the Revolutionary War*, I, 745–6.

18   The board consisted of Major Generals Greene, Stirling, St. Clair, Lafayette, Howe, and Steuben; and Brigadier Generals Parsons, Clinton, Knox, Glover, Patterson, Hand, Huntington, and Stark. Wayne was omitted, possibly

because André alluded to him, none too generously, in a satirical poem, the "Cow Chase" (Sargent, *André*, 236–45), but probably because of being on detached service (Fitzpatrick, *Writings of Washington*, XX, 107; Freeman, *Washington*, V, 213 n. 103; Stillé, *Wayne*, 234–5). For letters of Robinson, Clinton, and Arnold, see Sparks, *Writings of Washington*, VII, 533–5.

19 *Minutes of a Court of Inquiry upon André*, 17, 22–3.

20 Greene, *Greene*, II, 235; Gottschalk, *Lafayette and the Close of the American Revolution*, 140; Kapp, *Steuben*, 289.

21 Clinton to Washington, Sept. 30, 1780, in Sparks, *Writings of Washington*, VII, 539; Robertson to Washington, Oct. 2, 1780, in *ibid.*, VII, 541–3; Robertson to Clinton, Oct. 1, 1780, in Van Doren, *Secret History*, 488–9; Greene, *Greene*, II, 236–9.

22 Simcoe, *Military Journal*, 294; Lodge, *Hamilton's Works*, VIII, 28; Van Doren, *Secret History*, 366–7; Freeman, *Washington*, V, 217 n. 119.

23 "Autobiography of Ogden," in *New Jersey Hist. Soc. Proc.*, 2nd ser., XII, 23–4.

24 An excellent bibliography of André's last hours and execution is in Winsor, *Narr. and Crit. Hist. of Amer.*, VI, 467. See also Freeman, *Washington*, V, 221 n. 137; Abbatt, *Crisis of the American Revolution*, 69–76.

25 Washington to Rochambeau, Oct. 10, 1780, in Fitzpatrick, *Writings of Washington*, XX, 151; Arnold to Washington, Oct. 1, 1780, in Sparks, *Writings of Washington*, VII, 541.

26 *Ibid.*, VII, 540–1.

Chapter XXVI

ATTEMPTS AT INFLUENCE AND VINDICATION

1 *Lloyd's Evening Post*, Dec. 11–13, 1780.

2 *Pennsylvania Packet*, Sept. 30, 1780; André to Peggy, Aug. 16, 1779, in *Clinton Paps.* (WLCL); *P.M.H.B.*, XXV, 158, 160–1.

3 *Ibid.*, XXV, 162–3.

4 Arnold to Clinton, Oct. 18, 1780, in *Clinton Paps.* (WLCL).

5 Clinton to Germain, Oct. 30, 1780 in *ibid.* The expense money did not include the £210 paid by the British in July to Arnold's agent, Samuel Wallis. Arnold's investment arrangements with a London firm are explained in a letter from his broker, James Meyrick, Jan. 30, 1781, in *Mag. of Amer. Hist.*, II, 55–6.

How much Arnold received in current reckoning is an interesting question. A comparison of dollar and pound values in the 1780's and their equivalent in present-day purchasing power is a hazardous and uncertain enterprise since the interpretation depends upon the basis of computation, which itself may be open to criticism. Thus Carl Van Doren in 1941 figured that £6,000 was worth three or four times as much in the eighteenth as in the twentieth century. He therefore multiplied the £6,000 Arnold received by 3 and 4, and obviously gave the pound the 1941 round equivalent of $5.00. This would have meant, as he admitted, that Arnold received "roughly" between $90,000 and $120,000 (Van Doren, *Secret History,* 387). These figures seem excessive.

My own figure of $55,000, which, in turn, may be too low, was reached in this manner. In April, 1780, the Congressional committee working on Arnold's accounts figured in terms of a dollar-pound rate of 3 1/3 to 1, the dollar being in silver. Though 1780 and 1781 were years of great inflation, Arnold invested most of his money in good stocks and kept it there for years. Thus if one selects a "normal" year when the dollar had stabilized, it will give a truer picture of Arnold's price of treason than the inflated year of the treason itself. Accordingly I resorted first to the *Warren and Pearson Wholesale Price Index,* which has been compiled for the years 1749–1932. By this index prices rose from 92 (letting the years 1910–14 equal 100) in the "normal" year of 1785 to 95 in 1932, a year of acute depression. I then turned to the *Bureau of Labor Statistics Wholesale Price Index* to see how prices have changed since 1932. The *BLS Index* (letting the years 1947–49 equal 100) was 42 in 1932 and 112 in 1952, the increase being 2.67 times. In terms of the first index, therefore, one would find (by multiplying the 1932 index at 95 by 2.67) the 1952 index at 254. The difference between 1785 prices at 92 and 1952 prices at 254 is 2.76 times. Thus $20,000 (£6,000 x $3 1/3) x 2.76 = $55,200, the approximate equivalent today of the capital sum of £6,000. The assumptions used here concerning the dollar-pound exchange rate and the price increase since 1785 are conservative compared with Van Doren's. Still, even if one accepts the dollar-pound rate of 5 to 1, which was the rate Van Doren used, the result in terms of the price increase of 2.76 times is only $82,800, which is $7,200 short of his lowest estimate. Certainly, however, one can be reasonably safe in concluding that Arnold was given the equivalent of between $55,000 and $85,000 in modern dollars. Whatever the exact equivalent, he received a very respectable (?) sum indeed.

6 PRO, T. 64/291; Clinton's notes on conversation with William Pitt, Nov. 14, 1792, in *Clinton Paps.* (WLCL).

7 Letter of Edward Shippen, Sept. 19, 1806 in Arnold, *Arnold,* 413; *A List of the Officers of the Army,* published by the British War Office, April 28, 1783; Van Doren, *Secret History,* 384–7. The land grant has often been considered as having been given for service in the West Indies during the 1790's, but this is not quite true. As a Loyalist, Arnold was entitled to these lands, and he received certain pecuniary and residential exemptions because of activities in the West Indies. See PRO, C.O. 42/88, f. 867, 871.

8 *William Smith's Diary,* entry for Oct. 5, 1780,

9 In addition to Rivington's *Royal Gazette* for Oct. 11, 1780, Arnold's address to the American people may be found in Arnold, *Arnold,* 330–2.

10 The proclamation may be found in the *Royal Gazette* for Oct. 25, 1780, *Force Transcripts* (LC), and Arnold, *Arnold,* 332–4. For the gratitude of Mirailles's widow, see Maria Josera Elixis de la Puente to Arnold, July 8, 1780, in *Washington Paps.* (LC).

11 Arnold to Germain, Oct. 28, 1780, in *Clinton Paps.* (WLCL).

12 Washington to Rochambeau, Sept. 27, 1780, in Fitzpatrick, *Writings of Washington,* XX, 97; Lafayette to Rochambeau, Sept. 26, 1780, in Gottschalk, *Lafayette and the Close of the American Revolution,* 140.

13 Vergennes's letter is in Doniol, *Histoire de la participation de la France,* IV, 397; Andrew Elliot to Wm. Eden, Oct. 4, 1780, in *Add. MS.* (BM), 34, 417, f. 220. See Washington's letter to the Board of War to combat British efforts at sowing jealousy, in Fitzpatrick, *Writings of Washington,* XX, 256.

14 *New Jersey Archives,* 2d ser., V, 11; Moore, *Diary of the Revolution,* II, 327, 333, 337; Atwater, *New Haven,* 63–4; Palmer, *Steuben,* 234–5.

15 Scammel's comment is in Dawson, *André Paps.,* 67; Huntington's, in Burnett, *Letters of Members of Cont. Cong.,* V, 421; Wayne's, in Stillé, *Wayne,* 236.

16 Washington to Laurens, Oct. 13, 1780, in Fitzpatrick, *Writings of Washington,* XX, 173.

17 See Washington's comments in *ibid.,* XX, 264, 189.

Chapter XXVII

THE VIRGINIA AND NEW LONDON EXPEDITIONS

1 For a description of Arnold's activities, see the report to Eden, Oct. 7, 1780, in *Add. MSS.* (BM), 34, 417, f. 215.

2 Rodney to Germain, Dec. 22, 1780, in Hist. MSS. Commission Rep't, *Stopford-Sackville MSS.,* II, 193.

3 Damier to Germain, Oct. 13, 1780, in *ibid.,* II, 184.

4 Clinton to Arnold, Dundas, and Simcoe, Dec. 14, 1780, in *Clinton Paps.* (WLCL).

5 For the kidnapping plot, see corr. between Washington and Lee in Sparks, *Writings of Washington,* VII, 545–9; Lee, *Memoirs,* II, 159–87.

6 Arnold to the Officer Commanding the Party on Shore, Jan. 2, 1781, in *Arnold Paps.* (NYHS). The best account of the war in Virginia is Eckenrode, *The Revolution in Virginia.* For Arnold's part, see also Ward, *War of the Revolution,* II, 867–74; Carrington, *Battles of the American Revolution,* 584–97.

7 Arnold to Clinton, Jan. 23, 1781, in *Clinton Paps.* (WLCL); Fortescue, *History of the British Army,* III, 359.

8 Morris to Jona Hudson, Jan. 16, 1781, in *Arnold Paps.* (NYHS); R. H. Lee to Washington, Jan. 7, 1781, in Ballagh, *Letters of Richard Henry Lee,* II, 212–3; Freeman, *Washington,* V, 252–3.

9 Arbuthnot to Robertson, March 3, 1781, in *Clinton Paps.* (WLCL).

10 Arnold to Clinton, Jan. 23, 1781, in *ibid.;* Rochambeau to Washington, March 18, 1781, in *Washington Paps.* (LC); for comparison of Arnold's situation with that of Cornwallis, see W. B. Willcox, "Rhode Island in British Strategy, 1780–81," in *Jour. of Modern Hist.,* XVII, 317–21.

11 Fitzpatrick, *Writings of Washington,* XXI, 278.

12 The maneuvers of Lafayette and Steuben with Phillips are well described in Gottschalk, *Lafayette and the Close of the American Revolution,* 204–33, and Palmer, *Steuben,* 259–69. For Arnold's own account, see his letter of May 16, 1781, in *Clinton Paps.* (WLCL) and in Arnold, *Arnold,* 344–7. Dundas's opinion is in his letter of May 12, 1781, in *Clinton Paps.* (WLCL).

13 Jones on Clinton is in Jones, *New York during the Revolutionary War,* II, 206; on Smith, in *ibid.,* II, 209; on Arnold, in *ibid.,* II, 207, 177–8, 208, 333, 179. See also Mackenzie, *Diary,* II, 540, for military opinion.

14 Van Doren, *Secret History,* 419–20.

15 For Arnold's difficulties with Symonds, see Arnold's deposition concerning the agreement, in PRO, H.C.A. 32/299; Williams's petition, Dec. 4, 1781, in PRO, T. 1/570; the King's reply in W. Ellis to Treasury, March 23, 1782, in PRO, T. 1/570.

16 Officers' memorial to Treasury, April 8, 1782, and their letter of May 2, 1782, in PRO, T. 1/570; Collier to Arnold, April 16, 1782, in PRO, T. 1/570; Arnold to H. Strachey, April 19, 1782, in PRO, T. 1/570.

17 Lawrence, *Foot-Prints,* 71; Arnold's claim for prize money, April 3, 1783, in PRO, T. 1/590; claim on Williams's estate in *Arnold Paps.* (NYHS); Jones, *New York during the Revolutionary War,* II, 177.

18 *William Smith's Diary* for Aug. 1, 1781; Kyte, "A Projected British Attack upon Philadelphia in 1781," in *P.M.H.B.,* LXXVI, 379–93.

19 Record of 40th Foot drawn from War Office in London, in *Sesquicentennial of the Battle of Groton Heights and the Burning of New London,* 95–6.

20 "Stephen Hempstead's Narrative," in Harris, *Groton Heights,* 49; "Court-Martial," in *ibid.,* 113–5.

21 *Ibid.,* 35–7, 266–70. Ward places the onus on Lieutenant Colonel Buskirk of the New Jersey Volunteers (Ward, *War of the Revolution,* II, 627). But Buskirk was with the artillery, which did not get into the action; he did not arrive until after the fort had fallen (Arnold's report to Clinton, Sept. 8, 1781, in Harris, *Groton Heights,* 102).

22 *Ibid.,* 100 n. 1; Arnold's report in *ibid.,* 98–107; Clinton's General Orders in *ibid.,* 111 the spy's report in *Mass. Hist. Soc. Colls.* (*Heath Paps., III*), 7th ser., V, 265.

23 Quoted in Arnold, *Arnold,* 353–4.

24 Ward to Trumbull, Sept. 8, 1781, in *Arnold Paps.* (NYHS); Trumbull to Washington, Sept. 15, 1781, in Harris, *Groton Heights,* 163.

Chapter XXVIII

A New Start in England and New Brunswick

1 Clinton's memo of conversation, Nov. 5, 1781, in *Clinton Paps.* (WLCL); Shoemaker quotations in *P.M.H.B.,* XXV, 163; ship information in Lawrence, *Foot-Prints,* 71.

2 Sargent, *André,* 453; Franklin to R. R. Livingston, March 4, 1782, in Bigelow, *Franklin,* III, 48; Drake, *Historic Fields and Mansions of Middlesex,* 258.

3 Arnold's paper is printed in full as an appendix in Arnold, *Arnold,* 419–27.

4 *Ibid.,* 363–4; Van Schaack, *Peter Van Schaack,* 147.

5 Arnold's memorial to the commissioners and Stansbury's certificate are in PRO, A.O. 13/96 and are printed in Taylor, *Some New Light.*

6 Appraisals by Footman and Coxe are in *Miscell. Paps.* (HSP); Arnold's instructions to Shippen in *P.M.H.B.,* XXV, 452; Van Doren, *Secret History,* 268.

7 PRO, A.O. 13/96.

8 Quoted in Lawrence, *Foot-Prints,* 71.

9 Arnold's store was lot no. 1389. See *Land Deeds* (NBM); Sabine, *Loyalists of the American Revolution,* I, 550.

10 Arnold, *Arnold,* 392; Appendix IV above for Arnold's will.

11 Peggy to Edward Shippen, March 6, 1785, in *P.M.H.B.,* XXV, 453.

12 For evidence of Hannah's occasional residence in New Haven, see her note of Jan. 1, 1792, from New Haven on "Exchange for £15 Sterling," in *Gratz Coll.* (HSP). See also Peggy to Richard and Henry, Nov., 1802, in *P.M.H.B.,* XXV, 482.

13 Webster, *Historical Guide to New Brunswick,* 58; Maxwell, *An Outline of History of Central New Brunswick;* Arnold's real estate transactions in Fredericton are in *York County (New Brunswick) Records of Deeds,* I, nos. 120, 121, 122, 123, 185, 287, 383.

14 For difficulties with borrowers, see Nathan Miller to Arnold, Feb. 1, 1786, in *Emmett Coll.* (NYPL) and Arnold's letter concerning Capt. Abiathel Camp, Feb. 1, 1788, in *American Art. Assoc. Cat.,* Nov. 13, 1935; Shackford's account in Wells, *Campobello,* 446, and "Arnold at Campobello," Folder 23 (NBM).

15 For rent of house, see Arnold to Capt. John Colvell, Feb. 8, 1789, in possession of Mrs. Jean (Mrs. H. G. L.) Sweet of St. John, who kindly sent me a copy.

16 For suit, see the *Arnold-Hayt Paps.* donated by J. Fraser Winslow, K.C., to

the Library Archives, University of New Brunswick; Stockton, *The Judges of New Brunswick,* 65–70.

17 Peggy to Edward Shippen, June 30, 1788, and Edward Burd to Jasper Yeates, Nov. 15, 1789, in *P.M.H.B.,* XXV, 168; Arnold, *Arnold,* 372.

18 Peggy to Betsy Burd, July 5, 1790, in *P.M.H.B.,* XXV, 456–7.

19 *Ibid.,* XXV, 458.

20 Quoted in Arnold, *Arnold,* 374.

21 Hayt to Winslow, 1789, in Raymond, *Winslow Paps.,* 370; Webster, *Historical Guide to New Brunswick,* 16.

22 Original copy of power-of-attorney to Bliss and Putnam is in NBM.

23 Arnold to Bliss, Feb. 26, 1792, in *Odell Coll.* (NBM).

Chapter XXIX

LAST VENTURES AND DEATH

1 Cobbett, *Parliamentary History,* XXIX, 1518–9.

2 Peggy to her father, July 6, 1792, in *P.M.H.B.,* XXV, 461.

3 For duel, see Peggy's letter in *ibid.,* XXV, 461–2; Lord Hawke's statement in Arnold, *Arnold,* 380–1.

4 Arnold to Clinton, July 23, Oct. 17, Nov. 14, and Dec. 3, 1792; Peggy to Clinton, Nov. 13, 1792; Clinton to Arnold, Aug. 2, 1792; Clinton's notes made in Sept., 1792; Pitt to Clinton, Nov. 10, 1792—all in *Clinton Paps.* (WLCL).

5 Arnold to Bliss, Feb. 10 and March 19, 1794, in NBM.

6 Broglie, *Talleyrand's Memoirs,* I, 174–5.

7 Peggy to Richard Arnold, Aug., 1794, in *P.M.H.B.,* XXV, 464.

8 Sparks, *Arnold,* 334–5; *Gentleman's Mag.,* LXIV, 685.

9 Arnold to Bliss, Jan. 3, 1795, in NBM.

10 Fortescue, *Hist. of the British Army,* IV, 376. The best monograph on the subject is Willyams, *Campaign in the West Indies.* For an indication of Arnold's activities in supply, see the communication, dated Feb. 11, 1795, from John Jaffray, commissary general, ordering payment to Arnold of £2211. 6s. for fresh beef, in *Miscell. Paps.* (NYPL).

11 Arnold to Bliss, Jan. 3, 1795, in NBM; the resolution is in Arnold, *Arnold,* 388 n. 2.

12 Peggy to Bliss, Dec. 5, 1795, in NBM; Arnold to Bliss, Sept. 5, 1795, and Aug. 15, 1795, in NBM; Adair to Arnold, Aug. 8, 1791, in NBM; Arnold to Blakesley, Sept. 20, 1794, in New Haven Colony Hist. Soc.

13 Arnold to Bliss, Feb. 20, 1796 in *Odell Coll.* (NBM).

14 Arnold to Bliss, Sept. 5, 1795 in NBM; Arnold, *Arnold,* 388 n. 2 for his reply to the merchants' and planters' resolution; Peggy to Bliss, Dec. 5, 1795, in NBM.

15 Arnold to Cornwallis, Dec. 29, 1796, in Arnold, *Arnold,* 389.

16 Arnold to Spencer, June 1, 1797, and to York, April 22, 1798, in *ibid.,* 389, 390; Arnold to Liverpool, April 26, 1799, in *Liverpool Paps., Add. MSS.* (BM), 38,311, f. 9.

17 Application in PRO, C.O. 42/88, f. 875–6, 879; copy of Portland's order in PRO, C.O. 42/88 f. 871.

18 Arnold to King, June 19, June 24 and July 18, 1800, in PRO, C.O. 42/88, f. 872–3, 863–5, and 867.

19 For privateering information, see *P.M.H.B.,* XXIII, 188–92, and Peggy's letters in *ibid.,* XXV, 473, 482, 486, 488–9.

20 *Ibid.,* XXV, 473; Arnold to Bliss, Aug. 15, 1795, Jan. 7 and Nov. 25, 1797, Sept. 19, 1800, in NBM.

21 For information on the Arnolds' friends in London, see Taylor, *Some New Light,* 30–4, 58.

22 Arnold to Bliss, Sept. 19, 1800, in NBM; Peggy to Betsy Burd, May 10, 1800, in *P.M.H.B.,* XXV, 471.

23 Arnold's will is in Appendix IV above; Peggy to Richard Arnold, Aug., 1794, in Arnold, *Arnold,* 387.

24 Peggy to Edward Arnold, July 1, 1801, in Taylor, *Some New Light,* 59–60; Ann Fitch to Edward Shippen, June 29, 1801, in *P.M.H.B.,* XXV, 472–3.

25 Taylor, *Some New Light,* 25–7.

Chapter XXX

The Summing Up

1 Peggy to Edward Arnold, July 31, 1801, in Taylor, *Some New Light,* 61. From Peggy's letters to her sister and father, it would appear that she suffered from cancer of the womb. See *P.M.H.B.,* XXV, 486–7, 490, 491.

2 There have recently come to light bits of evidence, admittedly inconclusive, which indicate that Greene may have realized small private gains from selling to himself when he served as quartermaster general. See Freeman, *Washington,* V, 505–9.

3 Fortescue, *Hist. of the British Army,* III, 410.

4 Corner, *Rush's Autobiography,* 158; Pvt. Samuel Downing's comments are in Bolton, *Private Soldier under Washington,* 244.

5 The ablest British field commander was Lord Rawdon, later Earl of Moira and Marquis of Hastings. Howe had real ability but was too lethargic or politically disinclined to capitalize on the numerous advantageous positions he achieved over Washington. Clinton's caution killed his chances of bringing the war to a successful conclusion. Cornwallis could hit hard, but his blindness to sea power was fatal. Burgoyne, an unconventional soldier in his addiction to literature, was too conventionally-minded in a military way for

so difficult a campaign in northern New York. The officer most resembling Arnold in temperament was the cavalry leader, Banastre Tarleton, whose rashness led him into disaster at Cowpens. Potentially the best British officer in America was one who had scant opportunity to display command abilities thanks to the hatred of Lord George Germain, namely, Sir Guy Carleton, later Lord Dorchester, Clinton's successor as commander-in-chief in the last months of the war. In battlefield performance, none of these officers, as the saying goes, belonged in the same league with Arnold.

6   French, *General Gage's Informers*, 147–201; *Campaign of 1776, Memoirs of the Long Island Hist. Soc.*, III, 281 n. 2; Abbatt, *Crisis of the American Revolution*, 2–3; Einstein, *Divided Loyalties*, 3–50.

7   In the discussion of Burr, Vallandigham, and the World War Two traitors, I have found especially helpful Weyl's fine study, *Treason*, 110–62, 283–93, 342–7, 376–88, 392–6.

Appendix II

Was Arnold at the Battle of Freeman's Farm?

1   Wilkinson, *Memoirs*, I, 245; Livingston to Washington, Jan. 14, 1778 (the italics are mine), in Wharton, *Revolutionary Diplomatic Correspondence of the U.S.*, II, 414.

2   Gordon, *Rise, Progress and Establishment of the U.S.*, II, 250; Bancroft, *Hist. of the U.S.*, IX, 410; Stevens, "Benedict Arnold and His Apologist," in *Mag. of Amer. Hist.*, IV, 181–91; Channing, *Hist. of the U.S.*, III, 276–8; Montross, *Rag, Tag and Bobtail*, 225–7; Patterson, *Gates*, 155.

3   The letters of Varick and Livingston may be found in the *Schuyler Paps.* (NYPL) and are published in full or in part in Arnold, *Arnold*, 178–81, 189.

4   "Autobiography of Philip Van Cortlandt," in *Mag. of Amer. Hist.*, II, 286; Poor's letter is in Moore, *Diary of the American Revolution*, I, 497–8.

5   Winsor, *Narr. and Crit. Hist. of Amer.*, VI, 357; Arnold, "Benedict Arnold at Saratoga," in *United Service Mag.* (Sept., 1880); Guild, *Chaplain Smith and the Baptists*, 209; Neilson, *Burgoyne's Campaign*, 148–9; *Records of the Council of Safety and Governor and Council of the State of Vermont*, I, 176.

6   "Diary of Joshua Pell, Junior," in *Mag. of Amer. Hist.*, II, 109; Marshall, *Washington*, III, 277; Marshall, *Washington*, (revised edition), I, 201.

7   Riedesel, *Memoirs*, I, 150; Stedman, *Origin, Progress and Termination of the American War*, II; Botta, *Hist. of the War of Independence*, II, 11; Lossing, *Schuyler*, II, 344; Fiske, *American Revolution*, I, 327; Wilson, *Hist. of the American People*, II, 278; Dawson, *Battles of the U.S.*, I, 289–90; Carrington, *Battles of the American Revolution*, 342–4; Greene, *Revolu-*

tionary War, 116–8; Fortescue, *Hist. of the British Army,* III, 234–6; Nickerson, *Turning Point of the Revolution,* 308–16, 473–7; Ward, *War of the Revolution,* II, 506–12, 941–2. See also the critical discussions in Winsor, *Narr. and Crit. Hist. of Amer.,* VI, 315–6, 357 n. 2.

8 Arnold to Gates, Sept. 22, 1777, in *Gates Paps.* (NYHS); Wilkinson, *Memoirs,* I, 255.

9 Libby, "A Critical Examination of Gordon's History of the American Revolution," in *Annual Rep't of the Amer. Hist. Assoc. for 1899,* I, 367–88.

10 See M. DeLisle's comment in *Miscell. Paps.* (NYPL).

11 Dawson, *Battles of the U.S.,* I, 290; Trevelyan, *The American Revolution,* IV, 172 n.

Appendix III

Did Arnold Offer to Give Himself Up for André?

1 Sargent, *André* 375, 465–7; Abbatt, *Crisis of the American Revolution,* 64 n. 6.

Bibliography

A complete bibliography of Arnold would be almost as extensive as one on the Revolution. Hence included below are by no means all of the works that have been consulted or have proved helpful but simply those to which reference has been made.

As this book goes to press, an admirable study of the treason has appeared, James Thomas Flexner's *The Traitor and the Spy* (New York, 1953). It presents much new material on the early lives of André and Peggy Shippen, an area with which I have not concerned myself in a biography devoted to Arnold. I have discovered little in Mr. Flexner's book to induce me to alter my principal conclusions on Arnold; in fact, we agree at many points. Among minor differences, he raises a reasonable doubt as to Arnold's desertion from the army when a boy, but it is a point on which the evidence is too sketchy to obtain complete verification. At best, the desertion can be argued either way.

Adams, C. F., *Familiar Letters of John Adams and His Wife Abigail Adams during the Revolution* (New York, 1876)

Additional MSS., British Museum

Alden, C. S., and Westcott, A., *The United States Navy* (New York, 1943)

Allen, E., *Narrative* (Burlington, 1849)

Allen, G. W., *A Naval History of the American Revolution* (2 vols., Boston, 1913)

American Art Association Catalogue, Nov. 13, 1935

Appleton's Cyclopedia of American Biography

Arnold, B., *Minute Book,* June-August, 1768, New Haven Colony Historical Society

Arnold, B.—*Proceedings of a General Court Martial of the Line . . . For the Trial of Major General Arnold* (Philadelphia, 1780)

Arnold, B.—"Benedict Arnold's Regimental Memorandum Book," in *Pennsylvania Magazine of History and Biography,* VIII (1884)

Arnold, B., *Waste Book,* April, 1773—March, 1780, New Haven Colony Historical Society

Arnold Correspondence and Lieut. George Mathew's Narrative, in *Historical Magazine,* I (1905)

"Arnold's Investment of the British Subsidy," in *Magazine of American History,* II, Pt. I (1878)

"Arnold Letters," in *Magazine of History,* III (1906)

Arnold Papers, New York Historical Society

Arnold-Hayt Papers, Library Archives, University of New Brunswick

Arnold, E. S., *The Arnold Memorial, William Arnold of Providence and Pawtuxet, and a Genealogy of His Descendants* (Rutland, 1935)

Arnold, I. N., "Benedict Arnold at Saratoga," in *United Service Magazine* (1880)

Arnold, I. N., *The Life of Benedict Arnold* (Chicago, 1897)

Arnold, S. G., *History of the State of Rhode Island* (2 vols., New York, 1860)

Atwater, E. E., *History of the City of New Haven* (New York, 1887)

Baldwin, A. M., *The New England Clergy and the American Revolution* (Durham, N.C., 1928)

Ballagh, J. C., *Letters of Richard Henry Lee* (2 vols., New York, 1911)

Bancroft, G., *History of the United States* (10 vols., Boston, 1837–74)

Barbé-Marbois, F., *Complot d'Arnold et de Sir Henry Clinton* (Paris, 1816)

"Barnfare's Letter," in *Historical Magazine,* 2d ser., VI (1869)

Beardsley, E. E., *Life and Times of William Samuel Johnson* (New York, 1876)

Biddle Collection, Historical Society of Pennsylvania

Bigelow, J., *Life of Benjamin Franklin* (3 vols., Philadelphia, 1874)

Boardman, R. S., *Roger Sherman* (Philadelphia, 1938)

Bolton, C. K., *The Private Soldier under Washington* (New York, 1902)

Botta, C., *History of the War of Independence* (2 vols., New Haven, 1840)

Boutell, L. H., *Life of Roger Sherman* (Chicago, 1896)

Bradley, A. G., *Lord Dorchester* (Toronto, 1912)

Broglie, Duc de, *Memoirs of the Prince de Talleyrand* (5 vols., New York, 1891)

Bronson, H., *History of Waterbury* (Waterbury, 1858)

Burgoyne, J., *State of the Expedition from Canada* (London, 1780)

Burnett, E. C., *Letters of Members of the Continental Congress* (8 vols., Washington, D.C., 1921–36)

Burnett, E. C., *The Continental Congress* (New York, 1941)

Campaign of 1776, Memoirs of the Long Island Historical Society, III (1878)

Canadian Archives Reports

Carrington, H. B., *Battles of the American Revolution* (New York, 1876)

Carroll, C., *Journal* (Baltimore, 1876)

Carson, H. L., "The Case of the Sloop Active," in *Pennsylvania Magazine of History and Biography,* XVI (1892)

Caulkins, F. M., *History of Norwich* (Hartford, 1866)

Channing, E., *A History of the United States* (6 vols., New York, 1906–25)

Clark, G. L., *History of Connecticut* (New York, 1914)

Clinton Papers, W. L. Clements Library, Ann Arbor

Cobbett, W., *Parliamentary History of England from the Norman Conquest in 1066 to the Year 1803* (36 vols., London, 1806–20)

Codman, J., *Arnold's Expedition to Quebec* (New York, 1902)

Coffin, R. P. T., *Kennebec, Cradle of Americans* (New York, 1937)

Connecticut Gazette

Connecticut Journal and Newsboy

Continental Congress, Papers of, Library of Congress

Corner, G. W., *The Autobiography of Benjamin Rush* (Princeton, 1948)

Curtis, E. E., *The Organization of the British Army in the American Revolution* (New Haven, 1926)

Davis, M. L., *Memoirs of Aaron Burr* (2 vols., New York, 1855)

Dawson, H. B., *Battles of the United States* (2 vols., New York, 1858)

Dawson, H. B., *Papers Concerning the Capture and Detention of Major John André* (Yonkers, 1866)

Dawson, H. B., *Record of the Trial of Joshua Hett Smith, Esq., for Alleged Complicity in the Treason of Benedict Arnold* (Morrisania, N.Y., 1866)

Deane, J. W., Drowne, H. T., and Hubbard, E., *Genealogy of the Family of Arnold* (Boston, 1879)

Deane Papers, Connecticut Historical Society Collections, XXIII (1930)

Deane Papers, New York Historical Society Collections, XIX-XXIII (1886–90)

Decker, M., *Benedict Arnold, Son of the Havens* (New York, 1932)

Dictionary of American Biography

Digby—*The British Invasion from the North . . . with the Journal of Lieut. William Digby* (Albany, 1887)

Doniol, H., *Histoire de la Participation de la France a l'Etablissement des États-Unis d'Amérique* (5 vols., Paris, 1886–92)

Drake, S. A., *Historic Fields and Mansions of Middlesex* (Boston, 1874)

Dreer Collection, Generals of the Revolution, Historical Society of Pennsylvania

Eckenrode, H. J., *The Revolution in Virginia* (Boston, 1916)

Einstein, L., *Divided Loyalties* (London, 1933)

Emmett Collection, New York Public Library

Fiske, J., *The American Revolution* (2 vols., Boston, 1891)

Fitzpatrick, J. C., *Writings of George Washington* (26 vols., Washington, D.C. 1931–38)

Forbes, E., *Paul Revere and the World He Lived In* (Boston, 1942)

Force, P., *American Archives* (9 vols., Washington, D.C., 1837–53)

Force Transcripts, Library of Congress

Ford, W. C., Hunt, G., Fitzpatrick, J. C., and Hill, R. R., *Journals of the Continental Congress 1774–1789* (34 vols., Washington, D.C., 1904–37)

Fortescue, J. W., *A History of the British Army* (14 vols., New York, 1899–1930)

Freeman, D. S., *George Washington* (5 vols., New York, 1948–52)

French, A., *General Gage's Informers* (Ann Arbor, 1932)

French, A., *The First Year of the American Revolution* (Boston, 1934)

French, A., *The Taking of Ticonderoga in 1775: The British Story* (Cambridge, 1928)

Frothingham, R., *Life and Times of Joseph Warren* (Boston, 1865)

Gates Papers, New York Historical Society

Gentleman's Magazine

Gipson, L. H., *Jared Ingersoll* (New Haven, 1920)

Goodhue, J. F., *History of Shoreham, Vermont* (Middlebury, 1891)

Gordon, W., *History of the Rise, Progress and Establishment of the United States* (4 vols., London, 1788)

Gottschalk, L., *Lafayette and the Close of the American Revolution* (Chicago, 1942)

Graham, J., *Life of General Daniel Morgan* (New York, 1856)

Gratz Collection, Historical Society of Pennsylvania

Greene, F. V., *The Revolutionary War* (New York, 1911)

Greene, G. W., *The Life of Nathanael Greene* (3 vols., New York, 1867)

Guild, R. A., *Chaplain Smith and the Baptists* (Philadelphia, 1885)

Harris, W. W., *The Battle of Groton Heights* (Revised and enlarged by C. Allyn, New London, 1882)

Hart, A. B., *The Varick Court of Inquiry to Investigate the Implication of Colonel Richard Varick (Arnold's Private Secretary) in the Arnold Treason* (Boston, 1907)

Heath Papers, Massachusetts Historical Society Collections, 7th series, V (1905)

Hoadly, C. J., *Public Records of the State of Connecticut* (3 vols., Hartford, 1894–1922)

Irving, W., *Life of George Washington* (5 vols., New York, 1856)

James, W. M., *The British Navy in Adversity* (London, 1926)

Jones, C. H., *History of the Campaign for the Conquest of Canada* (Philadelphia, 1882)

Jones, T., *History of New York During the Revolutionary War* (2 vols., New York, 1879)

Journals of Each Provincial Congress of Massachusetts (Boston, 1838)

Kapp, F., *The Life of Frederick William von Steuben* (New York, 1859)

Kirkland, F. R., "Journal of Dr. Lewis Beebe," in *Pennsylvania Magazine of History and Biography,* LIX (1935)

Knollenberg, B., *Washington and the Revolution* (New York, 1941)

Kyte, G. W., "A Projected British Attack upon Philadelphia in 1781," in *Pennsylvania Magazine of History and Biography*, LXXVI (1952)

Lafayette—*Memoirs, Correspondence and Manuscripts of General Lafayette* (3 vols., London, 1837)

Lamb Papers, New York Historical Society

Land Deeds, New Brunswick (Canada) Museum

Lawrence, J. W., *Foot-Prints; or Incidents in the Early History of New Brunswick* (St. John, N.B., 1883)

Lawson, M. G., "Canada and the Articles of Confederation," in *American Historical Review*, LVIII (1952)

Leacock, S., *Montreal* (New York, 1942)

Leake, I. Q., *Memoir of the Life and Times of General John Lamb* (Albany, 1850)

Lee, H., *Memoirs of the War in the Southern Department of the United States* (2 vols., New York, 1869)

Lee Papers, New York Historical Society Collections, IV-VII (1871–4)

Libby, O. G., "A Critical Examination of Gordon's History of the American Revolution," in *Annual Report of the American Historical Association for the Year 1899* (2 vols., Washington, D.C., 1900)

Lincoln, C. H., *Naval Records of the American Revolution* (Washington, D.C., 1906)

Lintot's Letter, in *New Haven Historical Society Papers*, IX (1918)

List of the Officers of the Army, War Office, London, 1783

Liverpool Papers, Additional MSS., British Museum

Lloyd's Evening Post

Lodge, H. C., *The Works of Alexander Hamilton* (9 vols., New York, 1885–6)

Lossing, B. J., *Field-Book of the Revolution* (2 vols., New York, 1855)

Lossing, B. J., *Life and Times of Philip Schuyler* (2 vols., New York, 1872)

Mackenzie—*Diary of Frederick Mackenzie* (2 vols., Cambridge, 1930)

Mahan, A. T., *The Major Operations of the Navies in the War of American Independence* (Boston, 1913)

Mahan, A. T., "The Naval Campaign of 1776 on Lake Champlain," in *Scribner's Magazine*, XXIII (1898)

Marshall, J., *Life of George Washington* (5 vols., Fredericksburg, 1804–7; revised edition, 2 vols., Philadelphia, 1832)

Massachusetts Historical Society Collections, 2d series, IV (1816)

Massachusetts Historical Society Proceedings, 2d series, XII (1899)

Maxwell, L. M. B., *An Outline of the History of Central New Brunswick in the Time of the Confederation* (Sackville, N.B., 1937)

Meng, J. J., *Dispatches and Instructions of Conrad Alexandre Gerard,* 1778–1780 (New York, 1939)

Middlebrook, L. F., *History of Maritime Connecticut during the American Revolution* (2 vols., Salem, 1925)

Miller, J. C., *Origins of the American Revolution* (Boston, 1943)

Minutes of a Court of Inquiry upon the Case of Major John André (Albany, 1865)

Minutes of the Albany Committee of Correspondence, 1775–1778 (2 vols., Albany, 1923)

Miscellaneous Papers, New York Public Library

Miscellaneous Papers, Historical Society of Pennsylvania

Montross, L., *Rag, Tag and Bobtail, The Story of the Continental Army* (New York, 1952)

Montross, L., *The Reluctant Rebels, The Story of the Continental Congress* (New York, 1950)

Moore, F., *Diary of the American Revolution* (2 vols., New York, 1865)

"Morgan's Autobiography," in *Historical Magazine,* 2d series, IX (1871)

Muster Rolls of the New York Provincial Troops, 1755–64, New York Historical Society Collections, XXIV (1891)

National Cyclopedia of American Biography

Neilson, C., *Burgoyne's Campaign* (Albany, 1844)

New England Historical and Genealogical Register

New Brunswick Museum, for Arnold-Bliss and miscellaneous correspondence

New Haven Colony Historical Society, for Sherman's order for Arnold's arrest, Arnold's *Minute* and *Waste-Books,* and miscellaneous correspondence

New Haven Historical Society Papers, III (1882)

New Haven Town Records

New Jersey Archives, 2d series, V (1917)

Nickerson, H., *The Turning Point of the Revolution* (New York, 1928)

Norwich, Vital Records of (2 vols., Hartford, 1913)

Odell Collection, New Brunswick Museum

Ogden—"Autobiography of Col. Aaron Ogden," in *New Jersey Historical Society Proceedings,* 2d series, XII (1892–3)

Palmer, J. M., *General Von Steuben* (New York, 1937)

Patterson, S. W., *Horatio Gates* (New York, 1941)

Paullin, C. O., *The Navy of the American Revolution* (Cleveland, 1906)

Pausch—*Journal of Captain Georg Pausch* (Albany, 1886)

Pell, J., *Ethan Allen* (London, 1929)

Pell—"Diary of Joshua Pell, Junior," in *Magazine of American History,* II, Pt. I (1878)

Pennsylvania Archives, 1st series, VII (1853), IX (1854)
Pennsylvania Packet
Peters, S., *General History of Connecticut* (Edited by S. J. McCormick, New York, 1877)
Prerogative Court of Canterbury Wills
Public Record Office, for papers of Audit Office, Colonial Office, High Court of Admiralty, and Treasury

Reed Papers, New York Historical Society
Reed, W. B., *Life and Correspondence of Joseph Reed* (2 vols., Philadelphia, 1847)
Roberts, K., *March to Quebec* (New York, 1947) contains the journals of participants
Rockwell, G. L., *History of Ridgefield, Connecticut* (Ridgefield, 1927)
Royal Gazette (New York)
Rush, R., *Occasional Productions, Political, Diplomatic, and Miscellaneous* (Philadelphia, 1860)

Sabine, L., *Loyalists of the American Revolution* (2 vols., Boston, 1864)
Sargent, W., *Life and Career of Major André* (Boston, 1861)
Scharf, J. T. and Westcott, T., *History of Philadelphia, 1609–1884* (3 vols., Philadelphia, 1884)
Schlesinger, A. M., *The Colonial Merchants and the American Revolution, 1763–1776* (New York, 1918)
Schuyler Papers, New York Public Library
Sellers, C. C., *Benedict Arnold, The Proud Warrior* (New York, 1930)
Sesquicentennial of the Battle of Groton Heights and the Burning of New London, Connecticut (New London, 1931)
Silverman, A., "William Paca, Signer, Governor, Jurist," in *Maryland Historical Magazine,* XXXVII (1942)
Smith, J. E. A., *History of Pittsfield* (2 vols., Boston, 1869)
Smith, J. H., *Arnold's March from Cambridge to Quebec* (New York, 1903)
Smith, J. H., *Our Struggle for the Fourteenth Colony* (2 vols., New York, 1907)
Smith—*William Smith's Diary,* New York Public Library
Sparks, J., *Correspondence of the American Revolution: Being Letters of Eminent Men to George Washington* (4 vols., Boston, 1853)
Sparks, J., *Life and Treason of Benedict Arnold* (New York, 1847)
Sparks, J., *The Writings of George Washington* (12 vols., Boston, 1835)
Spears, J. R., "Benedict Arnold—Naval Patriot," in *Harper's Magazine,* CVI (1902–3)
Stedman, C., *History of the Origin, Progress and Termination of the American War* (2 vols., London, 1794)

Stevens, B. F., *Facsimiles of Manuscripts in European Archives Relating to America, 1773–1783* (25 vols., London, 1889–98)

Stevens, J. A., "Benedict Arnold and His Apologist," in *Magazine of American History*, IV (1880)

Stillé, C. J., *Major-General Wayne and the Pennsylvania Line* (Philadelphia, 1893)

Stockton, A. S., *The Judges of New Brunswick and Their Times* (St. John, 1907)

Stone, W. L., *Memoirs of Madame Riedesel, Letters and Journals Relating to the War of the American Independence* (Albany, 1867)

Stone, W. L., *Burgoyne's Campaign and St. Leger's Expedition* (Albany, 1877)

Stone, W. L., *Life of Joseph Brant* (2 vols., New York, 1838)

Stopford-Sackville MSS., Historical MSS. Commission Reports

Stryker, W. S., *The Battles of Trenton and Princeton* (Boston, 1898)

Stuart, I. W., *Life of Jonathan Trumbull* (Boston, 1859)

Sullivan Papers, New Hampshire Historical Society Collections, XIII-XV (1930–39)

Swiggett, H., *The Great Man* (New York, 1953)

Tallmadge-Sparks—"Correspondence between . . . Jared Sparks and Benjamin Tallmadge" (concerning Arnold and André), in *Magazine of American History*, III, Pt. II (1879)

Taylor, J. G., *Some New Light on the Later Life and Last Resting Place of Benedict Arnold and His Wife Margaret Shippen* (London, 1931)

Thacher, J., *Military Journal of the American Revolution* (Hartford, 1862)

Tower, C., *The Marquis de La Fayette in the American Revolution* (2 vols., Philadelphia, 1885)

Van Cortlandt—"Autobiography of Philip Van Cortlandt," in *Magazine of American History*, II, Pt. I (1878)

Van Doren, C., *Secret History of the American Revolution* (New York, 1941). Extensive use of the Clinton Papers

Van Schaack, H. C., *Life of Peter Van Schaack* (New York, 1842)

Van Tyne, C. H., *The War of Independence* (Boston, 1929)

Vermont, Records of the Council of Safety and Governor and Council of the State of

Von Eelking, M., *Memoirs, and Letters and Journals of Major General Riedesel* (2 vols., Albany, 1868)

Walker, L. B., "Life of Margaret Shippen, Wife of Benedict Arnold," in *Pennsylvania Magazine of History and Biography*, XXIV-XXVI (1900–2). Written largely from the Shippen Papers

Wallace, W. M., *Appeal to Arms, A Military History of the American Revolution* (New York, 1951)

Ward, C., *The War of the Revolution* (Edited by J. R. Alden, 2 vols., New York, 1952)

Washington Papers, Library of Congress

Waterman Family, The (2 vols., New Haven, 1939)

Webster, J. C., *Historical Guide to New Brunswick* (St. John, 1947)

Wells—"Journal of Bayze Wells of Farmington," in *Connecticut Historical Society Collections,* VII (1899)

Wells, K. G., *Campobello* (Boston, 1893)

Weyl, N., *Treason, The Story of Disloyalty and Betrayal in American History* (Washington, D.C., 1950)

Wharton, F., *Revolutionary Diplomatic Correspondence of the United States* (6 vols., Washington, D.C., 1889)

Wilkinson, J., *Memoirs of My Own Times* (3 vols., Philadelphia, 1816)

Willcox, W. B., "Rhode Island in British Strategy, 1780–81," in *Journal of Modern History,* XVII (1945)

Willyams, C., *The Account of the Campaign in the West Indies* (London, 1796)

Wilson, W., *A History of the American People* (5 vols., New York, 1902)

Winsor, J., *Narrative and Critical History of America* (8 vols., Boston, 1884–9)

Wood, W., *The Father of British Canada* (Toronto, 1916)

York County (New Brunswick) Records of Deeds

Zeichner, O., *Connecticut's Years of Controversy* (Chapel Hill, 1949)

INDEX

Johns, 44; proposes invasion of Canada, 45–6, 48–9; superseded by Hinman, 49; investigated by Massachusetts committee, 49–51; resigns command, 51–2; death of wife, 54; Ticonderoga accounts, 53, 56; New Haven visit, 55–6

Plans and organization for Quebec expedition, 57–63; sails for Kennebec, 61; leaves Fort Western, 65; tries McCormick, 65; writes important letters, 67–8; struggles with nature and starvation, 67–71; reaches St. Lawrence, 72; plans betrayed, 67, 73; crosses St. Lawrence, 76; fails to surprise Quebec, 76–7; goes to Point-aux-Trembles, 79; meeting with Montgomery, 79–80; quarrel with Hanchet, 70, 80–1; opposed by Brown, 81–2; assaults Quebec, 82–5; wounded in leg, 84–5, 91; maintains siege with courage and resourcefulness, 86–8, 91; appointed brigadier general, 88; quarrels again with Brown, 89–90; takes over Montreal command, 92; part in Cedars affair, 92–5; withdraws from Canada, 97–8; praised by Germain, 99; liked by commissioners from Congress, 100; seizes goods in Montreal, 97, 100; charges Hazen with neglect of goods, 100–1; Hazen's court-martial and BA's clash with court, 101–5, 347–8; Wilkinson's accusation, 104; Brown charges BA with plundering Montreal, 105–6; builds fleet, 106–8; upheld by Gates in controversy with Wynkoop, 107–9; Chase's warning, 109; begs for crews, 111; sails to Valcour, 112–3; Valcour Island battle plan, 113–4, 349; personally fires cannon, 115; escapes British, 116–7; destroys ships after Split Rock action, 118; Mahan's estimate of value, 119; praised by Americans and British, 119; criticized by Maxwell, 119–20; Brown's charges, 121–2, 349–50; judgment toward BA in Hazen's court of inquiry, 122

Ordered to Rhode Island, 122–3; loan to Oswald, 123; enamored of Betsy Deblois, 123–4; passed over by

Congress in promotion of brigadiers, 124–7; harries Tryon's retreat from Danbury, 128–30; promoted to major general at last but not to seniority in grade, 130; enraged by Brown's libelous handbill, 130, 352; seeks vindication in Philadelphia, 130; sympathy of R. H. Lee and J. Adams, 131; clearance by Board of War and Congress, 131; Canadian accounts, 132–3; again refused seniority by Congress, 133; resigns commission, 133; suggested by Washington as Schuyler's lieutenant, 134; sent to Schuyler, 134; still refused seniority by Congress, 135; works well with Schuyler, 140; volunteers for relief of Fort Stanwix, 141; use of ruse to relieve fort, 142–3; differs with Gates over Freeman Farm battle plan, 146–7; part in battle of Freeman's Farm, 147–8, 326–34; quarrel with Gates, 149–54; removed from command, 154; takes charge of battle of Bemis Heights, 155–7; hits Ball on the head, 155–6; wounded again, 157; Wilkinson's belittling comment, 158; Burgoyne's compliment, 158, 355; restored by Congress to rank in grade, 158–9

Convalescence, 160–1; suit rejected again by Betsy Deblois, 161; takes oath of allegiance at Valley Forge, 162; appointed to command of Philadelphia, 162; incurs anger of Philadelphians, 162–4; explores profit channels with Mease, West, Livingston, and Seixas, 164–5; involved in *Charming Nancy* affair, 165; supports Olmsted in the *Active* case, 166; borrows from Holker, 167; makes trading agreement with Duncan, 167; privateering investment, 167; West Indies scheme, 167–8; interest in education of Warren's children, 168–9; makes enemy of Reed, 171–2; marries Margaret "Peggy" Shippen, 172–4; buys Mt. Pleasant, 174; controversy with Matlack, 174–6; considers buying estate in New York, 177–8; charges preferred against BA by Council of

Set in Intertype Baskerville
Format by Marguerite Swanton
Manufactured by The Haddon Craftsmen, Inc.
Published by HARPER & BROTHERS, *New York*